SALAZAR

TOM GALLAGHER

Salazar

The Dictator Who Refused to Die

HURST & COMPANY, LONDON

First published in the United Kingdom in 2020 by
C. Hurst & Co. (Publishers) Ltd.,
This paperback edition first published in 2022 by
C. Hurst & Co. (Publishers) Ltd.,
New Wing, Somerset House, Strand, London, WC2R 1LA
© Tom Gallagher, 2022
All rights reserved.

Printed in Great Britain by Bell and Bain Ltd, Glasgow

The right of Tom Gallagher to be identified as the author of
this publication is asserted by him in accordance with the
Copyright, Designs and Patents Act, 1988.

Distributed in the United States, Canada and Latin America by
Oxford University Press, 198 Madison Avenue, New York, NY 10016,
United States of America.

A Cataloguing-in-Publication data record for this book
is available from the British Library.

ISBN: 9781787388291

This book is printed using paper from registered sustainable
and managed sources.

www.hurstpublishers.com

For James and Irene Armstrong, who have been boon companions and unceasing sources of encouragement and wise advice over many years.

CONTENTS

LIST OF ILLUSTRATIONS

The author and the publisher thank José Lourenço, editor of *Diário Insular* in the Azores, the Arquivo Nacional da Torre do Tombo (AN) in Lisbon, and the Estúdio Horácio Novais Collection of the Calouste Gulbenkian Foundation's Biblioteca de Arte e Arquivos in Lisbon for permission to reproduce their photos in this book.

LIST OF ABBREVIATIONS

ANP   National Popular Action
CCP   Portuguese Catholic Centre
CDS   Centre Social Democratic Party
DBR   Federal German Republic
ENT   National Labour Statute
FNLA   National Front for the Liberation of Angola
GNR   National Republican Guard
INTP   National Institute of Labour and Welfare
MFA   Armed Forces Movement
MIRN   Independent Movement for National Reconstruction
MPLA   Popular Movement for the Liberation of Angola
NGO   Non-governmental organisation
OEEC   Organization for European Economic Co-Operation
PAIGC African Party for the Independence of Guinea and Cape Verde
PCP   Portuguese Communist Party
PIDE   International Police for the Defence of the State
PS   Socialist Party
PSD   Social Democratic Party
PVDE   Police for the Vigilance and Defence of the State
SNI   National Secretariat for Information
SPN   National Secretariat for Propaganda
UN   National Union

INTRODUCTION

A TENACIOUS DICTATOR IN A LIBERAL AGE

This is a portrait of a pessimist. He dominated the political life of Portugal for forty years, never wavering in his scepticism about the ability of the Portuguese, and indeed wider humanity, to be virtuous and rational in political matters. An outlook sustained by thinkers from Thucydides to St Augustine and from Hobbes to Sigmund Freud convinced him that democracy was a dangerous innovation quite likely to end in disaster, except in a few exceptional countries like Britain and Switzerland.

He was a man whose outlook on life was shaped by the rural milieu into which he was born as well as by his particular family circumstances. This biographical study explores how he was influenced and formed by economic, religious and academic environments, what factors made him turn to politics and how, over a very lengthy period, he was able to bend the politics of his country to his own formidable will.

By the standards of the late 19th century into which he was born, Salazar would have been regarded as a rather conventional man. Austere and self-contained, he avoided close relationships and pleasures that got in the way of the work to which he was dedicated. However, his rise to power was unconventional and his retention of it for forty years was remarkable.

Salazar was from a peasant background, something he proudly acknowledged. He rose in the stratified world of pre-1920 Portugal on account of his intellectual gifts, becoming a professor of economics at the University of Coimbra when he was not yet thirty. In Britain today, where the professions are sometimes viewed as becoming once again preserves of privileged sectors of society, this would be seen as a noteworthy rise. But for someone with Salazar's conservative views on many matters, from the role of women in society to the unsuitability of government shaped by the masses, his rise is likely to appear an astonishing one.

What to a large extent explains his success, first in academia and later in politics, is his willpower. It was a characteristic noted by allies and adversaries in turn. He first showed it in overcoming career obstacles and then in presenting himself as a would-be saviour at a low point in his nation's fortunes, someone capable of rescuing the country from financial disaster and chronic political instability.

Those whom he had to convince were the military officers who had seized power in 1926. Their coup marked the end of over a century of a broadly liberal ascendancy in Portugal. The lieutenants of 1926 saw themselves as the guardians of the nation. But they had no clue how to address the critical challenge of the hour—how to overcome Portugal's severe indebtedness and avoid the country losing its financial independence by taking out a foreign loan (one likely to involve international supervision of the country's finances and perhaps even the confiscation of its colonies).

Salazar provided enough answers to be catapulted into government in 1928. In four years he showed himself to be an even more accomplished political wizard than an economic one. He civilianised an authoritarian regime when the politics of more and more countries were becoming militarised. By 1932, he had reached the political zenith. He was prime minister at forty-three and on the verge of creating a New State (Estado Novo) that would tear Portugal away from its liberal moorings.

The 1930s revealed a second trait which may explain his political endurance. That was a deep-seated caution. He declined to follow the examples of Hitler and Mussolini by establishing a totalitarian party-state. His dictatorship was one without a powerful mass party or an intrusive state busy indoctrinating the masses. Salazar's aim was the depoliticisation of society, not the mobilisation of the populace. If the New State wasn't a pure fascist manifestation, then Salazar faced the persistent accusation that he was presiding over a clerical fascist variant. In fact this former candidate for the priesthood kept the Catholic Church at arm's length. Given the strength of secular republican feeling in Portugal's cities, he judged it prudent not to restore to the church many of the rights it had lost under a predecessor regime. Salazar was a monarchist like his Spanish counterpart, General Francisco Franco, with whose regime he enjoyed a wary association. But he never contemplated restoring the monarchy as happened in Spain. Instead, his formula was to create a ruling alliance of conservatives, some moderate liberals and a few nationalist ideologues, kept in being by his political agility, and guaranteed ultimately by the armed forces.

The Communist Party, which came to dominate the opposition after 1945, was always beyond the pale. A vigilant secret police and a rigid system of press censorship were meant to curb its influence. But Salazar was careful not to create an army of martyrs through indiscriminate state violence. Those murdered at the hands of his security forces did, however, include General Humberto Delgado, who had mounted the biggest challenge to his rule. But the repression was limited and controlled; within a year of his regime being overthrown in 1974, more political prisoners were detained by its revolutionary successor than were rounded up at any point under Salazar.

His ability to tap into nationalist feeling undoubtedly also helps to account for his durability. First the Spanish Civil War and then, more crucially, World War II revealed his distrust of foreign powers and his ability to keep them at bay. He earned respect both at home and abroad for showing a high degree of skill in foiling various international designs on his small, strategically located country which was ill placed to defend itself in the murderous conflicts of the 1930s and 1940s.

Portuguese distrust of its larger Iberian neighbour, which had occupied it outright from 1580 to 1640, was legendary. Upon the eruption of war in Spain in July 1936, Salazar for once threw aside his caution and backed the nationalist right, the eventual victor. He then worked to keep Franco from throwing in his lot with Hitler after the latter unleashed a wave of military conquests in 1940.

Wartime relations were much smoother with Portugal's oldest ally, Britain, than with the new maritime power, the United States. He used subtlety and astuteness in keeping the warring European powers from trampling on Portuguese neutrality. But he needed to show fortitude and grit in preventing America's disdain for small countries that stood in its way, leading to a direct collision with Washington. He brought Portugal through the war intact, winning the respect of a range of international politicians and diplomats with whom he sparred.

The nerve-racking task of shielding Portugal from danger in World War II took its toll on Salazar's health. But he managed to impress foreign visitors then, and for many years afterwards, with his mental acuteness, which included a formidable memory for facts, numbers and people. His invariable politeness and capacity to charm and persuade softened the image of his regime. For Americans not unduly concerned with politics, he might have resembled a Hollywood character actor (a Claude Rains or Christopher Lee) able to calm an unruly land.

After 1945 he was ever more convinced that in a dangerous world he was indispensable for shielding the country from harm. The view even took hold among some committed democrats who got to know Salazar, that he was a dictator with a difference or that Portugal was a dictatorship without a dictator. Self-effacing, dedicated to his duties, shunning uniforms or bombastic displays, it was a benevolent autocrat who seemed to be in charge of Portugal. This was certainly the view that a busy public relations machine promoted. Salazar did not neglect propaganda, and the way the regime was marketed endowed it with a form of soft power. Unlike Franco's Spain, Portugal was later inducted into NATO as a founder member, joined the European Free Trade Association, and came to enjoy associate status with what much later became the European Union.

Salazar faced sharp opposition at different points but he was effective at promoting consensus, with himself seen as the indispensable arbiter of different elite interests. So his role as a balancer in a country which had been a byword for factionalism in modern times also enabled him to hang on.

Until well into his seventies, he was adept at handling a wide variety of different human types. He could work with a range of people without his opinions about their style, morals and outlook intruding. At times, it seemed that he ran Portugal very much like a punctilious head butler in charge of a sprawling country estate. He showed a painstaking attention to detail, checking administration to a minute level, but was also accessible to numerous people whose requests, in the form of petitions and letters, he patiently scrutinised.

Strict personal self-discipline must also account for his marathon span in power. He was careful not to encourage familiarity with allies and colleagues. He had close friends but ones which he had usually made before assuming power. He never married but he nevertheless enjoyed the company of women, and there were periodic relationships that ultimately never got very far. His three sisters were the closest family members who attended his funeral in 1970. Spurning marriage may have enabled him to avoid the family preoccupations which have often proven hard for authoritarian leaders to handle.

A schedule unchanged for over forty years enabled him to conserve his energy. Each autumn he cut himself off from politics by retreating to his village, where he tended the vines on his *quinta* (small estate). In Lisbon he developed a low-key routine in which he largely absented himself from public ceremonies and social occasions. For over fifty years he was looked after by Dona Maria, a dutiful governess who started out as an illiterate peasant girl and ended up as the most powerful woman 20th-century Portugal had known.

Being inconspicuous but firmly in control was very much how Salazar played things. He reacted with anger when the world intruded, banning *Time* magazine when it published an intrusive profile in 1946 and reacting angrily when the world's media highlighted the audacious hijacking of a cruise ship in 1961 by an opponent.

Usually, however, he had the self-belief, calm disposition, and sense of timing that enabled him to stay ahead of his foes. But rather than confront the new challenges of the post-1945 world, he retreated into his bunker. Distrusting most transnational initiatives, he showed no interest in adapting his regime to new times. He was reluctant to properly look after the millions of Portuguese whose conservative outlook mirrored his own. Education was not neglected as some critics have claimed. But many would emigrate when they got the chance to enjoy the social benefits which he feared would sap the work ethic of ordinary Portuguese.

Meanwhile, he persisted with the unwieldy corporative state which had seemed innovative in the 1930s but which grew into a patronage-ridden bureaucracy that enabled him to control much of the economy.

Reluctant to delegate, he also neglected to keep a close enough watch on the military, the ultimate guarantor of his regime.

Perhaps this lassitude stemmed from unhappiness that Portugal was becoming an anomaly in a world of democratic or else communist nations. It particularly stood out, by the start of the 1960s, owing to the regime's refusal to renounce its colonial empire, very large in comparison with Portugal's small European dimensions. Perhaps unavoidably, this led to partial ostracism during the era of decolonisation. A duel with the United States under President Kennedy occurred in the early 1960s which Salazar saw in very personal terms: 'Either the Americans succeed in killing me or else I die,' he said in 1963. 'Or else they will face years of struggle in order to put me under.'[1]

He told his doctor that 'the Americans in politics are childlike. Their anti-colonial complex harms them. They don't have any real idea of what is happening in the world.'[2] This anti-colonialism Salazar saw as a gimmick which could eventually give way to new forms of domination ultimately more pernicious than Portuguese colonialism in Africa had been. He saw America as another engine of liberalism, its brand of free-wheeling capitalism a threat, not a liberation, for much of the world.

He continued to swim against the conventional tide right up until he was felled by a brain haemorrhage in 1968. His successor, Marcello Caetano, lacking his political skills, was indecisive and dismantled most of the regime's defences. A short-lived revolution in 1974–5 carried out by junior army officers quickly led to the abandonment of Portugal's overseas empire.

In his early years in charge Salazar had enjoyed good fortune due to the low calibre of his opponents and favourable European political trends, but increasingly, from the 1940s, he made his own luck thanks to shaping the political order around his own needs and preferences as a ruler. Shrinking the political stage to dimensions which he could control enabled him to rise above adversity and ride out crises. By the 1960s, he appeared an exotic figure to be sought out, as he put it, by foreign visitors 'who want to glimpse the great dictator' and who, like the small child taken to the zoo, are disappointed if the elephant or the giraffe is not available to look at.[3]

Eventually, the Portuguese defied Salazar's warning that they were unsuited for democracy by rejecting revolutionary politics. The post-

1976 democratic republican regime has now surpassed his 'New State' in longevity. Its successful implantation suggests that the Portuguese were rather more prepared for multi-party democracy than Salazar, with his paternalistic outlook, had assumed. But its performance has been distinctly mixed. High-level corruption, poor management of the economy, and state incapacity in general have been hard to conceal. The parties have often been hard to distinguish from each other, perhaps standing out only through their prowess in developing strategies for acquiring the spoils of office.

Despite his manifold defects, Salazar has stood out against a drab political background. In 2007, 41 per cent of viewers of the TV series *Great Portuguese* voted for him as the greatest figure in Portuguese history.[4] He beat the nation's more illustrious monarchs and even the great explorers of the Age of Discovery. There was huge surprise and consternation among opinion-formers that Salazar remained such an important reference point. The assumption had been that he would be widely seen by Portuguese as a relic of a discredited past. After all, his belief that only political systems which made the national principle an overt basis for organising human affairs could ultimately work was starting to be seen as obsolete in influential quarters. The democratic wave had foiled communism, buried right-wing autocracy, and was now enabling nations across Europe to pool their sovereignty.

But the climate grew more propitious for Salazar's scepticism about majoritarian democracy. A growing cleavage arose between those who remained committed to power being exercised at national level and others who preferred power to be exercised through international networks and institutions. Global corporations, particularly in the advanced technology sector, made common cause with the middle- and upper-class left in promoting a progressive one-world order based on maximising personal freedoms and lifestyle choices.[5] A period of bitter contestation ensued as transnational institutions seemed to snatch authority from nation-states without wishing to be accountable to the wider citizenry.

This cleavage tended to pit highly educated, well-off people comfortable with globalisation against people of a conservative disposition, often less cosmopolitan in experience and outlook, who were unhappy with ceding power to faraway elites. It was the 'Somewheres' versus the 'Anywheres', people attached to local and national identities versus others content with an increasingly borderless world.[6] At first sight, it is not hard to imagine Salazar, a proven foe of transnational power, as a rallying point for conservative nationalists. But appearances can turn out to be deceptive. European national conservative movements have a strong attachment to elections whereas Salazar refused to invest power in the masses. Trends may change but it is hard to see someone with his approach to politics finding a place in any of the major populist parties that have formed on the right. They established a foothold in one European country after another following the onset of the post-2008 crisis in much of the Eurozone.

Salazar was opposed to parties of any kind, arguing that they were false harbingers of progress. He preferred instead to invest his hopes in elites that would offer impersonal rule dedicated to the national cause. Paradoxically, Salazar's distrust of the ballot box, belief in rule by experts, and readiness to endorse censorship in order to control the flow of ideas now enjoy more favour among globalists on the left than among nationalists on the right. It may even be possible to contend that as one of the main promoters of the corporate state in the 1930s, his belief in intra-elite cooperation found a strong echo in the 'Third Way' ideas promoted in Western Europe thirty years after his death.

Salazar may have distrusted transnational cooperation but he was in favour of government driven by bureaucratic experts and unencumbered by parliamentary oversight. His success in keeping such a ruling formula viable for forty years may give encouragement to some hyper-liberals whose ideological fervour makes them believe they can remake the world in their own image. Philosophers like John Gray have warned that this is hubris which threatens to topple a Western order containing meaningful freedoms and rights.[7] Salazar had few illusions about remaking even the small portion of the world over which he ruled. He was stubborn and deliberate in his approach and the only hubris that he ever displayed was the belief that he could halt the winds of change by retaining Portugal's overseas empire. He also believed, unlike a lot of modern politicians, that personal restraint was vital in order for major goals to be accomplished.

He could be ruthless but he lacked the crudeness and taste for blood of many dictators. Still, this fastidious intellectual who read the classics of literature possessed to the full the will to exercise power over an entire nation. In the ages of violent fascism and self-confident liberalism that coincided with his time in charge of Portugal, his exercise of power seems incongruous. Yet he conquered the political heights and stayed around for thirty-six continuous years as prime minister, a record in the annals of modern European politics. Inevitably, under this self-effacing but tenacious ruler, Portugal was much criticised for defying political conventions, but probably at no other point in the past three hundred years has Portugal been as influential as it was under Salazar.

Each of the fifteen chapters in this book deals with a chronological phase in Salazar's life. The first two explore his formative years. A lengthier trio follow which examine how he plunged into politics and, in a remarkably short period of time, established his political mastery over Portugal. Besides one chapter exploring his private life, the middle part of the book focuses on the peninsular and global challenges which increasingly absorbed his energies and enabled his political skills to become recognised well beyond Portugal. Chapters 10 to 12 explore the price he paid for putting aside his bold domestic plans as the world intruded on Portugal with unwelcome demands and innovations. An increasingly introspective Salazar, confronting hostile headwinds and forced to concede that Portugal was out of step with the world taking shape after 1945, emerges from these pages. But he showed agility and an acute instinct for survival especially in his duel with the United States, which is explored in chapter 13. Chapter 14 explores his battle to defy the conventional wisdom and retain an empire in Africa when every other European power was shedding its imperial role. A final chapter examines the continuing national and global interest in this conservative autocrat and why he continues to fascinate and divide the Portuguese in the fifty years since his death in 1970.

There is no doubt certain information and insights could have been gleaned by carrying out intensive work in the Portuguese National Archives at the Torre de Tombo in Lisbon, where Salazar's papers are kept. But the constraints of time, from the commissioning of the biography at the start of 2019 to its submission at the end of that year, ruled out lengthy archival work. However, a plethora of books and academic papers have been devoted to the material contained in the Salazar archive, which have been explored as the book has taken shape. This one relies on mainly secondary material as well as primary material gleaned from previous bouts of sometimes intensive work on Portuguese history and politics that stretch over a forty-five-year period.

Abundant raw material has been consulted, enabling a reassessment of Salazar's political personality, ideas, policies, short-term impact, and long-term influence to be undertaken. The book is far from an apologia, but it attempts to move beyond several of the interpretations which were influenced by the partisan politics that marked Portugal particularly in the 1970s. Dozens of books have 'Salazar' in the title but there have been few fresh portraits of the most influential Portuguese of recent centuries. This one is undertaken in the belief that enough time has elapsed since his death for it to be possible to step back and assess what was distinctive about him and may well continue to make him an object of interest as the memory of other autocrats fades.

I received indispensable help from various quarters in the year that I spent writing and researching this book.

José Alves Machado deserves special mention. He was a strong motivating force throughout and his own prowess as a researcher enabled me to obtain information on specific features of the Salazar story, easing the burden of my research.

Fernando de Castro Brandão has accomplished invaluable work separating fact from fiction in establishing the main outline of Salazar's life and political activities. Various reference works that he has written are likely to be essential for future historians. He was a hospitable host who proved generous with his time, candid in his assessments, and patient in dealing with several requests.

Jaime Nogueira Pinto is a veteran commentator on the conservative wing of Portuguese politics whose books, articles and, most notably, his 2007 television documentary on Salazar have kept the man and his political epoch continually in view. He took a constructive interest in my project and I benefited from conversations with him about it and from his reading of a draft of the text.

I owe debts to several libraries and their staff.

The municipal library in the charming city of Povoa de Varzim enabled me to make crucial headway with the book at an early stage. Warm thanks are due to Constança Marafona and her staff for their patience, great amiability and hard work on my behalf. Thanks to them I was introduced to the fascinating work recently carried out on the life of their city during the Salazar era and beyond by Steve Harrison, with whom I carried out a fruitful correspondence as the book was taking shape.

I spent less time at the municipal library in Cascais but I must single out Teresa Lucas for her energy and resourcefulness in gathering together materials for me from across the local library system. She put me in touch with the Espaço Memória dos Exílios in Estoril whose collection of materials on World War II and Portugal proved very helpful.

Staff at the National Library of Scotland in Edinburgh also proved efficient and helpful over an even lengthier period. During an intensive period of research, consulting the Iberian collection in the atmospheric building of the Casa Velasquez in Madrid, I received unstinting assistance from the library staff.

The Gulbenkian Foundation kindly extended permission to use three photos in their collection and grateful acknowledgment is made to Col. Estúdio Marío Novais for the photo upon which the cover is based and to Col. Estúdio Horácio Novais for three of its photos which are in the Gulbenkian Foundation. Other photos were purchased from the National Archive of the Torre de Tombo.

José Lourenço of the *Diário Insular* in the Azores kindly provided an electronic front page of their edition of 28 July 1970.

I warmly appreciate the calm environment and hospitality shown by various people with whom I lodged while in Portugal.

Firstly there was Tania Moreira and her father José, both warmhearted and obliging (Tania even fetching books from the Universidade do Porto library where she was carrying out her own research).

In Cascais, Isabel Calvário offered me delicious organic plums from her family *quinta* in Castelo Branco and kindly kept some books for me after I left.

At Vale de Juizo Steph and Dave offered a peaceful environment to work not far from the atmospheric Praia do Guincho.

This is an appropriate place to put on record my appreciation for the help and assistance provided by Iberian scholars Professor Kenneth N. Medhurst and Dr Joseph Harrison at the University of Manchester where my interest in this part of Europe was first awoken in the 1970s.

Naturally, any mistakes and inaccuracies are my own responsibility.

Tom Gallagher, Edinburgh   4 November 2019

1

THE BOY FROM VIMIEIRO

António de Oliveira Salazar was born at 3 pm on 28 April 1889. His home was a plain, single-storey building in the village of Vimieiro. It was separated from the larger town of Santa Comba Dão by the river Dão. A political figure always reticent about technological innovations in the 20th century was born next to the local railway station, a symbol of perhaps the most visible technological breakthrough of the 19th century. Nevertheless, it was a place where many of the 580 inhabitants still walked barefoot and oxen teams ploughed the fields.[1]

Vimieiro was located in the hilly province of Beira Alta. Portugal's largest peak, Caramulo, loomed nearby. The land was of variable quality and had to be worked hard to extract a living, but there was usually sufficient rain in contrast to the lands south of the river Tagus, which divided the country at the centre.

The south was the home of large estates which had been snatched from the religious orders after the triumph of a self-proclaimed liberal revolution in the 1830s. In the centre and north of Portugal, which were the most densely populated parts, the Catholic Church remained a social force. The stern Christian message asserting the need for correct living during one's short stay on earth, in expectation of an eternal afterlife, resonated with peasant Portugal, as it would with other rural communities across much of southern Europe.

Life expectancy was indeed short. In 1930, arguably the year when Salazar became the main national political figure, life expectancy was

46.5 years for men and 50.6 for women.[2] Salazar's parents, António de Oliveira and Maria do Resgate Salazar, married in 1881 when they were aged forty and thirty-six respectively. They had thus married very late in a peasant society. Both were literate in a country where the great bulk of rural dwellers were unable to read and write. Census findings, a year after Salazar's birth, revealed that 79.2 per cent of Portuguese were still illiterate.[3] The liberal republic which preceded his own regime saw illiteracy fall by less than 10 per cent. A substantial reduction in illiteracy only occurred during his years in power when there was a major drive to get the bulk of children literate and numerate.[4]

Salazar's parents came from families without much wealth but ones which had not been submerged into the subsistence rural economy. Education meant they could benefit from the innovations slowly beginning to penetrate the countryside. They had four daughters in fairly rapid succession and each of them would receive an education. The eldest, Marta (born in 1882) would herself teach arithmetic and grammar in the local primary school for forty-three years.

Salazar, the fifth and last child, was born into a household of hardworking, devout parents. António was a local estate manager. He was employed by the Perestrellos, who owned considerable lands in the region which were not intensively farmed. Their wealth enabled them to possess several houses. But there was little money to be earned from agriculture. Portugal had the classic profile of a still underdeveloped European country, lacking conspicuous industry and dependent for revenue mainly on primary economic products such as grains, fish, fruit, wine and cork. Many children did not long survive childbirth or else succumbed to ailments before they reached adulthood. Large families were common in all social classes in a situation where sudden death affected all social ranks. King Pedro V, seen as a promising young monarch capable of reviving the prestige of the royal family, would die suddenly in 1861, the victim of typhoid.

Arguably, Portugal had been ill led for many years. The Napoleonic invasion of 1807 had triggered a national crisis which would play out for at least the next fifty years. The country was plunged into chronic strife, deepening its economic backwardness. King João VI and the royal court had fled to Brazil as the French armies bore down on Lisbon. Large parts of Portugal were then the scenes of destructive warfare involving French and British armies. One of the decisive battles, which saw the Duke of Wellington defeat the French general Junot, occurred at Bussaco in 1810, a scenic ridge some distance to the west of where Salazar would be born nearly eighty years later. After the French had been driven out, a census in 1811 showed that the population had fallen by 15 per cent and it would be slow to recover (climbing to 3,411,454 by 1849).

By the middle of the 19th century Portugal was beginning to settle down politically. King João's sons Pedro and Miguel had become the standard-bearers of the liberal and conservative causes respectively. With British help the liberals had come out on top in the 1832–4 civil war. In the south the property and estates of the church and the Miguelite nobility were seized. José Mouzinho de Albuquerque, a purposeful finance minister, hoped that the land would be an invaluable source of wealth to mitigate the public debt. Instead, a new class of wealthy landowners emerged who were derived from the ranks of the liberal middle class.

Portugal resembled much of the rest of Iberia and Latin America in its political development at this time. Advanced constitutions heralding liberty, fraternity and equality were proclaimed in the midst of agrarian poverty, illiteracy and scant urban growth. Whatever liberalism had originally meant in their eyes, the newly ascendant forces often used it as an excuse to fall upon their enemies. Various power struggles occurred using slogans imported from France that often went above the heads of much of the population. As late as 1847, the then British prime minister, Lord John Russell, declared that 'the state of Portugal is in every way embarrassing and pitiable'. He deplored the 'spirit of tyranny and cruelty in the decrees and acts of Portuguese ministers without parallel in any part of Europe'.[5]

The possibility of meaningful political change and economic progress had been dealt a huge blow in Portugal when Brazil, its largest colony, declared independence in 1822. Hitherto Brazil had been the destination of Portuguese manufactures, which made up one-third of the trade going to the largest colony in the decades before the French invasion.[6] Sebastião José Carvalho de Melo, the Marquis of Pombal, a despot with some modernising instincts, had promoted manufacturing during his rule from 1751 to 1777. But after 1807, the basis for nascent industry collapsed. Under British pressure, Brazil's ports were flung open to foreign (mainly British) traders with grim effects for Portuguese manufacturers.[7]

As ruler of the country, Salazar was mindful of the severity of the blow to national fortunes constituted by the loss of Brazil. He put the point across to George Ball, the US under-secretary of state, when they had long meetings in Lisbon in 1963.[8] As an authoritarian leader, he was unusual in downplaying his country's wealth, resources and prospects, arguing that his statecraft was meant to keep a poor country afloat in a dangerous world. From the early 19th century onwards, Portugal was badly indebted and little wealth could be extracted from the people, 70 per cent of whom were involved in agriculture at a subsistence level. When even hearths were taxed in the late 1840s, it led to a revolt in the north, known as the Maria de Fonte uprising.[9]

Times had often been arduous for Salazar's parents, which perhaps explains why they married late. Much adversity needed to be overcome in order to acquire a semi-secure footing in society. They displayed a sense of common endeavour even though their personalities were hardly identical. Both were energetic and single-minded but António, despite his sound business sense, seems to have been fatalistic in outlook and not over-imbued with initiative. Undoubtedly, Maria do Resgate Salazar was the more single-minded of the pair. Her portrait reveals a face full of character, with dark penetrating eyes, a long, pointed nose and an expressive mouth, features which her son would inherit.

It has been said that if ill-intentioned people strayed onto their land, António's instinct would be to let the problem blow over while she would have no hesitation in confronting the troublemakers and chasing them away. She believed in order and propriety. Perhaps she felt that without them, a woman of good character would find it hard to enjoy any control over her environment. Her only son would also possess these traits. As leader of his country, when he decided he wished to walk on the railway tracks near his village, he was moved to apply to the railway company to provide him with a special pass to do so. He was fortunate in having as a mother someone who possessed an understanding of life beyond the confines of the village as well as a determination to make use of the advantages it brought, especially for her son.

Eventually, as Portugal's political leader, he would use the indomitability which had marked his family's story to define Portugal's relationship with the rest of the world and especially with the great powers. He would show the spirit of self-belief and critical awareness that was present in the couple who nurtured him and prepared him for adulthood. Portugal stood up against the major powers at critical stages during his years at the helm. Salazar would not be cowed or threatened during World War II. He developed a separate sense of Portugal's national interest which he never abandoned even if it collided with the preferences of the old and new powers. This was an unusual departure for a country where elites had so often displayed a sense of inferiority or an inability to define what was the true patriotic path that needed to be taken. Others had tried and failed to rise above the factionalism and irresolution that seemed to be endemic features of national life, to forge a unified response to critical challenges. Salazar did this most notably during the colonial wars that began in 1961. He reached out beyond his customary supporters in defying the emerging European consensus on swift withdrawal from Africa and bestowing independence on unprepared territories. It led to a series of unprecedented confrontations between Portugal and its allies, most notably the United States. Perhaps no other leader in Portuguese history defied international convention on an important issue with such determination and serenity, refusing to recede, particularly under American pressure, until the day that illness resulted in power being taken from him. It is far from fanciful to argue that this tenacity, staying power and sense of self-belief were the products of the experiences that he absorbed during his formative years growing up in Vimieiro.

By the time of António's birth, his parents were acquiring some financial stability. António senior supplemented his income by acting as a middleman in modest property transactions. Locally, he earned the nickname of being hard-headed and even crafty (*manhoso*) and it is likely that a large measure of his skill in negotiation and swift appraisal of a situation was passed on to his son. Certainly, the son later showed the ability of the clever countryman in shaping the pace and content of negotiations around his chosen preferences. It would never cease to be astounding to some that he would have the opportunity to run Portugal in the way that a competent steward managed a large country estate.

SALAZAR

So his father's occupation rubbed off on Salazar. But young António was always closer to his mother. As her youngest, he quickly became her favourite. He received none of the punishments that she occasionally meted out to her daughters. The arrival of a son gave fresh meaning to her life and meant that she could channel her hopes into his advancement.

2

THE MAKING OF A CONSERVATIVE

As the only boy in a family of girls, it is no surprise that Salazar is widely recalled as a shy and retiring child. It is perhaps understandable also in view of his mother being the dominant personality. She was adept at multi-tasking. She did manual labour in the fields, tended her home, raised her children and would later open a small inn with paying guests. As the family's financial position strengthened, she could leave the back-breaking work to others. She and her son drew closer, and he started to show signs of adopting her serious approach to life.

He helped her in the village inn, which appeared during his child-hood. The railway made it pay its way. The line's existence meant that the village was far less isolated than most. The young Salazar would have encountered people from the outside world, and for an intelligent and even precocious child it would broaden his horizons.

Away from the inn, Salazar preferred walks in the woods with his dog to playing with friends.[1] He would remain deeply attached to the local countryside throughout his life, breaking off from his political tasks to be on hand in the property he acquired, during the grape harvest and at other particular moments in the agrarian cycle. A village bricklayer who knew him well observed after his death that there wasn't a piece of earth in his *quinta* where Salazar had not placed his hand.[2]

His initial schooling was rudimentary but by his tenth year his father, urged on by Maria, had got him enrolled in the seminary at

Viseu, one of the largest towns in northern Portugal, lying 41 kilometres north of Santa Comba Dão. His upbringing at the hands of two hard-working parents would enable him to escape the village confines. Unlike other rural dwellers, they had managed to establish some control over their lives and were not tossed around by fate. They would have instilled in their son a familiarity with, and even liking for, hard work as well as a recognition of the need to plan and organise his affairs with care and precision.

It was customary for able children from poor backgrounds to be educated by the church. In 1899 there were around 2,000 seminarians but only roughly 110 ordinations. Salazar was soon learning French as well as Latin. His seminary years were ones of escalating tension. The monarchy was growing increasingly isolated. Republican agitation in the cities was increasing. In retrospect the differences between republicans and monarchists seem ephemeral ones.[3] Republicanism had put down solid roots in France after the empire of Napoleon III, and France was the supreme cultural model for the small Portuguese elite. Anti-clericalism was in vogue in late-19th-century France and it became the battle cry of ambitious politicians in Portugal who wished to break into the front rank of national affairs. Lacking any feasible economic programme, the middle-class radicals targeted the church. It was seen as a bastion of superstition and privilege, especially by the Freemasons predominating in republican ranks.

The Catholic Church was, however, strong across northern communities like Vimieiro and small cities like Viseu. Salazar encountered dedicated teachers in the seminary who offered him encouragement. Naturally, the study of theology figured prominently in the curriculum. The conservative outlook of the young seminarian was reinforced by what he studied as well as by the turbulent times he was living through. He would have known that the Catholic message of restraint and self-sacrifice in expectation of a higher reward was often mocked in the main cities. But the moral force of Catholicism provided rules for living in societies where there was much want and the absence of even a rudimentary police force until the first decades of the 20th century.

The enemies of the church saw its emphasis on order and tradition as imprisoning the masses in backwardness. The most ardent hoped to wipe out Catholicism in future generations. Salazar, for his part, believed the teachings of the church were a necessary foundation for guiding humanity towards a higher plane given the imperfections of human beings and the capricious nature of the world they inhabited. The student's self-belief grew as praise was bestowed upon him for his scholarship. He rubbed shoulders with people from different places and social backgrounds. Mário de Figueiredo was the first of the life-long collaborators in politics he got to know, aged sixteen. But his life extended beyond fellow seminarians and close family. He started to see on a regular basis a local girl two years his senior, Felismina de Oliveira. At that time he seriously believed that he was destined for the priest-hood and nothing came of the relationship.[4] Nevertheless, they remained longstanding friends, and as a school inspector she thought nothing of informing him by letter and in person of occurrences in the area that might otherwise be kept from him.[5]

1908 was Salazar's last year of study at the seminary. In February staff and pupils were shocked by the news of a terrible occurrence in Lisbon. King Carlos and the crown prince, Luis Felipe, had been gunned down as they travelled in an open coach across the capital's main square, the Terreiro do Paço. The regicide, carried out by anar-chists, left urban Portugal largely unmoved. But Salazar was prompted to write a letter of encouragement to João Franco, who had been given sweeping powers by the king in 1907 but who would not (politically) long survive his assassination.[6]

Salazar had been elected president of a student body two years ear-lier and in the spring of 1908 he would publish his first article. It was a piece in a local journal, *A Folha*, in which he criticised the indifference of Catholics towards the grave events which were shaking both church and nation.[7] By this time it is possible that he had encountered the writings of the influential conservative French polemicist Charles Maurras. Like most well-educated Portuguese, Salazar had acquired proficiency in French. This meant that he could read Maurras's com-bative newspaper, *Action Française*, in the original, where his doubts about liberal democracy's ability to guarantee social order and progress would doubtless have been reinforced. France, a republic for much of the time since 1792, had already witnessed the separation of church and state in 1905. Maurras and his followers had waged vigorous resis-tance to secular liberalism and their example took hold among conservative spirits in Portugal convinced that the republic offered only strife and misgovernment.

Some of those who knew Salazar were keen to advance the cause of such a promising young Catholic. As the monarchist regime hurtled towards extinction and the impending new one was imbued with anti-clericalism, few, if any, resolute Catholics were active in national life. Canon António Barreiros, the director of the Via Sacra college in Viseu, offered him a teaching post, which he took up in October 1908. He taught history, literature and mathematics and would remain there for two years. In 1910 he completed his pre-university schooling and now the time came when a crucial decision had to be made.

Should he go ahead and devote himself entirely to a life in the church or instead acknowledge the strong pull of worldly responsibilities and attachments? Against a background of menace and frontal danger for the church in Portugal, Salazar seems to have concluded that his vocation was not sufficiently strong for a life in the church. He took this decision after consulting with his mother and with church figures like Canon Barreiros, who had grown to respect him.[8] According to the writer Jaime Nogueira Pinto, he seems to have had doubts that, with his passion for politics, he could maintain the humility that the church demanded of its shepherds.[9]

Salazar's academic performance had been so stellar, getting maximum marks and winning an array of prizes year after year, that admission to the University of Coimbra seemed to be the next logical step for him. It was the country's only university, having around 500 students. It was a gateway to influence and authority within what was then a small and badly run state. Salazar decided to study law and was accepted, beginning his studies in October 1910. Financing four years of study was beyond the means of his parents. But the Perestrello family stepped in. Maria de Pina, the lady of the household, was his godmother. Salazar gave lessons to some of her younger children in return for payment which went towards financing his studies. He would also tutor other young people preparing for university. It was a start in the quest for the financial independence he would need if he was to advance in the world.

On 5 October 1910 the monarchy was finally toppled. A successful republican revolt resulted in King Manuel II fleeing to Britain. The republicans were highly visible in the university and even in conservative towns like Viseu until their disastrous record in office saw their support tumble. But even from the start of the Portuguese Republic they were not all-powerful at Coimbra. The monarchists were also numerous as were Catholic-minded students and professors.

Aged twenty-one, Salazar was several years older than most students. His maturity offered an advantage. He was already much better read than many of his peers. For the previous two years, he had enjoyed access to a well-stocked library in the college where he taught. It is likely there that he had the opportunity to refine his Catholic conservative worldview. He was already attached to the ideas of St Thomas Aquinas, who had become an influential figure in the history of Western thought by constructing a synthesis of philosophy and religion that sought to explain all life in a God-centred universe. According to the Iberianist scholar Howard J. Wiarda, 'Thomistic philosophy largely accepted Augustine's emphasis on organic order, of each group and person secure in his God-ordained station and (going back to Aristotle) on a hierarchy of social classes.'[10] The encyclicals of the recent pope Leo XIII, particularly *Rerum Novarum* (1891), were also an inspiration for the eager student. They accepted the onset of electoral democracy and laid down that Catholics should grasp the political opportunities to defend God, family and the interests of the nation.

At Coimbra, an Academic Centre for Christian Democracy had enjoyed an intermittent existence since 1901. At its reopening in 1912 after having been temporarily suppressed by the republican regime, Salazar gave what is his first known public address. He depicted himself as 'an obedient Christian Democratic soldier'.[11] With a young priest, Manuel Gonçalves Cerejeira, to the fore, the Catholic militants in Coimbra were determined not to cede any more ground to the republican regime.

In March 1914 Salazar headed a delegation which sought to appeal to the government not to turn a local church into the annexe of a museum. The government (then led by Bernardino Machado, a moderate) conceded, claiming that the church was too small for this purpose.[12] It would be the future prime minister's first visit to the national capital, at the age of twenty-five.

Salazar at Coimbra showed enormous capacity for work. Before he graduated in 1914 a committee of university professors, republicans included, had unanimously awarded him a prize in recognition of his scholastic prowess.[13] He was already developing his own independent sources of income. These came from offering consultancies on financial and legal matters to people needing advice on various commercial transactions. He now had enough money to augment his wardrobe with elegant clothes. He attended soirées and receptions and his circle of friends widened. Catholics and conservatives predominated but not all of them were from such backgrounds.

Fernando Bissaia Barreto, a medical doctor who was a near contemporary, became a lifelong friend. He would often travel down to Lisbon for Saturday lunch with Salazar when he was prime minister. But his political trajectory could not have been more different. As a medical student, Bissaia Barreto had played a prominent role in university agitation. He was a member of the secret society known as the Carbonaria and he got enrolled in a masonic lodge whose name was 'Revolta'. His credibility in radical circles enabled him to be elected to parliament in 1911. The next three years spent in Lisbon weaned him away from radical politics, however. When he returned to Coimbra in 1914 to qualify in medicine, he was a changed man. He had witnessed the divisions and confusions in republican ranks which had led to the swift decay of the republican cause. The unedifying behaviour of colleagues suggested not only to him that the Republic was far from an era of hope and improvement. The new regime inherited many of the structural defects of its monarchical predecessor as well as generating fresh ones. Dr Bissaia Barreto always remained republican-minded but he found common ground to establish a meeting of minds with Salazar that blossomed into a rich friendship. Both of them were involved in charity work, Salazar playing a role as an administrator and fundraiser in the Coimbra Misericordia, which was designed to help the poor and the sick. Over many decades, Bissaia Barreto would fling himself into work designed to ease the conditions of life for the poor. He built or reformed sanatoriums for tuberculosis sufferers, a leper colony, children's homes, natal clinics and holiday camps while performing his academic duties as the leading medic at the university.[14]

Salazar broke out of the predominantly male world of the university and Catholic ranks by striking up friendships with young women whom he encountered socially. Approaching the end of his law studies, he seems to have developed a strong emotional attachment to Julia Perestrello, the sixteen-year-old daughter of his godmother. Perhaps the most passionate and readable of the otherwise dry articles which he wrote for the Catholic magazine *Imparçial* was one which was simply entitled 'Ela' (She). It described the love for a beautiful young girl who lived in a fine house in a rustic location surrounded by nature's bounty but who was out of reach. In the case of Salazar, this would soon prove to be very much the case. He was tutoring Julia, and her mother was placed on her guard when he asked her to write an essay on the theme of love. Upon intercepting a passionate letter which the twenty-three-year-old Salazar had sent to her daughter, she took action to ensure that the relationship went no further. One biographer of Salazar has written: 'Her Julia was meant for the heir of another estate, not for the son of the manager of their lands in Vimieiro.'[15]

Father Cerejeira had tried to talk Salazar out of pursuing Julia and had been alarmed when he saw the best of the Catholic militants laying his emotions bare in the Catholic press.[16] He tried to steer Salazar away from 'frivolous' preoccupations even after he moved into the spacious former convent known as Os Grilos, where Cerejeira had set up his own community of like-minded souls. After Salazar got into the habit of smiling at the daughter of a law professor from the window of the Grilos, he even counselled him against thinking of marriage.[17] But Salazar, while having enormous respect for the priest's energetic work on behalf of their cause, was unmoved. He continued to have a circle of female friends to whom he was an adviser and a confidant. Elegantly attired, he would be seen with his close friend of the moment at the theatre or musical soirées. His feelings for these female friends would oscillate between friendship and something deeper. This handsome, well-mannered and fastidiously dressed young man was admired by them on account of his professional success as well as the public stances he had taken.[18] He was a good conversationalist, ironic and witty, but there was nothing superficial about this man with his considerable emotional depths.

The easing of political pressures on the church gave Salazar the space to pursue his personal interests and professional activities. The 1910 Revolution was not one that reverberated down through history as a harbinger of fundamental change like the Mexican one of the same year. Instead, it opened the way for internecine strife among the republicans. Few, if any, possessed the knowledge or capacity to build a nation on modern lines. Factional warfare intensified, and by the time it expired in 1926, there had been no fewer than forty-four governments.

Instability was greatly worsened after Portugal entered World War I on the Allied side early in 1916. The floundering state was unprepared for the commitment. No spirit of patriotic solidarity emerged. Instead, divisions between interventionists and neutralists hardened. The danger that Portugal's African colonies might be used as collateral in any compromise peace with Germany was an important argument for becoming involved. But German forces in Africa inflicted defeats on Portuguese forces, and on the Western front the Portuguese suffered desertions and high casualties. In total 10,000 soldiers were killed, many at the battle of Lys in April 1918.

In contrast to Portugal's disastrous World War I role, Salazar left nothing to chance as he sought to embark on an academic career. At the end of 1915, the university had announced a competition for new lectureships in a range of subjects. Salazar applied for the vacancy in the economic sciences. He spent the early part of 1916 preparing a thesis on 'the Problem of Wheat Production'. The submission was approved early in 1917. By now he was already on the staff. Indeed, he temporarily filled the chair of economics owing to the premature death of its holder, the quite left-wing professor José Marnoco e Sousa. He then proceeded to write a second thesis on the role of gold in Portuguese finances. He argued in both of these works against Portugal continuing to live beyond its means.[19] The gold thesis received a unanimous vote of approval in the faculty and Salazar went on to occupy the chairs of economics and finance at Coimbra.

In July 1918, the religious publication *Ilustracão Catholica* published a portrait of the young professor on its cover, predicting that shortly the nation would hear more of him.[20] He was thin, emaciated even, in appearance and, as men were being called up to fight in a war that meant little to most Portuguese, a military tribunal decided he was not eligible to take part. The clamour against the liberal Republic was reaching fever pitch as Salazar took up his teaching duties as a full professor in the autumn of 1917. Particularly forthright were a group of intellectuals from the upper and middle classes known as Integralists. Led by

António Sardinha, they offered a searching critique of parliamentary government. Their remedies were conservative and, indeed, authoritarian ones. Groups seen as embodying the continuity and vital spirit of the nation should exercise authority from the king down. They were nationalists before they were monarchists, according to one of their best-known activists, Hipólito Raposo.[21] For remedies to Portugal's national paralysis, they drew on the writings of 19th-century right-wing thinkers such as Auguste Comte and Gustave Le Bon. These French intellectuals, particularly Le Bon, were major influences on Salazar's own thinking, but the strong absorption of the Integralists in politics placed him on his guard. He preferred to see the answers for the chronic deadlock in Portugal as stemming more from administrative action. According to Cerejeira, Salazar would turn to him in 1918 and express his ambition to be 'the prime minister of an absolute monarch'.[22]

Portugal in that year was led by an authoritarian figure. The civilian Republic had been toppled in December 1917 and, until his assassination one year later, the country was ruled by a charismatic army officer, Major Sidónio Pais. He had a republican past but he rallied many of the Integralists to his side, as he did the younger officers. He was elected president on the basis of universal male suffrage and his regime was a forerunner, in some ways, of what followed after 1926. Integralists designed the regime's Senate, where landowners, aristocrats and army officers were numerous. But in the turmoil to be found all across wartime Europe, País was assassinated.

The most strife-torn period of the republican regime then ensued. Civil war swept parts of northern Portugal in the first months of 1919 as monarchists, led by Henrique Paiva Couceiro, sought to bring back the king. This uprising was suppressed with difficulty in a year when four governments held office. Another nine came and went in 1920. Salazar himself was not unscathed by the turmoil. In March 1919, along with three other professors, he was suspended from his academic post, accused of spreading monarchist propaganda while carrying out his normal duties.

In his appeal, Salazar mounted a vigorous defence, rebutting the idea that he had inserted his own political beliefs into the minds of his students. He claimed that it would be hard to tell from his lectures what his views on the constitutional position of the country happened to be.[23] He asserted that his engagement in politics only amounted to having cast a vote. He played down his own significance in Catholic ranks, scoffing at the claim that he was any kind of leader.[24] His accusers were unable to find any student willing to testify in their favour.

His defence, 'Minha resposta', was self-righteous but eloquent and skilfully couched. It was reprinted and has often been cited because it is seen as an early clue to his future intentions as a ruler. One passage reads: 'I am convinced that politics alone can never solve the great problems that demand solution, and that it is a grave mistake to expect everything from their evolution or from an arbitrary departure from their normal course. I am sure that the solution is to be found more in each one of us than in the political colour of a ministry. So far as I can, I try to make my students men, men in the best sense of the word, and good Portuguese of the type which Portugal needs to make her great.'[25]

The case was thrown out due to lack of evidence. Summer holidays in Vimieiro provided a respite from a turbulent year. By now Salazar's mother was suffering from an illness and would soon become an invalid. His closeness to Maria do Resgate Salazar had been shown years earlier by his decision to give precedence to her surname over his father's in his own name. In the Iberian peninsula it was normal to do the opposite, with children taking the surnames of both the mother and father and in that order.

Salazar's diffidence about politics was briefly dented when he decided to get involved with a new political party, the Centro Católico Português (CCP, or Portuguese Catholic Centre). The impetus behind it came from the Portuguese bishops who wished Catholics to be more visible in public life. From 1919 it would participate in elections, and it recognised 'legitimate authority' and promoted a message of social reconciliation.[26] Its first real successes occurred in 1921. Three deputies were elected for the CCP. One of them was Salazar, who had been persuaded to run for the seat in the northern city of Guimarães, regarded as the place where Portugal had been founded in 1140. By that time Salazar enjoyed undeniable prestige in Catholic ranks because of his academic success and growing influence as a conservative thinker. But it is likely that he agreed to suspend his academic career and opt for politics with deep misgivings. He would have been well aware that the parliament was dominated not only by political fixers, known in the Iberian peninsula as *caçiques*, but by dema-gogues also. They were the kind of angry tribunes who appealed to unreason and the spirit of revolt. He had read about how they had grown more prevalent in the political life of Western Europe in Gustave Le Bon's *The Crowd: A Study of the Popular Mind*, first published in Paris in 1897 and frequently reprinted.

Salazar took up his seat in July 1921 but he only remained two days in the capital. Lisbon was a city that he always had strong misgivings about even after it became his seat of power. Parliamentary sittings would not begin until the autumn, but Salazar had been elected to various committees, mainly concerning financial matters. He wrote to his friend Gloria Castanheira in August, 'I feel that politics will make me unhappy. I'm already getting stuck in the mud.' He could not reply in such terms to the Archbishop of Evora and the principal clerical advocate of a Catholic voice in politics, Manuel Conceição Santos, who wrote to him on 4 September, urging him to take his parliamentary duties seriously.[27] It is not clear whether Salazar ever replied to the prelate. His strong Catholicism did not mean that he was predisposed to display automatic obedience to religious superiors. In any event, the matter was soon taken out of his hands. On 19 October the conservative government of António Granjó was violently toppled. The prime minister was murdered in bestial circumstances as a dozen left-wing sailors hunted down their opponents in what was known as 'the Bloody Night'. The killings revealed a level of vicious anarchy and the reputation of the regime never recovered. Salazar refused to put himself forward again for fresh elections in 1922.

Salazar's surviving correspondence from 1921 shows him to have been prey to what may have been psychosomatic illnesses that summer. He must have realised that he would have been a fish out of water in the parliament. Perhaps his mild depression may have stemmed from a sense that, however appalling the regime, it would be very hard indeed to overturn a century of liberal influence on national life. But beyond republican symbols imported from France, the sitting regime had not sunk durable roots. It may have rejected Catholicism and monarchy, but it struggled to find anything to replace them with. There were no secular ceremonies which supplanted Christian customs. Compared with the liberal left movements in 21st-century

Anglo-Saxon countries which had bold plans to sweep away national loyalties and traditional group attachments in favour of a borderless world full of experiment, the Portuguese First Republic was a broken reed. Its adherents were powerless to resist a growing attachment to nationalism in keeping with the trend visible across much of post-1918 Europe. In Portugal new expressions of conservatism quickly sprang up.

The installation of authoritarian governments in Italy (1922) and Spain (1923) did not go unnoticed. These developments reflected a withdrawal of faith in the belief that political talent could flourish under democratic electoral systems and that effective government would result. Salazar may have shown an affinity for democracy in his 1919 statement when he referred to it as 'an historical fact, an unconquerable current ... perfectly compatible with Catholicism'.[28] But his absorption in the writings of early sociologists like Gustave Le Bon had bred within him scepticism about its claims. In 1919, he had invoked the French 19th-century political writer Alexis de Tocqueville when he spoke of the need for the practice of government to reflect its particular times and place.[29] With democracy entering a twilight age in Portugal in the mid-1920s, his sceptical outlook about its value would continue to be greatly reinforced by the trend of events.

3

SCALING THE HEIGHTS OF POWER

In early adulthood Salazar had landed on his feet in a country where brains, energy and determination were often no guarantee of career advancement for those from his background. His position might even be described as an enviable one by the early 1920s. Holding an academic post made him largely immune to political pressures, unlike many in the urban bureaucracies or commercial firms who knew their jobs and incomes could be imperilled by the vagaries of politics. He had not been traumatised by involvement in the war and his academic chair conveyed instant status in a country where the acquisition of a degree was seen as vital for professional advancement.

He threw himself into academic labours and Catholic politics and showed no inclination to start a family. But he had a circle of female friends alongside his male companions from the university. Correspondence shows him acting as an adviser or confidant to several of them.[1] From 1918, Gloria Castanheira was a close friend and formative influence.[2] Her home was a meeting place for writers, academics and lovers of music charmed by this concert pianist and music teacher. Salazar as a politician showed himself to be a man of refined cultural tastes, particularly in the musical field, and it is quite likely that this cultivated lady, almost twenty-five years his senior, helped to shape his journey from precocious country boy to sophisticated man of politics.

His correspondence with her reveals a man somewhat apart from the public image that would be fixed by the 1930s of an emotionally frozen public figure absorbed in his work.[3] The letters also show him to be melancholic and preoccupied by a range of minor ailments. But in public he cultivated an image of serenity and self-assurance. It was a profile that became more widely known especially after the second conference of the Centro Católico Português (CCP) held in April 1922. There he reaffirmed the view that all authority emanated from God and not from any kind of social contract. It was a Christian social order based on hierarchy, one ultimately guaranteeing the common good, from which authority flowed.

He also argued that Catholics in Portugal needed to be guided by the thoughts and goals of the Holy See in Rome. By now the Vatican had drawn back from confronting regimes hostile to church interests. Rome was not advising its adherents to try to topple its political enemies. Instead, the emphasis would be on seeking to restore the basic rights of the church where these had been reduced.

Salazar's message to fellow Catholics was one of obedience to the constitutional order. He had not ceased to be monarchist in outlook but he could sense that the cause was increasingly forlorn. King Manuel II, living in exile near London, had no heirs and many were still able to recall the poor quality of rule under the constitutional monarchy. But by the start of the 1920s, and partly modelled on the Action Française movement of Charles Maurras, a movement had sprung up in Portugal which advocated a more traditional and authoritarian monarchy. Lusitanian Integralism soon spread from right-wing youth to junior officers radicalised during World War I.

Salazar's decade as a senior academic at Portugal's premier seat of learning saw him grow in self-confidence as a political conservative He stood again for the CCP in 1925, the year in which Portugal would see the last election resembling a competitive one for the next fifty years, but he was unlikely to have been crestfallen at his failure to be elected. In 1922 he had said, 'I loathe Lisbon.'[4] Yet it was already becoming clear to some who knew him that he was being drawn inexorably into public affairs. He did not shrink from the exercise of power but at the same time his distaste for politics as it had been practised in Portugal was undiminished. He had stated in 1922: 'Look, I'm not, never was, and never will be a politician.'[5]

He would soon get to know Fr Mateo Crawley-Boevey, the Anglo-Peruvian priest who enjoyed influence during the papacy of Pius

XI. The priest related: 'he doesn't mislead me. Because behind that cold exterior, there is an inexhaustible ambition. He is a volcano of ambitions.' Fr Crawley-Boevey had been sent as an informal envoy to Portugal by Rome to test the extent to which the church could recoup its lost influence.[6] He arrived at a crucial point when Salazar, more overtly than ever before, was plunging into national affairs. Yet someone with Salazar's astuteness would have been aware that the Catholic Church no more possessed the key for acquiring power and influence than the monarchists did. The papal nuncio reported in 1929 that the Catholic Church had little presence among Lisbon's popular classes or even upper classes.[7]

If Salazar was to follow the path to national office, the military was likely to be his partner institution. Its influence was growing as that of the civilian Republic faded. A sign of its collective alienation from the political order came in the spring of 1925. In that year the trial took place of General Sinel de Cordes, a monarchist who had launched an unsuccessful coup. The general presiding at the trial, Óscar Carmona, was a republican but he had no hesitation in throwing out the charges, saying, 'the nation is sick'.[8]

Both Carmona and Salazar would play pivotal roles in the new political regime which closed down the parliamentary system in May 1926. Army units set out from the northern city of Braga on the 28th and soon they were in charge of the country, having met no resistance. The coup-makers were a heterogeneous alliance united only in their detestation of the fallen regime's lynchpin, the Democratic Party. For a brief time moderates were in the ascendancy. Commander José Mendes Cabeçadas became provisional president on 30 May. He was linked to Francisco da Cunha Leal, an energetic and strong-willed businessman located on the political centre-right. It has been claimed that Cunha Leal hoped to set up an authoritarian regime loosely based on Mussolini's model.[9] Salazar and two fellow Coimbra professors, Manuel Rodrigues Jr and Mendes dos Remedios, were invited to join the provisional government as ministers of finance, justice and education respectively. Salazar quickly withdrew—ostensibly on health grounds—noting the confusion and disunity among the coup-makers.

On 17 June it was the turn of Cabeçadas and the liberal republicans to be eliminated from the provisional government. The new strongman was General Manuel Gomes da Costa, a veteran of World War I. Politically inept, he was in turn ousted in a palace coup on 9 July. Fitful stability descended and, on 26 November 1926, General Óscar Carmona became acting president. He was a balancing figure, a republican, a Catholic and, it was said, at one point a Freemason. But any relief at the departure of the swarm of civilian politicians was tempered by confusion about what to do next. An institution that claimed now to be the nation's moral force had little idea where to take the counter-revolution. Senior officers found lieutenants who remained inspired by the example of Sidónio Pais to be volatile and demanding. Mutual suspicions, rivalries and unsatisfied ambitions beset the victors of 1926, and military figures who opposed them were soon plotting.

Salazar's retreat was only partial. He accepted an invitation from the minister of finance, Sinel de Cordes, to head a commission that was seeking to reform the tax system.[10] Over the next year he met a wide range of economic figures from across the country. These contacts would prove useful when the time came to unfurl his own economic model for Portugal. Relations soured with the minister when he declined to allow Salazar to make public his tax report. Meanwhile, the civilian was being courted by the minister of war, Abílio Passos e Sousa. Thanks in part to his leadership, the dictatorship survived a major bid to unseat it during February 1927. Many hundreds were killed in fighting in Oporto and then Lisbon. It was the bloodiest uprising witnessed in Portugal for over eighty years. In its aftermath, Salazar was invited to be the civilian expert in a new government. Young officers feared that another republican revolt might succeed if energetic action was not taken to deal with the chaotic national finances. Salazar held back, though. As he explained in a letter of 30 July 1927 to his Coimbra friend Joaquim Diniz de Fonseca, the intention of the dissidents was to leave him in the position of being a technocrat who was answerable to a military figure. He wouldn't have freedom of action to carry out vital financial restructuring. Moreover, he would have no opportunity to advance a fresh moral and political agenda at the heart of government.[11]

Events would soon show that he had sound grounds for reticence. On 12 August 1927 Lieutenant Alfredo de Morais Sarmento burst into a meeting of the government taking place in a military building in Lisbon. In later testimony from the president, he was described as being 'in a state of complete insubordination, forgetting the most elementary forms of discipline'. When Carmona tried to overpower him, a pistol that he was brandishing went off, and a bullet went through the trouser leg of a cabinet minister.[12]

A cross-section of impulsive civilians, along with junior officers, tried to fill the vacuum. Some were sent into exile in Angola, including two figures who would later play major roles in the Salazar regime, António Ferro and Henrique Galvão. The burlesque coup showed how precarious was the hold of the military regime. Salazar resolved to keep his distance, relating to Fonseca that if he joined the government in a subsidiary role, he would be at the mercy of diverging forces and could get little done.[13]

In the aftermath of what became known as the Golpe dos Fifis, Salazar embarked on his only trip outside the Iberian peninsula. He travelled by train to France and visited Paris, but instead of sight-seeing, he rapidly moved on to Belgium, then a stronghold of traditional Catholicism, the neo-Thomism which Salazar embraced and which would dominate official Catholic thinking until the 1960s. While in the country he attended a Catholic conference, returning rapidly to Portugal, where he started to comment acerbically on the regime's approach to economics.

The authority of finance minister Sinel de Cordes had frayed because of his failure to reduce the financial deficit. One obvious starting point was the military, which was top-heavy with senior officers.[14] But his hands were tied and, hemmed in, he appealed late in 1927 to the League of Nations for a loan of £12 million. A delegation sent to Geneva came back with the doleful news that a loan would only be forthcoming if the regime accepted what to one observer amounted to 'international control of Portugal's finances'.[15]

Salazar had rejected being a disposable technician. Now he went on the attack and, in a series of articles in the Catholic newspaper *Novidades*, he offered a critique of the handling of national finances as well as the loan idea. In the end, Sinel de Cordes rejected what he saw as this humiliating course, and the initiative now swung towards Salazar. He would emerge from the shadows when the newly appointed prime minister, Colonel José Vicente de Freitas, invited him to join the government. It was an overture Salazar could not spurn since those in charge of the military regime seemed ready to give him control of all government decision-making involving the spending of money.

But still he hesitated. With his friends in Coimbra, Fr Cerejeira, Mário de Figueiredo and Bissaia Barreto he mulled over the decision he would have to take. At one stage there was a histrionic outburst when he turned and said: 'So you wish me to go there alone and wake up at the bottom of a well.'[16] He also wondered if he would be able to bridge the gulf between the man of learning and the man of action. He later told a French journalist: 'Imagine if I had not succeeded in putting the state's finances in order. What would my pupils at the University have thought of me.'[17]

In the end it was Fr Crawley-Boevey who convinced him that he should rise to the challenge.[18] The terms that he thrashed out with de Freitas and Carmona showed that he had recovered his nerve. They were published in the newspaper *O Século* on 28 April 1928, the day he assumed the post of minister of finance: he would control the budget of each ministry and have a veto over all expenditure.[19]

It is astonishing to recall that a few months previously, Salazar's articles on financial matters were being cut by the censors. Now the country found itself confronted by an obscure civilian implacably determined to wield a new broom. This was revealed by the bluntness of his remarks upon being sworn in as minister. He declared on 28 April: 'I know quite well what I want and where I am going, but let it not be insisted that I shall reach the goal in a few months. For the rest, let the country study, let it suggest, let it object, and let it discuss, but when the time comes for me to give orders, I shall expect it to obey.'[20]

Salazar had been given the licence to be tough and outspoken. From Carmona down, the key regime figures well realised that their survival depended on a financial upturn. They also reluctantly accepted that for the financial recovery to go ahead, it must be within a new political framework. But defining a political direction when there was still no common ground in the military about any desired political end point was a tricky undertaking.

Salazar himself was initially uncertain about his political direction and it would take much thought as well as consultation with fellow conservatives before the path revealed itself. For now his labours were couched as patriotic work which would succeed in restoring order and dignity to Portugal. Obviously, many in the military liked what they had heard: on 9 June 1928 he visited army headquarters in Lisbon to thank its commander for the support already extended to him.

Neither did he neglect to work closely with the press so that newspaper readers could come to see the worth in his plans. For the rest of his life Salazar would attentively read the censored press and occasionally liaise with key editors. As new measures were rolled out, editors offered praise. On 27 July, the *Diário de Notícias* published the first of many adulatory articles. For the next forty years, its editor (for much of that time), Augusto de Castro, would be an assiduous promoter of Salazar's cause.

Salazar would soon learn that few figures in the military could be relied upon to offer equivalent loyalty. How long his political work would endure ultimately depended on the strength of his military support. On 20 July 1928, a small-scale coup was attempted in Lisbon, only to be rapidly quelled.

Salazar lived fairly openly at this time. His home from 1929 to 1932 would be a flat on Avenida Duque de Loulé not far from the strategic traffic junction at the Marquês de Pombal Square where more than one rebellion had been proclaimed. There he was tended by his housekeeper, Maria de Jesus Caetano Freire, whom he had inherited from his Coimbra lodgings. Dona Maria would give him unswerving loyalty over the next fifty years or more, guarding his privacy and usually ensuring a degree of domestic calm and a routine existence which he craved in his private life as well as in politics.

His transformation into a national figure occurred during his first months in government. On 27 July 1928, he issued a note promising that Portugal would stand by its foreign debt. On 1 August it was reported that his first budget envisaged a small surplus, the first for many years. During the rest of that month, he had regular meetings with the leaders of various economic interests whose support for his work was faithfully relayed in the press. His position was enhanced when, armed with special powers, he prescribed tough medicine that seemed to lift the sense of gloom that had long lain over Portugal. He balanced the budget and stabilised the escudo, hitherto one of Europe's most despised currencies. Ruthless centralisation, improved collecting and accounting methods, and cuts in expenditure, as well as some internal borrowings, made the books balance. He believed restoring financial equilibrium had to be rigorously adhered to before any financial expansion could occur. His line was reinforced when several civilian allies joined the government, including his Coimbra friend Mário de Figueiredo, who became minister of justice.

On his first anniversary in the post, Salazar published a long official note which revealed his vaulting self-confidence. He said that renouncing his good housekeeping would be a disaster and, besides, was now impossible. To show his seriousness he kept the heating down in his office and worked with a blanket draped around his knees. On 11 May he suffered an unexpected reverse when he slipped on a rug, badly breaking a leg. It required him to be hospitalised for several months. The celebrations marking the third anniversary of the 28 May uprising centred around the achievements of the convalescing finance minister. But out of nowhere a crisis revealed the persistence of ideological cracks within the regime, which briefly appeared to threaten his ascendancy.

On 11 June 1929, the civil governor of the town of Évora published an edict which prohibited civil processions and meetings without his prior authorisation. Moreover, this army officer ruled that the ringing of bells was forbidden after 9 pm. The local archbishop, Manuel Conceição Santos, lost no time in sending a letter of complaint to Figueiredo, the justice minister, who quickly ruled that church processions could go ahead without prior permission. Moreover, bells could be rung at any time. This local dispute in a quiet city just over a hundred miles east of the capital showed that church–state differences divided the military. Prime minister de Freitas overruled his minister. He spoke for those who believed Figueiredo's action violated the 1911 law separating church and state. Humiliated, the minister tendered his resignation.

As for Salazar, he played a masterful hand. The 'ringing of bells' (*toca dos sinos*), as the affair became known, was a secondary matter, he told his ministerial ally. But it was a major point of principle and he decided to submit his own resignation. This letter was conveniently leaked to the press, causing an uproar. On 4 July 1929 ministers gathered at the hospital where Salazar was still laid up, at the request of Carmona. Despite not being actively Catholic, he took Salazar's side. His work was too crucial for him to depart now. Instead, it was the prime minister and minister of war who submitted their resignations at the end of that day.[21]

It was Salazar who had prevailed in the first civil–military clash within the regime. On 9 July another government was formed under General Artur Ivens Ferraz, similar in his moderate republican outlook to his predecessor. Salazar was the only member of the outgoing government to stay on. There was then a bid by the general to seize the initiative from him. When he was absent from Lisbon on 4 October, Ferraz convened a cabinet meeting in which he announced an amnesty for many of the prisoners who had been deported from the mainland after the revolts in 1927. More seriously, he announced that 'a return to constitutional normality' was to be the objective of the dictatorship.

Upon his return, Salazar took up the cudgels and in the next cabinet meeting opposed Ferraz's plan for the dismantling of an authoritarian order then still in its infancy. Over the next three months a power struggle raged in which much of the Lisbon press helped Salazar to isolate his military foe. Salazar ultimately outclassed him when it came to infighting. While Ferraz was on an official visit to Spain, municipal chiefs came to Lisbon in a prearranged manoeuvre to heap praise on Salazar. At this event, he uttered what became a standard phrase of his regime, 'Nothing against the Nation, All for the Nation'.

He counterposed Ferraz's moderation with a plea for 'national regeneration' along what unmistakably looked like authoritarian lines. A meeting of the cabinet presided over by Carmona on 20 November issued a statement in which it endorsed Salazar's line of thinking on the future of the regime. The military moderate finally quit on 10 January 1930 after an acrimonious cabinet meeting from which Salazar had walked out.[22]

The ace in Salazar's hand of cards was undoubtedly Carmona. His position straddling the various fault lines in the military had contributed to him becoming president in 1928. Henceforth, he made it clear that no government would be approved by him unless Salazar was in it.[23] From the start of 1930 it meant that with the president's endorsement a civilian was now 'the strongman' of the regime. He played a major role in ensuring that it was General Júlio Domingos Oliveira who was invited to form a new government on 21 January 1930.[24] Oliveira was a dutiful but politically inexperienced cavalry officer who, like the president himself, was much involved with equestrianism. As he tightened his grip on power, Salazar was fortunate that these were the types of senior officers with whom he interacted on a regular basis.[25]

During 1930 Salazar was also interim minister for the colonies. He embarked on actions which revealed a lifelong preoccupation with territories none of which he would ever visit. He saw them as an extension of European Portugal and not as separate entities. Whatever the rest of the world thought, he was in no doubt that the Ultramar (after 1951, the official name for Portugal overseas territories) was indispensable for defining the nation and for creating a base that sustained Portugal's place in the world.[26]

However, in the uneasy peace of post-1918 Europe, these possessions were viewed as potential collateral in a bid to consolidate a rickety post-war settlement. They were discussed on the sidelines of the Versailles negotiations in 1919 and at the talks which gave rise to the Locarno treaty in 1925.[27] Besides the archipelagos of the Azores and Madeira, which were seen as districts of European Portugal, in Africa there was a string of territories of varying sizes. There was Cabinda at the mouth of the river Congo, Guiné further north and, offshore, a considerable number of islands, the most important of which were the Cape Verde islands and São Tomé and Principe. On the west coast of India there was Goa, whose official title was 'the State of India', and on the Chinese coast, directly opposite Hong Kong, there was Macau.

It was the position of the two largest colonies which preoccupied Salazar: Mozambique, a sprawling territory extending up Africa's south-east coast, and Angola, more compact but even larger. Indeed, it was fourteen times the size of Portugal and as large as the combined area of Spain, France and Italy. But in 1930 the territory (only lightly populated by settlers) appeared on the brink of anarchy. Its governor, Filomêno de Câmara, and his secretary, Lieutenant Alfredo Morais de Sarmento, were both volatile figures on the radical right. A murky power struggle in March 1930 led to the young officer being killed and his superior being recalled to Lisbon in disgrace.[28]

This kind of instability was the last thing that Salazar needed. He was in the final stages of drawing up a Colonial Act. It was designed to undo the autonomy allowed for under the toppled regime and reassert rule from the centre. There was a commitment to financial recovery but with the colony paying its own way. Salazar had already faced a challenge over Angola at home from a conservative rival, Cunha Leal. He was the governor of the Bank of Angola and had a different vision. He believed Angola could only be well run if it received substantial help from the centre.[29] Within forty-eight hours of his appointment, Salazar had ousted his outspoken foe from his bank position, and six months later he would be packed off to exile.

The Colonial Act was unfurled on 29 April 1930. It is seen as one of the defining documents of the regime. Salazar was greatly helped by a capable technocrat, Armindo Monteiro. He had invited him to be director-general of statistics in 1928 before making him his deputy in the finance ministry from 1929 to 1931. He visited Angola in mid-1930 and grasped that the lack of any financial order could trigger fierce unrest that might have unwelcome repercussions in Portugal itself.[30] Monteiro was one of the most self-possessed of Salazar's lieutenants. He relied on his ability to define priorities in Angola and impose financial discipline. Salazar is likely to have understood that a policy of national reassertion in Africa would do his credibility no harm among junior officers.[31]

The Act stipulated that the role of foreigners in the colonies was to be strictly limited. There would be restrictions on the purchase of property as well as investment and employment measures which favoured the Portuguese. Real fears existed in Lisbon that if a strong foreign economic presence sprang up, it could turn into an excuse for outright annexation of one or more of the bigger colonies. Salazar had no hesitation in standing up to the most visible contender, Britain, seen in some quarters as having already profited at Portugal's expense in southern Africa.

He refused to renew the contract of a British company which had been given a vast land charter in northern Mozambique. It was controlled by Lord Kylsant, a powerful figure in the City of London.[32] Pressure was brought to bear on the Portuguese politician by the British government. But he refused to yield. He sent a strongly worded letter to the British lord, denouncing the conduct of his company. The first example of Salazar's legendary stubbornness in international relations was thus directed at Portugal's oldest ally. He wrested control of a powerful special interest over a large part of Mozambique.[33]

Salazar had been aware of the company's poor conduct towards indigenous employees. But Portugal itself had very basic approaches to the issue of colonial labour, which the regime was in no hurry to modify. The priorities were to ensure that the colonies paid their way and were reserved for exploitation and development by Portuguese businessmen. Monteiro's biographer claims that he took the welfare of indigenous peoples into consideration.[34] But his reach is unlikely to have extended much beyond Luanda, and a shocking report submitted later to the National Assembly by a former Salazar loyalist, Henrique Galvão, showed how cruelly backward Portuguese rule could be.[35]

Salazar couldn't do everything even though the legend growing up around him suggested that he was a workaholic who slept little. He needed reliable subordinates who could execute tasks, warn him of dangers, and advise him on areas of policy he was still unfamiliar with. He retained many functionaries from the old regime if they fulfilled such criteria. Several of his chief helpers undoubtedly did. Antero Leal Marques, his chief of cabinet from 1928 to 1940, was one example.[36]

The head of the Portuguese foreign ministry until 1945, Luís Teixeira Sampaio, would be an even more valuable collaborator. This monarchist had a vast knowledge of diplomatic history and shared Salazar's innate distrust of career politicians.[37] Much younger people were also recruited. Marcello Caetano, an academically precocious right-winger, met Salazar for the first time in 1929, aged twenty-three. By 1931, when he obtained his PhD in constitutional law, he was already helping to draft the new constitution and in 1934 he started to draw up a new administrative code.[38]

Pedro Teotónio Pereira was another young Integralist who, like Salazar, was pessimistic about the direction of Western civilisation. He bemoaned the fact that for more than a century it had been under the sway of French liberal values. Portugal, he believed, had been turned into 'a second-rate France'.[39] His expertise in the area of insurance meant Salazar sought him out as early as 1928. He soon grew into a loyal collaborator—prepared to say (unlike Caetano) that when they disagreed, he always bowed to his superior judgement.[40]

Despite the military's size, relatively few soldiers emerged as close collaborators. Salazar had supporters among right-wing junior officers whom he preferred to deal with through intermediaries for fear of upsetting the command structure in a status-conscious institution. As he established himself as the regime's lynchpin, admirers flocked to his cause, some out of conviction, others from barely disguised opportunism. He mobilised his supporters in the business, municipal and media worlds when propaganda gestures were needed to show that he commanded real backing and was not just a dispensable technocrat. Accordingly, it made a lot of sense for him to formalise the backing for the change and renewal that he already personified in the eyes of many.

On 30 July 1930, three days after signalling his moving on from colonial affairs by resigning as interim minister, he took centre stage in an overtly political gathering. First of all, Domingos Oliveira announced the formation of a National Union (União Nacional). Nationalism was to be the fulcrum of the future politics, a version that was meant to be far removed from socialism. Salazar then took the floor, underlining that the era of disorderly parliamentarism was over. The family would be a vital building block of the new order. A central government with strong powers would direct it and there would be a tier of municipal government with real authority (though nothing came of that undertaking).

These were new times: 'there is peace; confidence abounds; and there is credit.'[41] The National Union (UN) would channel support for the government and defend the principles of the 1926 Revolution. Otherwise, little was said about the weight it would enjoy inside the regime. It is very likely that Salazar was still unclear in his own mind about the architecture of the system. For sure, democracy, as previously practised, was now inoperable as it contradicted 'the necessary hierarchy of values in a well-ordered society'.[42] It would be 'criminal' to imbue the UN with a party spirit. Salazar told an audience mainly made up of functionaries that it would be the antithesis of a political party.

The moderates who had been part of the original 1926 revolutionary movement now woke up to find there was no room for them. A transition to permanent authoritarian rule was instead in prospect. A parliament where parties would 'enjoy the right to elevate and topple ministers and cause obstructions in public life' was ruled out.[43] Revolts in both Madeira and Guiné in 1931 were duly quelled, the last armed moderate challenges faced by Salazar.

Time would show that the UN was to be an ancillary body, not a source of political power. At no stage did it appear that he wished it to fulfil the central role the Fascist party had acquired in Mussolini's Italy. This would have thrilled many on the growing far right, but it soon became clear to them that it was meant to be a platform of conservatism, not a revolutionary vanguard. The task of organising the UN fell, revealingly, to the ministry of the interior in subsequent months. Eventually, in May 1931, an organised structure was unveiled by the minister, who ingeniously observed that it was a political association independent of the state.

One month later the British Embassy reported: 'For some time past, he [Salazar] has been taking a leading part in every debate in the Cabinet and I am told that his voice has generally been decisive. A change of Prime Minister would therefore be a recognition of what is, in fact, the position of the cabinet today.'[44] But another year would elapse before Salazar's domination would enable him to become prime minister. Ardent supporters were not hard to find in the military, but most officers probably had a wait-and-see attitude towards politics. In his memoirs the veteran Salazar foe Cunha Leal wrote: '[Carmona] opposed his elevation to the Premiership for a long time and only consented with hesitations'.[45]

It is likely that there was great reluctance on the part of many in the military to see their dictatorship dissolved into a civilian one unless institutional guarantees were provided of continuing military influence. In the teeth of the Great Depression, Salazar's 1931 budget had been a stringent one and the military had faced cuts. The need to preserve symbolic power and be shielded from Salazar's financial zeal was bound to weigh heavily on officers with different ideological views.[46]

It was no mean feat for Salazar to domesticate a national institution which had never been far away from politics since at least 1820. In interwar Europe no financial expert came to wield his degree of power. Rather unusually, he combined technical skills with acute political intuition. This was a combination which was not easy to find in democracies and, over time, has grown harder to spot in politics generally.

Salazar proved to have the energy and tenacity, the clarity of expression, the necessary calm in moments of crisis, and the ability to tackle complex problems on a long-term basis that made it hard to keep him out of the premiership. By early 1932 a campaign was in progress for his elevation. Chambers of commerce, municipal councils and civil governors delivered eulogies. The main Lisbon newspapers published another round of approving editorials. In official visits beyond Lisbon, Carmona was left in no doubt about how great his chief minister's service to the nation had been.

On 28 May Salazar was decorated with Portugal's highest honour, the Tower and Sword, and his speech of thanks was broadcast on radio. A large crowd gathered in the Terreiro do Paço, Lisbon's large waterfront square, to hear it through special transmitters. In the same square the king of Portugal had been murdered twenty-four years earlier. Now it appeared that an undignified period of uncertainty and confusion stretching well back into the 19th century was drawing to a close. Finally, on 28 June 1932 the nation learned that there was a new government, this time led by the civilian 'dictator of finance' himself. Not perhaps since the implacable rule of the Marquis of Pombal in the 18th century had the priorities and judgement of one man come to determine the fate of Portugal and the direction it would take.

4

SALAZAR CONSTRUCTS HIS 'NEW STATE'

In political terms, it is possible to characterise Portugal in the early 1930s as a once densely forested tract where the trees had mostly been felled by a sudden and massive storm. What was left was a *tabula rasa*, a virgin land, in other words one capable of being redefined and built on by nimble and single-minded newcomers. It was Salazar who emerged from the pack of ambitious politicians, soldiers and intellectuals hoping to benefit as the dictatorship searched for definition and permanence. His background as a Catholic activist was unpromising but, during a time of rapid transition, he revealed himself to be a political entrepreneur unmatched in skill and effectiveness.

Within five years of arriving on the national scene, Salazar, through his management of budget allocations, brought the major part of the civilian bureaucracy under his direct control.[1] He then proceeded to place much of the nation's business and commercial activity under the sway of the regime. Much of Europe was already witnessing the centralisation of political power in even more unsettling ways, but this démarche was highly unusual in the context of recent Portuguese history.

The past was being relegated to a forlorn era as Salazar announced the arrival of a 'New State' (Estado Novo). How 'new' it would really turn out to be was, however, open to doubt. Just over forty years later, one not unsympathetic observer depicted the Portugal of Salazar as a modern, more complex, authoritarian extension of 19th-century managed politics under civilian, professorial leadership.[2] But there were genuine innovations which drew the attention of numerous analysts of European affairs whose gaze had rarely, if ever, alighted on Portugal.

In the eighteen months after Salazar became prime minister, a concentrated wave of law-making ensued. Work had been taking place on a new constitution from 1931. An *éminence grise* of the regime, Quirino de Jesus (1855–1935), had a major hand in drawing it up. His 1932 book, *Nacionalismo português*, revealed in some detail what would be the juridical framework for the Estado Novo.[3] By now an elderly figure, he assisted the 'dictator of finance' in breaking the hold on colonial affairs of Cunha Leal, who had comprehensively lost out in a power struggle with Salazar.[4] The historian António Sérgio referred to Quirino as 'the technical choreographer' of the dictatorship.[5]

Salazar's young lieutenants Marcello Caetano and Teotónio Pereira were also hired to work on the blueprint. As former Integralists, it is unlikely that they would have had much patience with a document portraying the state as a representative and democratic republic. This description had appeared in an initial draft, but in article 5 of the final version Portugal was described as a corporative and unitary republic.[6]

A costly propaganda campaign preceded a plebiscite on 19 March 1933 meant to ratify the document. Further publicity drives would extol it beyond Portugal itself for the rest of the decade. One of Salazar's intellectual mentors, the French sociologist Gustave Le Bon, had warned that 'enlightened constitutions and laws founded on reason' were usually of no avail in 'the Latin states' unless efforts were also made to improve 'the moral heritage'.[7] In a population of just over six million, around 1,200,000 people were eligible to vote. Officially, 719,364 approved the constitution while 5,955 voted against. However, about 30 per cent of the registered electorate (488,840) abstained.[8]

The 1933 Constitution was an eclectic document, a mixture of democratic and clearly authoritarian elements. The Integralists were bitterly disappointed and turned their backs on Salazar. Far from undoing the liberal inheritance which they felt had blighted the evolution of Portugal for over a century, they believed far too many concessions had been made to parliamentarism at a time when it was in eclipse elsewhere. But the veteran political thinker Quirino de Jesus seemed to think that Portugal needed something eclectic that transcended past divisions. He depicted the Constitution as being based on 'an ideology that was simultaneously liberal, nationalist and humane, but was firmly opposed to socialism, communism and "counterfeit" liberalism'.[9]

The liberal dimension was overtly expressed in the form of a National Assembly which would eventually sit from 1935 to 1974. It was a deliberative not a legislative body, its right to initiate legislation being subject to the proviso that no law or amendment might be proposed which would prejudice the national revenue. It had little influence on the formation or composition of the government, which became 'the exclusive attribute of the presidency of the Republic, the preservation of whose powers do not depend on the fate of any bills or votes in the National Assembly'.[10] The vote was confined to male citizens over twenty-one who knew how to write and had paid some taxes and to women with secondary education or who were family heads. It resulted in an electorate higher than the one before 1926. By 1942, owing to the slow decline of illiteracy, ten voters out of every 100 inhabitants could vote but, until 1945, only the National Union (UN) was able to nominate candidates.[11]

The National Assembly met for three months of the year, from November to February. The government could legislate by decree at any time without reference to the Assembly when it was not in session. When it was, Salazar had the power to suspend its sittings, should such action seem desirable.[12] He gave his own unflattering description of his creation in a 1938 interview: 'there are three months of the year when you have got to listen to parliamentary debates. Of course, there are occasional ideas of value but it is mostly fine phrases, just words! The present Council of Ministers is good enough for me; it's a small parliament in a way, and it's also useful and does something.'[13]

The Constitution made the president of the Council the dominant political figure. No longer was he first among equals.[14] It was a situation aptly described by Marcello Caetano as 'the presidentialism of the prime minister'.[15]

There was a head of state or president who in theory was the most important figure. In practice his function was to discharge largely ceremonial duties, leaving the prime minister with complete authority to run the country. Ministers were hired or fired on his recommendation to the president. The Constitution did not require the cabinet to meet in full session and, especially as he grew older or was in the midst of crises, Salazar preferred to work with ministers on an individual basis.

His constitution was a compromise between the conservative and authoritarian forces that had rallied behind him. Some were rooted in the pre-1926 system; others were opposed to it. They had shelved their differences in order to endorse someone who seemed capable of stabilising a social order which appeared to be collapsing next door in Spain, and who also displayed an unusual capacity for tackling national problems. Salazar promised an end to the situation where 'for many years in this country, politics killed administration: partisan fighting, revolutions, intrigues ... have proved to be irreconcilable with the resolution of many national problems'.[16] The term 'Salazarism' would enter the political vocabulary in the month that the Constitution was promulgated, perhaps an early recognition that his regime was ultimately a personal one.[17]

Article 8 of the Constitution listed basic rights and guarantees. Marcello Caetano set these out in what would be the key textbook on constitutional law for the next four decades. Among the rights enshrined were, for example, the right to life and personal integrity, property rights and basic guarantees of criminal proceedings. Added to these were freedoms typical of democratic regimes, such as freedom of expression of thought 'in any form', freedom of education, freedom of assembly and association, right of petition, complaint and complaint before organs of sovereignty, and right to resist orders violating fundamental rights.[18]

However, article 8 also entitled the state to prevent 'the perversion of public opinion' and 'safeguard the moral integrity of citizens'. It meant the state could regulate liberty of expression through a system of censorship directed from the ministry of the interior. Nor did freedom of association extend to allowing political parties. Moreover, 'crimes against the security of the state' became punishable by imprisonment. Finally, the state was also given the constitutional right to defend itself against 'all the factors that violated truth, justice, good administration and the common good'.[19]

Jorge Borges de Macedo, a historian who, after 1974, was often seen as a guarded defender of the Estado Novo, nevertheless argued that Salazar did not give sufficient attention to the practical means of ensuring the subordination of the state to law and morality.[20] But he was hardly under much pressure to do so given the discredit that democracy had fallen into even in some of its Western citadels. Professor Walter Shephard, president of the American Political Science Association in the year Portugal's Constitution was unfurled, called into question the viability of liberal democracy. 'Is it not evident', he asked, 'that the theory of popular sovereignty, the central idea of democratic ideology, cannot stand up under an objective political analysis, and must be abandoned?'[21]

Since the Constitution wished to correct 'the excesses of individualism', the presence of such authoritarian features is not surprising. In hindsight, Diogo Freitas do Amaral, who founded and led the only right-wing party to achieve prominence after 1974, believes the decision to embrace undemocratic politics was a misguided move given the concentrated support Salazar enjoyed in the Portugal of the early 1930s.[22] But few parts of the world witnessed the creation of new democracies at this time and Portugal had just emerged from the failed 1910–26 liberal regime (albeit one with elections fought on a very narrow franchise). Salazar, temperamentally an autocrat, would have found it hard to keep his coalition of interests intact and probably would have been lucky not to be swept aside in the resulting turmoil if he had sought to preserve a recognisably competitive form of politics in Portugal.

The father of this post-1974 politician, Duarte Freitas do Amaral, was a prominent figure in the Corporative Chamber (Câmara Corporativa). This was the regime's upper house and was staffed by representatives of various functional interests drawn from agriculture, commerce, industry, the military, the church, the universities, and various ministries and municipal authorities. Under the Constitution Portugal had been declared a corporative state. This doctrine saw the interests of various social classes as essentially complementary. It promised the abolition of strife between worker and employer, and even the end of capitalist exploitation. The body which would theoretically fulfil this aspiration was the corporation, supposedly meant to promote social justice and economic harmony.

The corporative ideal stretches back to medieval times when guild associations brought master and artisan together. In the 19th century it was refurbished by various thinkers alienated, to different degrees, from capitalism. From both right and left, capitalist individualism and the rise of the materialist state were decried. A historic breakthrough for the doctrine seemed to arrive with the triumph of Italian fascism.

Benito Mussolini placed the state at the heart of the corporatist ideal. Policy and administration came from an autocratic centre and not from 'the organic unity of all producers'. In reality this meant Mussolini himself. By 1939, when a corporative chamber finally replaced the old parliamentary system, he had made enough concessions to business and industry to nullify any innovative features of the doctrine. His corporations were little more than bureaucratic sinecures for fascist chiefs and their followers.

Salazar's nationalist regime had wanted to avoid copying a foreign experiment. The Portuguese system was supposed to centre around associations and not the state. The only external influence he readily acknowledged was that of the papacy. Two encyclicals were portrayed as cornerstones of his experiment, Leo XIII's *Rerum Novarum* (1891) and Pius XI's *Quadragesimo Anno* (1931), both of which stressed the desirability of labour and capital collaborating for the common good. In Portugal the law that sought to underpin this ideal was the National Labour Statute (ENT). Enacted on 23 September 1933, it was a charter for state control over life in the workplace. New labour organisations, known as *sindicatos*, were set up. They were controlled by the National Institute of Labour and Welfare (INTP—Instituto Nacional do Trabalho e Previdência). Their governing statutes and prospective leaders had to be submitted for state approval, and if they diverged from the ETN model they were dissolved.[23]

In time, figures from within the regime, such as António Castro Fernandes, conceded that, rather than treating capital and labour equally, the system perpetuated class antagonisms and favoured employers.[24] The right to strike was abolished but employers continued to enjoy much of their previous freedom of action. 'Anti-plutocratic' rhetoric employed by Salazar and his advisers failed to result in any deterrent action against exploitative capitalists. All employers were supposed to enrol in guilds centred around their area of economic activity and known as *grémios*. It was envisaged that they would work in unison with the *sindicatos*. But a *sindicato* required at least 100 members and most factories were small, family-run concerns. It was in the larger industrial concerns where the *sindicatos* were imposed, places where there had often been industrial unrest before 1926. By concentrating on industrial stress points, the regime demonstrated that it was more interested in social control than any innovative approach to industrial relations.

Economic interests in large-scale agriculture and fishing were obliged to join the corporative order, but in industry more exemptions were allowed. In the summer of 1934 Salazar publicly conceded that he did not want to force business interests into a straitjacket that might have the effect of strangling the economy.[25] But no such flexibility was shown in the labour field, where compulsion reigned. At the start of 1934, a rebellion had erupted, based in the glass-making town of Marinha Grande, against the 'fascist-like' corporativist order. It was swiftly put down, but significantly it would be the first challenge to the regime from the Communist Party.[26]

The thirty-one-year-old Pedro Teotónio Pereira was the architect of the corporative system. His base was the sub-secretariat of state for corporations and social affairs. It lay outside the cabinet and Pereira had hoped that this portfolio might be located within the prime minister's office, 'which would have given his agency more influence in the government system as a whole'.[27] Over more than three decades Pereira would prove himself to be a loyal collaborator.[28] He drew back from pushing through a full-scale corporativist revolution in the face of likely entrenched resistance from major business groupings; the armed forces and most of the state ministries remained outside the new ideological fold. Soon it was clear that 'a natural organic harmony' based on mutual voluntary collaboration between capital and labour was conspicuous by its absence.[29] The corporativist experiment certainly existed in the realm of public relations but its impact on governance was meagre. Portugal, to paraphrase Caetano (in 1950), was a corporative state in intention and not in fact.[30]

The corporative edifice offered a paternalist and micro-managing leader like Salazar several advantages. It enabled him to supervise and influence the pattern of industrial activity and limit developments that he disliked or feared. One of these was foreign intervention in the economy. New foreign investors were likely to have found the corporative structure disconcerting. The 1931 Law of Industrial Conditioning had already put curbs on foreign investment. But there was very little fresh domestic investment due to curbs on credit. Salazar's oversight of the economy was made easier the fewer the economic players there were. Despite the rhetoric condemning plutocrats, near monopolies grew up in several areas. Salazar could argue that rapid expansion would only overheat the economy and produce a cycle of boom and bust. But stagnation reigned in the first decades of his rule. State permission was needed to build a factory, add a new extension or move to a new site. Existing firms could intercede with the authorities to block approval.

How the system worked is well illustrated in the case of the industrialist Francisco Quintas, whose concerns were located in the northern coastal city of Povoa de Varzim. He had started a rope-making business in the 1920s and it soon became the nation's biggest producer. The government had been helpful. Sisal, the basic raw material, was obtained at fairly low cost from Portuguese Africa. The government also kept its price low, which boosted export sales. To discourage overproduction, licences were withheld from other competitors. But when he decided to branch into synthetic rope using plastic, he was rebuffed by the authorities, as another family firm in a nearby Portuguese city was already deeply involved in its production.[31]

Wolfgang Adler, a defender of Salazar's *dirigiste* economic approach, has argued that Portugal had been too prone to swallow foreign economic doctrines that were hardly suited to its long-term national conditions.[32] A dependence on foreign investment (which could result in agendas being promoted that suited powerful companies while leaving most citizens disadvantaged) had also arisen owing to Portugal's peripheral status between 1820 and 1930. Salazar did not go down the path taken by authoritarian Spain after 1939, which was to launch state firms to substitute for foreign investment and a weak private sector at home. Instead, he retained a competitive market approach to economics but with one vital qualification. All rules and decisions had to be subordinated to the 'superior interests of the nation' with the reduction of external dependence to a minimum being underscored.[33] This priority was realised 'through an extensive system of industrial licensing, which essentially mandated "prior authorization from the state for setting up or relocating an industrial plant. Investment in machinery and equipment, designed to increase the capacity of an existing firm, also required government approval."'[34]

The industrial workforce expanded from 1930 to 1940, rising from 478,000 to 602,000, and it grew even more rapidly in the following decade, rising to over 750,000 (an annual growth rate of 2.7 per cent). Employment in manufacturing grew from 12 per cent of total employment in 1930 to 19 per cent twenty years later.[35]

With few clouds yet on the horizon, Salazar admitted, in a speech delivered in February 1939, that the corporativist order had left many ordinary Portuguese empty-handed. There had been limited gains achieved by the workers in terms of salaries, social assistance and minimum wages.[36] Emergency conditions brought about by the world economic crisis and the war in Spain were offered as excuses.[37] By now Pereira had been away from the corporativist field for three years and was ambassador to Franco's Spain. The new agencies appear to have been used by Salazar to obtain oversight over different areas of economic life, suppress industrial agitation, and perhaps find a career outlet for university graduates whose support for the regime might otherwise slacken. Of the 4,000 university graduates being produced annually in the mid-1930s, over half were from the field of law, and the corporative bureaucracy was an area where many of them could be absorbed.[38]

In some quarters, an unhealthy signal was being relayed when his brother Luís became head of the important *grémio* of wine retailers and shippers in 1934.[39] But he was a respected figure in this commercial area, he was elected by fellow producers, and no breath of scandal seems to have been associated with his tenure. Affection for corporativism was likely to be sparse if it was associated with nepotism. Abuses in the system undermined the regime's legitimacy even when it seemed popular to foreign observers and, by the early 1940s, these would contribute to the Estado Novo facing unexpectedly strong opposition. With much of the world at war, a Portugal still at peace would see the corporativist institutions end up enforcing strict wartime rationing. For some it made it hard to recall Salazar's words of 1934 when he berated 'the modern tendency of unlimited State intervention to be a mistaken policy'.[40]

A shrewd person like Salazar, who was closer to his people than many other authoritarian leaders, never seems to have figured out that corruption would be difficult to avoid in the corporativist order.

Economic interests were already entrenched in various ministries and it was likely that lobbies and networks of power would seek to derive advantage from this new tier of bureaucracy. The British philosopher Herbert Spencer (1820–1903) had already warned how easy it was, in large state enterprises, for backstairs intrigue and sycophancy to determine selection, rather than merit.[41] In a country like Portugal where much state activity appeared to be based around the exchange of favours in what was known as the *cunha* system, perhaps Salazar needed no telling. He would receive and deal with petitions through his long political life, and perhaps the corporative system was an essential way for him to cement loyalty to his system. But as one historian remarked, it fashioned Portugal 'very much in the socialist way', leaving the Portuguese accustomed to a large state presence and very much dependent upon the state.[42] Indeed, in 1975 at the height of the left-wing revolution, one of its architects, the Coimbra professor José Teixeira Ribeiro, would be appointed a vice-premier in a communist-dominated government. His verdict back in 1945 had been that the legislation of the 1930s had created a 'corporatism of the state' and not a 'corporatism of associations'.

Surprisingly, in its aftermath, as veterans of the Salazar regime and its remaining supporters wrote about their experiences, very few bothered to devote much space to the corporativist system. One veteran regime insider, Idelino Costa Brochado, despite being a fervent admirer of its creator, was in no doubt that corporativism was 'opaque and illusionary'.[43] Such were its ambiguous features that variants of what was by then an unfashionable doctrine were later resurrected by European politicians, often though not exclusively on the left. In the aftermath of the New State, some democratic figures were drawn to interest group representation instead of a politics based around the cleavage of class.[44] Post-war corporatism (or 'neo-corporatism', to use Howard Wiarda's term) was far less authoritarian and intrusive than its interwar predecessor. But within the liberal democracies generally, trends after 1945 paralleled what had occurred in Portugal in the 1930s. There was a growing tendency among ruling politicians to ensure that issues previously seen as belonging in the political arena were removed and decided 'pre-politically' by NGOs, civil servants and the European Union. Experts drawn from civil society and elsewhere became important players in their own right just as the corporative actors in Portugal had been.[45] In return for having access to resources, enjoying honours, and being given admission to the political elite, they were sometimes expected to defend the government of the day in the media when it fell under attack. The beneficiaries of the corporative order in Portugal had also been expected to be cheerleaders of the regime whenever it faced unwelcome pressure from home or abroad.

Neo-corporatism ran out of steam as the careers of politicians associated with it faltered. But it remains attractive to mainstream figures such as the British academic Maurice Glasman. He is a member of the House of Lords in Britain and in 2017 he set out the argument for transforming the British parliament's upper chamber into an institution for corporate representation.[46]

Arguably, effective government capable of tackling serious problems in authoritarian Portugal and post-Cold War Europe suffered on account of the franchising of key tasks to ancillary bodies claiming to be either corporatist or civic. But in Portugal retribution was postponed for a long time because of the regime's ability to stifle opposition, by strong-arm methods if necessary.

Salazar called his new order a corporativist rather than a corporatist one because he wished to respond in an original and decisive way to problems which had distorted political development in Portugal over a long period. Politics had been relentlessly partisan, never more so than during the First Republic. Salazar laid out the charge sheet against parliamentary rule in 1934 when he wrote: 'The last democratic regime in Portugal did not effectively safeguard the interests of the individual nor maintain political liberty. In the past, free speech and the liberty of the press and of political association have always been subordinated to the interests of the party in power, with the additional drawback that in theory the law was one thing and in practice another.'[47]

It is clear from remarks that Salazar would make then and in the future that he regarded the defect as a general one. It was national in character and not confined to any specific political forces. In a speech he made twenty-five years after becoming minister of finance, he observed: 'We are prone to build on fleeting enthusiasms, due to our well-known character, and to abandon tasks we have just started for others. Now in the work we strive to do, we must progressively replace improvisation with study, fickleness in feeling with fidelity to a programme.'[48]

Salazar is unlikely to have disagreed much with the view of the Israeli political scientist Yoram Hazony when he wrote that 'where a people is incapable of self-discipline, a mild government will only encourage licentiousness and division, hatred and violence, eventually forcing a choice between civil war and tyranny. This means that the best an undisciplined people can hope for is a benevolent autocrat.'[49] His Constitution was the work of a paternalist who strove to replace bad old habits with a sense of national constraint. It aimed to ensure that there was little place in national life for 'men educated for the purely political struggle, the demagogic speculations, the emotional exaltations of the popular masses, and therefore inclined to reduce the life of the nation to agitation itself'.[50]

To remove destructive elements driven by their own appetites from political affairs, it was necessary to disable the chief source of their influence, the political parties. The 1933 Constitution was meant to be a 'system of cure' or a form of detoxification from the era of 'partyocracy' which Portugal had previously lived through. A dictatorship of the state was replacing a dictatorship of the parties, regime apologists contended, but one where citizens were offered greater opportunities to conduct their affairs without interference.

Plenty of dedicated and energetic people were needed if this fresh edifice was to have a meaningful impact on national affairs. The large numbers who were revolted by the sway that violence, demagogy and excitement had exercised over politics would need to be mobilised in order to draw a line under the past era of disruption and usher in a more successful one. But the occupational cartels imposed by corporativism did not provide an arena for people to develop a sense of responsibility or acquire familiarity with the arts of government at a practical level. Nor did the Constitution lay down a strong system of municipal government, long a staple demand of thinkers on the right. Salazar's formula of government was to be 'rule by the few'. It was what he was most temperamentally suited to. With his political skills, which included great powers of concentration and a strong retentive memory, he could provide momentum for such a system at least while his own physical and mental powers were strong.

His autocratic way assumed the existence of an elite schooled in moral principles that would provide an example to the wider society by the quality of its governance. He placed strong faith in the reliability of a benevolent and competent governing corps, perhaps one schooled in Catholic religious principles and devoid of the influence of post-1789 French radical thought. It is unclear whether he assumed in the 1930s that this elite would be far less vulnerable to the temptations of power than others had been elsewhere in Europe.[51] It would not have been unreasonable to assume that he hoped for a period, free of external preoccupations, to hone and perfect his form of guardianship. But he would not be granted the space to refine his design for governance in Portugal. International events would, arguably, blow the regime off course for almost a decade. Accordingly, when in the late 1940s there was the opportunity for a fresh look at the system of government, much of its sheen had faded and it was not just enemies of the regime who scoffed at the claims made for it.

5

THE ART OF PERSUASION

ALLIES AND RIVALS SUBMIT TO SALAZARISM

The death in Paris in July 1937 of Afonso Costa, the most redoubtable political figure from the 1910–26 era, marked the closure of any serious challenge to the Estado Novo from the liberal republican camp. The last remnants of the radical liberalism which had first welled up in the 1820s thereafter largely went unmolested as they huddled in the cafes of downtown Lisbon.

Increasingly, it was within Salazar's own support base, and the political right overall, that potential and actual challenges to his domination would spring. Outwardly, the Catholic camp appeared to be the most accommodating and least likely to pose challenges to its most favourite son's grip on power. By 1930 his close friend from seminary days, Manuel Gonçalves Cerejeira, found himself at the pinnacle of the national church. A bishop in 1929 at the age of only forty-one, he was chosen by Rome to fill the vacancy that opened up with the death soon after of the cardinal patriarch of Lisbon. It was just as meteoric a rise in the religious sphere for him as it had been for Salazar in secular politics. Enemies of the regime saw this as conclusive proof that a century of progress was being reversed and Portugal was becoming a clerical dictatorship.[1] But the truth would be rather different.

As a Catholic activist in Coimbra after 1910, Cerejeira had acquired the reputation of being 'an intellectual in combat'.[2] It would not assist the regime if he maintained this stance of being an aggressive defender of church interests. In 1933 he had complained to Carmona about the fact that the church was merely tolerated under the new Constitution and had been offered scant official recognition.[3] A year earlier, on Salazar becoming prime minister, a curious exchange between the two occurred which the dictator's semi-official biographer discusses but others have cast doubt upon. Cerejeira is said to have remarked: 'Do not forget that you are here by the will of God and with the support of the Church.' Salazar is said to have crisply retorted: 'I am here through the nomination of the President of the Republic and, from now on, our roads diverge. You occupy yourself with the Church and my place is in the State.'[4]

According to Franco Nogueira, henceforth both old comrades from Coimbra would look at each other in a different light and no longer see themselves as equals. As a conservative Catholic in a position of influence, Salazar saw his authority as partly emanating from God, but he did not wish to provoke dissension by being viewed as a Catholic militant in politics. His task was to extinguish political passions, and the political demobilisation of Catholics was needed for this to happen.

At the end of 1932, he bluntly made it clear in a speech that the era of Catholic politics in Portugal was over: 'The Catholic Centre [CCP] is an independent organization with a Catholic membership organized for active participation in politics. However, as its activities appear inclined to interfere with the progress of the Dictatorship, we must be prepared to introduce measures which ... will make the Catholic Centre superfluous.'[5]

On his side was the Vatican, which, after reaching a settlement with Mussolini in 1929 that put to an end over seventy years of confrontation with the Italian state, was urging Catholics in other places to reconsider an overt religious presence in politics. Instead of their being organised on a political basis, Salazar wished Catholics to throw their energy into charitable and educational activities.[6] These would reinforce the work of the state in restoring and improving Portuguese society, and to that end Portuguese Catholic Action was set up. Cerejeira was the driving force behind it, but he refused to fall into line overnight with Salazar's broader wishes. He was aware that some prominent figures saw the continuing need for a party that acted in defence of Christianity. Chief among them was António Lino Neto. He was unhappy at the prospect of Catholics being absorbed in the pro-government National Union (UN). He had been unconvinced upon seeing that the chief organiser of this body was the minister of the interior, a Freemason and a republican.[7] There was dissension also on the part of some bishops, but, in 1934 the church submitted. The CCP was dissolved and Lino Neto dropped out of public life (his son becoming a serious foe of Salazar during the 1950s).

At least eight Catholic colleagues who had been deputies before 1926, or prominent in CCP ranks, were elected to the National Assembly for the UN. From the outset, this national front was usually a docile instrument of Salazar's personal power. The first congress, held in 1934, was described as a 'ceremony in which the single command was authorised'.[8] A full decade elapsed before another took place. Meanwhile, the UN collaborated with the local administration to defend the status quo, or what was known in Portugal as *o situação* (the situation). In rural and small-town Portugal the *situacionistas* were often drawn from old families whose status derived from the land they owned or their business or professional weight. They had edged out the electoral bosses or *caciques* and, given the authoritarian times, were under little or no pressure from the wider society. In the larger cities it was harder for the UN to exercise prolonged influence. Here members of the liberal professions and small businessmen had sometimes commanded real respect. Even in a small town like Chaves in the north, a politician like Nicolau Mesquita had managed to use his 'pull' in Lisbon to bring a lot of improvements, mainly in the form of public works, to the place before the 1920s.[9] But under the Estado Novo there were few prominent figures who carried weight in a locality, region or economic sector in this way. The politically active naval officer Henrique Tenreiro, who acquired a dominant interest in the fish-processing industry and sat in the National Assembly for many years, was an exception.[10]

Instead, the political game was often restricted to rivalries involving personal interests, as one UN notable from the town of Fafe candidly admitted.[11] Such factionalism had already badly weakened the First Republic but, perhaps seeing it as an unalterable part of the national condition, Salazar channelled it into areas where it would not undermine the regime. But there was a price for having a facade party devoid of any real autonomy and energy. It would be paid when opposition revived to menace the regime.

Almost from the outset Salazar positioned himself as the impartial maestro conducting a varied ensemble of middle-class and traditional interests. He saw that the health and longevity of his regime was bound up with convincing the Portuguese that he was the steady and incorruptible conductor, free of compromising ties, whether it was with business networks or professional bodies or also the church.[12] He was sceptical about the ability of major Portuguese interests to behave responsibly if given free rein. His own remarkable political success may well have bred in him the view that the Portuguese were too immature to be left to their own devices. The bourgeoisie had shown its own incapacity to organise in both its own interest and that of the nation during the parliamentary era. He believed that order and progress would go hand and hand if political activity was diluted and poured into the empty vessel of the UN.

Most self-consciously Catholic Portuguese seemed prepared to accept Salazar's tight, paternalistic order. The country now had a recognisably Christian leader. His promised national restoration offered a degree of certainty in a turbulent world. For traditionalists there was much to appreciate. Class relations were frozen, seemingly on a pattern modelled on Salazar's own home town, Santa Comba Dão, 'with its rural, peaceful, static, hierarchical, mutually dependent, unchanging social order'.[13] Salazar's insistence that Portugal must learn to live within its means was bound to strike a chord with many Catholics. They were also bound to welcome the signing of a Concordat between Portugal and the Vatican, which was agreed in May 1940. Salazar kept a signed photo of Pope Pius XII on his desk. This pope, who reigned from 1939 to 1958, admired the Portuguese leader. At one stage he said: 'I bless him with all my heart, and I cherish the most ardent desire that he be able to complete successfully his work of national restoration, both spiritual and material.'[14]

But Salazar drove a very hard bargain with the church. 'God, Patria and Authority' might be watchwords of his regime but he was never prepared to turn Portugal into a confessional state. If Catholicism became the official religion with conspicuous state backing, he knew this would prove a rallying point for many opponents. He was likely to be aware that the large religious movement associated with the apparition of the Virgin Mary in the hamlet of Fátima was a deceptive indication of the strength of religion.[15] Nearly one million pilgrims may have gathered at the commemoration on 17 May 1931, but much of urban Portugal remained secular in outlook.[16] In 1931, the northern city of Braga had three times as many priests as much larger Lisbon.[17]

In public Salazar held aloof from the cult of Fátima and allowed the negotiations of the Concordat to drag out over four years. His tough approach to Rome meant that negotiations almost came to naught over the issue of civil marriage, which Rome was unhappy to see would be preserved. On 16 April 1940, a note from his office to the Catholic Nunciature announced that it had been impossible to reach agreement and accordingly the negotiations had foundered. The impasse had arisen over the Vatican's refusal to accept that each Catholic marriage in Portugal needed to be registered with the state. Salazar had already been unbending on a range of other points. He refused to accede to Portugal being officially recognised as a Catholic nation. He very well knew that the faith lacked sufficient implantation in national life. Nor would he agree to tax exemption for religious institutions or compensation for church property seized by the state in the early 19th century. The request to allow Catholic labour or employer organisations was also turned down.[18]

In the end it was the Vatican which blinked first after influential Catholics, particularly Mário de Figueiredo, succeeded in putting the negotiations back on track.[19] The agreement announced on 7 May 1940 maintained the separation of church and state, but the church was given a range of secondary privileges. Religious education was expanded and divorce was forbidden for those who had married in church. But civil marriage and civil divorce were maintained. The state was prepared to help pay for the construction of new churches if the rest of the cost was borne by the church. However, it did not put priests on the state payroll and only in Africa was real generosity shown to the church. Land was given to the missions along with subsidies for seminaries, and pensions for religious personnel seeking to Christianise indigenous inhabitants. Presumably the latitude was shown because the church was seen as a vital ally in spreading Portuguese influence beyond the coastal areas of Angola and Mozambique.

The Concordat defined the Catholic Church in Portugal as an organisation of moral and spiritual interests, but it had to submit to the requirements of the nation of which, naturally, Salazar was the primary interpreter.[20] A diplomatic historian has claimed that after 1940 'relations with the Holy See were characterised not by cordiality and trust but by suspicion and reserve'.[21] Salazar was only too aware how sensitive public opinion was in the major cities to any signs of partiality towards the church.[22] He preferred to risk a break with the Vatican to jeopardising the ideological balance of his regime. Rome's man in Lisbon in 1940, Archbishop Ciriaci, branded him 'a demonic incarnation'.[23]

There was no parallel between the national Catholicism of the Franco regime and the political truce which Salazar had painstakingly constructed between political camps whose quarrels had disrupted Portugal many years previously. The Concordat signed between Spain and the Vatican in 1953 ensured each diocese received financial support from the state and laid down that only a church marriage was legally binding. Under Franco, but not under Salazar, 'complete mutual identification' of church and state occurred.[24]

Salazar's relations with Cerejeira gradually cooled. The prelate had to balance international Catholic priorities, which grew more liberal after 1940, with domestic political imperatives at home. Ultimately, Salazar's old clerical friend from Coimbra never gave him serious trouble and was mostly absorbed in his religious responsibilities, usually doing his best to keep church adherents away from political controversy.

In his bid to heal deep-seated fractures in the conservative camp, Salazar could not overlook the monarchists. He praised them in his November 1932 speech outlining the direction of his regime: 'the forces opposed to demagogy could always count on the support of the monarchists'.[25] But many Portuguese, he recognised, had grown indifferent to the monarchy. He contrasted northern Europe, with its thriving constitutional monarchies, to the south where republicanism had made undeniable inroads. He argued that in order to forestall the threat of revolution in the future, monarchists should rally behind a regime like his which sought to preserve order. His efforts were assisted by the death in exile of King Manuel II, the last male member of the Bragança line. News of his passing, aged only forty-three, reached Lisbon on the day Salazar was sworn in as prime minister. A descendant of the

19th-century Prince Miguel, Duarte Nuno lived in southern Germany where he was an agronomist, but he only properly learned Portuguese in early adulthood. His marriage to a member of the female line of the Braganças reconciled the two estranged royal houses and he was allowed to settle in Portugal in 1950. But Salazar resisted attempts from allies like Fezas Vital, who had helped him draw up the Constitution, to groom Prince Duarte for kingship. There was no aristocracy of ideas associated now with the monarchy, which had narrowed into a sectional cause.

For twenty years monarchists and republicans collaborated in the UN. Salazar's powers of persuasion succeeded in effecting a truce between them. But not everyone was reconciled. The colonial hero and indefatigable plotter against the republic, Henrique Paiva Couceiro, turned against Salazar and was banished for two years in 1937. A letter he had written that Angola was on the verge of being snatched from Portugal had leaked out.[26] This staunch colonialist was responding to an initiative from an ex-British ambassador to Lisbon, Sir Claud Russell, who had publicly stated that Germany should be compensated with territory by different European powers including Portugal.[27]

As for the Integralists, they believed in monarchy. One of the most prominent of them, the lawyer Hipólito Raposo, was exiled in 1940, and deprived of his public offices, for insubordination.[28] His friend, the landowner Pequito Rebelo, kept open lines of communication with Salazar in the 1930s although holding aloof from the regime.[29]

Perhaps the greatest headache faced by Salazar as he consolidated his 'New State' came from the radical right. Chief of the ideologues who desired a vanguard party in tune with revolutionary developments in Italy and Germany was Francisco Rolão Preto. He had spent a lot of time in Belgium and France where he had pursued studies in law. His newspaper, *Revolução Nacional*, expressed the belief that a new type of 'political man', 'the fascist man', was poised to dominate the political stage from 1933.[30] In January 1933, Hitler's appointment as German chancellor was the subject of several laudatory front-page articles.[31] The newspaper was the main voice of the Blueshirt Movement—also known as the National Syndicalists—which became Preto's personal vehicle. He was bound to be disappointed in Salazar's unadventurous direction of travel. The leadership of the UN 'was a veritable college of cardinals composed of conservative notables from various strands of the Portuguese right'.[32] The Constitution, proclaimed as Hitler was smashing the power of German conservatives as well as the left, emphasised traditionalist and Christian principles.

Throughout his life Salazar shrank from releasing popular energies. He had a horror of revolution or agitation wherever it was manifested. This was in keeping with the type of politician that he was. He had an empiricist mindset, a leaning towards the concrete and the sensible over the dramatic, the far-fetched and the speculative. As the French political thinker Raymond Aron wrote in the 1960s: 'The government of Salazar tries to "depoliticize" men, that of Hitler or Mussolini to "politicize" or fanaticize them.'[33]

Thus, to have a somewhat reactionary leader imposing his will on Portugal in what were revolutionary times across much of Europe was a bitter blow to Preto. He was determined to set himself up as an alternative to the unflashy provincial dictator. While Salazar never had much time for big set-piece rallies, his radical challenger made these the basis of his bid for power. He toured the country speaking at public events and holding well-attended banquets. Young activists, drawn from the petite bourgeoisie, were attracted to them. The movement had a following perhaps amounting to 30,000 people.[34] It also had lines of communication extending to the presidential palace. Preto was received there in mid-1933 by Carmona, who reportedly assured him that 'all nationalists have a role to play in the new political situation created by the 1926 coup'.[35] Neither this careful arbiter of different tendencies within the regime nor the British Embassy, which observed around the same time an unprecedented growth 'in numbers and in strength' of the Blueshirts, was complacent about this rude movement led by a man who ostentatiously sported a Hitlerian moustache.[36]

But Preto was given no grounds for thinking that Salazar would share power or allow himself to be elbowed aside, as had happened to the conservatives in Germany. Prevented from holding a meeting in Coimbra, in January 1933 he went to a smaller place where he said: 'We have only one viva: viva the Dictatorship ... Whether they want it or not we are defenders of Dictatorship.'[37] Plenty of restive students were ready to take a bet on Preto's movement succeeding and bringing them influence and a state salary. Salazar's formula seemed to hold out no such automatic expectations. His desire to lower the temperature and restore predictability was not shared by a lot of young middle-class ultras.[38]

In a book-length interview published in 1934, Salazar poured cold water on revolutionary dreams: 'Our country's past is full of glory, full of heroism; but what we've needed, and especially in the last one hundred years, has been less brilliance and more staying power, something less showy but with more perspective. Anything that just makes an appeal to the heroism of our race without altering its general attitude of mind ... its way of doing things, all that may give us back for a moment our pages of glorious past.'[39]

Preto's movement became subject to censorship, and moves were made to detach his more promising lieutenants from the cause with offers of state jobs.[40] Speaking in Lisbon on 25 May 1934, Salazar bluntly spelled out that as long as he was in charge, Portugal would not become a pocket version of Hitler's or Mussolini's totalitarian order: 'we must put aside the inclination to form what might be called a totalitarian state. The state which in its laws, ethics, politics, and economy subordinates everything to national or racial interests would appear to be an omnipotent being, the principle and end in itself, to which all individual or collective action would be subject; it might even bring about an absolutism worse than that which preceded the liberal regimes, because the former, at any rate, did not sever itself from human destiny. Such a state would be essentially pagan, incompatible with the character of our Christian civilization, and leading sooner or later to revolutions like those which infected the older, historical systems of government, and, who knows, to religious wars more terrible than those of the old.'[41]

In the summer of 1934 a showdown could be postponed no longer. After making a particularly bold call for an overhaul, Preto was deported to Spain. On 29 July 1934 an official note announced the dissolution of the National Syndicalists and their merger with the UN. The assassination of the Austrian leader Engelbert Dollfuss had occurred days earlier (carried out by agents of Hitler), and this may have spurred Salazar into action. His corporativist Catholic regime offered close parallels with Salazar's own. The ruthlessness of the Austrian Nazis was bound to give him some food for thought. Some of

Preto's followers were sufficiently alienated from the uncharismatic regime to take up arms against it. But an attempted coup involving them and some anarcho-syndicalists (and army officers) collapsed within hours in August 1935. It lacked the backing of ultra-right-wing junior officers like Henrique Galvão, who had plotted in the past and would turn against Salazar in the future. In 1935, he was careful to write to Salazar 'in the face of the futile campaign of rumours and intrigues that have arisen, to express my warmest applause for Your Excellency's policy, which alone has merit and can take this country in the direction that is needed'.[42]

The influential law professor Luís Cabral de Moncada had been a Blueshirt member in 1932–3 and he later described it in these terms: 'it was a superficial phenomenon equivalent to the ephemeral lights sometimes visible on the waves in maritime conditions ... [Its] ... only function consisted of shouting ... and raising the right arm and hand in a Nazi or Fascist salute. These were actors not warriors.'[43]

A researcher examining requests for favours made to Salazar concluded that Moncada was assiduous in lobbying whenever he corresponded with the dictator. Salazar tolerated such approaches as they often disarmed potential troublemakers. Not surprisingly, he willingly threw open the regime to ex-Blueshirts who had shaken off their revolutionary ardour. From early 1934 a new body, Acção Escolar Vanguarda, was set up by the propaganda wing of the Estado Novo as an outlet for their energies. Much later some popped up in important posts. (One was Gonçalves Rapazote, the regime's last interior minister.)

The only other early direct political challenge to Salazar's emerging political order came from the ranks of the Portuguese Communist Party (PCP), which had been founded in 1921. It had around 400 members in 1935 and was increasingly the main target of the Police for the Vigilance and Defence of the State (PVDE). The PVDE had emerged from the ministry of the interior in 1932 and would still be an amateur force, lacking any specific training as a secret police agency, until later in the 1930s. In 1933 Salazar had characterised communism as a dangerous religious cult which had a twisted morality all of its own. He wrote: 'Communism is the synthesis of all the traditional revolts of matter against spirit, and of barbarism against civilisation. *It is the "great heresy" of our time* ... It tends to the subversion of everything, and in its destructive fury, it does not distinguish error from truth, good from evil, justice from injustice. Of little importance to it are the history and centuries-old experiences of humanity, the life and dignity of the intellect, the purest sentiments of the family, the honour of woman and her modesty, or the existence and grandeur of nations, as long as with its false conception of humanity it can succeed in man's enslavement and his worst subjection.'[44]

Being pessimistic by inclination, Salazar would most likely have not been surprised by the foothold the PCP acquired in a mainly rural society like Portugal, which still had only pockets of heavy industry. He was under no illusions that a regime like his, which had no special consideration for industrial working-class interests, could easily pacify the movement or buy it off. The PCP's first general-secretary, Bento Gonçalves, was treated as a dangerous foe. A worker in the naval arsenal in Lisbon, in 1935 he attended the first conference of the Comintern in Moscow. Arrested on several previous occasions, he was given a much harsher sentence upon being apprehended shortly after his return. He became one of the first prisoners sent to a rigorous detention camp that was opened in the Cape Verde islands at Tarrafal. It was an inhospitable place where the prison regime was harsh. Opponents of the regime did not hesitate to regard it as a concentration camp and Adriano Moreira, a minister of the government in the 1960s, described it as an awful place after paying a visit there following its closure in 1954.[45] Gonçalves died there in 1942, aged forty, appeals for an amnesty having been rejected.

The thirty-two prisoners who died at Tarrafal were almost all from a working-class background and would have had few people of influence ready to defend them. It was a different matter in the case of Álvaro Cunhal. He would replace Gonçalves as Communist Party chief following an interregnum of twenty years. In 1940, as a young militant but of impeccable middle-class origins, he was given a privilege very unusual in any country where the Communist Party had been forced underground. He had been detained in July of that year shortly before he was due to take his doctorate in law. His petition to take the exam in prison was passed on to the law faculty of the University of Lisbon. The faculty was dominated by Salazarist academics, including Marcello Caetano, then head of the regime's youth movement. Remarkably, it was agreed that the examination could proceed but that it must take place at the university. Besides Caetano, the chief examiner was Manuel Cavaleiro Ferreira, a future minister of justice. The subject of Cunhal's thesis was abortion and he advocated a liberal approach to something that was illegal in Portugal (as well as Russia at that time). He defended his thesis vigorously and the examiners awarded him his doctorate.[46] It was an unusual display of liberalism at a time when Europe was gearing up for terrible bloodletting in World War II. By now, the size of the Communist Party had also steadily increased in Portugal. The consideration shown to Cunhal not only highlighted the fact that academics played a prominent role in this authoritarian regime, but that class and status determined how even an enemy of the state was treated.

6

PORTUGUESE RUTHLESSNESS
IN THE STRUGGLE FOR IBERIA

Salazar may have been the central figure in Portuguese national affairs for forty years but, arguably, it was only in the 1950s that there was sufficient internal calm and wider geopolitical security for him to find the space to consolidate his regime. But by then he had been in charge for twenty usually eventful years. He was tired, had aged and had fallen into a routine which precluded a new wave of experimentation and reform. Fifteen years of crisis on the international stage had claimed his attention.

Without the eruption of the Spanish Civil War, his energies were likelier to have been directed at fine-tuning his Estado Novo. In such an eventuality, perhaps his outright dominance would have been avoided. The army's watchdog role might have been superseded as civilians assumed prominence. Some of them, if able and single-minded, might have withheld deference from Salazar. One who did was Manuel Rodrigues, the minister of justice, who, on the last day of 1938, wrote an intriguing article which appeared in the prominent Lisbon daily, *O Século*. It was entitled 'The Man Who Has Passed' and it was interpreted as a swipe at Salazar, a warning not to dream of entrenching himself in office indefinitely.[1] Rodrigues himself was no upstart but one of the Coimbra professors who had been invited in 1926 to join the military government and who had served in Salazar's government for an unbroken eight years, carrying out important changes in the area of justice.[2]

Accordingly, in the absence of external threats, fissures might have developed if Salazar had still tried to make his regime one of largely personal power. There were independent-minded figures, people needed by the strongman in order to help him manage a country which was by no means reconciled to meekly accepting, over the long term, a traditionalist regime. But the rebellion against the republican government in Spain which erupted on 18 July 1936 caused potential rivals to Salazar to shelve their agendas. The Spanish Civil War proved to be the start of a major emergency that deeply preoccupied regime-backers. It would rage for another decade as it became transformed into World War II, which, in turn, gave way to the Cold War.

The eruption of deadly strife in Spain would have come as no surprise to Salazar. As Portuguese politics were growing more conservative, Spain was the scene of an increasingly furious power struggle between left-wing, secular-minded republicans and a range of enemies on the right. The overthrow of the monarchy in 1931 had been a steep reverse for the Spanish right. But the republicans had been unable to consolidate their rule. The next five years saw not only frequent changes of government but rural unrest and a full-scale workers' rebellion in the coal-mining region of Asturias in 1934. These events were watched with anxiety by Salazar. He kept his distance from the republicans. He knew that Manuel Azaña, minister of war in 1931, later head of government, and finally president of the embattled Spanish Republic from 1936 to 1939 had 'encouraged, financed, and armed' those seeking to topple his own deeply conservative regime'.[3] From May 1936, thanks to a Spanish monarchist informant, he was aware that a coup (one involving a large part of the army) was being organised.[4] For his part, he was ready to allow right-wing nationalist conspirators to use Portuguese soil as a base for their activities. He felt he had little to lose. The republican camp was swinging ever closer to the left and promised sweeping land reform of the kind Salazar would never permit. The triumph of the left in Madrid was bound to embolden the opposition at home. Peninsular unity had been a rallying cry for radicals in both Spain and Portugal for nearly a century. The Spanish left was internationalist in outlook and Salazar feared that subduing Portugal would be one of the early objectives of a Spain under its control. Many middle-class radicals in Portugal backed Iberian federalism, some believing their country was too small for her agriculture to be modernised and industrialisation to occur.[5]

To the outside world Salazar tried to offer a benign view of Hispanic relations. He wrote in 1933: 'Portugal and Spain are like two brothers, each possessing his own home in the peninsula; so close to each other that they can talk over the wall, and even more friendly because each is independent and jealous of his autonomy.'[6] But this was just a facade. The narrow electoral victory obtained by the Spanish left in February 1936 plunged peninsular relations into crisis. Minutes of cabinet meetings in the spring of 1936 revealed that the biggest threat to Portuguese sovereignty was seen as emanating from extremist forces now in the driving seat in Spain.[7] Accordingly, Salazar felt he had no choice but to do his utmost to ensure victory for the rebels as the stand-off with government forces soon turned into a fiercely fought civil war. Portugal's leading industrialist, Alfredo da Silva, was encouraged to offer material resources to the rebels (which he later complained he was never paid for). Veteran army officer General José Sanjurjo, the titular head of the rebellion, was based in Portugal. He met with Salazar shortly before setting out to join the rebels, who had quickly captured most of the land adjoining the Portuguese frontier. But he was killed after his plane had crashed on take-off from an airfield at Cascais on 20 July.

The contagion effect that warfare in Spain could have on Portugal was shown on 9 September when mutinies erupted on board two of Portugal's biggest naval ships, the *Dão* and the *Afonso de Albuquerque*, when they were docked in the estuary of the river Tagus. The intention of the mutineers was to sail the vessels to a Spanish port and join the republicans. But the government was alerted before the ships could reach open waters. They had to pass within range of gun emplacements at the mouth of the estuary. Salazar ordered that the ships be destroyed if necessary to prevent the mutiny succeeding. Merciless gunfire rained down and the *Dão* ran aground after losing control. The leader of the mutiny reportedly committed suicide to avoid capture and the revolt on the other ship was quelled, leaving at least twelve dead.[8]

Six weeks into the Spanish conflict, Teotónio Pereira, the politician who, after Salazar, would play the most crucial role in the Spanish crisis, had already put forward an 'action plan' to facilitate the success of the uprising.[9] The Lisbon authorities did not flinch in sending back numerous Spaniards who sought sanctuary on Portuguese soil if they were identified as republicans. These included the mayor of the city of Badajoz and the local socialist deputy, who were handed back to the rebels and were promptly shot. A future Portuguese ambassador and diplomatic historian, Bernardo Futscher Pereira, reckons that it is improbable that Salazar or Armindo Monteiro was unaware of these incidents.[10] When Salazar was taking his customary drive or walk in the city during the evening, he would often stop at police headquarters to learn the latest news that had come out of Spain.

Britain and France had taken the lead in setting up a Non-Intervention Committee designed to try and limit foreign participation on different sides of the Spanish conflict. It was a futile exercise involving countries which were actively intervening already, sending arms and even troops and advisers. Eventually, it would have a twenty-four-strong membership with Portugal being one of the most awkward. For months Salazar held out against monitoring Spain's frontiers to try to prevent the passage of arms to the combatants. The other committee members had given their approval, but Portugal's was only forthcoming if they were dubbed 'observers' and not 'monitors'. This scheme of 'observation' was agreed in March 1937.[11] Foreign minister Armindo Monteiro was ordered to say that if Portugal's presence on the committee was seen as an embarrassment, then it would depart. Salazar was appalled that national sovereignty would be violated by an organisation of which Russia was a member. And even the Nazi Joachim von Ribbentrop was puzzled by his intransigence.[12] But within a short time, the British had retreated. Salazar's tenacity had seemed to pay off and his prestige in European diplomatic circles was high.

His government placed no obstacles on volunteers from Portugal being enrolled on the nationalist side in Spain. They were known as the Viriatos and estimates of their numbers vary. They had been organised by Jorge Botelho Moniz, an army officer and the owner of an influential radio station. Portugal undoubtedly played a substantial role in helping the rebels consolidate before Germany and Italy intervened on their behalf. By 7 November 1936, Madrid seemed on the verge of falling to the rebels, and at this point Salazar decided to become foreign minister, a job he would hold for the next eleven years.[13]

The objectives that he had communicated to Monteiro at the start of the conflict remained unchanged six months later: 'the support and servicing of the national camp in its struggle against the Republic, the preservation of the two Iberian states as autonomous actors but in association with the Atlanticist foreign policy of England, and the survival of the [Portuguese] regime'.[14]

Stabilising relations with the likely custodians of the new order in Spain was likely to be the main priority. He knew that it was not only the left but the right in Spain which was influenced by dreams of Iberian unity under the control of Madrid. While Armindo Monteiro was sent to London where his English language skills and diplomatic talents were felt to be most needed, a more challenging assignment was found for Teotónio Pereira. He was sent to Salamanca in January 1938 to be the unofficial diplomatic representative with Franco's forces.

This former Integralist, very right-wing in outlook, tall and self-confident in manner, was felt to be the most suitable member of Salazar's entourage to establish a rapport with rebels now under the undisputed leadership of General Francisco Franco. He was seen off from the Rossio station in central Lisbon by a large crowd of well-wishers. They were likely to have emanated from the more radical parts of the regime and would have included members of the Portuguese Legion (Legião Portuguesa). It had been created in the autumn of 1936 not long after Pereira had written to Salazar about the necessity of creating an 'offensive anti-communist force' drawn from 'trustworthy citizens'.[15] It took over the palace in the centre of Lisbon which had previously been the headquarters of the Portuguese Freemasons. The Masons had been driven underground. They would be a prolonged obsession for General Franco, who would detect their malevolent influence and that of other secret societies in unlikely settings.[16]

Salazar would find it difficult to strike up close ties with someone who saw the world through such a distorted prism. Pereira for his part had grown up hostile to the inordinate hold which French liberalism had exercised on Western civilisation. He was pessimistic about the prospects for a civilisation which, for more than a century, had revolved around French concerns. He complained that Portugal had been turned into 'a second-rate France', which had poisoned the blood of the people.[17] In his memoirs he describes taking direct action to remove some of the early novels of D.H. Lawrence from Lisbon bookshops when they had gone on sale in the 1920s.[18] So he would not be a fish out of water in the reactionary Spanish circles of Castile.

Nevertheless, he soon grew alarmed at the haughty disdain exhibited in these circles towards Portugal. A Spanish imperial mentality was alive and well reinforced, no doubt, by the territorial expansionism of Italy and Germany, the main backers of the rebels. Many officers had served in Morocco and were imbued with the need to reaffirm Spain's influence in the world. The centuries-old occupation of Gibraltar by the British remained an open wound. The Anglo-Saxon powers were seen as historical enemies of Spain, and Pereira often had to use all his persuasion to enable his Spanish interlocutors to see that the alliance with Britain made geopolitical sense for Portugal and should not be seen as threatening Spain.

He proved a more obedient subaltern than the strong-willed but querulous Armindo Monteiro in London, a man of independent wealth. If Salazar had feared that someone like Pereira might harbour leadership ambitions, any fears seem to have evaporated once he proved an effective defender of Portuguese interests while in Spain. He remained there for six years, a nerve-racking period during which the regime in Lisbon strove to persuade Franco to avoid taking any action which would turn the whole Iberian peninsula into a theatre of global conflict. Initially, he found little appreciation, especially within the influential Falange Party, for the help Portugal had offered the nationalists without ever being asked. Salazar was told that it was possible to count on the fingers of one hand the Spanish nationalists he had met who had genuinely warm and friendly feelings towards Portugal.[19] Franco himself, when interviewed by the doyen of the Portuguese press, Augusto de Castro, not long after he had crushed the republican forces, had said disparagingly of the Portuguese: 'but the truth is [by your help to us] you saved your skin, knowing what awaited you from the Reds'.[20]

Portugal gave *de jure* recognition to the Franco regime in April 1938. The Caudillo (as he soon came to be known) showed no interest in visiting Portugal after his victory. Neither did he hide from Pereira his reservations about his chief. At one point he said to him: 'Salazar follows outworn principles, in respect to gold and phantom taxes imposed by an English oligarchy dominated by Israelite forces.'[21] Pereira sought to use his diplomatic and interpersonal skills to cultivate close ties with monarchists and senior figures in the armed forces. His Spanish experience seems to have weakened his extreme-right outlook. The longer he stayed in Spain, the more he moved towards an anglophile position.[22] By the closing stages of his mission, in letters to Salazar he repeatedly called the Spanish ruler 'a Gallego', attributing to him some of the worst qualities Spaniards from Galicia were supposed to possess.[23] He wrote that he was of 'poor moral stuff', revealing that, unlike other Spanish generals, Franco was not scandalised by the Nazi–Soviet pact signed in August 1939 between Hitler and Stalin.[24]

Franco was opportunistic and cynical, particularly during World War II when he was guided solely by personal and regime survival. Salazar, by contrast, was influenced by higher national goals and interests, something which was recognised even by opponents who may have shared very few or none of them. Diplomats found him transparent and averse to double-dealing, in contrast to Franco, although nearly always a tenacious negotiator.[25]

Pereira probably had the good sense to hold back from his chief the wounding slights which Franco, in an unguarded moment, had made about the Portuguese leader, complaining that Salazar lacked courage, was irresolute and, in a word, was 'a weakling' (un timido).[26] He may have obtained this impression from his brother Nicolás, also a military officer, who would represent Spanish interests in the Portuguese capital for twenty years and whom Salazar grew to detest because of his inability to turn up on time for meetings.

Salazar was certainly not timid in the way he handled his own army, and this was perhaps never truer than during the Spanish conflict. Arguably, the army's power as an independent political force was curbed for at least a decade. The civilian leader caused a stir by appointing himself minister of war in May 1936. Never had a civilian held this position and salt was rubbed into the wounds when Salazar appointed a captain, aged only thirty-six, as deputy minister. As a young lieutenant, Fernando dos Santos Costa had met Salazar at Coimbra University, where he had been taught political economy by him. The 1926 Revolution then intervened and Santos Costa, busy with plotting, was actually failed by Salazar. Contact was resumed in the mid-1930s when the young officer was pointed out to him as a hard-working and capable soldier who knew more about the army and the war ministry than the senior officers who had lately been in the cabinet. In retirement, Santos Costa would claim that in 1936 President Carmona had been seriously considering appointing a foreigner to reorganise the ramshackle military and place it on a better footing.[27] In the past, non-Portuguese like Schomberg, Lippe and Marshal Beresford had performed this task. Carmona had an Englishman in mind for the assignment but, unsurprisingly, Salazar was completely against the idea.[28] It probably offended his own nationalist outlook and he took the job himself, holding it for the next eight years. Never once in that time did he appear in military uniform, unlike the other, better-known dictators of the era.

He and Santos Costa shared a common vision about the military. They did not see the point in having a permanent army large enough to ensure the defence of the colonies. In Africa 'the best army is made up of Africans under European command', the junior minister insisted. Both appeared to favour a relatively small, professional force that would gradually be modernised. Neither was probably surprised when there was outrage upon Salazar unveiling stringent economies at the start of 1938. After a decade, he finally felt strong enough to submit the military to his cost-cutting zeal. Many officers would be retired early and the higher ranks were to be substantially pruned. The twenty-three military bands in the armed forces were to be reduced to a mere eight. Until then spending on the army's musical section was about the same as that spent on the fledgling Portuguese air force.[29] Soldiers shut themselves in the military barracks in Lisbon demanding the removal of Salazar.[30] Danger threatened when Lisbon's military governor, General Domingos Oliveira, the officer who had assisted Salazar's rise to power, took up their cause. He went to see the president and demanded the cuts be rescinded. Carmona played a crucial role in defusing the crisis: he told his fellow cavalry officer that he supported the cuts and that, if necessary, he would stand down along with Salazar. Domingos Oliveira then heard from the prime minister a case for the cuts and he was won over, managing to defuse the incipient rebellion.[31]

From 1938, Salazar and his loyal number two kept the lid on the military by ensuring that loyalists were concentrated in the ministry of war, besides also being placed in charge of key operational units.[32] But tensions remained under the surface. Santos Costa had his admirers but grew to be hated in parts of a status-conscious military. As a mere captain he had become virtual dictator of the military. He was a monarchist, and enmity towards him was sharpened by the fact that he came from a humble rural background (much like Salazar's own). Later, he would be accused by the opposition of being pro-German in World War II (though, after Portugal joined NATO, he worked harmoniously with army officers like Bernard Montgomery who had fought the Nazis.)

Santos Costa claimed to me (in a conversation not long before his death in 1982) that he had been the creator of a modern army.[33] But steps towards reform of the military only really became visible once Portugal joined NATO in 1949. Salazar's overriding priority was to keep the military in their barracks. By 1939, the Portuguese Legion had around 40,000 men and its elevation suggested to some that the regime was veering in an openly fascist direction. But Salazar took care to ensure that the Spanish Civil War was seen as a unique challenge and that there was no need to emulate the militarism of the Franco regime.

In two speeches delivered to the National Assembly on 27 October 1938, when Franco appeared on course for certain victory, and on 22 May 1939, after this victory had been realised, Salazar took stock. The emphasis in both was that Portugal was 'a factor of peace' in an increasingly chaotic and disorderly continent. The country had done all that was necessary to prevent a neighbour falling under 'communist enslavement': 'we were from the very first what it was our duty to be, faithful friends of Spain and true sons of the peninsula at heart'.[34] 'We took our share of risk and suffering' but now the priority was to establish 'a true zone of peace in the peninsula'.[35]

No shocks could therefore be expected from Portugal. It would be steely and resolute in defending its sovereignty. As an 'Atlantic and imperial power' in its own right, it would follow a course that had helped to make it a constructive force in the world. This meant 'remaining faithful to the Anglo-Portuguese Alliance to secure the defence of our common interests'. But Salazar also stipulated (in his May 1939 speech) that Portugal 'reserves freedom of action and the right to form many other friendships' in matters that lay outside the alliance.[36]

As early as mid-1937 Salazar had told his closest friends that he thought another war in Europe was unavoidable.[37] In public, by contrast, he gave no clues about his apprehensions and in October 1938 spoke optimistically about the peace which Chamberlain and others had brought back from Munich.[38] But if conflict was unavoidable, he declared in that month that it was 'our firm resolve to spare our country as far as possible' from its horrors.[39] He hoped that Mussolini, the dictator whom he most admired, would opt for a similar prudent course. In the League of Nations, Portugal had defied him after he had invaded and occupied Ethiopia in late 1935. Salazar wished to preserve the territorial status quo in Africa and joined with Britain and France in imposing sanctions on Rome. Portugal even played a role in supervising the economic embargo slapped on Italy.[40]

In a private overture he had counselled the Italian leader to avoid adventures and continue to define Italy as chiefly a Mediterranean power. But at home, observers noted that the regime had adopted some of the trappings of the Italian fascist regime. On 19 May 1936 an official youth movement, the Mocidade Portuguesa (Portuguese Youth), was established. Membership was compulsory for children aged between seven and fourteen, who would be given military training and education of a patriotic character. A decree of 30 September, establishing its statutes, announced that it was complementary to the Portuguese Legion.[41]

The creation of a paramilitary youth movement and a fascist-looking militia occurred against the background of a crisis and war next door in Spain, which threatened not only the survival of the regime but perhaps Portugal's own independence. The Estado Novo's radicalisation would have gone down well with plenty of anxious supporters as well as others who had been frustrated by the dominant hallmark of traditional conservatism. Salazar and his ministers would be seen in public giving the fascist salute in the late 1930s (a practice not discontinued until the middle of World War II). But it is clear that Salazar tilted towards fascism from expediency, not from any real conviction. The state needed to be strong and vigilant, but generalised use of violence was not to be part of its armoury even when danger was on the horizon.[42]

So the radicalisation of the late 1930s had definite limits. An Italian Fascist party visitor observing Portuguese conditions noted in 1934 that the regime left people alone to lead their own lives and did not compel them to 'participate in the life of the state'.[43] In 1936 loyalty tests were introduced for public officials, but the Estado Novo remained low-key and unobtrusive compared with the major European dictatorships. To the disappointment of Teotónio Pereira, Salazar had retained a lot of bureaucrats from the pre-dictatorial era. One of these was Portugal's longstanding representative at the League of Nations, the former republican prime minister Augusto Vasconcelos, whose 'vast international experience was too precious an advantage to be renounced'.[44] Salazar had, it seems, brushed aside his eager lieutenant's warning that 'the state machine has a very diverse rhythm and tendencies survive that are hostile to our values'.[45]

The regime showed no sign of purging the bureaucracy or devolving any authority to radical political offshoots. The Legion was not allowed to acquire its own freedom of action or to terrorise enemies. To the chagrin of several of its civilian founders, its 40,000-strong membership had been placed under military control by 1937 and they promptly quit. Radicals who were Blueshirt in background had become prominent in the Legion and, in some places, friction with the National Union (UN) had ensued. The Catholic Church was also ready to speak out if figures whom it judged to be extremists over-reached themselves. Cardinal Cerejeira had strenuously resisted a request from the minister of education, António Carneiro Pacheco, that the church dissolve its own scouting movement.[46] A text by Cerejeira in the Catholic press was even cut by the censor around this time.[47] In 1938, further controversy erupted when the head of the Mocidade Portuguesa gave a reception for a visiting delegation of Hitler Youth. Francisco Nobre Guedes emphasised the parallels between the two movements, which evoked protests from the Catholic press. It was pointed out that in Portugal, unlike Germany, the state had no time for negative sentiments directed against the church.[48] Pressures from the church and moderate regime elements led to the scaling down of the number of visits by the Hitler Youth to Portugal and reciprocal ones by Mocidade members to Germany.[49] In 1940, Marcello Caetano was appointed head of the Mocidade. Church worries were allayed when under him a strongly Christian outlook became a pronounced feature.

Salazar wished to preserve equilibrium rather than strike out in bold and unpredictable directions. He may have admired Mussolini's political flair but he never displayed any wish to emulate his confrontational style either at home or abroad. He told his propaganda chief António

Ferro: 'Don't let us forget that Mussolini is an Italian, a descendant of the condottieri of the Middle Ages. And don't let us forget his own origin, his Socialist, almost Communist, upbringing.'[50] The 'pagan Caesarism' of Mussolini 'which recognises ... no moral or legal order' moved a critical Salazar to speculate whether the Italian and German regimes were compatible with Christian civilisation.[51]

Salazar kept a portrait of Mussolini on his desk until Italy entered the war in June 1940. As for Hitler, Salazar was usually extremely guarded in his remarks about his increasingly aggressive behaviour on the European stage while periodically praising the enterprise, skill and dedication to hard work of the German people. He had always found bellicose, headstrong and melodramatic figures uncomfortable to deal with, especially in the military, and several, in time, would cause him great trouble. His writings did not share the preoccupation of Hitler and Mussolini with militarism, territorial expansion, revolutionising society or asserting ethnic supremacy.

It is difficult to imagine either Hitler or Mussolini writing in such sceptical terms about their country and its need to pursue an unflashy course, as in Salazar's aforementioned remarks of 1934: 'Our country's past is full of glory, full of heroism; but what we've needed, and especially in the last one hundred years, has been less brilliance and more staying power, something less showy but with more perspective. Anything that just makes an appeal to the heroism of our race without altering its general attitude of mind ... its way of doing things, all that may give us back for a moment our pages of glorious past.'[52]

His ambassador in Berlin from 1933 to 1940 was the Count of Tovar, a diplomat opposed to German national socialism. It has been claimed he was hastily recalled to Portugal in 1940 when it looked as if he had been trying to alert the French, prior to Hitler's invasion, of his intention to bypass the Maginot line.[53]

Hitler took lessons from an actor to develop his repertoire of gestures and, as early as 1928, created a school to train members of the Nazi party to speak in public.[54] But with a thin and rather high-pitched voice when tense, Salazar shunned oratory. Rabble-rousing was not a road he was prepared to go down. But he did not neglect propaganda as a weapon to draw attention to the existence of the Estado Novo and extol its achievements. Far from it. Indeed it is possible to claim that the regime enjoyed an important degree of soft power in the 1930s and beyond because of its prowess in singing its own praises. This was very much down to one of the most original and talented people to enter Salazar's service.

António Ferro (1895–1956) was head of the Secretariat of National Propaganda (SPN) from 1934 to 1949. During the turbulent republican regime, he acquired a reputation as an innovative cultural figure keen to experiment with, and promote, new forms of expression, whether it be futuristic art or jazz music. He went further than others alienated from the chaos of the liberal order and was drawn to the cultural and aesthetic side of the fascism that was springing up in Mussolini's Italy. Full of energy and self-confidence and with a gift for public relations, he persuaded the Italian dramatist Luigi Pirandello to come to Lisbon in 1931.[55] On his travels he had built up contacts in the media, particularly in Paris. Salazar in time became aware of his presence. Ferro talked him into setting up the SPN but was disappointed that it failed to be given cabinet rank. Nevertheless, in his heyday he had more access to Salazar than most ministers who served him up to 1968. He persuaded him of the value of propaganda.

After all, he had unusual achievements to his credit in the depths of the Great Depression. He had made Portugal 'almost independent of international finance when at one point it looked as if foreign creditors might assume overlordship over the country'.[56] Mussolini understood the benefits of clever and well-aimed propaganda; the Spanish dictator for much of the 1920s, Miguel Promo de Rivera, had not, and it had accelerated his fall.[57] By embracing the very latest techniques of mass persuasion, the task of consolidating a conservative regime in a traditionally liberal country would be far easier. As a modernist steeped in avant-garde culture, Ferro made these arguments and talked Salazar into allowing him to be an impresario in the propaganda realm after their first meeting at the end of 1932.

Installed in an office just a few steps from the Chiado, Lisbon's central meeting point, Ferro got down to arranging the political marketing for Salazarist Portugal.[58] He used his connections in European journalism to lay on numerous interviews with, or profiles of, Salazar. Laudatory articles in *The Times* of London and the French media often appeared at politically sensitive moments when he needed to assert his authority. Interviewers were often paid with cash or else free excursions were provided within Portugal. Thus in a country where austerity would define the regime for many years, the budget for propaganda remained a generous one.

One of those whom he hosted in Portugal was T.S. Eliot, who fully shared Salazar's scepticism about liberalism's contribution to the human condition. A year after his visit to Portugal in 1938, the poet wrote: 'By destroying traditional social habits of the people, by dissolving their natural collective consciousness into individual constituents, by licensing the opinions of the most foolish, by substituting instruction for education, by encouraging cleverness rather than wisdom, the upstart rather than the qualified ... Liberalism can prepare the way for that which is its own negation: the artificial, mechanized or brutalized control which is a desperate remedy for its chaos.'[59]

Perhaps Ferro's most notable exploit was to market Salazar as a providential figure on the European political stage through publishing in book form a series of interviews with him that first appeared in the *Diário de Notícias* between 19 and 23 December 1932. In English it was known as *Salazar: The Man and His Work* and was translated into thirteen languages and distributed in sixty countries. The book centred mainly on the progress achieved in Portugal after forty months of financial dictatorship and the lessons for a Europe reeling from the great economic depression. Clever journalistic tricks were played. As Margarida Acciaiuoli has observed: 'At times he [Ferro] adopted a provocative and impatient tone; at other times he held back and adopted the role of a spectator ... the aim was to show the personality of the dictator from a variety of angles in the belief that this would shed light on what he was aiming to do.'[60]

There was an attempt to humanise Salazar and present an unostentatious and unusually transparent European leader. Towards the end of the book, Ferro observed: 'Here is Dr Salazar. His crime in everybody's eyes was that he never spoke; they said that he was self-centred ... but he brought himself to speak to me all right. Further, he submitted himself like a child to peremptory questioning on almost every angle of an extremely complicated problem, knowing that everything he said was going to be published.'[61]

The final page suggested the reader had overhead a candid conversation between a journalist and a remarkable person engaged in patriotic work: 'And now that we have heard of him, let each of us go back to our own life … Let us leave him to his work.'[62]

The book had in fact been a sophisticated and skilful exercise in propaganda. The text had been shown to Salazar before publication. He removed phrases and inserted other material, at the expense of the authenticity of the dialogue.[63] No less than 125,000 copies had been printed in the first Portuguese edition. In a country with an illiteracy rate exceeding 50 per cent of the adult population, this was a lot. One author has suggested that the size of the print run only makes sense upon realising that most copies were distributed through town councils in a well-coordinated operation.[64]

Ferro was a man of protean energy. During his fifteen years as propaganda chief, 'he turned the country into a theatre, assuming the role of stage manager. He organized modern art exhibitions, founded literary and artistic prizes, financed a number of films and many documentaries, prepared Portuguese stands at major foreign exhibitions, created a ballet company, drew attention to the potential to be found in popular art and established a museum of the people in 1948 to promote tourism. He concerned himself with improving hotels and restaurants, helped launch the state inns known as *pousadas*, gave railway stations a historic style of architecture, and in general was a motivating force behind strengthening good taste across the nation.'[65]

He was a plausible technician of manipulation who had persuaded a cautious and introspective ruler of 'the need to constantly hammer away at his ideas, strip away their stiffness, give them life and colour, communicate them to the masses'.[66] According to those who have researched Salazar's diaries, it is reckoned that between 1933 and 1939 Ferro had no less than 131 meetings with Salazar.[67] Thanks to his omniscient secret police, little got past Portugal's ruler so it is quite possible that he was aware of the persistent rumours that both Ferro and his talented wife, Fernanda de Castro, were bisexual. They enjoyed close ties with figures in the arts world assumed to be gay or lesbian. But Salazar was prepared to tolerate personal foibles among his backers as long as they did not get into the open. His seminary training, a decade as a university professor, and interaction with many different types of collaborators once he had reached power would have enabled him to see contrasting aspects of human behaviour. He himself was puritanical in his ways but, except during World War II when rationing was the norm, he did not necessarily expect others to adhere to his level of asceticism. His successor, Marcello Caetano, was different. He was prudish and Victorian in his outlook and 'on numerous occasions, complained about the protection Ferro bestowed on well-known homosexuals'.[68]

Ferro gradually lost his pivotal role in the regime as overt propaganda fell out of fashion following the defeat of the fascist powers. Some years after the SPN was renamed the National Secretariat for Information (SRI), Salazar appointed him (at the exhortation of his wife) as ambassador first to Switzerland in 1950 and later to Italy, two years before his death in 1956.

A French admirer, Christine Garnier, wrote that Salazar 'never strove to please the crowd. Few words. Few gestures ... He recoils from the warmth of the crowd.'[69] He was unwilling to be a hostage to the fickle emotions of the masses. He told Ferro: 'These good people who cheer me one day, moved by the excitement of the occasion, may rise in rebellion the next day for equally passing reason.'[70] He went on to admit: 'How often have I not been moved by the obvious sincerity of certain demonstrations! How often have I longed to speak to the people, to express my gratitude and my love! But when I am at the point of doing so, something holds me back, something which seems to say: "Do not commit yourself."'[71] He preferred a rhetoric of invisibility and silence.[72] This invisibility meant that he did not present an easy target for opponents. Ceremonial events were left to the president. His absence from the political foreground, along with his rather solitary personal life, probably assisted his longevity in power. His first major foreign policy challenge, the conflict next door in Spain, often left him with little time for pleasures or relaxation. But his private existence deserves exploration. It was far from being a void.

7

SALAZAR'S PRIVATE WORLD

The Estado Novo would go through various distinct phases, but perhaps Salazar's abiding hallmark was his self-restraint and composure. He had a settled routine, avoiding official visits abroad or attending conferences, and media exposure generally. For much of his premiership, his home was located above his office in a secluded building located next to parliament. His personal needs were attended to by a woman who kept an appropriate distance but was devoted to him. The calm and orderly environment in which he discharged his duties arguably benefited the quality of his decision-making. A leader whose physique was far from being the strongest enjoyed nourishing food and regular hours; his longevity in power may have been enhanced as a result. Hubris may also have been kept at bay because of simple living.[1] Salazar combined a readiness to assert his will with an essential modesty. He never acquired a proprietorial attitude to the state.

Micas, his adopted child, remembers tears welling up when she broke the news to him in May 1945 that World War II had come to an end. But he rarely betrayed conspicuous emotions except perhaps towards the end of his rule when responding to the challenges being posed to the survival of the Portuguese empire.

For four decades he developed a routine that enabled him to govern the country in an unruffled manner. He preferred to operate behind the scenes rather than adopt the high-profile role of head of state, into which some of his friends tried to push him as his rule approached its third decade. He told his foreign minister in the 1960s: 'I have only been able to remain in government for thirty years because I never slip out of a routine. How could one put up with thirty years of winning elections, answering parliament's questions, running to inaugurate things, etc.'[2]

Staying vigilant but keeping a low profile whenever possible became his survival formula. When being driven around in Lisbon, he insisted that his chauffeur keep to a normal speed and refrain from using a klaxon. Until his last fifteen years in power, he seems to have been kept well informed about conditions in a country where his appearances were usually few. He never visited the overseas territories but he made an effort to familiarise himself with facts on the ground through people who had earned his trust, such as the ex-minister, diplomat and businessman Jorge Jardim.

One of the rare occasions in which Salazar's routine was disrupted occurred on 4 July 1937. It was a Sunday morning and he was turning up to hear Mass in the apartment of a friend from Coimbra, the musician Josué Trocado. Unbeknown to those who guarded him, a bomb weighing around 40 kg had been planted in a sewer near where his car was expected to park.[3] The device had been prepared by anarchists, who had secured the cooperation of some communists in their bid to kill their arch-foe. Salazar was no longer seen as a transient ruler but as someone crucial for the survival of the regime. The conspirators hoped that his permanent removal would result in its swift decapitation. There was an assumption that turmoil in Portugal could help restore the initiative to the Spanish republicans. Certainly the plotters felt an obligation to try and halt the flow of weapons and supplies which had been reaching the Franco side in the conflict from Portugal for over a year.

Salazar then only had light security cover and the conspirators were confident of success. But the bomb failed to be placed in the exact location required if it was to destroy Salazar's vehicle. It exploded at 10.25 am as he was alighting from his Buick car. The loud blast shattered windows in many directions and a huge crater opened up in the road. But Salazar's car was not badly damaged and its main occupant was not even wounded. His would-be assassins, however daring and determined, had lacked the technical skill to accomplish their planned murder. Ironically, the authorities were even more incompetent. A slipshod investigation by the PVDE resulted in the wrong people being arrested, interrogated and tortured. Only another discreet investigation carried out by a different branch of the police led to the perpetrators being tracked down and arrested after some months.[4]

The next day the pro-regime *Diário de Manhã* wrote about the incident: 'without a single muscle of the face showing the slightest commotion ... with the usual serenity and without hurrying his pace, he entered the garden and went to hear the Mass'.

Reports of Salazar's composure in the face of such great danger seem to have been accurate. After having dusted down his dark suit, he said: 'Everything is over now. Let's go in for the Mass.' These were the only words that he seems to have uttered before disappearing inside.[5]

The bomb attempt did not coincide with one of the Estado Novo's calmest moments. The Catholic Church was unhappy about the far right indoctrinating young Portuguese and the army was seething over budgetary cuts. But the entire regime closed ranks as telegrams and messages of support flooded in from all points of the country. It was a moment which exposed the fact that this was a personal regime and, if its chief architect was suddenly no more, its prospects for keeping going were tenuous. Late the same evening thousands gathered outside the window of Salazar's house on Rua Bernardo Lima to show their appreciation that he had somehow escaped death.[6] He appeared at a window and waved to the crowds. It only emerged years later that some at the head of the army had been so traumatised by the incident that discreet soundings were taken among senior commanders about what needed to be done if there was another, but this time successful, bid to violently remove him. The idea came from General Domingos Oliveira and nobody outside the army (not even Salazar) appeared to be aware of the plans. The clear and unanimous response, according to the historian Fernando Rosas, was that the military should impose a military dictatorship to clean the house once again and afterwards entrust government to whoever merited confidence and could be relied upon not to destroy the work of 'national recovery' already carried out.[7]

On 6 July there was a military rally outside the presidential palace at São Bento to give thanks for Salazar's safe deliverance. A large open-air Mass with similar intent was held in the city exactly a week after the incident. In one of his few references to it, Salazar declared when speaking to military units on 6 July: 'It is not every day that one escapes an attempt on one's life hatched by an evil intelligence … but I don't see internal causes. Instead we should look above to the international scene, over-excited and loaded with a system of ideas that is a system of crime.'[8]

Attentive members of the crowd who had gathered outside his residence would have noticed two young girls gazing down from a balcony along with Maria de Jesus Caetano Freire, Salazar's housekeeper. They were her nieces, nine-year-old Micas and the younger Maria António. They had been born in straitened circumstances, and Salazar had taken the elder one into his home a year earlier (with her sister a frequent visitor). They informally became his adopted children and the news was announced to the Portuguese on 21 May 1938 in the weekend edition of the Lisbon newspaper *O Século*. The story was written by José Leitão de Barros, a talented journalist and committed supporter of the regime, who would go on to make several films. He described how a shy child from the north had arrived in the city, initially withdrawn and fearful but gradually striking up a close relationship with Salazar, whom she described as a warm substitute parent in her own memoirs written many decades later.[9] Until then information about Salazar had been released mainly for foreign consumption, and to many Portuguese he remained a distant and even mysterious figure.

The journalist Joaquim Vieira related that the Portuguese were now being introduced to the 'proto-familial' relationship in the austere dictator's household.[10] It included Salazar's housekeeper for what would be more than fifty years, Maria de Jesus Freire. She commanded real authority in household matters and was fiercely loyal to and protective of him. She had arrived in Coimbra as an initially illiterate young woman in her twenties and had gained employment in Os Grilos, the establishment where he, Cerejeira and others lived during a large part of the First Republic. He took her with him to Lisbon when his political career began. In time she would reveal herself to be an intelligent, discreet and self-possessed individual. Her position close to the leader of the country meant that she acquired much informal influence. People from parliamentary deputies to common citizens tried to go through her in the hope that she could intercede with Salazar on their behalf.[11] But there is no evidence that she used her role for self-aggrandisement or undermined the position of the man in whose household she acted as governess. She was discretion personified and strong-willed in her determination to shield the master, to whom she was devoted, from unnecessary bother. Ministers learned to treat her with respect and soon knew that if they upset her they were likely to upset Salazar also.[12] He was lucky to have by his side for so long someone with such a sense of devotion and service towards him. Maria de Jesus caused him none of the difficulties which high-powered assistants have brought down on the heads of powerful leaders in Britain, the US and elsewhere.

Salazar was unmarried, and perhaps rumours inevitably abounded that she and he had entered into a clandestine relationship. But claims that both had been lovers were scotched when a post-mortem carried out upon her death in 1981 revealed her to be a virgin.[13] She dedicated her life to Salazar, who, it has been said, she loved in a platonic manner. While he was an autocrat in the public sphere, he was a democrat in the domestic ambience, giving her free rein. Micas in her memoirs does not have especially fond memories of 'Tia Maria', who only mellowed upon the death of Salazar. He for his part shielded the children from her bad temper; Micas recalls that they had a regular time for playing games in a corridor, usually throwing hoops, and she would race him to the top of the house, he taking the lift and she bounding up the stairs.[14]

By this point the household had moved from Rua Bernardo Lima in the growing northern suburbs, where Salazar had lived from 1933 onwards, to a dwelling where he would spend the rest of his life. This was a residence perched fairly high up in the west of the city and located directly behind the National Assembly, which had been inaugurated in 1935 and was housed in the palace of São Bento. After the 1937 assassination attempt, a smaller building, dating from 1877, was renovated and expanded. Salazar paid great attention to the works, talking with the architects and builders and making detailed suggestions. It was to be a home which bore some resemblance to a stout manor house of the kind to be found in his part of Portugal. Salazar and his proto-family finally moved in during July 1938. It was also his place of work and the official meeting place where he received official visitors and held cabinet meetings.

São Bento and Salazar became indelibly linked for much of the 20th century. The house was divided into two parts. Visitors were received on the ground floor with its two reception rooms, one leading on to the other. To one side was Salazar's office, large but modest and functional. Next to that was a library where his secretary worked. His secretaries usually stayed in Salazar's employ for a long time, and several have written about their experiences with him. Usually he worked directly with them in the mornings, reading and responding to correspondence, occasionally making phone calls. Then at around midday the first audiences of the day commenced, meetings which usually finished by 2 pm or 2.30 pm. Lunch was taken, followed by a short siesta and some reading of the press or of books. At 5.30 pm some tea was drunk (never coffee, which he disliked) and from 6 pm he saw more people often until quite late. Alternatively the Council of Ministers convened at 6.30 pm and would go on for three or four hours. This was how Marcello Caetano, a close and observant colleague, recalled his typical day during the early 1940s when he faced particular pressures.[15]

A banqueting hall was the only other room on the ground floor but it was rarely used by the austere Salazar. An elegant staircase led to the first floor. Here were Salazar's quite modest private living quarters, a small office attached to his bedroom, a dining room, and a grand meeting room used for cabinet meetings. Micas recalls that the upper floor contained a lot of junk, including various trophies given to the leader by hunters. These included a stuffed crocodile, the large head and mane of a lion, and other artefacts from the colonies.[16] Salazar was careful to ensure a division of state and private property, and there were separate utility bills for the upper levels of the house, which were paid from his own pocket. Dona Maria supervised the whole house and employed up to six maids and other helpers. Her chief domain was the very large kitchen in the basement from where there was access to the garden. Its grounds were big and over the years different flowers, shrubs and small trees were added by Salazar, who was a dedicated plantsman. There was also a large pond. It was a place to relax near, which he did at the end of the working day, strolling around often in the company of Micas.

Salazar was not especially fond of Lisbon. It had dramatic prospects and a beautiful situation but, aesthetically, was not a distinguished city. The riverside had industrial buildings from which belched fumes day and night.[17] The weather was often sparkling in the spring and autumn but there were fogs and persistent rain in the winter months. In this city, he did not socialise much, and most of his friends were ones he had already made in Coimbra and the north. Occasionally, he would take afternoon or evening walks alone, usually in a northerly direction towards the Botanic Gardens with a light security escort in discreet attendance.[18] This was hardly the norm for a modern dictator.

The post-war US secretary of state Dean Acheson wrote of his surprise when he encountered Salazar by chance while on a visit to Lisbon on the eve of Lent:

> I had another glimpse of Dr Salazar ... Shrove Tuesday, Mardi Gras and throughout Lisbon the carnival was coming to a crescendo ... the park [at Castelo de São Jorge] was largely given over to children revellers in costumes and masks, chasing one another. In the midst of this gay bedlam we came on Dr Salazar walking with a man who could have been a guard or merely a companion. There seemed to be no other guards about. We stopped to exchange greetings but they were largely inaudible. While we stood there children dashed between and around us ... apparently unconscious of the presence of the "dictator" of Portugal. We passed on with a wave, my last glimpse of him as he strolled off being a tall figure in a swirl of midgets.[19]

But the 19th-century townhouse in the São Bento gardens would be his own world where, as he put it, 'I live in my own house with my own things'.[20] There he would find repose and domestic familiarity, while carrying out what he increasingly saw as his mission for Portugal during a time of acute disorder in the world.

The period from 1936 to 1945 was arguably when Salazar's responsibilities were heaviest. For the first four years he not only held down the premiership but was foreign minister as well as minister of war. It was a daunting burden of work and it left little time for new social relationships or the cultivation of old ones. Long periods sometimes elapsed before Salazar, normally an inveterate correspondent, was able to respond to letters from those whom he respected and admired.

Long gone were the occasions when, dressed smartly, he would venture out to take tea at a respectable downtown establishment in

Lisbon like the Pastelaria Benard. This haunt for the well-off had been the scene of a fleeting drama in the early 1930s which showed both the single-mindedness and self-discipline of an autocrat-in-the-making. The bachelor, now in early middle age, was due to meet a vivacious young woman who, unlike Salazar, enjoyed a life of wealth and ease.

He had been dating Maria Laura Bebiano for some time. He was possibly more serious in his attentions towards her than towards any of the other women with whom he had enjoyed platonic relationships or fleeting affairs. There was no lack of evidence that he enjoyed the company of women, towards whom he displayed a less austere and less humourless side of his character than the one shown when he appeared on the public platform. But for the workaholic Salazar, something rankled that day. His friend was over an hour late. To make matters worse, when she did arrive her attire was the height of extravagance. She was dressed in an expensive, brightly coloured costume that, as she admitted herself nearly fifty years later, made her appear coquettish.

Salazar was taciturn and distant, and when she asked what was the matter, after more silence he slowly exclaimed, beating his hand lightly on the table: 'Whoever I take in marriage will only wear the clothes that I can afford out of my own salary.'

'Oh you are insolent,' his friend replied furiously, 'and now you even dare to bring up the subject of marriage.'

And with that she picked up her purse, gloves and hat and hurriedly left, bringing an end to their affair.[21]

His social life revived after 1945, with Dona Maria exercising a watchful role over the correspondence which came in from female suitors, some of which was torn up and tossed in the bin before Salazar could even get a chance to see it.[22] There is no doubt, according to Manuel Lucena, that he liked women and he was venerated by many, but he presided over the most patriarchal regime of the century, never marrying and ensuring that his affairs with women remained secret.[23]

The other paradox is that the women who figured in his life as long-term friends or as more fleeting amours tended, more often than not, to have been persons of strong character, not lacking in initiative, and far from the dutiful women dedicated to family matters who were extolled in regime propaganda. One of them, Virginia de Campos, was a person of considerable standing in the small coastal city of Povoa de

Varzim north of Oporto. Salazar is known to have made several visits to see someone described as 'very beautiful, very elegant and chic'. He rarely ventured beyond her house with its beautiful garden, but the city, a fishing centre as well as a watering hole for the leisured classes, seems to have done well from his benevolent oversight. It acquired more educational facilities than was normal for a place of its size. In the 1930s the city council was given the right to build and operate a casino. A neoclassical building was completed in 1934 and the casino contributed much revenue to the city's coffers. But by the 1960s it was failing due to bad management. This caused four local men to approach Salazar to ask if the community could buy the casino owners out. At their head was a doctor, Alberto Moreira, who had spent much of his life working with the poor. The sum needed was arranged by going door to door and gathering small amounts from shopkeepers, cafe owners and other small businesses. Salazar gave the go-ahead for the scheme. Under the new community owners the casino was quickly put back on its feet and the profits were used partly to boost Povoa's tourist appeal. Steve Harrison, who has profiled this city in a recent book, described the initiative as 'a shining example of how communal capitalism could boost a town's prospects, bring in money and create jobs'.[24]

For relaxation Salazar preferred to return to his native village, sometimes for long periods. These usually coincided with important moments in the agricultural calendar. Only major crises prevented him being back in the autumn for the gathering-in of the grapes or the bottling of the wine on his small estate. Several of his sisters still lived in Santa Comba Dão but he purchased his own land and built a small but comfortable house. It is interesting to find that he was there during troubling periods for Portugal in World War II. Thus he supervised the planting of small trees at the start of February 1943. (Roosevelt and Churchill had just met at Casablanca and had agreed to step up the pressure on Portugal to allow the Allies military use of the Azores islands.)

If he was encountering problems in Lisbon and his collaborators were proving unhelpful, he would occasionally warn, 'There are trains every day for Santa Comba Dão', meaning that he had no intention to stick around at the centre of power if he wasn't wanted. It was a place for recharging his physical batteries and acquiring some detachment from the pressures and intrigues of Lisbon. Children wore shoes on the Sundays when Salazar would be expected at Mass.

In 2019 Elsa Amaral, an eighty-year-old retired nurse, recalled a figure who had been a familiar sight during her childhood: 'Dr Salazar arrived, always pleasant, and stayed, with a policeman at the front door, several others in the small farm and two PIDEs [secret policemen] stationed in the old schoolhouse.'[25] He did not have a retinue of officials or security people in his wake but kept to himself. Unlike other leaders from humble origins, neither did he single out his town for special recognition. There were no sports centres, improved roads or imposing buildings erected. No doubt his proximity meant that there were occasions when locals could approach him discreetly with a personal request for help. During his years in charge, perhaps hundreds of thousands of people wrote to him. One historian reckons that 'each month there were thousands of letters, petitions, complaints, "cunhas" [requests for interceding with officialdom], denunciations, proposals, reports and studies; he read everything, sending replies via competent channels.'[26] Often the unsentimental leader would leave the supplicants empty-handed. But he did not discourage such approaches and sometimes his response was quixotic. Such was the case in 1964, when shown a letter from a Syrian: 'I am going to marry on the 24th of May. I'd like to have the honeymoon in Portugal. But I see that such luxury is beyond my means. It would be a great kindness on your part if you found a solution that would enable my dream to be realised.' Salazar took the matter in hand and the couple were offered a stay in a state guest-house for five days free of charge.[27]

Salazar, a man of fixed principles, grew to appreciate the absurdity of life and he had no trouble cooperating with eccentric or atypical people, from António Ferro to Humberto Delgado (see chapter 12) or Jorge Jardim, as long as they were broadly loyal to the regime. He was, however, austere and puritanical in his own behaviour and did not let the high standards he set himself slip. It is no surprise that he chose to spend so much time in a small town where he had been formed. When they are added up, he must have spent up to five years in this unremarkable corner of provincial Portugal during his time in power. It was a device that enabled him to place a barrier between himself and those whom he particularly didn't want to see.

In the first decades of the regime, various families and interest groups managed to consolidate themselves in economic and financial terms thanks to his restoration of order and political stability, and his crackdown on industrial unrest. They included individuals and firms such as the Espirito Santo, Banco Português do Atlântico, the large industrial conglomerate known as the Companhia União Fabril (CUF), and the Champalimaud bank. They were some of the wealthiest elements in Portuguese society. Courtesy ties were usually retained but Salazar was never on intimate terms with the captains of industry, the financial moguls, or the large landowners of the south. He stayed away from their shooting parties in the sprawling Alentejo region, the breadbasket of Portugal, and he certainly did not attend the glittering occasions which marked various points in the Lisbon social year for the privileged set. One of the architects of the successor regime to his own, Mário Soares, believes that 'he left that clique of vultures ... uncontrolled, [able] to go on creating an inextricable web of political and economic connections'.[28] The conservative writer Jaime Nogueira Pinto disagrees. He thinks Salazar reduced their influence in politics and acted as a referee, preventing unwelcome accumulations of power.[29] There was no shortage of small and medium-sized companies, and while their profit margins were usually not high in the quiet economic conditions up to the 1960s, they held their own. Salazar also channelled subsidies to smaller firms to ensure their viability.

He was presiding over a form of state capitalism 'in which the government not only took it upon itself to start and stimulate business and accumulate capital for investment but to create a kind of officially sanctioned entrepreneurial class where none had existed before.'[30] He was a believer in capitalism but he may have had fewer grounds to be impressed by Portuguese capitalists. Perhaps most were averse to taking risks, preferring instead to see their capital tied up in London shares or else property in Brazil rather than economic projects at home. There was a lack of investment capital for new industries, which was paradoxical given Salazar's emphasis on economic self-sufficiency.[31] The caution of the entrepreneurial class was not lessened by the fact that Portugal had been relatively sheltered from the world depression of the 1930s on account of its not being a great exporter of primary products, whose value crashed.

He did, however, need men of wealth for various projects which counted in importance for the state. The one who stands out is Ricardo Espirito Santo, the heir of a large banking group. His father, the illegitimate son of a nobleman, grew up in the Lisbon poorhouse and he took as his wife a seller in the open-air market that used to exist in Lisbon's Figueira Square.[32] Adept at making money, he founded a bank and passed it on to his son. Ricardo not only had great financial acumen but a strong interest in the arts. His self-confidence and drive made him a leader within Lisbon society. From the 1930s, he would be an admirer, collaborator and confidant of Salazar, with whom he discussed and planned the most diverse initiatives, from supplying and extracting oil to arranging financial support for Germany after 1945.[33]

The dictator grew to rely on Espirito Santo for sensitive assignments in World War II, and although there was mutual admiration, he declined to benefit from the patronage of this or any other rich figure. Throughout his life he remained a byword for frugality. To keep heating costs down, he often worked with a blanket over his knees. His clothes were usually elegant and well made but they were often cut up later and recycled by Dona Maria.[34] He paid officials and even ministers small salaries, which meant that many whom he invited to join him in government refused because the pay was not enough to support a large family. Later, he would often place them on the boards of major companies as a reward for good service or as a means of getting them quietly out of the way. Upon his death in 1970 it was found that he possessed hardly enough in the bank to purchase a cheap apartment.

The paranoia, burn-out and high levels of mistrust which afflicted other dictators (and even some democratic leaders in power for a much shorter time) were kept at bay, perhaps because Salazar never became a total workaholic and instead developed psychological strategies for dealing with reversals and unsettling occurrences. So he was possibly disingenuous when he wrote to a trusted ally, Marcello Mathias: 'unlike other public men, I don't display a full and active life ... there is just the monotony of work.'[35] But Salazar did have a private life, he enjoyed social intercourse, and, perhaps more than other leaders, he could still meet a lot of people on a regular basis while insulating himself from the pressures which often bear down on ruling politicians. He enjoyed music (Bach being a favourite composer), adored cultivating plants and having beautiful flowers around him, and read works of classical literature. If a dictator could be an aesthete, then it is possible that Salazar fulfilled such a role.

Along with Salazar's tenacious and implacable defence of its neutrality, Portugal's geopolitical location shielded it from the storms which assailed much of the world in the 1930s and 1940s. The country's ruling autocrat grew even more inscrutable and out-of-sight in the early 1940s as he was almost overwhelmed by the scale of his governing duties in a time of world crisis.

8

WALKING EUROPE'S NEUTRAL TIGHTROPE, 1939–42

Long before the conclusion of the war in Spain, Salazar had come to see it as the likely prelude to a much bigger armed conflict in Europe. By now he was aware that conservative nationalists like him lacked power in Europe and were unlikely to shape its future. Mussolini was undisciplined and impetuous. Hitler had already shown signs of his unrestrained aggression. Salazar's mood about the world seemed to darken not long after Hitler had occupied Austria and absorbed it into the Third Reich.

He may well have guessed that foreign affairs would be his chief preoccupation for a long time to come and that he would thus have less time available to reconstruct Portugal according to his own tastes. European tensions thus had a real impact on the future direction of his regime, but Salazar was determined that he would remain an immovable rock in the approaching storm. So, as a prudent householder, he tried to take all possible precautions, combining the foreign affairs, war and finance portfolios (the last dropped in 1940).

He had various core objectives. The first was to keep Portugal out of a fresh European conflict; he was mindful of the calamities which had overtaken Portugal when it intervened on the side of Britain and France in World War I. Mozambique had been invaded by German forces, leading to nearly 10,000 fatalities.[1] On the main front line in

France an unprepared Portuguese expeditionary force had suffered large casualties and afterwards Portugal had gained little from the peace settlement. Indeed, at one point the American envoy to Portugal, Thomas Birch, had proposed establishing a form of international protectorate over Portugal owing to the level of internal disorder which participation in the 1914–18 conflict had exacerbated.[2] This was the kind of humiliation which Salazar hoped to avoid. He knew his country was weak in terms of armaments and resources but he was determined to preserve its independence and freedom of action.

It was not a quixotic gesture on his part. As Europe got ready to plunge into another vortex of destruction, he knew that Portugal counted as an actor more than it had in the past. A political context favouring authoritarian regimes, combined with his own skilful diplomacy, had given the Estado Novo and its head a vaulting reputation. He was taken seriously in Berlin and built up a rapport with Germany's envoy in Lisbon from 1934 to 1944, Oswald von Hoyningen-Huene. He was a German conservative who refrained from joining the Nazi party.[3] He was never required to deliver ultimatums to Salazar or, it seems, speak harshly with him because Hitler's interest in Portugal was only a momentary one. Portugal's stock would have risen in German eyes because of its total commitment to achieving a military victory for the nationalists of General Franco, whom many in Berlin viewed as a fellow fascist.

In the late 1930s Portugal behaved on the world scene as a relatively independent actor with its own will.[4] As passions were unleashed by Spain, Salazar gingerly tiptoed through a diplomatic minefield. Even when he aligned with Germany and Italy in seeking to crush the Spanish republicans, he never lost the confidence of Britain. He reassured London that preserving Portugal's Atlantic orientation remained its central strategic objective. Salazar had no wish to see the collapse of British power. It is unlikely that he relished a future for Portugal in a Europe dominated by Hitler's New Order. From his first months in power, the Führer had given ample evidence of his ruthlessness towards other regimes which were not so far apart from his own. Britain, meanwhile, had been loath to intervene in Portuguese politics for over a century. There had been moves in some policy circles to treat what were regarded as badly run Portuguese colonies in Africa as bargaining chips in a naive bid to buy off Hitler. But they had never assumed seriousness and did not shake the alliance. Inevitably, the regime possessed Germanophiles, but they lacked ties with Germany, whose economic links with Portugal were scanty.

One of Salazar's most independent-minded allies, Armindo Monteiro, was ambassador in London for seven crucial years until 1943. Conversations between him and Lord Halifax, the British foreign secretary from 1938 to 1940, were frequent and his strong ties with his successor, Anthony Eden, played a crucial role in the wartime Anglo-Portuguese story. Salazar himself calmed any British nerves about Portugal being another wobbly piece on the European chessboard with a speech that he gave on 22 May 1939 in which he offered assurance about his fidelity to the Anglo-Portuguese alliance and defence of common interests. He stated that 'it was always this way for centuries … with a fundamental basis in geography, history', not something 'easily discarded like many marriages of today'.[5]

Upon the outbreak of war, an official note was released in which 'the Government considers that the greatest service it can perform … is to maintain the peace for the Portuguese people'.[6] With Britain having no idea about the length of the war or the direction it would take, there was no pressure on Salazar to abandon or modify neutrality. Nor was there any kind of similar push from the German side. According to Bernard Futscher Pereira: 'The Führer considered Portugal so strongly intertwined in the English alliance and saw that a defence of its interests was dependent on it, that only force could detach Portugal from England.'[7]

Portuguese neutrality had its attractions for those in London who believed it imperative to keep Spain out of the war. Any formal intervention by Madrid would be on the German side given the ideological character of the Franco regime and the fact that, to no small degree, it owed its victory to Hitler's military backing. If German power was established in much of the Iberian peninsula, then Britain would have found it almost impossible to hang on to Gibraltar. The loss of what was a key to British sway in the western Mediterranean meant that retaining Malta would be impossible and the way was open to the loss of Egypt. In this grim scenario, Britain's Middle East possessions and, above all, India would only be accessible by way of the long and arduous voyage around the coast of Africa, which was already infested with German U-boats.

Among British political figures there was no firmer defender of Salazar than Sir Samuel Hoare (later Lord Templewood). He had been a well-known appeaser as foreign secretary in the mid-1930s, making a pact with his counterpart in Paris, the later wartime French collaborationist Pierre Laval, designed to dilute international action against Mussolini's seizure of Ethiopia. In the middle of 1940 he became Britain's envoy to Madrid. He seemed to regard it as a thankless task given the entrenched pro-German feelings in Spanish ruling circles. For some time after his arrival on 29 May, 'a British airplane was maintained for his personal use at Barajas airport in the event that a sudden Spanish declaration of war might require an abrupt exit'.[8] Hence he was bound to view Salazar positively thanks to his determination to keep his larger Iberian neighbour out of the conflict. A non-aggression pact had been signed shortly after the end of the civil war in March 1939, which committed both countries to come to one another's aid in the event of an outside attack. The initiative came from Salazar. He had been informed by his watchful envoy in Spain, Teotónio Pereira, of the disparaging attitude towards Portugal within the nationalist camp and the desire to annex the country exhibited by senior figures in the Falange movement. In a meeting with Rámon Serrano Súñer, Franco's brother-in-law, on 26 June, the Spaniard had told Pereira that 'Hitler would no longer tolerate the independent existence of an ally of Britain on the continent and that Spain might soon be forced to permit the passage of German troops to invade Portugal … Súñer strongly suggested that Portugal should make a gesture that would enable Spain to protect it, clearly implying a move toward making a satellite of the neighbouring country.'[9]

In June 1940, at a time when Salazar believed that Portugal faced 'consistent and total peril on every side', a breakthrough occurred in bilateral ties. An additional protocol to the existing treaty was added whereby Lisbon and Madrid pledged to consult each other to safeguard their mutual interests in the face of any threat to their security or independence.[10] The ambassadorial presence in Lisbon of Franco's brother Nicolás was a boon. This sybaritic figure was more pragmatic than Súñer, who would shortly be appointed foreign minister.

Salazar's apprehension that the situation in Iberia might soon render any treaty with Spain a dead letter had been heightened by the entry into the war on 10 June 1940 of Mussolini's Italy. He had written to the Duce some years earlier urging him to remember that the Mediterranean was his sphere of influence and that he should try to avoid over-reaching himself, only to receive a sarcastic response that could be summed up as 'Nothing is too much'.[11]

No longer was a photo of Mussolini to be found in Salazar's study. But there was a groundswell of support in Spain to emulate Italy so as to enjoy the spoils of a conflict that seemed destined to quickly end in total German victory. Spain immediately moved from a position of neutrality to non-belligerency. Pereira warned his superior of the likelihood of German pressure to intervene. Germany did not, however, adopt this course even after Franco sent the head of his army to Hitler with a letter in which he offered the Führer whatever Spanish help would be regarded as useful.[12]

Hoare was bound to be relieved at Portugal's deft handiwork to prevent Franco crossing the Rubicon. His appreciation was laid bare in a memoir published a year after the ending of the world conflict. He wrote:

> With Salazar I had the first of many long talks during my visits to Lisbon. I had met in the last thirty years most of the leading statesmen of the continent. When I think of their various qualities and characteristics and try to classify them, I place Dr Salazar very high on the list of those who left a lasting impression on me ... I would compare Dr Salazar for singleness of purpose and simplicity of life with President Masaryk. Both were political ascetics ... [who] lived the plainest of lives, indifferent and indeed hostile to any ostentation, luxury or personal gain.[13]

In a desperate hour, the British wooed Salazar by means of their soft power. In June 1940, he received a telegram from Lord Halifax, chancellor of the University of Oxford, requesting that he accept an honorary doctorate in civil law. Salazar accepted, but to go in person to receive the award was obviously out of the question. Yet just a month earlier, Walford Selby, the British ambassador in Lisbon, seemingly panic-stricken by the German blitzkrieg in Western Europe, had urged London to plan for the seizure of Portugal. His view was disregarded as Selby was seen back home as faltering in his judgement. London sent out a number of capable and energetic men to take over most of his diplomatic functions.[14] Sir Marcus Cheke was a highly active press attaché. Far more important was David Eccles, who arrived as economic counsellor in the embassy in April 1940. This cultivated and self-assured businessman knew the Iberian peninsula well. One writer has claimed that Eccles 'got on splendidly with the donnish dictator, sharing his love of philosophy and of Europe's conservative traditions'.[15]

Twenty years later himself a member of a British Conservative cabinet, Eccles wrote in the early 1960s:

> The Salazar I knew was by any standard a great man, from whom I learned many scraps of wisdom that became treasures in my memory. I accept that he stayed in office far too long ... he allowed the secret police to do things we all regretted. But, in the early days of the war, when defenceless neutrals were easily persuaded that the defeat of Britain must follow the collapse of France, he never concealed his hope that we would win, and he took risks on the assumption that someday, somehow, we would.[16]

The socially agile envoy even related an incident which revealed a humorous side to Salazar, one that few foreigners had ever encountered:

> One morning after having met a dark beauty on a deserted beach, I invited her to lunch, afterwards to discover she was not French, as I thought, but the daughter of the German military attaché. Salazar was informed about this incident and much more. He had heard, he said, that I was enjoying the society of Lisbon. He had a suggestion to make. If I were thinking of giving a ball he would have put at my disposal a rose-tinted palace not far from the city. He seemed perfectly serious, indeed he was never anything else. But what a gesture at a time when Britain's fortunes were at their lowest![17]

Perhaps the most effective collaboration between them occurred on 22 June 1940 when Eccles drew up a proposal to send to Spain, afflicted with terrible food shortages, 100,000 tons of wheat before the end of that month. Salazar quickly agreed to be the intermediary with Madrid. In return the Spanish government was asked to provide certain assurances regarding its neutrality. A cabinet meeting was called in

Madrid and the proposal was swiftly accepted, so chronic had the food situation become.[18]

But the rigours of war would increasingly test the Anglo-Portuguese relationship and Eccles would find Salazar a daunting negotiating partner. So did Selby's replacement as ambassador at the end of 1940, Sir Ronald Campbell. W.N. Medlicott, the historian of British economic warfare from 1939 to 1945, reckons that 'In Portugal, Great Britain had at once a closer political friend and a tougher economic antagonist than in Spain. In economic warfare matters Portugal was in a curious position; she was still dependent on Great Britain for overseas supplies, but on the other hand she had much to interest the Germans, in particular wolfram … Dr Salazar was much more inclined to reproach than to assist the ancient ally.'[19] Wolfram was vital for creating the tungsten needed to produce high-precision armaments and Portugal had by far most of the accessible mines in Europe where it could be extracted (Spain having a smaller number). Until late into the war, Salazar insisted that denying sales of the mineral to Germany jeopardised Portuguese neutrality and invited possibly terrible retribution from the skies.

Economic factors in the end curbed the pro-fascist spirit among many of the Spanish victors. But it was not immediately clear that caution would prevail in Spain. From October 1940 to September 1942 Súñer would be foreign minister. He was described by the historian Stanley Payne as 'arrogant and almost incredibly overweening, puffed up with his self-importance'. Payne believes he 'aspired to become the master of Spanish politics and government', perhaps like Salazar or Mussolini, neither of whom was a chief of state.[20] Teotónio Pereira grew to detest him, confiding in Salazar that during one conversation, he could barely resist the temptation to smash him in the face.[21] He feared that the Spanish lawyer's combination of excitability, arrogance, harshness, megalomania, and lack of scruples could lead Spain to a catastrophe. Pereira would not have been surprised to learn that, on a visit to Berlin in August 1940, Súñer had referred to Spain's tutelary role regarding a semi-satellite Portugal, claiming (in Payne's words) 'that in looking at the map … one could not avoid the realization that geographically speaking Portugal really had no right to exist'.[22] Pereira claimed that when, on a fresh visit to Berlin at the end of September 1940, Súñer, in an audience with Hitler, set out his territorial demands in Africa, the Führer replied: 'If you people want all this, why don't you take advantage of the moment and absorb Portugal along with its colonies.'[23]

The Allies were already aware of Spanish benevolence towards the Axis cause. Navigation stations in Spain were at the service of the Luftwaffe, German destroyers were being secretly refuelled at night in bays on the north-west coast, and the Abwehr, the German military intelligence, was allowed to operate throughout Spain.[24] Accordingly, it wasn't a neutral leader whom Hitler journeyed to meet at Hendaye on the French–Spanish frontier on 23 October 1940. Franco was a potential ally, but at the meeting he was left with the strong sense that Germany lacked the means to turn Spain into an effective military partner.[25] During many hours of negotiations, the Spanish leaders stated openly that their desire was for Hitler to win. According to Stanley Payne, 'they identified with his cause and wanted to enter the war; but … they were absolutely forthright about the assistance they needed.'[26] Franco insisted that a shattered and hungry country needed large amounts of food and materials without which it would be impractical to go to war so soon after the ferocious one fought on Spanish soil. Neither was he over-awed by Hitler. It made little difference that, in previous months, the Germans had achieved conquests that only Napoleon had surpassed in modern times. For his part Hitler was unimpressed by Franco's inflated sense of destiny.[27] He seemed a garrulous, crafty but ultimately parochial nonentity. He compared him to a 'narrow-minded chatterbox "with the manners of a sergeant major". "With me such a man would not even have become a Kreisleiter [local leader]."'[28] A frustrated Hitler departed, saying that he would rather have had three or four teeth removed.

It is clear that in order to knock Britain out of the Mediterranean, a German invasion had been seriously considered by Hitler in the first half of 1940 and it would take a year before the idea was shelved. The benefits, not just military ones, were considerable. Normal rivals in the Nazi power structure, Hermann Goering, the head of the air force, and General Erich Raeder, the chief of the navy, tried to persuade Hitler that an Iberian strike should be given top priority. The Suez Canal could be captured and the Balkans and Turkey cut off from their remaining links to the West.[29] Lord Alanbrooke, chief of the Imperial General Staff of the British Army (1939–43), wrote that this was precisely the strategy feared the most by those seeking to remain in the war and prevent the Germans from overrunning Britain and its colonies.[30]

Four armoured divisions were stationed on the other side of the Pyrenees ready to pour into Spain at short notice. An apprehensive Salazar sought to offer no excuse to Nazi Germany, and it was the fear of attack from that quarter that, for a long time, made him reluctant to bow to Allied pressure for bases in the Azores. The Portuguese island chain had been discussed on 22 July 1940 in the British cabinet. The government had decided that both they and the Cape Verde islands should be seized only if it became clear beyond a reasonable doubt that Portugal or Spain intended to collaborate with the Axis powers against Britain.[31]

The looming danger to Portuguese sovereignty increased on 12 November 1940 when Hitler issued the directive for 'Operation Felix'. It envisioned a German intervention in the Iberian Peninsula with the purpose of driving the British out of the western Mediterranean. To secure this objective the Wehrmacht was ordered to take Gibraltar and close the Straits.[32] The directive further stipulated that the 'English should be prevented from gaining a foothold at another point of the Iberian Peninsula or of the Atlantic islands'.[33] Operation Felix would not be undertaken until preparations for the seizure of the Atlantic islands had been finalised.

Two days later (on 14 November) Hitler again discussed the question of occupying the Azores in a conference with Raeder. The admiral reminded him that Portuguese neutrality contained its uses for Germany. The Führer's interest in, and knowledge of, American affairs was sketchy and he was told that any breach of Portugal's neutrality by Germany was likely to antagonise public opinion in the US. Moreover, it would result in the immediate occupation of the Azores, perhaps also of the Cape Verde islands and of Angola, by Britain or the US.[34] However, Hitler was not to be deterred. He maintained that the Azores would afford him the only springboard for attacking America, if the US should enter the war. He envisaged the US east coast being struck by a newly designed German warplane; he believed that threatening the US in this way might make Roosevelt reconsider extending military help to Britain.[35]

Events in October 1940 were to distract Hitler's attention from the western Mediterranean, however. In a bid to emulate his senior ally's triumphs, Mussolini mounted an ill-planned invasion of Greece which soon ended in disaster. Hitler, who had not been given prior notification, had to divert German forces to Greece to accomplish Mussolini's objective. At the end of 1940, a meeting of the Superior Council of the Army in Spain advised Franco to keep out of the war. But Operation Felix remained under serious consideration in Germany. It only receded as a serious option owing to Germany's deepening entanglement in the Balkans in April following a pro-Allied coup in Belgrade, which resulted in a swift occupation of Yugoslavia. A large military push in Iberia was finally ruled out after Germany declared war on the Soviet Union in June 1941.

Salazar regarded the Soviet Union as the pre-eminent European danger but he was guarded in his public comments about the invasion. In Spain, by contrast, there was huge enthusiasm, and on 17 July Franco launched a violent diatribe against 'the Western plutocracies and predicted a German victory'.[36] Salazar's preference remained for a compromise peace between the combatants who had gone to war in 1939. He continued to try and win round Franco to his cautious view, and his best chance to do so came when, seemingly at short notice, a meeting was arranged between the two men on 12 February 1942. No minutes were kept of the meeting whose details Salazar conveyed to the British ambassador while keeping his own ministers in the dark. He had slipped unobtrusively out of Lisbon along with the secret police chief, Agostinho Lourenço. They drove directly east to Estremoz, where they picked up Teotónio Pereira. Their destination was Seville, and before crossing the frontier, they stopped to have an impromptu lunch by the roadside.

The two leaders were of a different stamp, Franco a soldier who had won power by the exercise of often brutal force, and Salazar an academic who had risen to the top by cunning statecraft and dedication to his public duties. What they shared in common was deep-seated prudence and a powerful survival instinct. The mission of the Portuguese was to convince his Spanish interlocutor not to abandon his country's non-belligerent stance in the conflict. The grounds for their cooperation were still tenuous and there was plenty of room for misunderstanding. At the meeting, Franco told Salazar of his belief that an Allied victory was absolutely impossible.[37] On that day the British had suffered a huge military defeat when their base at Singapore fell to the Japanese. Such a setback was likely to have rekindled Franco's hopes that, under him, Spain could profit from what he hoped would be the demise of the Anglo-French hegemony which had kept Spain in a subordinate position for over two centuries.[38]

Franco had met Hitler (and Mussolini in February 1941) before he had sought out Salazar. This was perhaps a sign of the coolness in bilateral relations. But in the event both men got on well. The Spaniard was impressed by Salazar's intellectual qualities. Interpreters were not required as he spoke in Gallego, the language he had grown up with. Given its closeness to Portuguese, Salazar had no difficulty in following him and any tensions subsided as it became clear that no precipitate action was being planned by Franco. There were already signs that Hitler had over-reached in his invasion of the Soviet Union and the quick knockout blow that would sweep away the communist regime was never going to materialise. Súñer, who had described Salazar in 1940 as 'a very dangerous anglophile' and as 'the last friend England had left in Europe', dropped his disparaging view of the Portuguese leader.[39] In an interview with the German ambassador upon his return to Madrid, he described him as 'a very engaging person, extremely well-educated, distinguished … and possessing perfect dignity'. But it no longer mattered much that Súñer now saw Salazar as a man of the first rank, as his own star was in eclipse and soon he would no longer count in Spanish decision-making.[40]

By now the United States had entered the war following the Japanese attack on its main naval base in Hawaii on 8 December 1941. Hitler had long underestimated America's capability as a military foe. He refused to listen to a former adviser, Ernst Hanfstaengl, familiar with the United States and its martial culture.[41] Believing instead that it was rotten to the core because of the influence of Jews and the presence of a large black population, he declared war immediately afterwards on America.

From a conservative perspective, Salazar also had misgivings about America and its growing ascendancy in world affairs. The widening of the war was a reverse for his hope that a compromise peace could occur as a result of the chief West European combatants determining that outright victory for either of them was impossible. Russia remained the primordial threat. It was a view some British diplomats with regular access to him may well have grown weary of hearing. He certainly regretted the alliance forged between Britain and the Soviet Union after June 1941, and in a radio address on 25 June 1942 he publicly attacked it. He also persisted with the view that liberalism as a practical doctrine had been superseded.[42] His public stand was badly received in London, but Salazar may have felt that the time had come when he needed to show that he was not about to embrace expediency and ditch his conservative authoritarian outlook. The emergence of large new power blocs whose fulcrum lay outside Western Europe troubled him. He believed that in a world divided in this way, his regime would be hard put to find any secure place.

He seems to have had few confidants within wartime Portugal with whom he could discuss Portugal's options in the war and the direction the conflict was likely to take. Throughout his years in power, he was never close to any military figures (with the exception of his alert guardian of the army, Santos Costa). Intellectual figures within the army with a grasp of military strategy were hard to spot. With his ambassador in London, Armindo Monteiro, he had increasingly strained relations, and until after the war Washington was seen as a secondary diplomatic posting.

With one person he was able to unburden himself about his views on the direction of Europe and those nations aiming to shape it. This was the Swiss political thinker and historian Count Gonzague de Reynold. They exchanged letters over a twenty-five-year period from 1934 to 1959, some of which are kept in Salazar's archive in Lisbon. De Reynold had written a book on Portugal in 1937 in which Salazar was extolled for being a Christian leader who was paternalist without being Caesarist or totalitarian.[43] But, unusually for a foreign admirer of the New State, he was also critical of features of national life that the regime seemed in no hurry to alter. He drew attention to the poor health conditions of much of the population, the prevalence of infectious diseases, and the high rate of illiteracy.[44] But notwithstanding these strictures, Salazar chose to treat him as an intellectual equal and even a soulmate. Upon the book's appearance, Salazar congratulated him, writing that his 'observation of facts and interpretation of events are simply impeccable'.[45] They were both traditionalists in spirit and instinct, convinced that the French Revolution had profoundly impaired Europe's development. There was, however, a looming issue where their views failed to coincide. While de Reynold was a vigorous champion of a united Europe, Salazar thought the concept was utopian and an admission in some quarters that Europe was exhausted and incapable of renewal. He preferred to see a Europe of cooperative nation-states, closely aligned on a range of practical issues.[46]

In two very lengthy letters to his Swiss friend, written on 1 September 1941 and 29 October 1942, Salazar enunciated some of his views about the war and his attitude to the chief combatants. He held out for a compromise peace long after the idea seemed to be impractical to Monteiro in London. He recognised that Portugal's longstanding ally, Britain, was the chief opponent of such a peace. Britain, he believed, was a far less disciplined and well-organised society than Germany but he admired its staying power and believed it could retain much of its empire and avoid being elbowed aside by the US. How a financial expert like Salazar could have made this assumption, given that Britain had to liquidate most of her foreign reserves and sell almost all of her foreign assets during the war, is not altogether clear.[47] The letters breathe suspicion towards the United States and fear and repulsion towards Russia. He may have chosen to make largely commonplace remarks about Germany (ones that he had made to others) since he knew there was a risk that correspondence crossing occupied parts of Europe might be intercepted. But he did express alarm about Germany's authoritarianism and Hitler's insatiable appetite for territory, especially to the east, and he despaired about the eclipse of Europe as most people had known it.[48]

Ten days after his second downbeat epistle to his Swiss friend, Salazar got the most direct indication that the tides of war were rapidly shifting. Late on 7 November 1942, a Saturday evening, he was telephoned to be told that the British ambassador required an urgent meeting. Simultaneously, the American minister in Lisbon had contacted President Carmona to also press for a meeting. Neither man would be put off until the next day. Why were the two chief figures in the Portuguese state the objects of such a démarche? The likeliest explanation seemed to be that the Western allies were poised to occupy the Azores. Instead, the diplomats representing Britain and America had sought out their Portuguese hosts to inform them that a major military landing in north-west Africa was imminent. Known as Operation Torch, it was designed to drive German forces out of the whole of North Africa. Germany had just suffered its most serious military reverse as a result of the British defeating General Erwin Rommel's Afrika Corps at the Battle of El Alamein in the Egyptian desert. The French Vichy forces in Morocco and Algeria were quickly overwhelmed in a landing that represented the greatest amphibious operation since Xerxes crossed the Hellespont in 480 BC.[49]

The British Foreign Office hoped that the North African landing would tilt Salazar towards interpreting his country's neutrality decisively in favour of the Allies. He would successfully urge prudence on the new Spanish foreign minister, Francisco (Count) Jordana, who paid an official visit to Lisbon in December 1942 that was widely judged to have been a success. Franco himself remained troubled about the concessions which Portugal was being pressured to make to the Allies. Salazar stated to his ambassador in Madrid: 'In spite of our loyalty and the correctness of our procedures, Spain feels we have embarked on a path that is not to its benefit.' He offered the observation that 'we, the Portuguese, in general are Anglophiles out of love. The Spaniards are Germanophiles on account of their Anglophobia out of rancour, not to mention hate.'[50] But relations with Spain steadily improved. The flashpoint for Portugal would be relations with Britain and America. For the next eighteen months they would often encounter a stubborn Portuguese leader who was intransigent in basing his actions in the external sphere around what he considered was best for his vulnerable country's national interest.

9

NO SAFE HARBOUR FOR SALAZAR OR HIS REGIME

Previously long removed from the major highways of history, with the outbreak of world war Portugal's capital suddenly found itself 'the only major gateway between warring Europe and the world outside'.[1] As well as being a hotbed for espionage, Lisbon was the largest port of embarkation in neutral Europe and the main link for civilian flights between Great Britain and the United States. It was also the chief distribution port for International Red Cross Committee relief supplies to prisoner of war and internment camps and a transit point for multitudes fleeing the conflict.

Harvey Klemmer, known for evocative writing on how Britain struggled to survive in 1940, wrote in 1941: 'I came to Lisbon from the London blackout … Lisbon bursts on anyone coming from England like some half-forgotten splendor out of another life.'[2] But he warned in the *National Geographic Magazine*, 'before these lines appear in print, Portugal may only be a memory and Lisbon a ghost town of the Second World War. There is a special risk in attempting to write about a small neutral possessed of rich territories, owning strategic islands, and lying on the flank of a continent in flames.'

Remarkably, the war in Europe did not deter Portugal from marking two important anniversaries. 1940 was the 800th anniversary of the birth of the country and was also 300 years since the escape from sixty years of Spanish captivity. The 'Exhibition of the Portuguese World' would be the cultural high point of the Estado Novo regime.[3] Work froze for one month in September 1939 only for Salazar to decide to continue regardless of the war. Normally one to carefully husband the nation's finances, he decided to mark both occasions with celebrations that lasted a full six months. Its architects were two of the regime's most original characters. Propaganda chief António Ferro was responsible for selecting the exhibits and defining a message that Portugal had a civilising mission in a ravaged world. He used the official catalogue to underline that 'at a moment when frontiers are falling like houses of cards ... Portugal is a peaceful nation whose borders have remained unaltered over centuries.'[4]

The minister of public works, Duarte Pacheco, was the other driving force behind the 1940 exhibition. Thanks to him, for nearly a decade Portugal witnessed a spurt of architectural creativity which saw new highways, railway stations and monuments composed in an innovative Portuguese style with little of the harshness or bombast to be found in Italy or Germany.[5] The infrastructure of the country began to be transformed and his work would go on, though at a less frenetic pace, after his death in a car crash in 1943. His 'enormous capacity for work and the demands he placed on others enables him to stand out historically'.[6] Like Salazar too busy to spend much time on personal relationships, he was criticised for ruthlessness and megalomania. Thus, he cleared inhabited areas around the Lisbon waterfront in preparation for the 1940 exhibition. Compensation to affected property owners facing expropriation was often deemed inadequate and no legal appeals were allowed.[7] Ironically, he never fell into disgrace after 1974 and a major Lisbon transport route continues to be named after him.

A self-confident message was conveyed in the exhibitions. Firstly, Portugal was proud of its struggle to rule itself and this desire was as strong as ever. Secondly, economic and political conditions were normal. But there were major anxieties beneath the surface. If different military and strategic decisions had been taken by the chief combatants, Lisbon could easily have been occupied or else militarily damaged.

Portugal was at the mercy of events completely outside anyone's control, including Salazar's. He must have known that, and observers noticed how the leader, by now in his early fifties and under immense and competing strains, was starting to age perceptibly.[8]

Perhaps the gloomiest member of his ruling circle was ambassador Monteiro in London. He warned Salazar in October 1940 that 'unfortunately we are now in the line of conquests and, only by a miracle, could Portugal escape the torrent of madness that is sweeping across the continent'.[9] But his formula for survival was regarded as folly by his cautious boss; Monteiro was suggesting that the alliance with Britain needed to be enacted: 'we need to prepare an evacuation of the Government to the Azores or the Ultramar, from where, even with the country under occupation, we can continue to direct the nation'.[10]

Salazar was unmoved by what he saw as a dangerously impractical approach from his otherwise effective London ambassador. Besides, Britain had already thrown him into a potentially embarrassing situation thanks to the arrival in Lisbon on the eve of the exhibition of the ex-King Edward VIII, now known as the Duke of Windsor. His brother the Duke of Kent was the official British guest at the event and, on 21 June, Salazar felt it necessary to tell the British ambassador that 'it would be inconvenient and undesirable' if the two men were to be in Lisbon at the same time.[11]

One duke's visit was held back while Salazar strove to ensure that the ex-king, who had previously exhibited Germanophile views, did not compromise Portuguese neutrality. To this end, his banker friend, Ricardo Espirito Santo, was of enormous use. He had persuaded the Windsors to lodge at his sumptuous house on the Lisbon coast where dinner parties in their honour were organised with the local elite in attendance. He kept Salazar informed of the private conversations that took place. This, along with the detailed written reports of the PVDE, would mean that Salazar knew and understood how the plans of the duke were likely to unfold.[12] So it was bound to have been a relief when the duke left Portugal on 1 August to live out the war years as governor of the Bahamas.

Soon after Salazar had to contend with a newly appointed ambassador to Germany who, within hours of landing in a capital that was already being bombed by the British RAF, decided it was not the place for either himself or his young family. Nobre Guedes belonged on the Germanophile wing of the regime and he had been asked several times by Salazar (ever keen to preserve some ideological balance) to join his government. But he had refused, claiming the salary was too low.

Whatever had possessed a politician without overt diplomatic skills to accept, he soon bombarded Salazar with letters asking to be recalled. However, a leader with a strong sense of duty expected it to be displayed also by subordinates. When Nobre Guedes effectively walked out of the ambassadorship in early 1941 and acted as if the gesture was of no great significance, Salazar flew into a rage. Not only did he refuse to see him but he barred him from all state employment and spread the word that he would regard it in the worst light if someone gave him a job in the private sector.[13]

Salazar had warned about the 'pagan Caesarism' exhibited by Hitler in the mid-1930s. He knew there were Germanophiles in his government such as Santos Costa, who admired the Wehrmacht's fighting qualities, and the navy minister, Ortins de Bettencourt. But no minister challenged his wartime decisions and he was left to work out what was driving Hitler on his mission of destruction. At the end of 1941 he was reading *Mein Kampf* the better to understand him.[14] But if he had been aware of the furious tirades that Hitler was delivering around this time to intimates about institutions like the Catholic Church, which Salazar still held dear, the Portuguese leader might have cast the book aside.[15]

Hitler's cruel onslaught against nations and ethnic groups which he held in contempt increased the workload of the leader, who was also his country's foreign minister, as tens of thousands of desperate people tried to enter Portugal. Monteiro beseeched him to climb off the fence. Early in the war, he wrote, 'Only God can save us.' The best hope: 'a fragment of local autonomy in the grand machine directed draconically from Berlin'.[16]

Meanwhile, Salazar was briefly faced with insubordination from a wayward consul in Bordeaux, Aristides de Sousa Mendes, who, in time, would become the most famous diplomat in Portuguese history, one who had been defying a ministry ruling that prior authorisation from Lisbon was required in order to issue visas to certain categories of applicants. Bordeaux had abruptly become a diplomatic hotspot as France was overwhelmed by Nazi Germany. Many thousands tried to get away after what seemed, to some, like a catastrophic demise for Western civilisation. It was in this despairing context that the picaresque figure of Aristides Sousa Mendes was briefly thrust into the limelight. According to the legend that has built up around him, he defied an authoritarian regime and tirelessly issued visas enabling thousands of people, including many Jews, to escape the Nazi clutches. Moreover, he paid a stiff price for his valour. He was investigated by his political masters, denied a diplomatic career, left with little money to survive, only to die broken in health and spirit in 1954.

In reality, this coda to Portugal's wartime story is rather more complicated. Sousa Mendes comes across as a charming misfit who would not be out of place in a novel by Graham Greene or John Le Carré exploring personally conflicted officials in the unsettled conditions of 20th-century Europe. Sousa Mendes was a devout Catholic whose amorous ways more than once interfered with his career. He had a habit of rule-breaking and had to hurriedly leave a posting in Brazil in 1918 after appointing a close relative to the consular staff.[17] His behaviour there resulted in a two-year suspension that lasted until 1921. In 1923, while stationed in San Francisco he had badly fallen out with members of the local Portuguese-American community and was obliged to leave the United States after Washington withdrew its official recognition from him.[18]

Between 1911, when he joined the consular service, and 1940, he received eight reprimands and faced five disciplinary proceedings.[19] As an official in a more liberal European state than the Portuguese Estado Novo, it is quite likely that he would have struggled to avoid dismissal for capricious behaviour. But he may have been given his longest diplomatic posting—in Antwerp, where he served from 1929 to 1938—out of consideration for the fact that he had a large family and it was a place where extra income generation was good due to the amount of Portuguese shipping.[20]

After the outbreak of World War II, countries of all kinds, neutral and non-neutral, had introduced measures to keep certain categories of refugees from entering their jurisdictions, to which Sousa Mendes would have been expected to adhere. Circular 14, sent to all Portuguese consulates in November 1939, laid down that consuls would need to get prior approval from Lisbon for applicants who could not freely return to their countries of origin or who had no visible means of support. The relevant passage stated that this needed to be the approach 'in the case of "Foreigners of indefinite or contested nationality, the

Stateless, Russian Citizens, Holders of a Nansen passport, or Jews expelled from their countries ... The consuls will, however, be very careful not to hinder the arrival in Lisbon of passengers going on to other countries.'"[21]

But Portugal never closed its frontiers to refugees—unlike other neutral states—after September 1939. The author Neill Lochery has argued that it was economics rather than ideology which prompted the authorities to tighten up.[22] Portugal was a country with limited resources. Its regime did not distinguish between Jews and non-Jews but rather between immigrant Jews who came and had the means to leave the country, and those lacking them. Avraham Milgram is just one of a number of historians to claim that modern anti-Semitism failed 'to establish even a toehold in Portugal'.[23] Adolfo Benarus, the honorary president of the Jewish community of Lisbon, claimed in 1937 that 'happily in Portugal, modern anti-Semitism doesn't exist'.[24]

In 1938, Salazar sent a telegram to the Portuguese Embassy in Berlin, ordering that it should be made clear to the German Reich that Portuguese law did not allow any distinction based on race, and that therefore Portuguese Jewish citizens could not be discriminated against.[25] The historian Irene Flunser Pimentel has suggested that in 'a compilation of propaganda texts, entitled *Como se levante um estado* (1937), Salazar, without actually naming them, criticised the Nuremberg laws that had recently been passed in Germany. He considered it "regrettable" that German nationalism was "damaged" by such pronounced racial features that it meant "from the juridical point of view, there was a distinction between the citizen and the subject—giving rise to dangerous consequences".'[26]

Portugal was not alone in showing concern about taking in people who could be a drain on its resources or a source of agitation and unrest. Sousa Mendes got into trouble at home because of his quixotic approach in a sensitive posting. Long before the crisis of May 1940 he had been issuing visas to people whose right to stay or not was the foreign ministry's responsibility. The numbers increased in June 1940 but fell far short of the thousands of visas which his later admirers claimed had been issued by him.[27] Evidence that his efforts were especially directed towards fleeing Jews is also speculative. British, Portuguese and American citizens, often people with means, figured prominently as recipients of visas.

Sousa Mendes was also erratic in his work habits. This led to an aide-memoire being sent to the Portuguese government on 20 June 1940 from the British Embassy in Lisbon. The complaint was made that its Bordeaux consul was failing to honour an undertaking made by Salazar to enable fleeing Britons to receive the transit papers that would enable them to enter Portugal. Some, it was alleged, were even being charged an inflated rate and payment to a Portuguese charity was requested.[28] In his defence the consul dismissed the charity claim as 'absurd'.[29] At the boiling point of June 1940 Salazar would have been averse to provoking one of the major combatants, and one source alleges that it was the British complaint which may have led Lisbon to move against the consul.[30]

Arguably, issuing a visa was not yet equivalent to saving a life, as it would become in 1944 and 1945 when the existence of the Holocaust was increasingly well known and several Portuguese consuls endeavoured to save Jews and others. Posthumously, Sousa Mendes became a secular saint, perhaps the most notable Portuguese of World War II after Salazar himself. Much of his standing derives from the alleged privations that he faced in his bid to ease the distress of people fleeing war. But his punishment was relatively mild. On 30 October 1940 he was suspended by the foreign ministry for one year on half-salary due to failure to properly exercise his duties. This was hardly a case of persecution. His French mistress, Andrée Cibial, had given birth to his child weeks before this ruling. Sympathetic writers describe her as an unstable character who made public scenes and succeeded in estranging Sousa Mendes from most members of his large family (which by 1940 consisted of eleven mainly grown-up children out of an original family of fourteen).[31] His disorderly private life, and how it may have affected his work, was never made an issue by Salazar (his supposedly very straitlaced boss).

Similarly, the authorities were remarkably lax when it emerged that Sousa Mendes had forged a passport for Paul Miny, a deserter from the French army (who wasn't a Jew), before hostilities had ceased in 1940. This was an offence that carried the penalty of two years in prison and expulsion from the public service.[32] But the foreign ministry sat on its hands, describing it as a police matter. The PVDE, the secret police, did accuse the consul of passport forgery. Ultimately, no action was taken by a ministry directly under the control of Salazar (whom several of Sousa Mendes's admirers characterise as a supremely vindictive figure).[33]

Sousa Mendes was never actually expelled from the foreign service. However, a foundation instrumental in keeping alive his memory claims he was 'stripped of his diplomatic position and forbidden from earning a living'.[34] It seems that ill health prevented him from returning to diplomatic work and he figured on the roll of diplomatic staff up to his death. This makes sense since he was paid a full salary by the state until the end of his life. One of his most sympathetic biographers, Rui Afonso, has reckoned that he continued to receive a salary at least three times that of a teacher.[35]

His last years were bitter and frustrating but it is hardly apt to claim, as the Sousa Mendes foundation does, that 'what was once an illustrious and well-respected family—one of the great families of Portugal—was crushed and destroyed'.[36]

In 1995, when former belligerent countries were marking fifty years since the end of World War II, Portugal staged a week-long series of events commemorating the role of Sousa Mendes in 1940. The majority of Jews who crossed the Franco-Spanish frontier in the early summer of 1940 to eventually reach Portugal did so undoubtedly owing to his intervention on their behalf.[37] But it is perhaps equally fair to contend that it was Portugal's flinty leader who employed state power to save a much greater number of Jews and other refugees. At the outset of the war, he permitted 200 Gibraltar Jews, along with the rest of the British territory's civilian population, to be resettled on the island of Madeira. In June 1940 he gave his approval for the Europe office of HIAS-HICEM, the main Jewish relief organisation, to be transferred from Paris to Lisbon. Though it was treated with suspicion initially by the Portuguese authorities, there was growing cooperation to ease the plight of refugees and enable them to receive humane treatment before the opportunity arose for them to be resettled elsewhere.[38]

Still hardly appreciated was the role of a future minister of education in rescuing European Jews later in the war. Francisco de Paula Leite Pinto was at that time the general manager of the Beira Alta Railway, which operated services from the Portuguese coast to the Spanish frontier. He organised several trains that brought refugees from

Berlin and other European cities to safety in Portugal. Salazar had been persuaded to instruct consuls in territories under Nazi occupation to validate all passports held by Jews even though the documents were known to be far from reliable.[39]

The man who seems to have exercised a definite influence on Salazar's approach to Jewish refugees was himself a Jew, Moisés Bensabat Amzalak. He was a supporter of Salazar's regime and he rose high in Portuguese academia through his expertise in economics and marketing. He has been credited with persuading Salazar not to turn away the refugees given visas by Sousa Mendes (in violation of the rules), making life tolerable for the Jews seeking shelter in Portugal, and for also obtaining his backing for Leite Pinto's rescue mission.[40]

Yet there is one awkward fact about Amzalak that has been aired more than once during the era of commemoration for Sousa Mendes. In 1935, the German ambassador in Lisbon recommended to his superiors that Amzalak be awarded the medal of excellence from the German Red Cross. António Louçu wrote a book hostile to Amzalak on the basis of this gesture and the fact that the daily newspaper which he co-owned, *O Século*, allegedly had Germanophile ties at one period.

Upon its appearance in 2007, Esther Munchkin, one of the leaders of the Jewish community of Lisbon, mounted a defence of Amzalak. She argued that the deeply terrible nature of the Nazi regime was not yet apparent in 1935.[41] Earlier, the well-known historian José Freire Antunes had asserted that without Amzalak it is impossible that 150,000 refugees would have reached Portugal during the Nazi epoch.[42] One of the best-known, the Austrian writer Stefan Zweig, was a guest in the home of Amzalak before moving to Brazil where, in 1942, he committed suicide out of despair at the fate of European civilisation.[43] Thanks to Amzalak, Sousa Mendes and others, Lisbon became the European capital for those without a homeland.

Accordingly, seeking to discredit someone on the basis of fleeting associations in one of the most turbulent points of modern European history is largely a futile exercise. Towards the end of his life Sousa Mendes was linked with opponents of Salazar, but for much longer he had been sympathetic to the dictatorship installed in 1926 and, before that, the monarchy. But it seems ridiculous to cast doubt on his actions in 1940 because of past political behaviour.[44]

Far more people could have been rescued and saved if Salazar had had more time at his disposal to focus on the peril into which European Jews had been cast. But, arguably, he was no more negligent than Churchill or Roosevelt who, in public, played down the deadly attempts to kill off millions of Jews when the true extent of their plight had become known to the Allied leaders by 1942–3. There is no evidence of either of them showing deep emotion about the destruction of a large part of European Jewry. But Salazar did, weeping in front of Amzalak when forced to tell him, late in the war, about the likely fate of 4,304 Jews in the Netherlands, many with Portuguese surnames.[45] Berlin turned down his plea that they be designated as of Portuguese origin in order to enable them to avoid the concentration camps and be ferried instead to Portugal.[46] It is wrong to ignore the good that Portugal under Salazar did, which stands up well in comparison with the stance of the other European neutrals. Some of them, more closely situated to the scene of Nazi butchery, were finally more energetic than Portugal as the war reached its end and the fate of Jews being pursued by Nazis and their collaborators became hard to overlook.

In the Hungary of 1944, delivered into the hands of the ultra-fascist Arrow Cross movement by the German occupiers, Carlos de Liz-Teixeira Branquinho, the chargé d'affaires in Budapest, played a pivotal role in saving up to 1,000 people from the Nazi death camps.[47] His case differs from that of Sousa Mendes in a number of respects. He was deliberately setting out to save Jews, he had the full backing of the authorities in Lisbon, and he was risking his life in a city controlled by local fascists. Yet he has been largely overlooked perhaps owing to the fact that he was coordinating his actions with Salazar (and highlighting his case weakens the core argument in the Sousa Mendes legend that he was defying a tyrannical superior). Arguably, *both* Salazar and Sousa Mendes displayed ethics of responsibility towards the plight of refugees, many of them Jews, during a terrible period in European history. Neither were they alone in that regard, and the disproportionate attention given to Sousa Mendes suggests that wartime history is in danger of being used in contemporary Portugal as a political weapon.

It was the attempt to preserve control over Portugal's dispersed territories which probably occupied the bulk of Salazar's time during World War II. The fate of the strategic mid-Atlantic Azores islands was perhaps his main concern. Germany's plans for their seizure have already been discussed. Long before the US entered the war, President Roosevelt publicly expressed strong interest in their fate. He declared an unlimited national state of emergency on 27 May 1940, and, in a radio address that evening, stated: 'Unless the advance of Hitlerism is forcibly checked now, the Western Hemisphere will be within range of the Nazi weapons of destruction ... Equally, the Azores and the Cape Verde islands, if occupied or controlled by Germany, would directly endanger the freedom of the Atlantic and our own American physical safety ... Old-fashioned common sense calls for the use of strategy that will prevent an enemy from gaining a foothold.'[48]

There had already been a rapid build-up of Portuguese troops on the Azores and the Portuguese government expressed its determination to do all it could to defend its sovereignty against any attack (though insisting that none was anticipated).[49] Luckily for Salazar, it soon proved that American military chiefs were no more enthusiastic about invading the Azores than the German military was.[50]

It was Portugal's most far-flung colony, Timor, which was the sole casualty of the war. Unexpectedly, on 4 November 1941, British foreign secretary Eden had pointed out to Portugal the vulnerability of Timor's strategic position for Australian defence.[51] On 17 December, when ambassador Monteiro arrived at the Foreign Office to continue discussions, it was only to be told that a Dutch–Australian force had already landed on Timor. Earlier, before the United States and Japan went to war on 8 December 1941, Salazar had agreed to accept Allied military assistance if Timor was attacked. But a Japanese attack had yet to occur. The Australians moved (along with the Dutch) out of fear that a Japanese seizure of an island so close to their northern coast could have grave consequences. Salazar, for his part, feared that the presence of Allied troops on Portuguese soil would encourage Berlin to tighten pressure, perhaps even leading the Germans to seize the Azores. A glacial Salazar confronted ambassador Campbell, who later wrote that the incident had 'placed a strain upon Anglo-Portuguese relations such as had not been experienced since Lord Salisbury's ultimatum of 1890'.[52] Britain was asked by Salazar whose order to send a defending force it had been and when it would be countermanded. Monteiro, once again out on a limb, urged Salazar to take 'big decisions' as 'our neutrality is expiring' (by which he meant to formally join the Allies).[53]

Instead, at a swiftly convened meeting of the National Assembly on 19 December 1941, Salazar provided facts and dates that suggested British bad faith. A memorandum was then delivered to London, expressing profound consternation.[54] Simultaneously, in a message to Tokyo, the Japanese were informed that the violation of Portuguese territory was a 'pure act of force, carried out without the assent of the government or local authorities'. The Japanese launched a brutal invasion in February 1942 and it has been reckoned that 60,000 people were killed (around 15 per cent of the population) during the Japanese occupation. By August 1945 the place was in ruins and would be slow to recover.[55]

The British seem to have considered Salazar's fury an over-reaction without taking into account his fears that the seizure of Timor represented a precedent which could result in much of Portugal's empire being lost in the international maelstrom. Sir Ronald Campbell wrote in early February 1942: 'We cannot allow ourselves to ignore the strange man with whom we are dealing. Notwithstanding his undeniable Christian virtues ... he is capable of falling into a black rage from which he only slowly emerges ... if we give him cause, a second time, to feel that we have ill-treated him, I am convinced that he will break with us completely and forever, either throwing himself into the arms of the Germans, or, more likely, resigning from government.'[56]

Despite frustrations with him at the top of British government, Salazar continued to receive favourable coverage in Britain. Ronald Bodley, a Briton who had escaped from France back home via Portugal, published a book in 1941 in which he wrote: 'Oliveira Salazar is one of the few politicians, if politician he can be called, who has been completely sincere in his ambition to see his country regain its position as a power which counts. He has never wanted anything for himself; he hardly ever appears in public; he has invented no musical-comedy uniform and dresses like any man in the street, and he lives modestly in the upstairs apartment of the prime minister's fine residence and works as hard as when he was teaching at the university.'[57]

But the divergences between two old allies continued. From January 1941 a British undercover mission existed in Lisbon led by Jack Beevor, who was installed in the British Embassy. From at least September 1941 Salazar had been aware of its existence and that, in the event of the war reaching the Iberian peninsula, its role would be to carry out acts of sabotage, provide armed resistance, and furnish propaganda.[58] By early 1942, the British network had been penetrated and destroyed by the PVDE. Some Britons who enjoyed diplomatic cover were interrogated by the secret police, Salazar confronting Campbell about them.[59]

The Battle of the Atlantic, being waged not far off Portugal's shores, increasingly preoccupied the British. On the Allied side over 72,000 naval and merchant sailors were killed, 3,500 merchant ships and 175 warships sunk or damaged, and 741 aircraft of the British RAF lost.[60] Already by 1942, the severity of the losses had prompted Allied military chiefs to conclude that bases on the Azores were essential to extend air cover over the mid-Atlantic 'gaps' where U-boat wolfpacks could tear at the convoys without interference.[61] Urged on by his senior officers, Churchill was ready in the words of the head of the British Foreign Office, Sir Alexander Cadogan, 'to ask Portugal for these facilities, and to intimate that if not freely granted, they would be taken anyway'.[62] However, he was persuaded by Eden to rely on negotiation. But soon there was huge consternation in London when it was learned that Portugal had struck a fresh deal with Germany over the sale of wolfram.[63] In June 1943, Salazar finally conceded that, in principle, the facilities on the Azores could be used, but pointed out that negotiations were bound to take time. He was chiefly concerned with the need to prevent German reprisals. When the British invoked their ancient alliance with Portugal, a deal was struck in October, but wolfram sales continued. A major Allied landing in Western Europe was being prepared and there was anger that lethal German weaponry was being fashioned by this Portuguese mineral. Finally, after broadcasts critical of the Portuguese regime began to be transmitted on the BBC, Salazar (after protracted haggling) agreed to an embargo on wolfram production just days before the D-Day landings on the Normandy beaches in mid-1944.

It is clear that in London ambassador Monteiro was viewed with far more favour than his occasionally intractable boss. Eden concluded that Salazar was 'a very complicated man', his ambassador in Lisbon recognising, from frequent bouts of lengthy negotiations, that there were depths to Salazar that at times could seem unfathomable.[64] How sensitive Salazar's London envoy was to British needs was shown by an effusive speech from Eden on 15 August 1943 when he declared that in the sombre months of 1941–2, he had been the only ambassador who had the openly declared conviction that Britain would prevail.[65] Earlier on the same day, he had been decorated with the Order of the Bath, the highest British honour that can be awarded to a foreigner. At a luncheon attended by diplomatic heads of mission in London and the ambassador's many friends (Churchill included), Eden said: 'Dr Armindo Monteiro: your country needs you. Other destinies await. At this time, you can count on all your friends here being on your side.'[66]

There is no evidence that the British sought to supplant Salazar at this time, even though they had a far more amenable successor to hand. The terms of trade he offered Britain were far more generous than those of some of the other neutrals. While Sweden and Switzerland always demanded gold in their trade with Britain, a bilateral 'payments agreement' signed in October 1940 enabled Britain to use sterling to buy Portuguese goods and receive credit for escudos. The agreement meant that Britain could compete with Germany for Portuguese goods at a time when Britain was short of gold and hard currency. While the British paid for wolfram with a credit, Salazar expected the Germans to pay with gold, which they did in very large quantities.[67]

As his energies were pressed into international statecraft, almost imperceptibly Salazar began to grow weaker at home. He no longer appeared in public so much. The last time a major crowd glimpsed him was on 28 April 1941. On that day crowds had massed in front of the ministry of finance where a bust of the leader was being unveiled. They had come voluntarily or else had been bused in from right across the country, and they soon filled the waterfront square, the Praça do Comércio, in Lisbon. Portuguese military bands kept them entertained until, at 6 pm, Salazar appeared from a ministry window. He delivered a speech that was more in the form of a dry lecture than a fascist rallying cry. He was heard in respectful silence, followed by prolonged applause.[68]

Eighteen months later, serious unrest had broken out in Lisbon and it would take several years before it would fully abate. The trouble arose from dissatisfaction over mounting shortages and rapidly increasing prices for the basic staples that were available. From the summer of 1942 supplies of oil, electricity and coal began to diminish along with foodstuffs. In a country with unreliable harvests which depended, even in good years, on imports of key household products, Salazar struggled to get a grip on the situation. The production of grain did not cover half the country's needs and many cattle had to be slaughtered owing to its unavailability.[69]

The Battle of the Atlantic determined how much oil and food products could reach Portugal in neutral or Allied shipping. The pauperisation of the lowest income groups was starting to occur as scarcity and high prices for whatever was available took hold.[70] But the regime was far more concerned about the intermediate classes in towns and countryside.[71] Its ability to shield owners of small property and capital from disruption and acute want had kept it in office during turbulence across the world in the 1930s. Accordingly, Salazar's mystique as a benevolent ruler took a sharp dent in the middle of the war.

Strikes in October 1942, particularly those affecting the transport sector, were the first signs of unrest. Twelve hundred people were arrested before calm returned.[72] But with conditions having worsened in the meantime, a far bigger strike wave was unleashed in July 1943. The trigger was news that Mussolini had fallen on the 25th. It produced an explosive effect on the very same day. A wave of strikes erupted in Almada on the south bank of the Tagus estuary, which quickly reached Lisbon. On 29 July, the managers of the transport and telephone companies considered the climate was pre-insurrectional and the factories most affected were occupied by the Portuguese Legion.[73]

The underground communists were showing prowess as agitators. But there were cracks within the regime itself that were most visible on the Catholic side. No longer was the sole posture of Catholics one of gratitude to Salazar for ending republican persecution. Catholic activists who were engaged in charitable work were among the first to become aware of the collapse in social conditions. Two strong-willed priests in particular, Abel Varzim and Joaquim Alves Correira, inspired groups of Catholics who were now ready to break completely with the regime.[74] As early as 1938 Varzim had denounced the *sindicatos*, or state trade unions, for failing to defend the workers. Then the head of the Catholic Workers' League, Varzim produced *O Trabhalador*, which ventilated church concerns about the conditions of the poor.[75]

The Estado Novo's ideological legitimacy also suffered because it was the corporative bodies that were called upon to manage scarcity. Previously seen as an iconic feature of the regime, after 1939 they fixed prices, enforced wage freezes, allocated quotas, and levied fines. In the midst of this unexpected maelstrom, Salazar received conflicting advice about how best to maintain control at home. From Spain, Teotónio Pereira said in late 1942 that a tough response from the PVDE was justifiable. Soon, he would be urging Salazar to dump his successor as head of the corporations, Trigo de Negreiros.[76]

The Communist Party chief, Álvaro Cunhal, felt sufficiently emboldened to write in the communist newspaper *Avante* that a putsch should not be ruled out. Carmona, he thought, could be a prime mover and, if a post-Salazar government liberalised, it should not face an immediate assault (very much his initial stance thirty years later when the Estado Novo did fall).[77] He might have been strengthened in this view if he had become aware of the long letter which ambassador Monteiro sent to Salazar in 1943. He pleaded with him that now was 'a unique occasion' for Salazar to begin with 'honour and advantage a new political departure' which would result in a modification of the regime and the removal of pro-German figures (though no names of politicians were mentioned).[78]

Salazar did not take well to advice that went completely against his reading of the position. In a letter written shortly before Monteiro's permanent recall from London in 1943, he wrote: 'one day when you return to read letters of which you certainly have copies', you will see them as 'unjust' and 'pretentious' where you 'ignore facts or else are led astray by English left-wing views'. In a barbed remark Salazar observed: your letter conveys the impression of 'a grand senhor living in London, mixing with the leaders of the world and patronising a poor man from Santa Comba'.[79]

As the war approached its end, Salazar's regime prepared itself for a trial of strength. A British diplomat was told by deputy João Mexia of the new-found brazenness of agricultural labourers in the Alentejo region who boasted about the land soon being theirs.[80] A secret police report from February 1943 mentioned that many regime supporters were despondent that the Estado Novo could be swept away.[81] But the regime was less brittle than Mussolini's fascist state. It had husbanded its resources and avoided high-risk adventures. May 1944 saw the greatest popular challenge in the form of strikes and demonstrations. However, there was far greater readiness on the regime's part to defy its opponents. There were mass arrests and the most dangerous agitators were placed in the Campo Pequeno bullring in Lisbon.[82] Nevertheless, it was a scary moment for the *situaçionistas*. Nothing like the May 1944 strikes would be seen until 1974. The PCP had displayed its hold over a sizeable part of the working class. The direction of the war, and the transformation of its guiding star, the Soviet Union, into a major world power enhanced the significance of communism.

Salazar had plenty to weigh up in the final phases of the war. His deep attachment to neutrality collided with the determination of the Americans to win the war by almost any means. When the British were granted access to the Azores in 1943 for military purposes, Portugal could be seen as a co-belligerent. Salazar's argument to the Germans was that he had no alternative on account of Portugal's historical dependence on British maritime power. Berlin appeared to accept this. But Salazar could not argue that he was beholden to America in a similar way, and it would take several dangerous confrontations before the US was granted equivalent military facilities there.

Fortunately for Portugal, when relations came to a boil with the US in 1943, a rare soulmate, George Kennan, with whom Salazar could have serious intellectual conversations, was in temporary charge at the US mission in Lisbon. This top-flight strategist was traditionally minded. They both regretted the war, admired firm conservative leadership, and Washington's envoy also had misgivings about Roosevelt's foreign policy (which he is unlikely to have revealed to the Portuguese leader).[83]

On 10 October 1943, Salazar had broken his regular autumn holiday to come down to Lisbon to receive the envoy. Kennan had been instructed by his superiors to say that the US respected Portuguese sovereignty 'in all colonies'. But minutes before he was due to meet him, this instruction was rescinded, which was bound to concern Salazar. Thinking quickly, Kennan decided to embark on a discussion about the broad nature of the Luso-American relationship in the light of the war situation. 'Then', as one of Kennan's biographers relates, 'on the 11th another cable arrived instructing Kennan "by direction of the President", to "request" the American use of Azores facilities on a far larger scale than anything the British had asked for ... Convinced ... [it] would provoke Salazar's wrath—if not his resignation—Kennan ... refused to carry out a White House order and asked permission to return to Washington to explain why, if necessary, to the President himself.'[84]

Kennan realised that the facilities being demanded by the Americans on the Azores amounted virtually to a US occupation.[85] At the Pentagon defence officials gave him a roasting. Rather than buckling under, Kennan got in touch with the president's chief of staff, Admiral William D. Leahy, who arranged for him to see Harry Hopkins, Roosevelt's chief diplomatic adviser. Very rapidly Kennan found himself before the president himself. Roosevelt 'listened cheerfully to the whole story, told Kennan not to worry "about all those people in the Pentagon" and drafted a personal letter to Salazar ... "I do not need to tell you the United States has no designs on the territory of Portugal and its possessions ... I do not think our peoples have been in close enough touch in the past."'[86]

An upgrade in bilateral relations to embassy level followed, and Kennan hoped that by patient engagement Salazar could be induced to offer the US facilities on the Azores. He was undoubtedly one of the small number of American diplomats posted to Lisbon who got through to Salazar. A decade later, Aaron S. Brown, another diplomat based in Lisbon, described the importance of the human dimension there:

> A proud, sensitive people who after a long period of decline are now experiencing a national renaissance as a result of the policies and accomplishments of the Salazar regime, the Portuguese, while not lacking in realism, are most susceptible to friendly human gestures, particularly when not accompanied by obvious quid pro quo strings. 'O factor humano' is a phrase constantly used in their conversation and reflects the ever present Lusitanian yearning for friendship, understanding and consideration. The personal element, therefore, in creating an atmosphere conducive to the realization of our objectives in this country, cannot be discounted.[87]

But Kennan was soon posted elsewhere. His replacement, Henry Norweb, was, by contrast, seen as coarse and unintelligent.[88] Over subsequent months tensions built up. Matters reached a crunch point on 6 October 1944 when Norweb received instructions, personally approved by Roosevelt, to present an ultimatum to the Portuguese authorities. According to the note, the US government considered the Portuguese attitude 'a very grave obstacle in the prosecution of the war'. Unless Portugal took all necessary steps to facilitate the building of an airport, Washington threatened to suspend economic help.[89] This was no idle threat. Portugal was dependent on external food supplies and oil to maintain vital services and prevent unrest spilling over into revolt.

The ultimatum was not mentioned by the ambassador to Salazar on the advice of Teixeira de Sampaio, his chief adviser. He feared what his reaction would be. More weeks of prevarication on the Portuguese leader's part followed. Eventually, on 28 November 1944 an accord was signed. The Americans went ahead and built their base.[90] Salazar was a reluctant landlord. He asked for no rent. Portuguese workers did not participate in its construction. This allowed Portugal to show its reservations to Spain and especially to Germany about having US bases anywhere on Portuguese soil.

In October 1943, when the British had been allowed to use the Azores militarily, Salazar feared the worst. A blackout was imposed on Lisbon in case of a German air attack. The military made plans to try to defend Lisbon from Spanish military occupation until British military reinforcements could arrive. But after a secret meeting in Spain that month with Franco's foreign minister, Count Jordana, Salazar managed to persuade him that no threat to Spain was implied. Similar deft footwork on his part meant the Germans confined themselves to making an energetic protest.[91]

The strain of trying to prevent Portugal from being consumed in the inferno of world war accelerated the ageing process in Salazar. A photograph of him at a memorial service for President Roosevelt on 13 April 1945 suggested a man who looked rather older than his fifty-six years. His official biographer, Franco Nogueira, wrote about his wartime appearance: he is 'emaciated; his features are lined; the face sharp and wan; his hair greying ... Above all, there is the insomnia.'[92]

On the advice of his friend Dr Bissaia Barreto and his own physician, various drugs were tried to conquer insomnia but they proved unavailing. Undoubtedly the calm domestic environment provided by Dona

Maria, and his affection for the child Micas, who became a teenager during the war, provided some relief from the pressures that he faced. But quixotically the governess decided to convert part of the grounds of the prime minister's residence into an urban farm. The rationale was provided by the acute food shortage. Salazar wasn't thrilled by this intrusion, but he acknowledged that in the domestic realm, her decisions and preferences enjoyed pre-eminence over his and he never put his foot down.[93]

Upon the announcement of Hitler's death on 4 May 1945, flags were ordered to be flown at half-mast in Lisbon. The instruction came not from Salazar but from Teixeira de Sampaio. A similar gesture, supplemented by a visit to the German legation in Dublin by Ireland's leader Eamon de Valera, had led to an angry exchange of words between him and Churchill. But the British were now stoical towards Salazar. They had been fully exposed to his legalistic mind but were also convinced that on no account could he be seen as a foe. Even at the most fraught point in bilateral relations, Salazar was treated respectfully. He was not to be browbeaten as the British did in wartime with the nominally independent King Farouk of Egypt or treated as a subaltern, which was the fate of the Polish government-in-exile in London. The idea of a palace coup in which Carmona played the role of King Michael of Romania, who tricked the Romanian dictator Marshal Ion Antonescu into coming for an audience in August 1944 only for him to be arrested and later shot (by the Soviets), was never likely in the case of Portugal. The British instinctively felt that Salazar was a guarantor of order in an unpredictable country of whose chronic instability before 1930 diplomats still had vivid memories. Placing him under house arrest in his home village or bundling him off to distant exile in the colonies were expedients liable to cause damage far into the future. So Salazar was to be left in place. The amount of support he would receive after the war would depend on the new global constellation of forces.

Warm words of mutual respect were exchanged when a banquet was held in honour of Sir Ronald Campbell upon the diplomat's retirement a few weeks later. Salazar was now preoccupied with how to prevent his regime capsizing in the tsunami which resulted in the eclipse of the major fascist powers. Their official demise came with the proclamation by the Allies of Victory in Europe Day on 9 May. Salazar agreed to authorise demonstrations, and the anglophile outlook of the Portuguese (which had largely remained unchanged for the past six years) was shown by the huge turnout of joyful people in Lisbon.

It was a shrewd move by Salazar to allow the people to release their emotions. He had yet to lose touch with them in psychological terms but he was disorientated by the furious pace at which new power alignments had arisen in Europe and the wider world. He may also not yet have realised the true depths of Hitler's wickedness, as shown by his temporary decision to censor the information coming out in the spring of 1945 about the real extent of the Holocaust.[94] The Führer had not only ended his life by his own hand but he had also beaten much of Europe into insensibility through years of war lust and violence directed at Germany's real and imagined enemies. The conservative order which Salazar had grounds to hope would accompany his work of reconstruction in Portugal for many decades had also crashed to dust everywhere outside the Iberian peninsula. It was a chastened Salazar who now confronted a menacing and unfamiliar world, which he soon discovered was out of sympathy with the low-key nationalism that his regime insisted on retaining.

10

LOW SPIRITS, 1945–52

At the apex of his World War II triumph, Britain's prime minister Winston Churchill received a crushing rejection at the hands of voters in the July 1945 general election. In 1943, Franklin Roosevelt had warned him of the serious danger of defeat. He pointed out that this would be his likely fate unless he presented his voters with a post-war offer from which they materially benefited. Roosevelt had just unveiled a massive benefit plan for returning American veterans that promised to usher them into the post-war middle class and he was comfortably re-elected in 1944.[1]

It is not unreasonable to assume that Churchill expected to be re-elected in a wave of patriotic feeling. Likewise, Salazar's gaze had been directed away from domestic considerations for much of the 1939–45 period. He also received frank advice about the need to shore up his national base. It came from Marcello Caetano, who, in 1944, urged his chief to create a ministry of social assistance, which he offered to head.[2] The purpose was to respond to high levels of poverty and economic distress before these issues could be exploited by the opposition. Caetano believed in the principles of the regime but he felt that for paternalism to be an enduring formula, it needed to include a strong social component. In a radio broadcast in July 1943, he had put aside any sycophancy by daring to say that Salazar had provided a good service but was not always right.[3]

But Salazar was unconvinced about the need for such a new departure. He seems not to have actively considered that the global conflict
might have produced a sharp backlash against his regime even though
he had spared the country most of its horrors. But, like Churchill, he
decided to waste no time in testing his strength. Elections for the
National Assembly were brought forward by a year and announced for
18 November 1945. In a speech of 7 October 1945 he stated: 'I hope
finally that there is sufficient press freedom so that the acts of the government can be judged without restriction along with the political
ideas put by the candidates before the voters.'[4]

This gesture appeared to indicate that he wanted Portugal not to be
completely out of step with the revival of electoralism in different
parts of Europe. Simultaneously, an amnesty for political crimes was
announced along with some mildly liberal measures. (A fitful effort
would also be made to describe the regime as an 'organic democracy'.)[5] In his speech Salazar acknowledged that the mood had turned
against the regime in Lisbon. He complained that too many in the capital had forgotten that the improvements in public works were disproportionately located there.[6]

But he had forgotten the three years of rationing in the capital. The
price of potatoes had risen threefold between 1939 and 1945 with no
corresponding rise in incomes.[7] The regime's response was often unin-
spiring, as when Fernanda de Castro, wife of the propaganda chief
António Ferro, arranged for a book of recipes to appear which showed
how to make snacks without meat—one of its contributors writing,
'there's no point in eating steak sandwiches every day.'[8]

Salazar also rebuked the opposition for the tenor of its campaign:
'The greater part of the mental activity of the numerous enemies of the
situation has been devoted to insults of a personal order, of which the
largest percentage ... have been directed at myself.'[9] Perhaps assuming
that the elections were unlikely to throw up any rude surprises, Salazar
then left for his regular autumn trip back to his village. However, he
was there hardly a week before he was recalled to the capital. The
National Union (UN) turned out to be in poor shape even for the
limited electoral combat Salazar permitted. According to Caetano, a
spirit of combat was absent.[10] To make matters worse, the minister of
the interior, Júlio Botelho Moniz, was proving inept. He had tried to

replace the head of the PVDE, Agostinho Lourenço, only to discover that this nimble secret policeman had plenty of intelligence on regime figures. In the ensuing power struggle, Moniz's protégé ended up in prison.[11] With the onset of elections, the hapless interior minister went on to replace the civil governors, meant to direct the regime's campaign, with new people to his liking, who were, however, often unfamiliar with local conditions.[12] An officer (who would later cause far worse trouble for Salazar) also issued violent threats, which were exploited by the opposition.[13]

Back in the saddle, Salazar moved against the opposition, impeding their ability to campaign. He must have noticed the lukewarm support from his old ally Cardinal Cerejeira, who, in a sermon, said the main criterion that Catholics needed to keep in mind was not to vote for people hostile to the values of their faith. He declined to be drawn on which party merited Catholic support, the UN or the opposition alliance known as the United Democratic Movement (MUD).[14] Much later it emerged that he had even made discreet preparations at this time for a new Christian democratic party to be founded in case conditions for Salazar's autocracy came to an end.[15]

Election day was accompanied by driving rain in Lisbon and the turnout slumped. The opposition had withdrawn days earlier in protest at restrictions. The gap between the ideals of the regime and the tawdry reality had grown too wide during the wartime era. Salazar's ministers enjoyed little respect and he was more withdrawn than ever. A feature on Portugal which *Time* magazine published in July 1946 was unflattering: 'Unlike all modern dictators he hates parades, pomp or cheers. When he rides to ceremonies with President Carmona, the old soldier preens and beams; Salazar slinks back in the car, a scowl on his handsome face with the Savonarola hard mouth.'[16]

A post-mortem on the regime's electoral performance was held over several days early in December 1945. Caetano did not hesitate to go on the offensive. He argued that the regime's political arm had decayed. Indeed, it had no inner life and was now largely composed of clients of the political system.[17] According to a close ally, João Costa Leite, Salazar had been wounded by these remarks, which several other ministers endorsed. The prime minister reputedly told him that he had spent a sleepless night during which he contemplated resignation only to decide that his duty was to carry on.[18]

Time would show that there was nothing to be done about the UN. It was not the arena where a new 'political man' was being groomed who would defend Salazar's prudent autocracy and sternly repulse the totalitarian communists.[19] Salazar corresponded with the main voice of the intellectual far right, Alfredo Pimenta, but he was disinclined to tolerate an organised radical nationalist faction within the Estado Novo that might have given the regime a sharper political edge.[20] The UN accordingly remained a tepid force even after Caetano was persuaded to take charge of it in the late 1940s. The control exercised by the regime bureaucracy over the UN meant it was a body 'always on the periphery of the state and the government, outside the former and in the hands of the latter'.[21] Caetano's worry about the drift at the heart of the regime was endorsed by another of its founding figures, Teotónio Pereira, who wrote from Brazil (where he was ambassador) that the optimism about 'our government' had evaporated.[22] He had been the chief architect of the corporative system in the 1930s. By the mid-1940s an anonymous article written by 'Lusitano' (and attributed to Caetano) argued that the system had lost its social peace and justice roles.[23] The most serious study of corporativism at this time came from Castro Fernandes, an ex-National Syndicalist. His conclusions were withering: rather than treating capital and labour equally, the system perpetuated class antagonisms and favoured employers. On the strength of his slim volume he was made corporations sub-secretary.[24]

Salazar himself chose May 1945 to offer the pious hope that 'cleansed of some abuses and excesses, [corporativism] will return to the purity of the principles from which to some extent, through wartime circumstances, it has departed'.[25] But Caetano thought having a ministry of corporations was as absurd as there being a minister of liberty in a democratic regime. Even António Ferro admitted at the end of 1945 that widespread dissatisfaction with the corporative system sprang from 'favouritism' and the fact that in many areas 'private selfish interests had prevailed over the public good'.[26] But Salazar showed a stubborn refusal to dismantle the corporative edifice. He was usually never one to retreat for the sake of expediency but he did agree to an inquiry into the failings of the corporative system headed by Mário de Figueiredo. It proved to be no whitewash. In the words of Howard J. Wiarda: 'the population was invited, through press and other advertisements, to convey their grievances ... The commission compiled all the horror stories and published a report which was so devastating that the government refused to give it any official attention.'[27]

Despite the disrepute into which the Portuguese 'third way' had fallen—one that had earned international plaudits in the 1930s—Salazar set his face against offering a 'new deal' to the population. He saw himself as a strong leader, dedicated to the public good, whose primary role was to offer security in a dangerous world and with an irresponsible opposition once again making trouble at home. He failed to support Daniel Barbosa, minister of the economy for just over a year in 1947–8, when he led the effort to increase the pace of the economy through industrialisation. The northern businessman also argued that basic staples essential for the Portuguese diet should be subsidised in a bid to lower prices. But he was too innovative for Salazar, with whom he would nevertheless correspond about economic matters well into the future. The menacing international situation made him averse to taking any major economic initiatives until the end of the 1940s. If there was a boom, in Salazar's eyes it was likely only to be temporary.[28]

He and the regime were lucky that, in the words of the British ambassador, Owen O'Malley, the opposition lacked 'leaders with ability, experience and national prestige' as well as a serious programme for governing Portugal.[29] In a naive gesture, the opposition figurehead, António Sergio, wrote to the influential British Labour Party intellectual Harold Laski asking him to help appoint a British ambassador to Portugal who was anti-fascist and who would support the Portuguese democrats and intervene alongside the armed forces to remove the regime.[30] But with the arrival of the Cold War, London was not about to ditch Salazar. Visits of British, American and French naval squadrons to Lisbon in 1946 were seen by Salazar as encouraging goodwill gestures.[31] He had publicly warned about the threat of Soviet hegemony in May 1945. The scale of the challenge perhaps explains why, on the same occasion, he remarked that World War II had been 'the last time in which we could and ought to be neutrals in a European conflagration'.[32]

No longer did British observers view dictatorship in Portugal as 'a temporary measure, with Dr Salazar somewhat in the position of a schoolmaster over an extraordinarily difficult class. The pupils have been so extremely naughty that they now must be treated like

143

infants.'[33] John Colville, a deputy head of mission in the Lisbon embassy from 1949 to 1951, before becoming private secretary to Churchill when he returned as prime minister, saw Salazar as a figure of European stature but his criticisms were also stinging:

> [He] failed to achieve ... an acceptable level of social justice. The rich were only moderately so in comparison with other countries. The middleclass was a growing body, flourishing contentedly in what had become a predominantly consumer society, sustained not by agriculture or industry, but by the accumulation of war profits, the remittances of Portuguese citizens ... and the produce of the African colonies. The poor, however, were miserable and destitute ... I doubt whether in his ivory academic tower he had any conception what dire poverty means. Nor indeed have many of us; but we may have a clearer vision of it than an isolated university professor ...[34]

Salazar's firm belief that communism was the pre-eminent threat to the Estado Novo meant that only firmness could weaken its impact. Many hundreds of detentions occurred between 1943 and 1949.[35] In the winter of 1946–7, food shortages and high prices led to a spike in dissatisfaction among some of the poorest groups. Civil governors regularly submitted alarming reports that the inefficient distribution of food supplies was leading to severe hardships and reducing the capacity of manual labourers to work.[36] The PCP attempted to launch a general strike at this time but a state crackdown snuffed it out. Cunhal himself was arrested in 1949 and would remain in prison until 1960. Beforehand, he had managed to raise his international profile on the left. In 1947 he had slipped out to Yugoslavia before going on to Prague weeks before Czechoslovakia succumbed to a communist coup in February 1948. By then he was in Moscow, where he met Mikhail Suslov, in charge of communist activities across the world and a man who would be vital for his career.[37]

From 1949, the number of arrests for political militancy decreased as the regime entered a calm period. However, maximum vigilance was maintained and this was particularly true of the universities. A crackdown had already got under way in 1947 with the appointment of an uncompromising hardliner as minister of education. Fernando Pires de Lima, a law professor at Coimbra University, harshly quelled protests in the medical faculty of Lisbon University. Two dozen professors were expelled. Caetano, himself a law professor at Lisbon, was indignant when he read about it in Berne, where he had been attending a conference of the International Labour Organization (ILO). Caetano later wrote an unflattering portrait of the minister in his memoirs where he contrasted his harshness with his own attempts to be suave and conciliatory towards students sceptical about the Estado Novo.[38] Perhaps the best-known of the professors to be purged was the mathematician Bento de Jesus Caraça, who, dying the following year aged only forty-seven, became something of a martyr on the left.[39]

The regime for its part exercised special vigilance in Portugal's three main universities because its own personnel, unusually for any political regime, were in large part drawn from the academic field. Moreover, its origins could be traced back to university struggles. The University of Coimbra in particular was viewed as 'the university of the regime'. Salazar had described it in the early 1930s as a 'moral reserve of the nation' and a 'lighthouse of patriotic virtues'.[40] But it gradually ceased after 1945 to be important for the regime.

Salazar's rigid stance towards the opposition suggested Portugal was under the heel of an absolutist ruler. A 1949 CIA report meant for President Harry S. Truman talked of 'the palace factions' being managed 'with a draconian firmness' by Salazar.[41] But appearances could be deceptive. When it came to arranging a government reshuffle early in 1947, it emerged that Salazar (at that time at least) was not really master in his own house. He was standing down as foreign minister but he got an unpleasant surprise upon being informed that his preferred replacement, Luís Supico Pinto, lacked sufficient backing within the armed forces. The bearer of this unwelcome news was Fernando dos Santos Costa, the minister of war (and later defence). Salazar may have had no alternative but to heed the warning. Santos Costa had been, and would continue to be, a trusted aide who kept a careful oversight of the military mood.[42] Officers had not been insulated from the wartime hardships and, as sub-secretary of finance, Supico Pinto had played a key role in setting prices and allocating supplies. Such a role was bound to have made him unpopular, but it is not for certain that it was the source of the military's ire. His biography stood out from the staid and conformist norm in the upper echelons of the Estado Novo. Recently married, he had previously sired a child out of wedlock. While Salazar may have appeared a stickler for formalities in public, there is evidence that he was relatively liberal in such matters. But pillars of the regime such as the Catholic Church and the officer corps of the military were unlikely to display similar latitude.[43]

Santos Costa was probably wise to advise Salazar to abandon the idea. The main significance of the casting of its veto was that it showed the military had returned as a strong player within the regime. Its influence revived as the relevance of the UN faded. Politics began to be played out in the army as the elderly president Carmona approached the end of his days. Notable among the plotters were ex-zealots for the Estado Novo, such as Jorge Botelho Moniz and David Neto, who may have abandoned the regime due to disappointment with the progress of their careers.[44]

Carmona seems to have shown favour to military conspirators before their arrest in April 1947. This emerged at the trial of several of them in 1949.[45] An earlier sign of his disenchantment with Salazar had been manifested in October 1945 when he agreed to receive a delegation from the opposition MUD. This was the first audience that he had granted to anti-Salazarists for many years. One of the delegates, José Magalhães Godinho (Portugal's first Ombudsman after 1974), recalled later that at the meeting Carmona had stated that if it became clear to him that the opposition had the support of the army, then he would have no hesitation in dismissing the government.[46] However, he said he could do nothing without army backing.

The head of the 1947 conspiracy, General José Marques Godinho, never stood trial. Suffering from a heart condition, he died in custody on 24 December 1947. The opposition claimed that he had been treated harshly by Santos Costa because he had letters in his possession suggesting that the minister had been pro-Axis before 1945. Much later, Santos Costa broke a long silence in which he denied having had any role in Godinho's death.[47] Correspondence between him and the minister of justice Manuel Cavaleiro de Ferreira in 1947–8 has been published which shows how both men disagreed over the manner in which the affair had been handled.[48] However, the regime was unnerved by this affair. It followed an attempt by an armoured column led by Captain Fernando Quiroga to march on Lisbon in October 1946. But the revolt soon collapsed when nobody else joined the rebel column. Two years later, new laws were enacted providing much stiffer penalties for rebellious civil and military functionaries. The minister of justice even ordered the arrest of General Godinho's widow and the family's lawyer, Adriano Moreira, was also detained for two months.

Carmona was elevated to the rank of marshal and relations improved as Salazar renewed the weekly meetings that previously had taken place between the two men. In 1949 he would even be nominated for a fourth presidential term. Salazar was emerging from four tough and wearying years, ones which would have broken the willpower of a lesser figure. His sense of dejection had been made clear at the meeting of the UN in late 1945 when he was heard to murmur: 'God help us. God help us! … nothing has changed in the mentality of this people, nothing at all! It was in vain that we worked all these years to educate them politically, to stop them wallowing in party intrigues and to give them a feel for the bigger national issues.'[49]

Salazar's morale would not have been boosted when poor harvests after 1945 compelled him to use up increasing amounts of gold reserves in order to pay for expensive food imports. His dejection was understandable not just in relation to the picture at home. He had sought to impose a low-key regime of settled order in Portugal exactly at a time when disorder and terrible brutality and carnage swept across much of Europe. The ascendant values that were central to the new international order were uncongenial ones. At that time there were no figures to whom he could reach out for counsel and encouragement. Teótonio Pereira was a permanent diplomat, Armindo Monteiro had retreated into business, Duarte Pacheco had died in a car crash in 1943. As for Caetano, he was energetic but peevish, and his belief in greater economic liberalism and a relaxation of the regime's coercive features hardly appealed to his chief. Salazar had lost much of the self-confidence that he exhibited in the 1930s and was apocalyptic about the future. Henrique Veiga de Macedo, who was in government through the 1950s, recalls him saying in 1946: 'the time will arise when the Portuguese will split over how to serve the Nation. Perhaps the time is approaching when the great split will be between those who serve the nation and those who deny it.'[50]

Both Caetano and Franco Nogueira have argued that Salazar was in a state of acute demoralisation at this time. His young ward Micas, who continued to spend much time in his company, doubted this view.[51] She recalls an incident in 1947 which suggests that he was far from wrapped up in his own troubles. She had fallen ill with appendicitis. After her successful operation Salazar appeared at the hospital and wished to settle the bill. After the doctor said nothing needed to be paid, Salazar threatened to cut relations unless he was presented with a bill. Eventually a bill for a symbolic amount reached him.[52] However, in the same year, it is notable that a man who scrupulously filled his work and appointments diary kept it blank for around five weeks in September and October 1947. 'At home' was written in pencil from 12 to 18 October; and shortly afterwards he met several doctors.[53]

Allies of Salazar, perhaps fearing that he might walk out and leave a political vacuum, tried to show consideration for his achievements in public. Thus a volume was published on the twentieth anniversary of his entry to government, which extolled him as a figure of European stature. The Coimbra law professor Luís Cabral de Moncada wrote: 'Gentlemen! Salazar knew to save Portugal from the stupidest and most ferocious of all the wars in history. Under his government, our country was the oasis of Europe and a land ... of refuge for all those who, during five years, came from devastated lands, their homes destroyed by the mother of all cataclysms.'[54]

It may have been that the likes of Moncada clung to the hope that incipient drives towards inter-state European cooperation would preserve a haute-bourgeois culture in a Europe now overshadowed by communism. But Salazar lacked enthusiasm for the early European movement. One of the first practical steps taken in the story of continental cooperation was to impose a rigid embargo on Franco's Spain. Despite its brutal origins, it was a nationalist regime not very different from Salazar's own. In 1947 most European democracies had withdrawn their ambassadors as a sign of their revulsion over Franco's hardline rule. But Portugal (along with Britain, Switzerland and Ireland) maintained diplomatic representation. The 1939 security pact would also be renewed in October 1948 and, in his dealings with Britain and the United States, Salazar often warned against fully ostracising Spain. He regularly made clear his view that integrating the whole of the Iberian peninsula in initiatives to defend the West against dangers from the East was only elementary prudence. His alliance with the Franco regime stemmed not from any doctrinal ties but from such a shared understanding. There were occasions when he was ready to place his regime somewhat apart from the Spanish one. Thus in 1952, at a meeting with US ambassador Lincoln MacVeagh, the views of Salazar were summarised in the following way: 'the Portuguese Government has no particular love of, or ideological affinity for, Franco. Portuguese interest in Spain, he said, is purely a matter of geography; the defense of Western Europe and particularly the security of Portugal is incomplete without the active integration of Spain in the over-all defense system.'[55]

Despite never really warming to Franco, who had come to power in a completely different way to Salazar, the Portuguese leader nevertheless always argued the need for Spain to be brought in from the cold. The security platform enabling Portugal to promote its own geopolitical outlook was the North Atlantic Treaty Organization (NATO). At its launch on 4 April 1949 Portugal was one of the founding members, but its path to membership had been far from straightforward.

The coup in Prague on 22 February 1948, which delivered Czechoslovakia into the hands of the Soviet Union, sharpened awareness of the need to create a viable transatlantic security shield against further Soviet expansion. An area of 1,400,000 square kilometres with approximately 87 million inhabitants had fallen under Soviet domination in the previous three years in 'a conquest without war'.[56] Portugal was approached about participating at the start of 1949. A senior British diplomat has written that Salazar thought Portugal would be asked to participate in drawing up the draft treaty for what would become NATO.[57] However, soon after, it was decided that as speed was of the essence, it was best to confine this task to a nucleus of governments. It was assumed that inclusion of all the prospective members would complicate and delay the negotiations.

On 18 March 1949, Portugal, along with Denmark, Iceland and Italy, was invited to join NATO. Each of these governments accepted without qualification. But Salazar held back. Fears arose in his mind that the direction of this alliance might ultimately weaken Portuguese sovereignty. By now he would have been in no doubt that its chief sponsor, the US, was firmly opposed to the retention of European empires such as Portugal's in Africa. The US was informed that

Portugal was unhappy that the alliance was to be for a minimum duration of twenty years. Salazar asked for Portugal to have the right to join on condition that it could withdraw after ten years. According to Sir Nicholas Henderson, the Portuguese were just interested in the anti-Soviet dimension and 'this they regarded as a short-term problem. They were not interested in establishing some long-term system of security for the North Atlantic area.'[58]

But Albano Nogueira, a former Portuguese ambassador to NATO, has offered a different view. He believes that the founding document was insipid in Salazar's eyes. He criticised its 'hesitation' and 'imprecision'. Absolute criticism of communism was not enough. There needed also to be assertions 'more in conformity with the agreed principles of a civilization that ought to be defended'.[59] He was also nervous about Portugal ending up being committed 'to intervene in intimate European skirmishes ... in the formulation of which we took no part'.[60] Ironically, the first shots that NATO would fire in anger would occur in what might be seen as just such an internal conflict, one that involved the violent break-up of Yugoslavia.

With such concerns, Portugal found itself out on a limb. Other impending members wanted the minimum period for engagement with NATO to be longer than twenty years, and Portugal found no support for joining the Atlantic alliance on its own terms. On 22 March 1949 the US secretary of state, Dean Acheson, wrote to Salazar explaining the difficulties with his approach and expressing the hope that Portugal could join as a full and original member.[61] But it wasn't until 31 March that Salazar replied. During the intervening period Portugal had been negotiating with Spain to ensure that good relations were not ruptured by the inclusion of one and the exclusion of the other in a landmark security initiative. Spain, for its part, decided there was no point in publicly objecting to the Portuguese accession to NATO, though privately it was unhappy.[62]

Salazar agreed Portugal could be one of the twelve founding members of NATO but he expressed resentment about 'having received the Pact for signature without having been given the opportunity to suggest amendments to the text'.[63] Salazar's proven record of being an exacting negotiator may well have been a factor that prompted the central players in the birth of NATO to avoid having protracted discussions about its founding basis.

When on 25 November 1949 Salazar met Averell Harriman, a senior diplomat who was then US special representative in Europe, he remarked that forming NATO was probably the most important single international step taken in modern times. A US embassy official noted that the prime minister smilingly commented, 'We shall see.' 'To this Mr. Harriman immediately retorted, "You seem to be somewhat skeptical. May I ask why?" Dr. Salazar replied, "I am not really skeptical, but you Americans are apt to entertain an optimism about your sincere intentions and altruistic plans which has at times gone unjustified by results."'[64] Harriman would later emerge as a strong foe of Portugal's African presence, remarking to the French politician Antoine Pinay in 1966 that it was intolerable such a small country ruled over a territory as vast as Angola.[65] But Salazar would conclude that the overtly anti-communist nature of the pact meant that it was pointless for Portugal to stay outside.

Perhaps he had also learned a lesson from his initially very sceptical approach to the Marshall Plan, proposed by the US secretary of state George C. Marshall in 1947 in a bid to revive Europe's economic fortunes. The US planned to offer assistance to much of Europe in the form of loans and grants that ultimately would total over $12 billion. Salazar had always seen foreign aid as a source of political interference and the initiative is unlikely to have excited him. Indeed, on 24 September 1947, the foreign minister had stated: 'the happy internal condition of Portugal permits me to say that my country does not need external financial help'.[66] Soon after Portugal was hit by a balance of payments crisis thanks in part to the increase in the cost of basic staples which it imported.[67] Its reservations about the US initiative receded and over a four-year period Portugal received $90 million worth of grants and loans. This was a pittance compared to what other wartime neutrals would receive.[68] It hardly had the revitalising effect seen in bigger states where American aid helped put heavy industry back on its feet. Portugal still lacked a steel industry, which hampered some of the regime's building programmes, and a more enthusiastic response to this seemingly altruistic US gesture could well have led to aid for more valuable projects. Interestingly, it has been claimed that between 1947 and 1960 Spain received ten times more financial assistance from the United States than Portugal would do in that period.[69]

Salazar resisted most American offers of aid in return for investment by US firms in Angola, but American aid and expertise helped advance some infrastructure projects, particularly in the energy field.

The Spain which Salazar visited as Franco's personal guest in the summer of 1950, having been denied Marshall Aid and not yet in receipt of ultimately more generous bilateral US support, was going through a long period of grinding hardship. But it was a moment of repose in the relations between the two states. The threat of communism was receding in Portugal owing to the vigilance of the secret police, now renamed the International Police for the Defence of the State (PIDE). The excesses being carried out by Russia's Stalin across the eastern half of Europe also appalled many Portuguese who otherwise thought Salazar had long overstayed his welcome. In Spain, the Caudillo was by now very much in control. One year earlier, in October 1949, Portugal had been the location for Franco's first (and only) state visit abroad.[70] Banquets were held along with concerts and a bullfight was staged in the Lisbon bullring.[71] A special train took Franco north where he attended Mass at the shrine of Fátima. The next day a Rolls Royce took him to Coimbra where the university awarded him an honorary doctorate. The youngest law professor at the university, Guilherme Braga da Cruz, then still in his early thirties, gave the oration. He invoked Cardinal Cerejeira, who was attending the ceremony also, extolling his academic work for having shown the underlying Christian mission shaping Iberian civilisation. Braga da Cruz asserted that the ceremony was an academic recognition of Franco's military qualities and statesmanlike virtues.[72] Never, at least in Portugal, was Franco so warmly extolled in public as he was by this young traditionalist. His oration confirmed Coimbra as a stronghold of nationalism and anti-communism. Braga da Cruz would be rector of the university during the 1960s, having earlier turned down several invitations to join the government. He pleaded the responsibility of bringing up a large family in order not to move to Lisbon and try to subsist on a relatively small ministerial salary. But he would be a dedicated upholder of the Estado Novo's values, usually operating from behind the scenes.[73] A year before his death in 1976 he was expelled from the university along with several other conservative professors.

Franco's had been not only a protocol visit but a kind of ideological celebration between two unapologetically right-wing Iberian regimes.

As Franco headed home, the two men warmly embraced at Lisbon airport. A photo of the occasion would have perhaps suggested a ten-year age difference between them. Salazar, though just sixty, looked years older, while Franco, aged fifty-seven, could have passed for a younger man.[74] The economic situation would remain bleak in Spain for nearly another decade, but Franco did not wear himself out by micro-managing economic matters as Salazar did. Nor did he have to exercise too much concern about events beyond his frontiers. Spain no longer had an extensive colonial empire, unlike Portugal. Both countries would be denied membership of the United Nations through a Soviet veto until 1955, but Spain was relatively unperturbed while for Salazar it was a cause of some alarm as anti-colonialism quickly turned into a central issue in international relations.

Through the 1950s Spain also quickly emerged from the diplomatic isolation it had endured in the late 1940s. In 1949 Churchill had swum against the West European tide by stating in the House of Commons that excluding Spain from NATO left 'a serious gap in the strategic arrangements for Western Europe'.[75] Unlike Salazar, Franco, having begun by sharing the same deeply sceptical views of the United States, decided to focus on building up strong bilateral ties with Washington. Senior American generals such as General Omar Bradley, head of the Joint Chiefs of Staff, expressed the view in 1948 that the Iberian peninsula could well be 'the last foothold in continental Europe' that might be held if the Soviet Union mounted an invasion.[76] A geostrategic partnership gathered pace in the 1950s, leading to Franco ceding the Americans the right to establish three airbases and a submarine base on Spanish soil (a concession unacceptable to Salazar in terms of his own relations with the US). Outside NATO, dictatorial Spain seemed more confident about its place in the West than Portugal under Salazar, especially on account of the increasingly problematic status of its colonial empire.

In a speech given in May 1945 Salazar seemed positive about the establishment of the United Nations. This is surprising given that the new global body would have a Security Council that would be confined to the great powers and would be able to take action on major international issues. Salazar at the time may not have properly worked out that a body in which Russia played such an influential role was an ill omen for Portugal. Nor that the Soviets and their allies would use anti-colonialism as a weapon to harass European countries like Portugal with large overseas empires.[77]

But there were also rumbles of discontent at home about conditions in the empire. During his quarter of a century as bishop of Beira in Mozambique, Sebastião Soares de Resende was increasingly bold in publicly raising sensitive political and social themes which sometimes provoked conflict with the state.[78] In 1946, he may have been the first public figure to call for the abolition of forced labour and the *indignato* status given to most blacks. In his diary entry for 6 June 1946, he described these forms of discrimination as 'an excrescence ... [neither] human nor justified in our times of liberty and responsibilities ... The authorities want the savage black to continue as a beast of burden.'[79]

Someone whose criticisms troubled the regime far more directly was Henrique Galvão. As a radical right-winger, he had been exiled to Angola for his role in a revolt. From 1927 he immersed himself in Africa, which had a profound impact on him. It stimulated the writing and political work of a man of action and a talented intellectual. He possessed a vision for the colonies shared by few others, and one writer claims that he dreamed of the eventual emergence of a Euro-African continent.[80]

The early 1930s had been a period when the colonies were rekindled in the national consciousness, and Galvão had played a leading role in this exercise. Michael S. Peres has written: 'The empire was therefore conceptualised as a Pan-Lusitanian community, geographically scattered but fused into one political, economic, cultural and spiritual unity. Colonial autonomy, experimented with in the early twentieth century, was abandoned and the African territories again tightly bound to the Lisbon government. Colonial policy had for its ultimate goal the integration of the overseas lands with the mother country via a common economy and the eventual spiritual and cultural assimilation of African populations into Portuguese citizenship.'[81]

A sleepy and unimaginative colonial bureaucracy had never produced anyone quite like Galvão. This Africanist was a hunter and explorer who ventured into remote parts of Angola and ran the journal *Portugal Colonial* from 1931 to 1937. Colonial themes were to the fore when he diversified his portfolio of responsibilities, taking charge of the national radio from 1935 to 1940. He was the driving force behind the 1934 Oporto Exhibition, which sought to instil a colonial consciousness in the public and to encourage a sense of transcontinental Portuguese identity.[82] He was the author of the slogan 'Portugal is not a small country', which 'neatly encapsulated the main thrust of the [Oporto] event and was illustrated by his own ingenious cartographic construction intended to impress the gargantuan dimensions of the empire onto the public's mental conception of national identity. By superimposing the outlines of Angola and Mozambique over the map of Europe, Galvão conveyed, visually, the point that imperial Portugal occupied a geographic area larger than that of Spain, France, England, Italy, and Germany combined.'[83]

From 1936 to the late 1940s he was also inspector general of colonial administration, which ran in parallel with many other activities.[84] It is unlikely that someone with his absorption in the colonial world would have been overjoyed with the torpor that had reasserted itself in colonial affairs from the mid-1930s onwards. He worried that outdated and inhumane practices would result in Portugal losing its colonies in a fast-changing world. An opportunity to influence policy seemed to arrive when Marcello Caetano was appointed minister of the colonies in 1944. In the following year he was asked to carry out an investigation to see whether native legislation which outlawed abuses was being properly adhered to. Caetano had become aware that the heavy wartime demand for colonial products had intensified abusive practices. He feared that they would become ingrained unless Lisbon firmly stamped upon them.[85]

The course of history was perhaps changed when, instead of reporting back to Caetano, Galvão decided to submit his report to the National Assembly. Perhaps he thought change could occur more quickly by taking that route. He had, after all, been elected to that body in 1945, representing Angola as an independent on the UN slate. So, on 22 January 1947 the report was duly submitted and discussed at the body's seventeen-member colonies commission. Those politicians who cared to study it closely would have found in its fifty-two pages a detailed account of systematic abuses. Africans were 'herded' (the term deliberately used by Galvão) by the colonial authorities and made to work for private companies. These 'contract workers' faced appalling conditions ranging from poor diet and low wages to beatings. He found that the mortality rate among them could be as high as 35 per cent and reckoned that the system was worse than slavery since their owners had more of an incentive to look after slaves.[86]

Perhaps Galvão hoped that in changing times influential people would take notice when he was able to show that the Colonial Act's basic guarantees to Africans of 'protection and defence in accordance with the principles of humanity' and legal punishment for 'all abuses against the person and property of the natives' were being systematically flouted.[87] To drive home not only the disgrace but also the danger for Portugal, he argued that having jammed the colonial machine, the regime was inviting subversives to move in from neighbouring territories where anti-colonial movements were already active.[88]

But his hopes of galvanising sleepy Lisbon into action were unavailing. His report was shelved instead. A furious Caetano abandoned him. His anger at not even being sent a copy of the report that he had commissioned from Galvão is perhaps understandable. Both men had come to believe that greater autonomy, especially for a colony the size of Angola, was becoming increasingly hard to postpone. But in an angry letter from Caetano, the mercurial captain was rebuked for the way he had released a report which, he was told, could only assist Portugal's enemies at home and abroad.[89]

For Galvão there was no going back. The man who in 1937 had dedicated a book to Salazar, praising him for 'his thought and his work which made the rebirth of the Colonial Idea possible in Portugal', now turned against the regime on humanitarian grounds but also for career reasons.[90] He was not going to quietly disappear, compensated by sinecures, which was the case with numerous others whom Salazar dispensed with. In February 1949 he raised the issue of Angola again in the National Assembly. A debate occurred followed by a vote in which no other deputy took his side. He had been under the surveillance of the PIDE since 1948 but, incredibly, he was able to keep his civil service role until the end of the 1940s and Salazar even thought of offering him a second term as a deputy. Galvão accepted, then withdrew, and in November 1949 crossed the Rubicon in a violent press polemic directed against a senior regime figure, Mário de Figueiredo, who led the UN in the National Assembly.[91] This notable demanded a harsh punishment and persisted even when Salazar urged him to forget the matter.

This latitude was more often than not how Salazar preferred to handle dissent from within the regime itself. Galvão was on a collision course with the regime he had once championed. It would face grave consequences when the officer's warnings that colonial mistakes could jeopardise its retention of the overseas territories seemed to be confirmed by events in 1961.

Galvão had already shown that he was ready to cross over to the opposition when he spoke up in court for his friend and fellow 'Africanist', Carlos Selvagem, who was one of the military officers put on trial for sedition in 1948.[92] By 1951 he was fully aligned with the opposition. The lawyer Vasco da Gama Fernandes (the first president of the democratic parliament from 1976 to 1978) was impressed by his zeal and efficiency. He singled out the ex-Salazarist for being the tireless main organiser of the opposition's presidential campaign of 1951: 'he showed himself to be an extraordinary polemicist from whom the best initiatives arose'.[93]

However disparaging the non-communist opposition was about Salazar's record and his methods of rule, few objected to his determination to hold on to Portugal's African territories. The empire was seen as the work of the nation as a whole and was not the monopoly of the Estado Novo. It was General José Norton de Matos's renown as an energetic governor of Angola in the 1920s that contributed to his being chosen as the opposition candidate in the 1949 presidential election. He criticised Salazar for his short-sighted approach to colonial matters, especially his mania for centralising so much practical administration in Lisbon. Oppositionists would argue that Salazar was jeopardising Portugal's independent existence as a European country since the colonies were central to preserving a national *raison d'être*. Many of Salazar's foes nevertheless supported his bid to quell the Angolan revolt of 1961 and remain in Africa. They might even have agreed with Salazar when he confided to Franco Nogueira in the 1960s: 'it's certain to me that the duality of the peninsula only works due to the existence of the Portuguese Empire; without it, Portugal's independence from Spain will grow precarious'.[94]

Bitter memories of years of heavy-handed and exploitative rule over local Africans could gradually be erased, Galvão thought, by membership in a Euro-African federal republic of Portuguese states with Lisbon as its centre.[95] Belated acknowledgement from the regime that the status quo was untenable came in 1951 when the 1930 Colonial Act was scrapped. A new law substituted the term 'ultramarine provinces' for colonies and the 'Ultramar' for 'Empire'. But there was no endorsement of administrative decentralisation. Instead, 'integrationism' was imposed as the new official doctrine underpinning Portugal's overseas role.

After seven years in the doldrums, the Salazar regime received a boost when NATO held a major conference in Lisbon during February 1952. By the time the city was filling up with political notables from across Western Europe and North America, Salazar's spirits had revived. He was in the early stages of a rewarding platonic friendship with the vivacious French conservative writer Christine Garnier. The communist threat had been contained. Nothing further would be heard from Galvão until 1959 as he was arrested weeks before the NATO summit and later placed on trial. With a major war raging in Korea, where an international force sought to halt a communist advance, and ominous tensions emerging in divided Germany, Salazar's warnings about the scale of the communist threat seemed to enjoy credibility even on the moderate European left. He had influential backers within NATO, such as the US secretary of state Dean Acheson and André de Staercke. As chef de cabinet of the Belgian prime minister-in-exile, de Staercke first got to know Salazar after he escaped to Portugal from occupied Belgium in 1942. He spoke up for the Portuguese leader's moral, political and intellectual rigour whenever doubts were cast about Portugal's suitability for NATO membership. In 1956, he managed to persuade Salazar not to impose the veto that would have prevented Paul-Henri Spaak, a Belgian socialist, from becoming the secretary-general of NATO. But when once he asked Salazar: 'Do you never think that one day it will be possible to crown your work by giving political liberty to the Portuguese and, for example, permitting parties to be active?', the autocrat immediately reacted: 'There you go too far.'[96]

At this early stage in the Cold War Salazar might have obtained some grim satisfaction as he saw some of the wiser Western leaders recoil from the impact of communism on their world. Few were left unaffected by the fact that in France and Italy, continental Europe's most emblematic countries, it was the Communist Party which was easily the largest political force. Salazar could seem anachronistic and unbending. But the capital which they found during the summit was clean and orderly.

Of the leaders in Lisbon for this gathering, it was Dean Acheson who later provided the most detailed perspective about Salazar. He was obviously greatly taken with him, describing him as 'the nearest approach in our time to Plato's philosopher-king'. He wrote:

As soon as our hats and coats were taken, we were shown into Dr Salazar's connecting study. The room was of medium size, was lined on three sides with books and paintings above them, and furnished with a desk and upholstered leather chairs. I saw no telephone, file or papers on the desk ... everything about both rooms was non-official, comfortable, simple and unpretentious.

At the door a slight and very handsome man smiled a welcome to us. A long and thoughtful face topped by short-cut, greying hair, was given both a melancholy and quizzical cast by mobile eyebrows arched towards their inner ends. His manner, easy yet dignified and serious, did not suggest authority or the faintest trace of pomposity. As we sat down ... he sank into his chair until his crossed knee was almost level with his shoulders. With elbows rested on the chair arms, his hands first clasped before him began to move with his talk, carving figures out of the air. Then one noticed the beauty of his hands, delicately formed with long tapering fingers, sensitive hands appropriate to a sensitive face ...

With the talk off to a good start, the ambassador kept it going by leading Salazar in to the economic and political theories of his policies ... No gloss was applied; no effort made towards self-serving statements; no trace of personal ambition appeared ...

Our talk stretched far beyond the time allotted by the Prime Minister's office, but no one intervened to stop us. The ambassador finally rose, saying that we had trespassed too long. I left knowing that I had never spent a more revealing hour, and had met a man unique in his time, the possessor of a rare mind and even rarer charm ...[97]

The Lisbon summit saw changes in NATO which 'moved it from improvised arrangements to institutional forms'. It was also a high point of post-war Luso-American relations. But good relations failed to solidify. Salazar thought the great powers were likely to use Portugal as a pawn and that it would be expendable when the chips were down. His request that the Portuguese overseas territories be included was rebuffed (as he might have expected) and he got nowhere with his advocacy for Spain to be included in NATO.[98] His reluctance to believe that Portugal's voice could really count in NATO was perhaps later borne out in 1961 when the Atlantic alliance refused to spring to its defence upon India (then a pro-Soviet neutral state) invading the territory of Goa in December of that year. He was always apprehensive about NATO becoming a corridor which would enable the United States to acquire sway over Portugal. For years he was reluctant to host NATO bases: his terms were accordingly limited and transactional. His suspicion of the motives driving the newest of the great powers increased as his interaction with Washington grew. He is unlikely to have demurred from the view of Marcello Mathias, his ambassador in Paris at the height of the 1956 Suez crisis, that America was 'a nation without history' that blindly stumbled forward, 'either driven by puritan idealism or by mercantile egotism'.[99]

Salazar had always found the idea that politics could shape and improve the human condition to be dangerous nonsense, and at the start of his third decade in charge of Portugal, he was able to reach out to some Western leaders who did not dissent from his view. For twenty-five years, there had been no ideological competition allowed in Portugal. He saw most of the ideologies as being nothing better than falsehoods about human nature. From his perspective, it was the political parties and their rancorous spirit which disrupted the natural order of things. They drove citizens to chase after unrealisable goals and group themselves into bitterly antagonistic factions. Liberty and justice, he believed, were best guaranteed by individuals exercising self-restraint and investing their hopes in a limited state which guaranteed order and security and avoided trying to redefine human nature. But Salazar's conception of such a prudent state had been undermined through the 1940s, and as Portugal entered the 1950s, the destination of the regime seemed increasingly bound up with his own biological fate.

11

THE GOLDEN AFTERNOON OF THE ESTADO NOVO, 1952–58

Except for the crisis of 1958, the 1950s were easily the most settled period in Salazar's nearly forty-year tenure at the helm of Portugal. Externally, political conditions improved. Churchill returned to government in Britain in 1951. In 1952, the US Republicans won a majority in Congress and Dwight D. Eisenhower, their candidate for the presidency, won the first of two electoral victories. A socially disruptive period also drew to a close at home. Living standards slowly recovered. The pace of economic life quickened through the 1950s and would not diminish until the replacement of the regime in 1974. The Estado Novo was already a familiar element which maintained hegemony not so much through force but simply by being a continuous presence in society that stretched into decades. Salazar's golden rule, 'Let things be to see how they work out', seemed particularly apt for the sleepy 1950s.[1]

Throughout the 1948–68 period, Portugal avoided the currency fluctuations and crises that periodically troubled the lives of many citizens in more powerful countries. The escudo was a strong currency that maintained its value throughout Salazar's era. It was perhaps the most tangible proof of the financial success of the ruler, who had ended a prolonged era of crisis which meant that Portugal had fallen far behind much of the rest of Europe, compared with its position in the

17th and 18th centuries.[2] Financial stability was underpinned by a strong balance of payments outlook and large reserves of gold and foreign exchange. Salaries for those in public employment were low, but they kept their purchasing power due to the virtual absence of inflation in the last decades of Salazar's rule.[3] In fact, at the close of his government, Portugal's gold reserves were about 2.25 per cent of the world's total. Possessing one of the most robust currencies in the world made Salazar conclude that Portugal did not need to join the International Monetary Fund, formed in 1945, until 1961. By that year, the escudo was tied to the US dollar. It had been indexed to the pound sterling until 1949, but the latter's devaluation by the British Labour government required Portugal to accept the predominance of the United States, at least in the financial sphere.

The hitherto small middle class was growing, as shown by the expansion of Lisbon northwards in the early 1950s. Well-designed suburbs like Alvalade encompassed stylish and functional architecture that, seventy years later, still retains its appeal. New quarters for workers were created; these could not conceal scenes of poverty and social misery, especially in the countryside, and were still capable of shocking foreign visitors. However, 'both nutrition and the public health system improved between the 1940s and the 1970s, with the result that during this period life expectancy soared, from just over 50 to 71 years.'[4] This was the end of a long period of economic decline which had begun in the first half of the 19th century, and which had left the Portuguese the shortest people in Europe by the 1890s.[5]

The Estado Novo was far from being a monolith. Government service was open to individuals from beyond the left seen as having something to contribute. Cabinets were heterogeneous in composition, which often hampered effective coordination, according to one historian.[6] Some ministers offered their service at a price. Paulo Cunha, an effective foreign minister from 1950 to 1958 until felled by a heart attack towards the end of his tenure, initially resisted repeated overtures from Salazar to join the government. This wealthy liberal law professor at Lisbon University would only accede on being assured by Salazar that purges would end in the academic world and a new building would be constructed to house his law faculty.[7]

The National Union (UN) was made up of different factions. In 1949, there was a groundswell of feeling that Salazar ought to consider assuming the presidency after decades in an executive role. Salazar lost no time in squashing that idea. He had no appetite for a ceremonial position. He was also aware that a head of state used to giving orders but shorn of power in his new role was bound to find cohabitation with a younger executive head of government difficult. Aged eighty by now, Carmona was persuaded to go forward for yet another term. Salazar's customary speech at the start of the parliamentary session in November 1949 showed that he had no intention of going anywhere. Much of the detail concerned economic changes that were in the pipeline. In 1950, a new post was created, the minister to the presidency, which was meant to remove some of the administrative burden from his shoulders. None of the holders would be able to turn it into a new power base despite each of them being a senior regime figure.

Carmona's death on 18 April 1951 did, however, produce a breach in the regime which was not entirely filled until the summer of that year. The monarchists were the largest faction in the National Assembly and they took advantage of the uncertainty to agitate for a return of the monarchy. Franco's Spain had passed a law of succession in 1947 which described Spain as a monarchy under a regent. From 1950 a royal prince, Dom Duarte Nuno de Bragança, would live permanently in Portugal. He was a direct descendant of King Miguel, the conservative standard-bearer in the civil war of the 1830s. He had grown up in Germany but was not hardline in his political outlook. His character was hardly a regal one. In the words of the historian Vasco Pulido Valente, he was 'a German gentleman who spoke Portuguese badly and harboured the secret desire to be an agronomist'.[8]

The Monarchist Cause was an embryo party that was well entrenched in different parts of the regime. Being a monarchist at least by sentiment, Salazar would hardly have impeded its participation in his system of rule. But he wanted to be the one who made the major decisions on the direction of the regime and he did not think that its consolidation could be aided by bringing back a form of government which had not been blessed with success when previously tried. However, for a while it looked as if matters might be taken out of his hands. There was a tie among the six chief civilian heavyweights of the regime when he gathered them together to discuss the preferred future direction after Carmona. The president of the National Assembly,

Mário de Figueiredo, was the most outspoken in favour of the monarchy, believing that a king could unite the Portuguese. He was challenged by Marcello Caetano, who reminded him that monarchies were slowly going out of fashion and that in Portugal there was still a strong republican sentiment.

However, Figueiredo was not to be dissuaded and, on 24 April, he ensured that deputies passed a constitutional amendment that indefinitely postponed the election of a new president. These malcontents seemed to be hoping that Salazar would agree to becoming the strongman in a monarchical regime. The possibly dangerous impasse was broken with the intervention of Santos Costa, the minister of defence. He had retained his monarchist sympathies while Caetano, the man who had become his chief political rival, had dropped his. But he candidly pointed out to Salazar that the armed forces were unlikely to endorse the proposed change.[9] In political iconography, the military origins of the regime gave the armed forces a special symbolic role. In practice, the military had not acquired the practical influence which it had in mid-20th-century authoritarian regimes, from the one in Spain to the Turkish and Egyptian regimes. The officer corps was not distinguished by strong professionalism as the deputy head of NATO, the British general Bernard Montgomery, observed in the early 1950s.[10] Santos Costa saw it as his primary role to stifle any unrest in the army which could jeopardise the regime. He was effective in this role, even ready to be ruthless at times, but it meant that there were few obvious candidates to succeed Carmona as head of state.

For a self-avowed nationalist, Salazar seemed content to have a small-scale army. It was one that only grew in size and resources during the last stages of the Estado Novo. It has been claimed by a long-term backer that in 1951 he would have much preferred a civilian to be head of state.[11] Albino Soares dos Reis, the chief moderate republican in the regime, had the gravitas to fill the role, but the National Union in 1951 was too riven with tensions for him to be acceptable to all sides. After some weeks, and at the defence minister's suggestions, a hitherto obscure officer was appraised to see if he would be willing to stand for the UN as head of state. This was General Francisco Higíno Craveiro Lopes, who came from a line of military governors in Goa and who was seen as an officer who had avoided intrigue and was likely to confine himself to the ceremonial duties central to the office. He was elected president on 11 July 1951 and inevitably he found it hard to stay apart from speculation and intrigue about who, and what, should come after Salazar.

The succession was now the issue which took up the time of diplomats and journalists when they filed their reports as the third decade in power for Salazar began. The Belgian NATO official André de Staercke, who got close to him at this time, once asked him straight out:

Mr President: Do you think you are eternal?

Salazar: Why that?

De Staercke: Because I wonder who will come after you.

Salazar: Me too. I ask myself this often ... When asked, I tell people: 'I have given years of good government. After me, they will have to find the means to consolidate what I have accomplished.'

De Staercke: But Monsieur le President, this is not a Christian perspective, this is a fatalistic outlook.

Salazar: You know there is a lot of Arab blood in this country.[12]

The fractious conduct of his entourage in 1951 may only have encouraged him in the belief that he had to persevere in his national mission until he no longer had the physical strength to do so. He spoke in somewhat unflattering terms to the writer Christine Garnier about the Portuguese elites a short time afterwards: 'As for the elites, they can be summed up as prone to criticism and at each moment they feel it necessary to define their independence and their personality.'[13] Caetano had often shown such recalcitrance, but balanced against his obduracy was the fact that he was a technocrat of proven ability who had grown up with the regime. He was usually unafraid to speak with candour to his chief about matters that affected the well-being of the regime. Thus in a letter dated 4 March 1949, which he signed off with 'from your most dedicated and admiring friend', he described the state of affairs in the Serpa region of the Alentejo province, declaring that 'You should urgently pay attention to conditions.'[14]

Soon afterwards Caetano was made president of the Corporative Chamber, where he had some influence but little real power. Many ministers would have confined themselves on visits to the provinces to simply consorting with local notables and would have returned to Lisbon with an inadequate view of conditions on the ground. Salazar may have seen Caetano as an awkward but indispensable servant. He tried not to surround himself with mediocrities or sycophants, but Jaime Nogueira Pinto has written that 'someone who knew him close up believes Salazar had a strong disdain for many of those who served him. He knew they were opportunists but, having a strong stomach, he nevertheless used them.'[15]

Salazar viewed his government as a traditional conservative one. Lacking a strong party or an intrusive state, it was not fascist nor did he think he could be described as a dictator. One long-serving minister, Henrique Veiga de Macedo, recalls a meeting of the Council of Ministers probably in the 1950s where he heard Salazar say: 'It is not true what is on some lips, namely that I am a dictator. Scrupulously abiding by the law and applying myself to its spirit is a permanent preoccupation.'[16]

In a 1944 profile of Salazar, the Office of Strategic Services was more accurate than some of the reports later carried by its successor, the CIA, when it described him as an anomaly among Latin leaders and dictators owing to his temperate personality and sober governing style.[17] When informed by a Canadian newspaper, the *Ottawa Citizen*, in 1954 that 'certain sections of the US media are used to calling you a dictator. What is your response?' Salazar replied: 'I can't help noticing that figures who stand out far more in world politics are described in more neutral and even cordial terms. I refer to President Nasser, Marshal Tito, and Mr Khrushchev who the same press organs can treat with reverence. An epithet is reserved for Portugal which does not correspond to the facts nor to the constitutional position ...'[18]

Salazar expected his ministers to be thorough and professional especially when allocated important tasks. Someone who observed the regime from the inside wrote that he was accustomed to telling his closest helpers: 'Follow my indications and bring me always work that is well done.'[19] But he was a motivator rather than a martinet. He was careful to balance factions and avoid making enemies. A regime without parties rather than one with an all-powerful party had its obviously repressive side. The law could be flung aside when circumstances merited it, opponents of the regime could be—and were—tortured and even killed. But the death penalty was never restored, and those who had sought to kill Salazar in 1937 were mostly freed after serving no doubt tough sentences in Portuguese jails though avoiding the fate of being sent to the concentration camp of Tarrafal in the Cape Verde islands. It was closed in 1954 and penal conditions were sufficiently relaxed for major foes of the regime like Cunhal and Galvão to be able, later, to escape from detention. In democratic Italy between 1948 and 1962, the police caused ninety-four deaths when breaking up protest events, but nothing remotely comparable happened in Portugal at any point in the regime's existence.[20] It was a different story in Africa, however. During 1953, in the colony of São Tomé hundreds of creole labourers would be shot when protesting against inhuman labour conditions.[21]

Unlike the age in which this book is being written when the degree of intransigence between competing liberal, radical and conservative ideologies allows no forgiveness when anyone errs in word or deed, in the Portugal of the 1950s there was usually room inside the regime for former opponents who had repented of their ways. At least one ex-member of the opposition MUD in the mid-1940s, Jacinto Nunes, was the deputy budget minister from 1955 to 1959.[22] Salazar might even be compared to the Russian conservative writer Alexander Solzhenitsyn in his disdain for ideologies. The political thinker Daniel J. Mahoney has written of the Russian: 'He adamantly refused to replace the primordial human distinction between good and evil with the pernicious ideological distinction between Progress and Reaction. He refused to subordinate human beings to ideological abstractions.'[23]

For Salazar, General Charles de Gaulle's view that in the long run 'ideologies pass but nations remain' may have very much defined his own outlook. As he grew older, he never became a prisoner of any faction or powerful individual in the regime. He is likely to have grasped that his own monarchists were burnt out, dominated by busybodies and others who may have embraced this option because it seemed the best way of obtaining a sinecure.[24]

The conduct of several of the regime monarchists meant that gradually they ceased to be a factor of any serious weight within the regime. Salazar worked increasingly closely with civil servants and technocrats. Following fifteen years of international preoccupations, and with Africa yet to be an issue of front-ranking importance, he was able to devote more attention to the economy in the 1950s than at any other point in his rule. In 1952, the First Development Plan was launched. This was

against the background of pressure from pro-industry regime supporters.[25] The plan identified low labour productivity, low incomes and
unemployment as barriers to growth. Perhaps several years of very
poor harvests partly help to explain why agriculture was not seen as
worth investing in. Instead, the emphasis was on infrastructure, primarily electric power generation and improvements in the transport
system. The main promoter of industrial policy was the economist José
Ferreira Dias, who had been patiently seeking to make it a priority for
the Estado Novo since the 1930s. He had earlier been responsible for
a law of Industrial Reorganisation in 1945, which identified what were
seen as industries essential for Portugal's well-being. They were iron
and copper metallurgy, and the production of ammonium sulphate,
calcium cyanide, and cellulose.[26] These were industries of sufficient
importance, he argued, that the state should use its own resources to
promote them. The 1945 law also allowed for state intervention if
existing industries of strategic importance were being mishandled.

The so-called 'forty families'— the largest family-based holding companies that were in charge of major firms—benefited from this new-
found emphasis on industry. Some, including Banco Espirito Santo,
Banco Burnay, and Nacional Ultramarino had few industrial holdings or
would only acquire industrial subsidiaries much later. However, there
were others—Banco Português do Atlântico, Companhia União Fabril
(CUF), Banco Pinto e Sotto Mayor, and Banco Borges e Irmão—which
had been more heavily invested in industry since early in the Estado
Novo's existence.[27] They had few ties with foreign capital, which is
hardly surprising since Salazar had been careful to pass laws, such as the
one on the nationalisation of capital dating from 1943, that curbed
direct foreign investment in certain industries.[28]

Left-wing critics of the regime presented the frugal Salazar as a tool
of rapacious economic interests concentrated in a few families. But it
has been argued that Portugal lacked a coherent business class organised to defend the interests of a few privileged groups. One analyst has
written of the 1950s: 'Looking at the broader business community, the
key decision-makers within Portuguese industry were actually heterogeneous in socio-economic origin, social mobility, education, manage-
rial styles, and [their] enterprises varied in terms of their technological
complexity, relations to the state and foreign capital.'[29]

Moreover, there is evidence that Salazar took pains to ensure there was a degree of economic balance, with small and medium-sized producers being protected from ruthless competition on the part of bigger firms able to use their access to capital to drive out competitors. His system of rule, with occasional voting rounds, depended on small property owners not being alienated. Predictably, however, it was the bigger economic players who counted the most. They were able to evade being part of the cumbersome *gremio* system. Instead of fading away, the corporative system lurched back into prominence when the corporations were formally established in 1956. By now a vast body of corporative laws had grown up to regulate the economy, collective contracts and, of course, labour–employer relations.[30] Semi-state agencies would grow even more numerous as the state acquired greater responsibilities in areas like health care and social welfare. Thus in 1957, a National Institute for Blood was set up which would be monitored by the Corporative Chamber along with numerous other semi-state bodies.[31] By 1963, Howard Wiarda writes, 'there was more attention to social issues—and virtually no talk of corporativism. Pensions, holidays, work breaks ... these were the concerns.'[32]

Corporativism was seen as hopelessly anachronistic in the social democratic 1950s, but forty years later it was ruling social democratic politicians in northern Europe who would emulate Salazar by creating a large web of para-state bodies to regulate and oversee an expanding public sector. By his last year in power the number of functionaries had reached 205,000, of whom 161,000 were in the central administration, a fivefold rise since 1930.[33] This power enabled his regime to distribute jobs and concessions on a vast scale. This was also the appeal of corporatism for some clearly democratic politicians. As with Salazar, the power of patronage extended their grip on power, but they faced less criticism than he did for going down this road.

The Corporative Chamber was dominated by agents of the state, some of whom were efficient professionals, others regime loyalists, and a floating number of out-of-office politicians and administrators whom the regime kept loyal by retaining them on the state payroll. Undoubtedly the best-known figure in the corporative world was Admiral Henrique Tenreiro. He dominated the *grémios* in the fishing industry for much of the post-war period. He is seen as an almost demonic figure by some on the left, active in the Portuguese Legion and allegedly displaying pro-Axis sympathies in World War II. He married into a Brazilian banking family, which may, in part, explain the wealth that he was able to exhibit during his years as a businessman-cum-administrator of one of the main Portuguese industries.[34] But this hard-driving and energetic figure also modernised the industry and made sure that fishermen, especially in the arduous and dangerous long-distance fishing industry, were treated far better than agricultural workers in the southern wheatfields. He never attained his ambition of becoming a minister in the government, perhaps because Salazar feared that he might be a lightning conductor for the opposition to base a campaign around. After 1974, he was imprisoned and his business affairs minutely investigated by a state tribunal of inquiry, but it was impossible to make any charges of corruption stick.[35]

The rural world continued to be overlooked in 1950s. It was explicitly stated that the purpose of the construction of dams, at the centre of the 1952 development plan, was to promote industrialisation, not to benefit agriculture. Henrique Veiga de Macedo, who was in the government through the 1950s, later criticised Salazar for not including any provision for land reform at this time. He wrote many years later: 'The major irrigation works in the Alentejo [were deficient] in the sense that there was no provision for giving landless labourers and rentiers access to the land, and in a situation when many big landowners were absentee ones, ones who had forgotten the social function that private ownership bestowed upon them.'[36]

To sanction land reform, the agrarian latifundists would have had to be cut down to size. Salazar could have done so if there had been a consistent emphasis on rural improvements, which was sometimes a feature of traditionalist regimes. Overall, the agrarian estate owners contributed little or nothing to the national economy and their arrogance was sometimes harmful to the modest self-image of the regime. But Salazar left them undisturbed, and ironically it was Caetano, the technocrat who hailed from Lisbon, who seems to have been the regime figure who was most outspoken about rural conditions. His stint as head of the National Union in the late 1940s enabled him to glimpse conditions on the ground. In a letter to Salazar after his visit to Trás-os-Montes in the north-east, he wrote: 'I saw magnificent works but I cannot say it comforted me to see the rest: a lot of poverty, low wages … the exploitation of minors …'[37]

Rather surprisingly, Salazar seems to have been unaware of the doctrine of distributism, which had been conceived by the English Catholic writers G.K. Chesterton and Hilaire Belloc. To combat the evils of industrialism, they promoted small-scale family farming, small units of trade, and industry and various crafts.[38]

By 1955 Caetano was minister of the presidency and presumably he thought his influence over the ageing Salazar could result in the pace of economic change quickening. Planning for a second development plan got under way, but to the chagrin of Caetano, after thirty months of work, Salazar sharply cut back on the amount of funding being allocated. His minister insisted that the funds existed while António Manuel Pinto Barbosa, the minister of finance, agreed with his boss that it was necessary to lower economic ambitions. Caetano complained bitterly in a memoir written later in exile that some of the most interesting innovations required by the Portuguese financial market were mutilated, and there was an unacceptable delay in the setting up of a state development bank.[39]

Involvement in this scheme had brought Caetano into contact with lots of people from the economic world, including some on the left, but it had revived conflict between what he saw as the regime's 'renovator' and 'immobilist' wings. He wrote ruefully: 'I was stranded. It was the result of two years or more of conscientious labour and jealous forces had thwarted this effort.'[40] When he left his role as Salazar's chief ministerial aide in 1958, he told his successor, Teotónio Pereira, not to harbour any illusions about being able to steer Salazar away from any fixed path that he was determined to go down.[41]

While Salazar was beset by intermittent doubts about promoting rapid economic growth, his views on the wisdom of European integration seemed to be uniformly negative. In 1951, after the treaty launching what would be the first decisive step in supra-national cooperation, the European Coal and Steel Community, had been signed, Salazar was unenthusiastic. He believed the concept of a European federation was a fragile one when placed alongside the nation-state and warned about likely problems that it would be difficult to easily overcome.[42] In 1953 he reiterated that the Portuguese economy should answer to a national command even though there were no alternative economic alliances then in sight that could substitute for the emerging Common Market. In September 1958, by which time the European Economic Community (EEC) had come into existence, he reiterated his scepticism in an interview with *Le Figaro*: 'Western Europe is so heterogeneous. History, the [different] languages, colonies, economies, institutions, I cannot see how all these factors that separate the [European] nations, can come together in an effective union ...'[43]

What in particular seems to have placed Salazar on his guard was the enthusiastic backing that the United States was giving to European integration. The momentum behind the concept appeared to arise from what was seen as the typically immature and short-sighted approach from across the Atlantic as well as the chronic weakness of France for much of the 1950s. Salazar couldn't see how the European peoples would accept the loss of national sovereignty and feared that the Soviet Union would try and exploit the new course for its own dangerous advantage.

Yet a more subtle and ultimately more influential figure in policy-making terms, José Gonçalo Correia de Oliveira, made far more headway than Caetano in coaxing Salazar to retreat from dogged economic nationalism. He was helped by the fact that he was the son of an influential poet who was admired by Salazar. His influence began to be felt when the application for Marshall Aid was submitted. It meant that Portugal became involved with the main body coordinating US funds, the Organization for European Economic Co-operation (OEEC), created in 1948. According to Wolfgang Adler, what this meant in practice for the Portuguese 'was an invasion of the expert class'.[44]

Correia de Oliveira was shrewd enough not to directly confront Salazar on economic policy, but he pushed him towards growing European engagement by appealing to the pragmatic side of his economic make-up. Salazar would probably not have promoted industrialisation in fits and starts if he had not acknowledged the importance of the European market for Portuguese goods and the growing economic interdependence of national economies after 1950. His foreign trade adviser was a member of the government from 1955 to 1969, first joining as deputy minister for budgetary affairs and leaving after four years as economics minister. He and the diplomat Ruy Teixeira

Guerra acquired a deep knowledge of the technical issues shaping European inter-state cooperation. His sway over Salazar was shown when his chief declared on 19 January 1956 that he was prepared to 'defend and support an increasingly deeper cooperation … without loss of national autonomies'.[45] But he was frustrated by Salazar's reluctance to allow him to coordinate foreign trade strategy across the different ministries. This ran counter to Salazar's preference to concentrate such decisions in his own hands. As the new European economic architecture took shape, he was always required to report back to his chief, who was loath to give him discretionary negotiating powers.[46] Nevertheless, Correia de Oliveira pulled off the coup of obtaining founding membership of the European Free Trade Association (EFTA) for Portugal in 1960. This was against the initial unwillingness of the lead country, Britain, to sanction Portuguese participation due to its weak economic indicators and the fact that agriculture would be excluded from the trading arrangement.[47] But smart diplomatic footwork by Portugal's European team of negotiators, well described in Felipe Ribeiro de Meneses's life of Salazar, overcame Britain's reservations. A diplomatic offensive by Correia de Oliveira and his team won over sceptical EFTA members and Portugal was given protection for key industries that were hardly competitive at an international level.[48]

Salazar was persuaded also of the need for Portugal to be implicated in these European negotiations while retaining its freedom of action. Correia de Oliveira even dangled before him the hope that Portugal's overseas territories could be integrated in EFTA. But this was a slim hope and the focus of attention slipped from EFTA to the EEC when Britain began negotiations for entry into that already far more important entity in 1963. Portugal didn't follow suit, but shortly beforehand Correia de Oliveira had managed to win agreement for Portugal to apply for associate EEC membership.[49] His preference would have been for full EEC membership, but he was isolated within the government on this issue.

What was probably decisive in tilting the balance away from autarky towards growing economic engagement with much of the rest of Western Europe was the need to quicken the pace of the economy so as to find extra revenue to fund the wars in Africa being waged from 1961 onwards. Even though Correia de Oliveira never displayed any scepticism about Portugal remaining in Africa, this radical shift in economic priorities would in a short time strengthen those regime currents who wanted Portugal to concentrate on a European role when the continent appeared to be undergoing momentous economic and political shifts.[50] The Europeanists in the main were associated with major economic groupings able to benefit from the post-1945 trends in European political economy. A lot of smaller firms without their political clout nevertheless had very different priorities and needs. They depended for their viability on the large (and growing) market for their products in the colonies. The clothing industry, centred in the north of Portugal, is perhaps the main example.[51] But these smaller capitalists lacked political influence. Salazar followed a pro-colonial course because of his own ingrained nationalism and his continuing ability to remain in charge of an authoritarian regime undergoing subtle modifications.

Ironically, it was only in the 1950s that the empire started to impinge on the consciousness of greater numbers of Portuguese. This arose from a number of factors. One was the quickening pace of emigration to Portuguese Africa, especially Angola. From 44,083 Portuguese settlers in 1940, the size of this community of Angolan Portuguese rose to 78,826 in 1950 and 172,529 in 1960.[52] Many of them hailed from the north of Portugal and they searched for commercial opportunities which were unavailable in the still-stagnant provincial economy back home.

Fewer numbers moved to Mozambique, Portugal's second-largest colony but further away from the homeland or the metropole. But the pace of immigration similarly quickened in the 1950s. One of the newcomers was an individual who would enjoy a very singular influence on relations between Lisbon and the colonies during the final decades of the imperial story. This was Jorge Jardim, who became under-secretary for the economy in Salazar's government in 1948 at the age of twenty-nine. He came from a fairly modest background and would always retain the common touch. He was unconditionally loyal to Salazar, with whom he built up a special rapport. When Salazar was felled by a stroke in 1968, it was Jardim who was one of the first people he asked to see after he made a partial recovery. Jardim would undertake various special missions for him in southern and central Africa during the

1960s meant to dissuade newly independent countries from permitting guerrilla fighters to use their territories to challenge Portuguese rule. He proved very successful with Dr Hastings Banda, ruler of strategically placed Malawi. He built up more influence in Mozambique in particular than senior colonial officials because of his direct access to Salazar. Yet when Salazar had met his new minister in 1948, it did not seem such a rapport could be easily established.[53]

Jardim was accompanied by Salazar to the door of his residence and, upon noticing that he was hatless, Salazar asked why, only to be told by the new minister: 'I don't wear one.'

'Then start to wear one, I advise you to go out and buy a hat.'

With a growing family, Jardim decided to abandon government in 1952 and took the then radical step of moving to Mozambique. His energy and drive meant that he soon became an influential local businessman and a community leader. Salazar rarely invested special trust in his colleagues, but he grew to have confidence in Jardim's judgement on African matters, and a durable alliance sprang up between them.[54]

The growing threat to the Portuguese overseas territories made Salazar conclude that unconventional approaches were needed in order for Portugal to hang on in Africa. The decision of the British to withdraw from India in 1947 and partition the subcontinent thrust sleepy Goa, Portugal's oldest colony, abruptly into the limelight. Known officially as 'the State of India', it was promptly claimed by the Nehru government. As early as 1946, the renowned pacifist Mahatma Gandhi had asserted that 'in free India, Goa will not be able to continue as a separate entity'.[55] In 1954 the first clashes arose when, following uprisings in the remote enclaves of Darda and Nagar, India took them over. Portugal then suspended diplomatic ties in 1955. This was the year when the non-aligned movement of countries wishing to remain apart from the Cold War sprang up, following a conference held in Bandung, Indonesia. Anti-colonialism was the motivating force behind this alliance whose leaders were Nehru of India and Marshal Tito of Yugoslavia.

Portugal was disappointed, but perhaps not overly surprised, when Britain sought to accommodate itself to the anti-colonial spirit rather than defy it. The last serious resistance had ended in ignominy with the fiasco of Anthony Eden's attempt to seize control of the Suez Canal in late 1956; the Anglo-French invasion of Egypt collapsed due to American hostility. Eden was replaced as prime minister by Harold Macmillan, who shared the American worldview of promoting the rapid independence of African colonies as the best way of countering rising communist influence.

Treaties signed with Portugal in 1661 and 1899 had committed Britain to defend her overseas territories.[56] But the slowly evolving crisis over Portuguese Goa showed the asymmetrical nature of this alliance.[57] London gently rebuffed Portuguese requests for Britain to mediate or offer it public support in its tussle with India. Neither could Portugal expect any help from the Americans. John Foster Dulles, the US secretary of state, may have told journalists in 1955 that 'as far as I know, all the world regards it [Goa] as a Portuguese province'.[58] But in practice US officials were advising Britain to cajole Salazar into offering concessions to India with respect to sovereignty. The Portuguese feared that conceding to the Indians over Goa was likely to require bigger concessions in Africa before long.

When confronted with the US stance on Goa in 1954, the US ambassador was told by Salazar's foreign minister, Paulo Cunha: 'we were profoundly wrong if we thought anti-colonialism the antidote for communism, and anyway Goa not a colony but, after 400 years, on a level with rest of Portugal and with culture distinct from India as admitted by even Nehru. Present situation, moreover, not one involving freeing colonial people but of open imperialistic aggression by India against another sovereign state.'[59]

As early as 1945 Salazar had concluded that world trends would make it harder to preserve Portugal's pluri-continental status. In a speech made on 9 November 1945 he had set out his rather bleak view of world developments: 'The world which is coming, the society in which we are destined to live, will be far more diverse than the present ... Major social transformations will happen abruptly ... and everyone will see how things are altered that it was assumed had a permanent form. Our understanding of life, our relations with others, the function of wealth and labour, the hierarchy of traditional values in society will change until the day arises when almost none of us can understand how we thought differently from ancient times.'[60]

Salazar seemed to fear a regression to ancient tribalism. But he could be faulted for placing so little emphasis in practice on what he saw as Portugal's civilising mission in Angola. Settlers there grew disgruntled in the 1950s as Lisbon's investment plans seemed to overlook the largest colony, where a strong opposition vote would be registered against the regime in 1958.

Portugal's embattled position in Africa received much-needed ideological reinforcement in the 1950s. It came in the form of a new way of framing Portugal's long-term engagement in diverse lands across the southern hemisphere. The theory of Lusotropicalism affirmed that a new type of civilisation had originated thanks to the voyages of discovery which the Portuguese had embarked upon in the 16th century. It was a symbiotic one merging European and tropical cultures. The mestiço or mixed-race dimension underlay a tropical civilization, which first took shape in Brazil but had imitators in Portugal's main African territories.

Lusotropicalism was devised not by a Salazarist propagandist, echoing the style of António Ferro, but by a respected Brazilian anthropologist, Gilberto Freyre. He had already obtained scholarly renown with books such as *Casa grande e senzala* (1933), which laid the groundwork for the central theory associated with him. For a long time he had belonged to the political left, which is perhaps normal in a society where racial exclusivism was associated with the political right. In the 1940s he had openly praised communism as a cause around which the most respectable Brazilians 'of intelligence and character' had gathered to fight 'Nazi-fascism'.[61] In 1948 he had been one of eight social scientists from across the world invited by UNESCO to host a conference on 'the tensions affecting international understanding'.[62] But, influenced by the harsh features being displayed by communist movements which had taken power, he moved to the right.

In 1950 he accepted an invitation from Admiral Sarmento Rodrigues to spend seven months travelling across the Portuguese world in order to expand his thoughts on the evolution of colonial society. There were no strings attached and Freyre indicated later that the invitation, from the ministry of the overseas, 'could not have been more clearly apolitical'.[63] Freyre was effusively received in Portugal before beginning his voyage. Many opposition figures such as General Norton de Matos hailed him because his work upheld the 'integrity of the pluri-continental nation'.[64]

On arriving in Portugal, he had several meetings with Salazar, whose 'acute intelligence' and ability to listen impressed him. One source has claimed that 'although he criticised the system of censorship, he also wrote that the regime in Portugal was superior to others, "apparently more democratic".'[65]

It was a coup for Salazar's Portugal that arguably the most distinguished Brazilian intellectual of his day was ready to argue that the racial mixing which arose from Portuguese colonial expansion gave rise to a new civilisation in the tropics. Lusotropicalism made its debut as the overtly racialist apartheid regime was being consolidated in South Africa, only to generate a chorus of protest that did not ease during its forty-year history. Freyre never denied that slavery and exploitation were major aspects of the Portuguese imperial story, but he gave them a new dimension, arguing it was too easy to overlook the fact that the conquest of races also had a peaceful dimension in which the European character of the process in time blended into a Lusotropical one. For his part, Salazar would gradually adopt the view (more and more explicitly) that Portugal was a multiracial, pan-cultural, and plural continental agglomeration of peoples. At his funeral in 1970, the state-influenced press emphasised that it was an occasion for Portugal as a multi-ethnic nation to be on display.

The most visible exponent of Freyre's ideas in Portugal was Adriano Moreira. He had started out as an opponent of the Estado Novo and never overlooked its oppressive features overseas. In 1954, he had submitted a dissertation on 'The Prison Problem in the Ultramar', which was examined by Caetano and Joaquim Silva e Cunha, a future minister of the Ultramar.[66] He combined a nationalist outlook with a belief that Portugal needed to adapt its approach to the African territories in order to have a positive long-term role. Perhaps no other figure became as familiar with conditions in each corner of Portuguese Africa during the 1950s as Moreira.[67] The regime was slow to embrace his formulas to raise up the non-white population from subordinate status, but it did not impede his intellectual work. Increasingly, as the anti-colonial clamour grew, Moreira represented Portugal at sessions of the United Nations, where he supported the position being worked out by Franco Nogueira, opposing decolonisation but arguing that Portugal accepted the need for modernisation in Africa and that it was happening.[68]

Salazar was ready to defy the winds of change by insisting: 'We have been in Africa for 400 years, which is a little more than having shown up yesterday. We stand for a doctrine which is different from being governed by an interest. We have the authority to execute and defend a policy, which is distinct from abandoning human destinies to the winds of change.'[69]

Perhaps the event that best symbolised the tenuous calm and repose that defined Portugal for most of the 1950s was the state visit made by the young British monarch, Queen Elizabeth II, in February 1957. Portugal then displayed an atmosphere of tranquillity that compared well with the divisive and febrile atmosphere in Britain, where the Suez crisis had ended just weeks earlier.

An age gap of nearly forty years separated the British head of state from Salazar. It is quite likely that she would have been advised that the decisive and energetic ruler of the 1930–45 period was now fading into history. Salazar's inflexibility, his hostility to many aspects of the modern age being embraced in Britain, and his scepticism towards democracy, might well have been underscored instead. The family friends with whom the Queen stayed near Sesimbra on the private leg of her visit, lasting two days, might have offered a different perspective. She might have been told that on occasion communists were badly tortured or even shot. But Portugal lacked the hallmarks of a totalitarian fascist state and certainly was far removed from the grim 'people's democracies' of Eastern Europe. Indeed, regime insiders had grown fretful about Salazar's increasing disinclination to instil the precepts and ideas of the Estado Novo in the next generation. He seemed to shrink from creating the 'emergent class of capable men' which H.G. Wells thought was needed to direct society.[70] He might have been described as a quirky figure, unmoved by the complaints of the opposition, but ready to read letters of political prisoners requesting clemency.

The Queen might also have been informed by the British Foreign Office and her local friends that Salazar was a good listener, a trait that the Queen would develop to a remarkable extent over the next sixty and more years on the British throne. She was unlikely to find conversation difficult as Salazar possessed charm, especially when engaging with women. Besides, they were likely to discover that they had certain things in common. For one thing, they were both devotees of country life. It was said throughout her reign that the Queen enjoyed the opportunities to retreat to Balmoral, her country seat in the Scottish Highlands, where she enjoyed outdoor pursuits free from protocol. This Highland castle hardly compared with Salazar's simple house in Vimieiro. But they were both drawn to a life far removed from the bustle of their official roles.

Teotónio Pereira, Portugal's ambassador in London for most of the 1950s, would have been able to mention to Salazar details of her life at Balmoral. Rather unusually for ambassadors, he had established a strong rapport with the Queen and members of her family. As a result, he accepted an invitation to spend time at Balmoral outside his official role and as a family friend.[71]

An unexpected point of convergence between the Portuguese leader and the monarch of the United Kingdom might have been the strong commitment to their public duties which they both often displayed. Several times, Salazar spurned opportunities to settle down, get married and pursue a family life, because it would get between him and his job as the steward of the nation to which he was primarily wedded. At the time of writing the Queen and her consort Prince Philip have been married for over seventy-three years during which they have had four children. But, in her case, it has been argued that her strong devotion to official duties meant that family life often took second place.[72]

The visit, in the late winter of 1956–7, took place without any hitches. The weather was benign until its final stages, and pictures of Salazar and the Queen showed them to be relaxed in each other's company. It is unlikely that he would have subjected the British visitor to any lecture about the glories of Portugal. This was not Salazar's way. He was a self-deprecating figure but tough in negotiations, as shown when he had recently bested British negotiators in ensuring that the vast fortune bequeathed by the Armenian oil magnate Calouste Gulbenkian would primarily fund an arts foundation in Portugal and not London. Indeed, the scale of this wealth enabled the Gulbenkian Foundation to largely fund much of Portugal's cultural activities over subsequent decades.[73]

If the Queen had drawn him out on the nature of life in Portugal, it would have been in character if he had interpreted his country in a low-key and modest manner, as he did a few years later in an interview with the Italian newspaper *Corriere della Sera*: 'We are a strange country,' he told the eminent journalist,

Fig. 1: Salazar and President Óscar Carmona in Braga for the tenth anniversary of the revolution which had begun there. 1936.

Fig. 2: Salazar looks on as President Carmona converses with Navy Minister Ortins de Bettencourt, and (far left) Pedro Teotónio Pereira converses with the German ambassador. Late 1930s.

Fig. 3: An animated Henrique Galvão and President Carmona, with Duarte Pacheco on the left. 1930s.

Fig. 4: Salazar facing a large crowd on Lisbon's Praça do Comércio. Date unknown.

Fig. 5: One of the largest pro-regime demonstrations in Lisbon. Spring 1941.

Fig. 6: General Humberto Delgado with opposition allies including ex-Blueshirt leader Francisco Rolão Preto (second from left). 1958.

Fig. 7: Foreign Minister Franco Nogueira with Richard Nixon. Early 1960s.

Fig. 8: Salazar with Cardinal Manuel Gonçalves Cerejeira and President Américo Tomás. 1960s.

Fig. 9: Front page of *Diário Insular* (Azores) marking Salazar's death. 28 July 1970.

contradictory in various ways: small within the continent of Europe, vast overseas; poor in terms of production with huge potential riches; kind and pacific in its local habitat but at the same time capable of struggling bravely and without ulterior motive for noble ideas: the integrity of the territory, the freedom of the people ...; Portugal believes in its ... civilizing role ... This certainly requires railroads, highways and dams but kilometres of motorway and tons of concrete are not needed ...

What we strive for is to be ambitious in our modesty; nothing should be promised that cannot be delivered; nothing should be stated that doesn't exactly correspond to the problems as they exist.[74]

Large and appreciative crowds turned out for the special British guest, from the touristic fishing town of Nazaré to the centre of Lisbon. Franco Nogueira would write later: 'During three days the nation intensely experienced the royal visit, in a haze of gentle affection, of pride, of sentimental hospitality, and with a trace of charming provincialism also.'[75]

It was a minor diplomatic triumph for the regime, which would play host to other state visits from the rulers of Ethiopia, Thailand and Indonesia. These visits dented the view that Portugal had no friends in the developing world, but Salazar was likely to be realistic enough not to invest too many expectations in the British royal visit. It was a protocol occasion symbolically reaffirming the world's oldest bilateral alliance between two states. There were already clear signs that Britain would be unlikely to rush to the defence of its ally if a crisis arose in any of Portugal's overseas territories. But before the colonies became yet another of the world's trouble spots, it was in Portugal itself that Salazar would face a surprisingly intense challenge to his continued rule.

12

TORN CURTAIN, 1958–61

FRIENDS DESERT THE REGIME AND ENEMIES STRIKE

Portugal offered an appearance of calm as it entered the second half of the 1950s. Opposition threats appeared to be minor, and abroad the Cold War entered a less intense period after the Suez crisis and the crushing of the Hungarian revolution. Salazar doubted if an East–West collision was imminent. He believed it far likelier that the Soviets would advance their goals through subversion. He was pessimistic about whether the liberal democracies were alive to the long-term danger posed by this threat.[1] Thus he saw no need to attend the NATO summit to which heads of government of member states had been summoned at the end of December 1957. It would only be a circus for journalists and the new world of television, he thought.[2] He was the only one to stay away, sending Caetano instead.

The national calm which prompted Salazar to set aside more time for social life was deceptive. There was simmering discontent about the slow pace of economic progress, the often stifling character of the state bureaucracy, and the concentration of economic opportunities around Lisbon.[3] In a 1956 report, the French ambassador wrote about 'a shocking contrast between the concentration of wealth in the hands of a few families and the misery which persists as much in the countryside as among the proletariat, and which is even found among the petite bourgeoisie of the towns.'[4]

After he left government in 1948, the Oporto businessman Daniel Barbosa would continue to write to Salazar, pointing out that there was plenty of discontent due to economic stagnation and general backwardness.[5] As long as the secret police were able to muzzle the opposition, Barbosa's warnings did not seem to preoccupy him.

The discontent which bothered Salazar the most occurred within the ranks of the *situaçionistas* or partisans of the regime. They were becoming increasingly fractious. Sniping between monarchists and republicans did not abate. In July 1957, press agencies claimed monarchical restoration had been on the agenda at talks between Salazar and General Franco. Caetano then issued a statement to United Press stating that 'there is no issue with the regime in Portugal'. His chief's reaction was prompt. He ordered censors to remove any mention of what Caetano had said and told him that his intervention had been unfortunate. His argument was that the monarchists were quiet and satisfied with the remote possibility of restoration; and to maintain this state of affairs it was necessary for the regime not to make a declaration of its republican faith.[6]

In his job as minister to the president, both men spoke nearly every day. US diplomatic circles thought that Salazar had finally decided to train a successor.[7] But Caetano felt frustrated: his responsibilities often involved secondary matters and he was unable to interfere in the departmental work of ministers.[8] But when not preoccupied with tasks like preparing for the British royal visit, Caetano sought to build up his own power base.[9]

Caetano also succeeded in inducting the president into his political camp. The stiff Craveiro Lopes floundered in an atmosphere of political intrigue. In the end Salazar reached the conclusion that it was too risky to nominate him for a second term. He had said to the president on several occasions that sometimes he felt really tired and the idea of quitting grew attractive. Perhaps on occasion this was merely subterfuge on the part of a wily Salazar. At one audience, he proposed three possible successors of which Caetano was one, to which the president said, 'Why not.'

Salazar looked at him meaningfully when asking: 'Would he then be the heir apparent?'

To which he replied: 'And why not?'[10]

The president had already fallen out with his original sponsor, the defence minister Santos Costa. Towards the end of his term, he was not even receiving invitations to attend military ceremonies despite being commander-in-chief of the armed forces.[11]

Craveiro Lopes's hopes for a second term crashed after what an admirer of his described as 'a disastrous audience' which he conceded to a combative defender of Salazar, Mário de Figueiredo. The president put it to him: 'And, if against all our desires and expectations, Dr Salazar was forced to quit, who ought to replace him?' Figueiredo's response was implacable: 'I refuse to accept that the question will arise. Only in death will Salazar leave São Bento.'

Craveiro Lopes then made things worse for himself by saying: 'This is hardly a reasonable position to take ... I have talked several times with the President of the Council on this subject and I have to say that his is not the position you have taken. It is my understanding that in the case of a vacancy arising for the head of government role, it is Dr Marcello Caetano who ought to be nominated.'[12]

Craveiro Lopes refused to accept Salazar's face-saving formula that he write a letter saying it had been his own decision not to go forward for a second term. Nor would Caetano agree to deliver a letter to the president breaking the news that the National Union (UN) would not be nominating him again. Salazar had not always been sure-footed in his handling of the army, and he must have expected that there would be repercussions inside that institution.

Salazar rebuffed Caetano's suggestion that he should fill the vacant presidency. This had also been the preference of his then fierce rival, Santos Costa.[13] Similarly, this advice was delivered but with almost brutal frankness by the ex-minister of finance Daniel Barbosa. In several letters to Salazar written from Oporto, he described a regime that was increasingly isolated from the population and which only survived because of military backing. Moreover, he stated that if the elections had really been free, the unexpected military challenger, General Delgado, would have been the winner. Salazar was offered a sobering diagnosis of the blockages in the regime in the areas of economic development, distribution of wealth, bureaucracy, overseas policy and the 'fragmentation in the camarilla'.

In what was a stinging rebuke, Barbosa didn't hesitate to place responsibility for this dangerous malaise directly at Salazar's door—a

Salazar who refused either to change or to go. The ruler was told that in order for the regime to hang on, it was necessary for him finally to move up to the presidency and to designate a vice-president with effective powers. He terminated one of his letters in a tone of direct challenge: the lives of 'our sons' and social peace are in your hands: 'you can no longer duck this responsibility and it is important, Your Excellency, to know what you decide.'[14]

The regime played safe by appointing as its official candidate for the presidency a low-key naval officer, Américo Tomás, who had been minister for the navy since 1944. Unlike Craveiro Lopes, he did not know the overseas territories and few could remember him having made a noteworthy decision. But if it had been assumed that opposition would be containable, the regime was due for a rude awakening. The UN candidate faced a challenger in the person of Humberto Delgado, the youngest general in the Portuguese armed forces, who threw his hat in the ring. Compared with Tomás, he had done much in his fifty-two years. He had been linked to the radical army groups that sustained the dictatorship after 1926, he had negotiated with the British over the granting of a wartime base in the Azores, and he had held diplomatic posts in North America and represented Portugal at NATO gatherings.

In the eyes of many, Delgado was a volatile and uninhibited personality. This may explain why Santos Costa never placed any troops under his command. Francisco da Costa Gomes, a later Portuguese head of state, who had worked with him in NATO matters, recalled that Delgado 'sounded me out about having been invited by a group of businessmen in the north to run for President. He had undoubted qualities but he lacked sufficient good sense and tact to be an effective President.' Costa Gomes thought he had been ill advised to say that he would 'obviously dismiss him' when asked what Salazar's fate would be if he were elected president. The gauntlet had been thrown down at a press conference in the Chave d'Ouro cafe in Lisbon on 10 May 1958. Such a promise electrified his campaign.[15]

Delgado's declaration of revolt should not have been a complete surprise. Correspondence with which he had bombarded Salazar for several decades revealed a narcissist who was unhappy that his particular talents and dedication had gone unrecognised.[16] Fierce written attacks on the critics of the regime and, in particular, the work of

Salazar had burst forth from the early 1930s.[17] He became associated with the para-military Portuguese Legion.[18] As late as 1941, he was writing about Hitler as 'the painter and former corporal' who 'will go down in history as a brilliant revelation of human possibilities in the political, diplomatic, social, civil and military fields'.[19]

The watchful Santos Costa was sufficiently impressed by his energy to give him various assignments, where he undoubtedly showed competence. But he was unstable and impulsive, as shown in an incident related by Costa Gomes, himself a future president. Delgado had asserted, on the eve of running for president, that his preferred career option had been to be appointed director of the NATO Defence College. The job had slipped through his fingers because he had alienated one of the members of the appointment board, the British admiral Sir Michael Maynard Denny. Incredibly, Delgado could not resist teasing the admiral by constantly pulling the abundant hair coming out of his ears. Unsurprisingly, the admiral detested these jokes and vetoed Delgado's appointment. The cerebral Costa Gomes had warned him such irreverence would cost him dear, but he was reportedly told by Delgado that he could not help doing it.[20]

This quixotic military figure, who in time would find cooperation with other foes of Salazar impossible, was nevertheless the focus and embodiment of an unexpectedly strong challenge to the status quo in Portugal. Clichés about the country started to be revised when huge crowds greeted him on the campaign trail. Hitherto, any rebelliousness in Portugal was often viewed as having been curbed by the strength of a traditionalist culture. It was summed up by the three 'Fs', football, fado, and Fátima.

Salazar was hardly ever seen at Fátima, where the veneration of Our Lady was largely regarded as the preserve of the Catholic Church. It is claimed that he disliked fado because of the enervating effect of this Lisbon soul music on the human spirit.[21] And as for football, it was a mass urban spectacle; according to one writer on Portuguese football, the sport sat uncomfortably with the traditional, nostalgic and rural outlook of the Estado Novo. Salazar and his regime displayed deep suspicion towards everything that possessed a mass popular character, that was able to excite the multitude and, in the euphoria of collective emotion, enable them to switch their opinions instantaneously.[22]

Weariness with the regime burst forth onto the surface for many reasons. But it was clear that the provision of order, stability and slow-moving progress was now eclipsed by a desire for freedom and, above all, an assault on poverty. Some Catholics who were encouraged by the religious hierarchy to protest in the mid-1950s about the absence of essential freedoms in communist-controlled Eastern Europe, had riposted that in Portugal a number of the same rights were also absent.[23] Significant numbers of people stood up in 1958 and declared that Salazar's services were no longer required. He might be a dictator with a difference—frugal, honest, retiring and understated—but he still relied on coercion to trample opposition. His strictures against the chaos and venality of multi-party politics were believed for several decades, but the behaviour of the ruling camarilla that had grown up around him in the 1950s now greatly lessened the force of his arguments.

The vast size of the crowd which greeted Delgado when he began his electoral tour of the country in Oporto on 14 May 1958 came as a dreadful shock to regime adherents. His enthusiastic reception in what was seen as the capital of Portugal's conservative heartland was bound to strike panic among many. Joaquim Trigo de Negreiros, the minister of the interior, found it all too much for him, and defence minister Santos Costa took charge of his internal security functions. On 16 May, Delgado evaded a PIDE roadblock to reach the city of Povoa de Varzim by back roads. This coastal spa and fishing centre had done well under Salazar and was seen by some as a showcase city for the regime, but warm and vocal crowds turned out to greet Delgado there.[24] Salazar was warned by his indefatigable correspondent Daniel Barbosa about how fast the tide was now shifting against what his regime stood for. In a letter dated 18 June, he wrote: 'far more than the agitation in the streets, far more than the interest in seeing, hearing and "living the novelty" it is necessary to recognise the receptivity of a great segment of the population towards someone, without particular recommendations to *his* credit, who nevertheless has opened up new pathways and directions for people …'.[25]

The underground communists had initially made much of Delgado's past fascist dalliances and his time in North America convinced their propagandists that he was the 'Coca Cola General'. Their preferred candidate was Arlindo Vicente, a lawyer. But seeing the strength of the mobilisation around Delgado, the communists ditched their candidate and rallied around the man who was soon rebranded as 'the General without Fear'.[26]

In the small world of Portuguese politics it was impossible for opposition and regime figures to stay completely apart. Santos Costa and the fiercely anti-Salazarist novelist Aquilino Ribeiro hailed from the same corner of the north and had remained friends despite their differences. At the height of the election fervour, the defence minister ran into the novelist in a Lisbon bookshop. There, he asked him: 'But do you think that type of man is suitable, one day, to carry out the role of President?'

'Evidently no, my dear friend,' came the reply from the writer. 'We need someone who will open the door for us.'[27]

Santos Costa replied: 'But it is necessary to weigh up the price, Master Aquilino. It would be so steep that I don't think even our carefully managed national treasury could support it.'[28]

This remark may only have strengthened the determination of Salazar's military watchdog to firmly resist the opposition wave. He had been critical of regime decisions and was prepared to speak frankly to Salazar. Later he would state that Salazar 'had an in-built resistance to consulting ordinary people who tilled the soil ... he would never accept that men who tilled the soil had the same right to vote as an educated man.'[29]

But Santos Costa felt Portugal would be lost if his regime went under, given that the communists were the best organised force waiting in the wings. Accordingly, he unified the army and the police under his command in order to prevent the centre of Lisbon being taken over by the opposition, as Oporto had been. He stationed four tanks in the Praça do Comércio on the Lisbon waterfront to prevent ministries there being assailed (to the consternation of Caetano).[30]

Large crowds that had assembled to greet Delgado's train as it arrived at Santo Apolónia station on 15 May were dispersed by forces of the National Republican Guard (GNR). Officers and men on horseback, under the control of Colonel António de Spínola (who sixteen years later would play a fateful role in hastening the end of the regime), proved effective in breaking up the crowds. But for several days intermittent violence persisted in Lisbon.[31]

189

Delgado may have concluded that his adversary was unlikely ever to grant him an electoral victory. So in the midst of campaigning he tried to organise several coup attempts.[32] But he was unable to persuade military colleagues to act. It was a huge gamble to take on a regime which showed every sign of not going down without a fight. What if a coup met with resistance from other units and serious fighting erupted? Few officers with career prospects were willing to risk them, and the stability of the country, by backing such a mercurial colleague (however much he had tapped into national dissatisfaction).

Salazar saw Delgado as a subversive. He had burned his bridges by bluntly promising to get rid of him if he won the election. His ego and the pull of American culture had turned him into a demagogue of the kind whom Salazar had entered politics years earlier in order to supplant.[33] He saw the turning away of former supporters of 'the situation' in terms of a bigger global rejection of authority. Speaking soon after the campaign, he declared:

> The world is reeling from all aspects of a grand and rapid transformation. The severity of the problems that confront us is not going to diminish but increase many times over. And the task is so great that I do not know how there are those who do not feel it and do not want to serve it. Leaving that aside, we are a small country, of a population limited in size, with modest forces and certain structural weaknesses. Two things for us are always necessary: a strong government and a nation united around the idea of perpetuating itself and growing stronger.[34]

On the eve of voting, during a speech given for Admiral Tomás, Salazar had promised that he would not cede any ground to his enemies, however difficult it proved for him. Speaking at the approach of midnight on 4 June in the main Lisbon sporting arena, he threw down the gauntlet:

> I see the coming of times in which greater sacrifices than the vote will be demanded of all for the defence of the common good ... There may come a time when one must be willing to fight, and hard; and happy will be those who have someone to rally them, to lead them, to show them the way and to ensure, with his contribution, that victory is theirs ...[35]

The fact that, on the advice of moderates like Caetano, the regime had used controlled force to repel the Delgado wave enabled the initiative to stay with it.[36] Santos Costa is reported to have remarked to

Salazar at the height of the crisis that 'in such a country as ours, one without consistency or political awareness, to have the troops on your side is all you require'.[37] It was now up to the UN, civil governors and, where really necessary, the regime's security apparatus to ensure that a satisfactory result was delivered.

Unlike past opposition candidates, Delgado did not withdraw before election day claiming foul play. Instead he pressed his challenge up to and beyond the vote. Official figures gave him 236,528 votes as against 758,998 for Tomás: he had polled just under a quarter of the vote in a restricted ballot. Massive anomalies were revealed in this result. In Oporto, where Delgado had received his greatest welcome, only 27,107 out of a round 400,000 eligible citizens contrived to vote for him. In Lisbon the picture was hardly different, with only 105,978 votes being recorded for him out of a population of 900,000. However, Delgado managed to win in some areas where the regime may not have envisaged strong support for the opposition candidate. These districts included the select Lisbon suburb of Sintra, Bragança, the capital of remote Trás-os-Montes, Rio Maior and Vila Franca de Xira, as well as many parts of Angola and Mozambique.[38] If the opposition had managed to win in such outwardly unpromising places, it is possible to conclude that Delgado's support in Portugal's two biggest cities was far greater than the official estimate.

By August of the following year, the decision had been taken to abolish direct presidential elections. The Constitution was revised so that the president would henceforth be chosen by an electoral college drawn from members of state bodies at national and local level. In the face of this Salazar was adamant that his regime still enjoyed credibility. He told the French journalist Serge Groussard in 1961: 'If democracy consists of a process of levelling down and refuses to acknowledge natural inequalities; if it believes that power emanates from the masses and that government ought to be the work of the masses and not of the elites; then in truth I am convinced that democracy is a fiction.'[39]

He was evidently untroubled by any adverse publicity from scrapping presidential elections on a limited franchise, having stated much earlier, in 1938, that 'the good people who acclaim me today, gripped by momentary passions, are capable of behaving otherwise the next day, if moved by other passions'.[40]

It is perhaps also worth quoting his 1934 remarks on the unreliable and, indeed, permanently dangerous features of Portuguese liberalism (in his mind), so as to understand how unaltered was his view of the opposition nearly twenty-five years later:

> Our liberalism, suave and false was always intolerant and jacobin. If it was able to inveigle its way back into power tomorrow, it would be not only anti-Catholic but anti-Christian, irreligious, furiously atheistic, leaving it so divorced from the things of the spirit to be amoral in theory and practice. Its fatal habit of exploiting the masses without them receiving any palpable benefit … means that they end up hating everything that is superior in virtue, intelligence and beauty.[41]

A later conservative critic of Salazar wrote that the 1959 move revealed that the regime had 'lost its already very tenuous connection with democratic principles'.[42] However, the autocrat is unlikely to have felt any self-doubt. He was the custodian of the national estate and toughness was the only way to drive out intruders. Besides, the example of other countries showed some of the essential weaknesses of democracy.

The 1958 crisis in Portugal had erupted just after the collapse of the divided and rudderless French Fourth Republic. A new Fifth Republic designed to suit the preferred leadership style of its founder, Charles de Gaulle, was centred around a powerful executive ruler who faced election only every seven years. Relations soon warmed up with the new conservative president, and Paris would prove a source of support, particularly on the international front over the next decade.

Similarly, relations with the German Federal Republic (DBR), which had been on a good footing since 1949, weathered the 1958 crisis. Salazar had earlier reached out to the post-Hitlerian state with financial help and, in turn, envoys sympathetic to his regime were sent from Bonn. Franz Josef Strauss, the defence minister, made two official visits in 1960 and 1962. Reciprocal use of military bases was agreed and the DBR supplied Portugal with armaments necessary for its growing military role in Africa. It is reckoned that both France and the DBR placed a high value on the importance of Portugal for the Atlantic Alliance. In both capitals the fear that an unravelling of the Portuguese Empire would spell the end of the Estado Novo, and perhaps usher in a communist regime, was keenly felt among some decision-makers.[43] The pinnacle of Luso-German relations post-1945 was reached in 1961, otherwise not a propitious year for Salazar: the West German minister of economic affairs, Ludwig Erhard, arrived in Lisbon with a large delegation. He 'praised Portuguese financial policies under Prime Minister Salazar' and stated that West Germany wanted to 'facilitate, by every means, the more rapid economic development of Portugal'.[44]

Franco Nogueira, the architect of foreign policy through the 1960s, claimed that admiration for Salazar in the ruling Christian Democratic Union ran all the way up to Chancellor Konrad Adenauer, whom Erhard succeeded in 1963.[45] By no means could this be said of Portugal's oldest ally. High-level ties with Britain went into decline. Tony Benn MP, later an influential figure, urged that the alliance with Portugal simply be scrapped given the nature of the Portuguese regime.[46] Even an ambassador who personally respected Salazar like Sir Nigel Ronald, stationed in Lisbon from 1947 to 1955, was morose about political conditions by the time of his departure. In a memorandum he had written:

> The influence of the major industrialists and bankers really seems to have grown since the Development Plan was launched in 1953. Different friends, influential Portuguese, share my opinion that it is deplorable that Salazar gives the impression of listening less and less to the advice of ... liberal cardinal patriarch of Lisbon and increasingly to Dr Ricardo Espirito Santo whom I always considered to be a mandarin at the level of the [French] Second Empire.[47]

By 1958 British opinion had grown hostile to Salazar due to his reactionary image and his unyielding response to the Delgado challenge.[48] Once the general had lost his official positions and been expelled from the air force, it was Britain which allowed him to campaign against the regime there while France and West Germany both denied him entry.

Salazar could also rely on the goodwill of Spain, which took more than passing interest in the political tremors which rocked its smaller ally and neighbour in 1958. Relations were, however, for a time stormy with Brazil. This was due to the presence in Lisbon as ambassador from 1956 to 1959 of Álvaro Lins, who did not hide his animosity to the government to which he was accredited. This literary critic made common cause with dissident intellectuals and gave refuge to Delgado in

January 1959. However, Lins was outmanoeuvred by Salazar, who used his strong ties with the Brazilian president, Juscelino Kubitschek, to neutralise him as a troublemaker. In his last years in office, Salazar could rely on the firm backing of the military regime installed in Brazil after 1964. But for much of his time in office, relations with Brazil were lukewarm. During World War II there had been strains. The United States had considered requesting the civilian dictator Getúlio Vargas to occupy the Azores, Brazil having renounced neutrality to declare war on the Axis in 1942. Overall, Brazil had never offered the high-level backing for the Estado Novo that could be found in France for much of the period from 1932 to 1970.

Salazar's most important move after the 1958 election was taken not with any of Portugal's close partners in mind but with the need to reassert the authority of the state and his own pivotal role within it. A substantial ministerial reshuffle took place on 14 August. Both Caetano and Santos Costa stepped down. Rumours suggested that the scale of their disagreements meant that Salazar was forced to replace them to heal fractures that had opened up at the top of the regime. But their own testimonies indicate that both men left voluntarily. Caetano had not been happy in his position. On 4 August he had met Salazar, who had raised the possibility of his staying in government.

Caetano said he didn't think he was a good choice despite being a friend. Salazar retorted that friendship was not at issue and he did not have this problem because he was nobody's friend. There was a tense silence and then, according to Caetano, Salazar said, again in a sad tone: 'I can't have friends. I am nobody's friend.'[49]

On the day that he quit, Caetano went to see the new president and presented his resignation from the Council of State, saying that he was abandoning politics.[50] Then he sent a letter to Salazar in which he said he considered himself exonerated by the UN. On arriving home, there was already a letter from his former chief. He was thanked from the bottom of his heart for precious collaboration and Salazar expressed his hope that, after a necessary repose, he would continue to work for a regime to which he had so much to contribute. According to Caetano, this affectionate gesture from a man who said he had no friends meant he feared a political rupture.[51]

Caetano was a versatile technician who had built up considerable influence, but his departure did not leave a vacuum. As for Santos

Costa, his stepping down did leave a void as he had been a dominant figure in the military for over two decades. He had been turned into a bogeyman by opposition propaganda, and the Communist Party celebrated his departure as a great victory. But although he could be harsh in his management style, it is perhaps too easy to assume that his influence had been wholly negative. He had sought to modernise the army and had overseen the construction of NATO air bases in Portugal.[52] He had also ensured that a cadre of officers had been sufficiently trained so as to assume NATO responsibilities. Perhaps one judgement on him has to be that he had found it impossible to create an army staffed by officers who were loyal to the regime in good times and bad. Upper-class Portuguese shunned the military as a career. Many officers were drawn to the military because it offered financial security and a degree of social respectability. They hailed mainly from the middle classes and from the ranks of the aspiring provincial bourgeoisie. They were patriotic, as were most Portuguese, but were not yearning for combat roles.

Salazar and Santos Costa were ageing traditionalists who found there was a shortage of people who shared their values. The military man had made too many enemies in an institution short of cash and with limited promotional opportunities, and several protégés later showed a willingness to strike against the regime. Salazar had been told, via Tomás, that he was no longer representative of the army. But when Santos Costa announced that he was going, Salazar is supposed to have said to him: 'You gained the elections. The country won't understand if you quit now.'[53]

A biographer of Salazar, Franco Nogueira, reckons that he was relieved that his military right-hand man was leaving even though nobody would ever really replace him. More than ever, he knew that his authority depended on his relations with the armed forces.[54] He may well have drawn some comfort from the belief that if he no longer had the strength to exercise complete dominance over the armed forces, they still lacked the capacity to remove him.[55]

Both Santos Costa and Caetano had, in different ways, given a lot of service to the Estado Novo and they had not always been used in an effective manner. Salazar never trusted Caetano sufficiently to proceed with reforms and social improvements that could have blunted opposition offensives like the one which had just erupted. Salazar also seems to have had a contradictory approach to the military. He recognised that it was the regime's main pillar of support but he showed himself averse to familiarising himself with its conditions and taking steps that would reduce its threat to the regime in adverse circumstances. His political soulmate in Madrid, General Franco, would probably have been amazed that he agreed to Botelho Moniz becoming defence minister in 1958. He had grown apart from Salazar, had refused to be considered as a military candidate for the presidency in 1958 because he disliked those in Salazar's entourage, and (like Delgado) had fallen under US and NATO influence.[56] Franco would have sent such a figure to command a remote garrison and not be the man who gave orders to his military.

Calm was slow to return after the electoral tumult. On 13 July 1958 the bishop of Oporto, António Ferreira Gomes, wrote a long and very critical letter to Salazar. In it he described searing conditions of poverty in his diocese and suggested that Salazar should no longer be seen as a conservative idealist but as a hoarder of personal power. He described the recent election as a turning point which revealed that a church which had remained silent about the regime's damaging record was paying the price by losing the support of dedicated lay activists.

The bishop seemed to write more in sorrow than in anger. He recalled how his view of Salazar had been very different in the 1930s: 'I remember well the excitement … with which we accompany the beginnings of your career … I must still have a sack of paper in which I religiously kept every word of yours … In addition to everything else we felt as Portuguese … [your elevation] was a kind of gift that the Church made to the Motherland at a crucial moment.'[57]

What was a private letter entered the public domain in unknown circumstances during the following month.[58] Salazar referred neither to it nor to its author when he addressed the UN on 6 December 1958. But he threw down the gauntlet to the church, warning that if the hierarchy proved incapable of preserving a united front between the Estado Novo and the Catholics, then the 1940 Concordat might have to be altered.[59] The speech showed Salazar to have been stung by the rebelliousness of Catholic activists. But he had not forgotten the mutinous bishop, who was turned away from the frontier on 18 October 1959, the beginning of ten years of exile.[60]

The scholar Manuel Lucena wondered if Salazar had not, by this point, become detached from the church, relying not on a religious institution for legitimacy but instead on a strong state to carry out his will.[61] His contacts with Cerejeira, who struggled to prevent a breach between radicalised laity and the regime, were scaled down, although they dined each Christmas Day. Usually depicted as a reactionary, Cerejeira was quite liberal in the way he governed his church. He was loath to take disciplinary action against critics of the regime or radical spirits within the church.[62] So there was hardly a partnership between church and state during the heyday of both men.

Salazar had shown the church the iron fist inside the velvet glove. None of Portugal's forty-nine bishops stood up for their Oporto colleague or dared to intercede with Salazar on his behalf. In a pastoral letter issued in January 1959 they reminded Catholic Action, the chief lay body, that its constitution required it to steer clear of politics. The statement went on to say that the church's task was to preach the gospel and the state had the obligation to build its institutions on the basis of a Christian social programme. But the statement did not clarify whether the bishops felt that the government had been fulfilling the obligation or what the role of Catholics should be who were convinced that it was no longer doing so.[63]

Catholic activists turned out to be the ones up to their necks in a revolutionary bid known as 'the Cathedral Plot', which was due to be launched on 11–12 March 1959. It was not an old-fashioned military conspiracy but was led by Manuel Serra, a senior Catholic youth leader. He was in charge of some 300 armed civilians, many of whom sprang from Catholic workers or Catholic student groups. Several of the junior officers involved had a background of Catholicism, and it was in the crypt of Lisbon cathedral that their weapons were stored. It was the most elaborate conspiracy mounted against the regime for many years and at the heart of it were radicalised Catholics.[64] After he had seen one of the regime's main allies gripped by disaffection, it is perhaps no surprise that Salazar turned on the bishop of Oporto later in 1959.

The start of this year already brought the unwelcome news for Salazar that Henrique Galvão had evaded his guards and escaped from the Santa Maria hospital in Lisbon to which he had been transferred from prison due to the sixty-three-year-old's ill health. He was in detention from 1952 before finally being sentenced to sixteen years in prison in March 1958 for subversion. Yet despite the brutality of this sentence, Galvão enjoyed mild conditions. His then friend Delgado, along with Caetano and others, intervened to allow him to have a type-writer in his prison hospital even though he continued to write articles considered to be defamatory of Salazar.[65] On escaping, he managed to obtain sanctuary in the Argentinian embassy from which he was given safe passage to Argentina after the authorities promised he would not be permitted to pursue anti-Portuguese activities. Salazar was reluctant to assent but he did. 'We shall regret it a thousand times,' he stated. 'He is far more dangerous than Delgado.'[66]

Even before the pressures started to bear down on him from many different sides, Salazar had started to take medication apparently to raise his spirits. From April 1956, he was taking Eucodal, related to heroin, on a regular basis.[67] The intense work rate followed by Salazar for all but a month or so each year was bound to have taken its mental toll. From being a conservative with a global following in the 1930s, he had become a byword for European reaction. His shifting reputation reflected as much the changed times that had arisen in the West as his own conduct in office. There was occasional official recognition, however. Upon his seventieth birthday on 28 April 1959, he was congratulated by President Eisenhower, Queen Elizabeth II, de Gaulle and the Pope. Coimbra University bestowed on him an honorary doctorate. A month earlier he had received an invitation from the university to give a final lecture. This came hard on the heels of an open letter in which a hundred citizens said his final lesson to the nation should be to step down.[68]

A period of uneasy calm persisted for most of 1959 and into 1960. Salazar enjoyed regular extended autumn holidays in his village retreat. A smooth working relationship was established with the new president, Américo Tomás, who was diligent in carrying out his official duties and avoided involvement in intrigues. He was unusual among Estado Novo dignitaries in acquiring close ties with influential figures in the Franco dictatorship, sharing the Caudillo's love of hunting and hosting his deputy, General Agustín Muñoz Grandes, who kept an eye on the stability of the Salazar regime.

But the world was making ever more unwelcome demands on Portugal, especially concerning its territorial presence in Africa. 1961 delivered a series of hammer blows for Salazar and his regime, which quickened media interest in the previously long-overlooked country, producing forecasts that his days were numbered.

The first one struck on 22 January 1961 when Galvão and twenty-three Iberian revolutionaries seized a Portuguese cruise liner, the *Santa Maria*, which, along with its 600 passengers, was about to set sail from Curaçao to Florida. The aim of what the hijackers dubbed Operation Dulcineo was to ignite a general uprising in Angola. It was hardly a secret, in the light of the dramatic violence which had erupted in the Belgian Congo in 1960, that Angola was a tinderbox. Galvão placed his hopes on the Portuguese whites rising up and that a chain reaction of events would drive a much-weakened Salazar from power. However, the liner never reached Angola, where a revolt did erupt in Luanda on 3 February 1961 but among some of the city's black population. A full-scale rebellion in rural northern Angola then followed in which many thousands lost their lives. Understandably, this crisis soon eclipsed the 'Santa Maria affair' in importance but the latter was an embarrassment for Salazar while it lasted. Over thirteen days, dozens of the world's journalists tracked the odyssey of the hijacked ship as it headed for Brazilian waters. Portugal's image as an oasis of calm was gravely undermined. Salazar was indignant when the Brazilian government granted the hijackers political asylum after the ship docked in the port of Recife.[69]

Salazar had been furious when Portugal's oldest ally interpreted Galvão's operation as an act of rebellion under the Geneva Convention on the High Seas. By abstaining from condemnation, Britain seemed to be opening the way towards treating the revolutionaries as legitimate representatives of Portugal.[70] But soon even greater displeasure was shown by a much stronger ally of Portugal. On 13 March 1961, the United States voted with numerous African and Asian countries in supporting a United Nations resolution condemning Portuguese colonialism. Two days later the bloodiest phase of the Angolan events began when hundreds of white settlers were killed and thousands of Africans from elsewhere in Angola who worked on their estates were massacred, in an uprising centred on the Bakongo region in the north-west.

The response in Lisbon was sluggish, and it wasn't until 13 April 1961 that Salazar appeared on television to make a dramatic broadcast that he was assuming the post of minister of defence and that Portuguese troops would be sent rapidly and in large numbers to regain control of a situation, one which had led to bloody counter-massacres carried out by enraged local whites with the help of mixed-race Portuguese.[71]

Belatedly, Salazar was carrying out advice that had been insistently given to him by Santos Costa. In letters dated 3 and 6 April he argued that the deployment of up to 10,000 troops in rebel-held areas of northern Angola was vital in order to contain the uprising. He pleaded with Salazar to exercise authority and not to 'suggest' but to 'demand' and 'order'.[72] However, Salazar's hands were tied at this point. Defence minister Botelho Moniz appeared more concerned with compelling him to modify his 'hardline' stance opposing self-determination in the African territories. In a letter to his chief written on 27 March he insisted that the time was overdue for sweeping changes at government level which would enable reform of the military to take place. He claimed to have the overwhelming backing of military colleagues and he had the opportunity to put his views to Salazar in meetings held on the 27th and 28th.[73] But Salazar played for time, probably aware by now that his minister was seeking to oust him. He would have got confirmation of this from President Tomás, who met with Moniz twice on 5 April, when he was told that he should politically neutralise, or else dismiss, Salazar as the military was poised to take control of the country.[74] Rumours of what was afoot spread in political circles, but despite the audacity of his plans, Moniz would take time off to enjoy an Easter break in the Algarve.[75]

He had briefly fallen ill but his departure from Lisbon may be indicative of the mood of confidence he and his fellow plotters possessed about the likely success of their enterprise. Moniz brushed aside the advice of a close collaborator, Colonel Carlos Viana de Lemos, to mobilise middle-level officers as well. It was to be a palace coup organised by senior ranks and the evidence suggested the army was solidly behind it. The navy was peripheral and only the air force, where Brigadier Kaúlza de Arriaga was active, proved hostile.

Nearly a week after signalling his intentions to Tomás, he returned to see the president on the 11th. Perhaps he assumed that the naval officer would fall into line with what seemed to be the consensus that

Salazar's time in charge was over. Tomás is often disparaged as a nonentity and has been underestimated in the historiography of the Estado Novo.[76] But he remained loyal to Salazar while giving little away to the conspirators, whom he met a second time that night when their demands were even more insistent. Salazar (who had received another letter that day from Santos Costa saying that action was imperative as the conspirators were poised to strike) was kept informed by the president of what was afoot.[77] Salazar understandably fell into low spirits. He said to foreign minister Mathias that 'it is likely, the pair of us will meet up soon in Aljube', a Lisbon prison.[78] He may also have doubted whether the president could find the resolve to hold out against such an internal rebellion. His spirits were kept up by Luís Supico Pinto, who had turned into an *éminence grise* of the Estado Novo. His wife, who would become a redoubtable figure in the last phase of the regime, described him as discreet, trustworthy, and extremely well-informed.[79] Salazar seemed to prefer to have him as a watchful adjutant rather than as a minister, and it is easy for his importance within the regime to be lost sight of. After the president's backing was confirmed on the night of the 11th, Salazar turned to him and said: 'Well, my dear sir, it would seem that I have to continue ...'[80]

What might also have encouraged Salazar were the messages which he got from former fierce opponents such as Armando Cortesão and Cunha Leal, who closed ranks behind Salazar in his bid not to let Angola go. Salazar sent a letter of thanks to Cunha Leal, a foe for over three decades, praising him for his love for the motherland.[81]

On the 12th Salazar had a long meeting with Tomás, who was told by him that he was going to remove the plotters and assume the defence job himself. Tomás agreed to officially ratify the changes the next morning. He also sent a letter to Moniz saying that he had full confidence in the prime minister. This was not long after the defence minister had told the American ambassador, Charles Burke Elbrick, that 'Dr. Salazar is old, has less energy, no longer takes command of situations as he did previously'.[82] By now backers of the status quo had been able to mobilise within the armed forces. Kaúlza de Arriaga of the air force played a decisive role. On 12 April there had been stormy scenes when he was called in by the defence minister, who soon raged at him to 'get out immediately, you big rascal'.[83]

Moniz doggedly persisted with his plan, which now included the removal of the head of state. (An aircraft was on standby to spirit Salazar off to exile in Switzerland.)[84] The conspirators all gathered in the Cova de Moura palace on 13 April. They were joined by ex-president Craveiro Lopes, who brought his marshal's uniform with him. He was with the rebels heart and soul and planned to change into the uniform when the goal of removing Salazar had been accomplished.[85] Before their deliberations got under way, the state radio broke into its normal schedule to announce that the minister of defence and senior colleagues had been removed. Soon after, the head of the air force, General Albuquerque de Freitas, pointed out to his colleagues that technically they were now acting outside the law and it was his view they could not count on the backing of the majority of military units. Therefore, he had decided he was unable to take part.[86]

The coup collapsed at that point. Already telecommunications had been cut by members of the Portuguese Legion who had surrounded the palace. If the high level plotters had persisted, it would probably have been impossible to avoid clashes between backers and opponents of the takeover, perhaps even resulting in intervention from Spain, which had contingency plans to act if the regime was toppled. Salazar, for his part, decided to take no action against the plotters, who were retired or else reassigned (but nor did he promote Kaúlza de Arriaga, his instinct for preserving a balance in the military remaining acute). One of those able to continue their military careers was Colonel Francisco da Costa Gomes, deputy minister of the army. He was the only one to comment publicly in the aftermath of what was known as the 'Abrilada' when he published a letter in a Lisbon newspaper in which he offered a defence of the army's role. He rebutted critics who claimed the army had been caught unprepared in Angola and that its response had been inadequate, and he went on to say that the Angolan problem was not a simple one and that the military part of it was far from being the most important dimension.[87]

The government was reinvigorated by new members. Salazar had met with Caetano and offered him the post of minister of economic affairs. There had also been rumours that he had connived in Moniz's action and it was known that he figured in the plotters' plans for the post-Salazarist future.[88] According to several accounts, Caetano had known about the coup but did not want to get involved.[89] He turned down the invitation to return, which is perhaps the reaction Salazar had anticipated, according to Franco Nogueira. His biographer, who entered the government not long after, reckons that he wanted to show that Caetano had no right to criticise the government when he spurned an important post.[90]

By the autumn of 1961 the revolt in northern Angola, which had been launched by Holden Roberto's Union of Angolan Peoples, was ended. The sense of acute crisis receded but Salazar remained preoccupied with the plotting of Delgado and Galvão. Soon they would fall out. Galvão was accused of exhibitionism by Delgado, who complained: 'When you want to make a revolution, you do not announce it on rooftops.'[91] Delgado's closeness to the communists repelled Galvão. He was convinced that it was their intention to turn Portugal into 'just another colony of Russia'.[92] It has been reckoned that

> personality and ideological differences were key factors in the breach. Galvão's cold and cerebral temperament was diametrically opposed to Delgado's mercurial and emotional character. Despite common characteristics—former supporters of the New State, men of action and professional soldiers—they had grown apart ideologically. Galvão remained consistent in his conservatism, expressed in unswerving anti-communism and a personal commitment to colonialism. Delgado, on the other hand, was more pragmatic, moving closer to the PCP and accepting the principle of self-determination.[93]

Delgado was involved in a revolt that erupted in the military garrison in the southern town of Beja on New Year's Eve 1961. It was led by a hard-boiled foe of the regime, João Varela Gomes, who had retained a position in the military despite being involved in plotting since at least 1959. He was wounded, but the under-secretary of the army, Tomás de Fonseca, was accidentally shot and killed by his own side.

The last major flashpoint in 1961 had been Goa. Salazar had ordered its governor, General Manuel Vassalo e Silva, to fight to the death along with his men. Adriano Moreira, minister for the Ultramar at the time, later wrote that the loss of Goa 'wounded most profoundly the popular consciousness due to the link with historic values, and the association with the *Lusiads* [the great work of 16th-century Portuguese literature by the poet Luís de Camões] in the shaping of Portuguese identity'.[94]

But in a confidential report made for the Portuguese authorities in 1956, the left-wing geographer Orlando Ribeiro argued that there was little racial mixing, the Catholic Church was in a weak state, and Portuguese culture overall was poorly implanted.[95]

On 10 December 1961 Salazar decided to formally invoke the Alliance and ask Britain to come to the aid of Portugal if its territory was attacked. But by now ties with India had primacy over any obligations created by the Anglo-Portuguese alliance.[96] The British prime minister, Harold Macmillan, noted privately: 'it was absurd of the Portuguese to try to hold on to it [Goa]'.[97] But Washington believed that Portugal's claim to Goa was sound in international law. On 8 December the secretary of state Dean Rusk had issued the Indian government with a strong warning against launching a military assault.[98] J.K. Galbraith, one of the president's most radical advisers, who was US ambassador in New Delhi, stated privately: '[I] hardly imagined that I would be undercut in such an ... incompetent manner by our own government.'[99] On 18 December, Britain declined to associate itself with an American resolution at the UN strongly condemning India. Lisbon had been previously informed that Britain would be unable to permit Portugal landing rights for military planes at its bases in Libya, Mauritius and the Maldives.[100]

Macmillan had written to Nehru on 13 December, warning that occupying Goa would squander India's global credibility and risked igniting a series of regional conflagrations.[101] Indonesia was mentioned but not India's Himalayan frontier, which Chinese troops violated ten months later in a short war which India lost.

The invasion of Goa, launched on 17 December 1961 by 30,000 troops, quickly saw the territory overrun. Salazar was disgusted that the Portuguese commander disobeyed his order to lay down his life to defend what for him was a precious heirloom that had been part of Portugal for over 400 years. Leonid Brezhnev, a senior Soviet figure, expressed pleasure at being in India, and thus on hand, to witness 'the liberation of the land of India from the last remnants of colonialism'.[102]

Salazar had come to see himself as the custodian of the Portuguese nation, the defender of its sovereignty against all comers. But it is uncertain how numerous were the Portuguese who shared his perspective. Unlike the cases of Angola and Mozambique, there were now very few direct ties binding them to the first territory acquired by Portugal in the Age of Discovery.

Speaking to the National Assembly a few weeks later, Salazar described British diplomacy as 'a very devious school' which always strives, 'even in the gravest of circumstances ... to obtain concrete commitments in exchange for vague promises'.[103] He argued that the seizure of Goa had been an even bigger reverse for Britain and also the US because it showed the impotence of these mighty powers in upholding justice.[104] The closing part of the debate on Goa was interrupted by cries from the gallery of 'death to Nehru', 'down with the Alliance', 'bandits'.[105] A vote for an eventual change in foreign policy if deemed necessary to defend the interests of the nation was passed unanimously. His close ally in the press, Augusto de Castro, wrote just after the Goa invasion that Portugal should realise that the English alliance was no longer an instrument of effective reciprocity.[106] But Salazar was not heading for a break with Britain. He remained something of an anglophile, and in an interview with *Le Figaro* in Paris he declared that 'the English, whom we very much like ... remain our allies'.

The multi-faceted nature of the challenges faced by Salazar between 1958 and 1961 was unprecedented. The dictator seemed to dismiss the likelihood of a concerted challenge from below. The people might be prey to political fashion and novelty but they did not pose a threat to the regime. A tiny minority had fallen under communist influence but this was a future danger, not an immediate one. As for the military, its spasms of restiveness could be contained, as in the past.

The threats Salazar was most vigilant about seemed to emanate from abroad: communist subversion, the hostility of the United Nations, unrest in Africa, the defection of one or more previously close allies. He seems to have discounted a challenge in which an ambitious military figure used the electoral mechanism to rally the opposition and establish a working relationship with the underground communists. But this is what happened with stunning rapidity in 1958. Moreover, it was an officer known to Salazar and in whom he had placed trust. It was a harsh verdict on his ability to judge the soundness of those with whom he had worked. But perhaps in his defence he would have argued that the human material he was forced to deal with often proved variable.

The Estado Novo wasn't tested to breaking point but it was badly stretched, particularly in the first and last of these years. Portugal had become a more complex place to govern, and Salazar's own effectiveness as a ruling autocrat was eroded by his diminishing physical and mental strengths.[107]

Previous challenges to his authority had mainly arisen from circumstances beyond his control—economic depression, war in Spain, World War II, the Cold War, and the drive to dissolve European overseas empires. Human agency had also played a role. This would be the case after 1958 also, but by now a key source of the regime's difficulties was internal. It could even be argued that Salazar had prepared a rod for his own back by failing to adapt to changing circumstances. This did not necessarily mean embracing a conventional party-based democracy. Dismantling his authoritarian regime had few advocates within the Estado Novo, and its main communist opponent was arguably far more dictatorial than the Estado Novo would ever be.

Salazar could have been far more innovative in adapting his regime to new political times without embracing a form of governance which he despised. He could have introduced more consultative elements especially at local level (which was an integral part of the Portuguese right's programme before 1926). He could have grasped the nettle of the succession question and thrashed out a formula in advance that would apply upon his death or incapacitation. Arguably, he had dealt with far more challenging matters when consolidating his authority in the 1930s. Instead, this task was to be left to a president chosen for his willingness to be a largely decorative element at the top of the regime.

Selecting a president from the military proved to be a huge vulnerability for the regime by the late 1950s. Salazar asserted that the armed forces were the guarantor of his system, but arguably he had not managed this institution well. He had been more adept at controlling the factions within the regime's broader family, but friction, stemming in large part from the succession, in time dragged the military back into politics.

Perhaps his biggest error was not to properly look after the millions of Portuguese whose conservative outlook mirrored his own. As in Spain under Franco, economic development was centred on major urban conurbations where support for the regime was meagre. Salazar neglected agriculture and rejected advice from ministers to invest far more in health and social programmes aimed at small town and rural Portugal, where most people still lived in the 1950s.[108] Such an approach might well have blunted opposition efforts to detach Catholics from the regime, and made it far harder for Delgado to enjoy such popular momentum in 1958. But it would have run counter to Salazar's flinty philosophy that adamantly opposed an intrusive state promoting ambitious social programmes which would (in his eyes) only soften the character of the people.

There would be a large and growing state, but it existed to supervise the workings of the economy and to protect the regime from its enemies. The post-1958 crisis showed that the regime retained an important nucleus of adherents who were prepared to rally to its defence. This support base wasn't primarily ideological. In the 1930s Salazar had been careful to avoid officially sponsoring a militant movement. It took little imagination to see how a Portuguese version of the Spanish Falange might slip from the control of a temperate and low-key paternalistic ruler. But it is less easy to see why there was such complete neglect of political education after 1945. Perhaps Salazar thought the easiest course was to try and embrace depoliticisation. This course, however, meant that power gravitated to small knots of people in the ruling circles who sometimes abused their position.

Important degrees of passive endorsement for the regime remained in Portuguese society. Despite the corrosion of its authority in the 1950s, it was not blown away by the eruption of strong internal opposition. Numerous Portuguese still had vivid memories of the unrelieved chaos before Salazar's time. They retained respect for his ability to pacify the country with a moderate degree of force and would have shared, at least in part, his view about the disorderly state of mankind needing to be contained by firm authority. Salazar was an instinctive follower of the English philosopher Thomas Hobbes who argued that peace could only be preserved by a ruler who had a firm control over 'opinions and doctrines'. These views would become fashionable once more during the early 21st century retreat from untrammelled liberalism but in the late 1950s they were growing distinctly unfashionable. Fewer and fewer of his own countrymen were prepared to accept his message of austerity, especially in light of rapid improvements elsewhere in Western Europe. Therefore, Salazar was increasingly swimming against the tide when he argued that progress was fleeting and easily reversible and that democracy could be a false friend because it left countries that placed too much emphasis on the ballot box defenceless in a dangerous and capricious world.

The septuagenarian Salazar showed agility in playing off different individuals. He could work with a wide range of people without his opinions about their style, morals and outlook getting in the way. Two examples suffice of this pragmatism: the trust that he placed in the liberal-minded republican José de Azeredo Perdigão who ran the Calouste Gulbenkian Foundation for many decades from its inception in the mid-1950s; and his ability to work with the social-democratic-minded Jacinto Nunes, who had a major influence on financial policy in the last dozen years of Salazar's rule.

He was different in this respect from Marcello Caetano, whose preference was for a homogeneous support team. Despite facing bouts of illness in the 1958–61 years, Salazar kept his nerve and showed Olympian calm when confronted by each of the challenges of those years. First there was Delgado, then defectors from the Catholic camp, followed by senior military figures, and finally former reliable partners Britain and America. But no formidable opposition movement took shape. Henrique Galvão observed wryly that Salazar easily oversaw the dance of the opposition and 'the opposition danced'.[109]

His ability to rally adherents during periods of crisis was impressive. His appeal for solidarity was basically couched in nationalist terms. Initially, many people were prepared to endorse the regime's bid 'to defy the winds of change' in Africa. Salazar was thus far from unrepresentative in his wish for Portugal to remain implanted in Africa. But the Ultramar was not the obsession for most Portuguese that it would become for him during his last years in power. How far he could defy the liberal spirit of the age, exemplified by Europe disengaging from Africa, would soon become clear as the 1960s got under way.

13

CONTRASTING ALLIES

PREDATORY AMERICA AND AMENABLE FRANCE

The United States made a radical reappraisal of its ties with a fellow founding member of NATO with startling speed. Speaking of Salazar and his regime, President Eisenhower told Charles Burke Elbrick, his envoy in Lisbon, on 9 November 1960 that 'dictatorships of this type are sometimes necessary in countries whose political institutions are not so far advanced as ours'.[1] In May of the same year he had paid an official visit to Portugal where the press was informed that 'my talks with President ... Salazar have been conducted in a spirit of complete mutual understanding'.[2]

Yet, less than a year after these words had been uttered a new administration was actively involved in trying to unseat Salazar with secretary of state Dean Rusk and ambassador Elbrick keeping in close touch about the progress of a looming coup and the CIA's Lisbon bureau frenetically involved in the background. A new president had taken over in the meantime. John F. Kennedy, the Democratic Party's narrow victor in the November 1960 election, believed that a rapid transfer of control from European powers in Africa to local elites was necessary to prevent the Soviet Union from turning Africa into a dangerous new theatre of the Cold War. By taking the lead in harnessing African nationalism, he expected that a firewall could be built that would keep the Soviet foe out of Africa. The Portuguese would have been aware of his hostile disposition to their overseas role from at least 1956 when Kennedy became the first chair of the US Senate's Africa Subcommittee, which gave him the opportunity to meet many of the continent's rising politicians.[3]

Salazar would be composed in the crisis that quickly followed. Surprised US officials in the 1960s would refer to his apparent serenity when under pressure. He had come to expect inconsistency from the US, which he had bracketed as an insensitive and grasping ally as soon as regular contacts arose in World War II. Franco Nogueira, his steely lieutenant in the duel with Washington, saw the people whom Kennedy had recruited from academia to reshape his policy as wielding a malign influence. He wrote later: 'The intellectuals and theoreticians of Harvard took over Washington. Alliance solidarity, moral pledges, legal principles, everything was swept aside.'[4]

But even the Portuguese were likely to have been astonished at the ferocity of the cold wind from Washington. On 20 February 1961 Liberia had requested an urgent meeting of the United Nations Security Council following an outbreak of violence in Angola. The Portuguese representative at NATO headquarters in Paris delivered a note to Portugal's partners asking that their governments oppose the Liberian motion. Portugal regarded events in its overseas territories (the Ultramar) as a strictly internal matter. But the Kennedy administration informed Lisbon that there was deep concern 'over the deteriorating position of Portugal … in Africa'. As a result the US pressed Portugal 'to undertake major adjustments in her policies which as presently constituted seem to us headed for very serious trouble'.[5]

Portugal needed to prepare its African territories rapidly for independence to avert more violence and the United States stood ready to help. Dean Rusk requested that the new US position be communicated at the highest level of the regime. Burke Elbrick confessed to being 'jumpy' before seeing Salazar on 7 March 1961. But there were no histrionics on Salazar's part. Salazar was impassive as the new course was explained to him. When he spoke, he stated that he was not surprised by what he was hearing and, no doubt as the ambassador expected, was utterly unbending. He told Elbrick that it was 'manifestly impossible to be an ally of Portugal in Europe and an enemy in

Africa'. He would not allow Portugal to be influenced by the US, whose stance towards Africa was naive and dangerous. Elbrick was told that the Russians were 'attacking Portugal via Africa and it would appear that the Americans are ingeniously playing their game'.[6]

Perhaps Salazar was, in Elbrick's words, 'calm and very self-possessed' throughout the interview because he had inured himself to facing American capriciousness. A Portuguese diplomatic historian believes that Salazar's view of the Americans was permanently coloured by his dealings with their wartime president, F.D. Roosevelt. He was exasperated with FDR, who 'believed ingeniously that his intentions were well-meaning ... [but] had unfathomable ignorance of foreign sensitivities, especially those of small nations'.[7]

Roosevelt believed that the mid-Atlantic island chain of the Azores was defined by the Monroe doctrine as an American sphere of influence, and the Portuguese territory was almost seized by the Americans in 1941.[8] Towards the end of the war, the senior British diplomat Frank Roberts observed that Washington reveals 'a predilection to treat the Portuguese as people of no importance and to ignore the existence of the Anglo-Portuguese alliance'.[9]

The priority for Salazar was to keep America out of Portugal's internal affairs as much as possible and make sure it did not establish a permanent foothold on any portion of the national territory. His experience with US envoys only strengthened him in this view. That with George Kennan, who was acting minister in Lisbon in the middle of the war, was atypical. They were both conservative scholars who had entered public affairs. At one stage Kennan disarmingly mentioned to him that American inexperience at the highest levels of world politics meant it had something to learn from Portugal.[10]

Lincoln MacVeagh, a classical scholar, was in the post from 1948 to 1952 but he failed to empathise with Salazar. He wrote that Portugal is 'what we call, in modern terms, a fascist state, which is itself only a new name for the kind of state exemplified by ancient Rome in the scandalous days of the later Republic'.[11] The high point of his diplomacy was an agreement with Salazar that gave the US a military base on the Azores. The Lajes base became a centre of communications between the US and Europe, an air, sea and submarine vigilance post, as well as an air bridge in time of crisis.[12] The Americans would have preferred a long lease, but Salazar made sure it was a short one that had to be renewed every five years. This was a far-seeing move especially given that a base which steadily increased in importance for NATO as the Cold War intensified could be used as a bargaining tool against a disruptive US government.

Salazar showed his willingness to defy Washington as the US–Soviet crisis over Cuba was approaching boiling point in 1961. He turned down flat the US government request to install a radar installation on the other Portuguese island of Madeira, so as to improve detection of high-altitude nuclear tests conducted by the Soviet Union or China. He wrote in his own hand: 'We should not do anything, for now, that aggravates the United States ... But denying their requests will show our legitimate resentment and I think that, as far as they are concerned, it will encourage them to be prudent in their relations with us.'[13]

At the end of 1961, with Goa having been seized by India, the foreign minister, Franco Nogueira, summoned ambassador Elbrick to his office and warned him that if America was as unhelpful over this matter as it had already been over Angola, 'Portugal would be obliged to reconsider its relations with US and this would necessarily involve a complete change in status of those relations. He did not mention NATO relationship or Azores base, but there was no misunderstanding as to exact meaning of his declaration.'[14]

Salazar had been stung by the failure of the US to publicise its private view that it considered Goa to be an integral part of Portugal and that it was opposed to India acquiring the territory by force. A month before his invasion, Nehru had been received with much fanfare in the White House during a state visit in which Kennedy made no mention of the Goa question.[15]

George W. Ball, under-secretary of state in the early 1960s, tried to convince Salazar that the American position was not based on 'narrow self-interest but on an anxiety to preserve the values of our civilization'.[16] However, the Portuguese leader was usually withering about the American contribution to civilisation. Ronald Campbell, Britain's wartime ambassador in Lisbon, wrote that Salazar considered the Americans as 'nouveaux riches, followers of mammon, amoral in all respects' and totally incapable of 'grasping the intricate problems of Europe'.[17]

The Azores thus were vital in restraining what was seen as US bullying. Secretary of State Dean Rusk would spell this out to Kennedy on 12 June 1962: 'United States interest in retaining the Azores is the only lever by which the Portuguese can hope to obtain a modification of our African policy. They will attempt to use the lever to maximum advantage. It is expected that they will not press this advantage to the full immediately, but will maintain constant pressure down to the termination date of the Agreement and beyond in seeking to obtain modification of United States policy.'[18] The agreement was just months away from renewal. In an article written shortly before, influential US foreign policy adviser Dean Acheson had characterised the Azores as 'perhaps the single most important [set of bases] we have anywhere'.[19]

Salazar might have mellowed towards the United States if he had been regularly interacting with figures like Acheson and Kennan, whom he would have seen as possessing a 'European sensibility'. Instead, long before the 1961 crisis, there was distressing evidence that America had a casual approach to ties with Portugal. One of the more incisive ambassadors, James Bonbright, recalls the lack of interest that secretary of state John Foster Dulles had shown when briefed about Portugal before holding a meeting with its foreign minister in Washington in 1955. When Bonbright pointed out that the Azores was a sensitive issue, Dulles said, 'Why don't we just tell them that we'll pull out?' After he could get a word in edgeways, the ambassador said: 'Mr Secretary, you just say that to the foreign minister, and you will make Dr. Salazar the happiest man in Portugal.'[20]

Salazar declined to renew the agreement for military use of the Azores when it expired in January 1957. He made it clear to the US envoy, Bonbright, that the refusal stemmed from the US breaking with its European allies during the Suez crisis in order to advance the process of decolonisation. He told the ambassador that there were advantages in cooperating with his country when their interests converged but 'nobody should be left in any doubt that we cannot cooperate when our rights or interests run the risk of being destroyed by the very one that makes an appeal for our good will'.[21]

The embassy was not a senior diplomatic assignment. Evidence for this arises from the appointment of Robert Guggenheim as ambassador in 1953. He belonged to a major US financial dynasty and according to a junior diplomat in Portugal at that time, he created havoc during his tenure: 'He was the Mr. Harassment, chased the secretaries around, even very pallid old maid-looking secretaries ... In Lisbon he dropped a little coffee spoon down the bosom of the wife of the Foreign Minister, who was very beautiful, and said, "Excuse, madam, can I rescue that?" And that was when the cup overflowed, and they [the Portuguese] asked ... that he be removed.'[22]

Under Bonbright, the ambassador from 1955 to 1958, decorum was restored. 1958 would be the year in which a settlement was reached after complex and protracted negotiations over the fate of gold which the Nazi German authorities had paid to Portugal in exchange for wolfram and other militarily important materials. Much of the gold had been looted from private individuals by the Nazis. But Salazar was disinclined to hand over the large sums demanded by a 'Tripartite Gold Commission' set up by the Allied democracies to negotiate with neutrals who had traded with Germany. He insisted that the money had accrued to Portugal through normal commercial transactions. His obduracy meant that the sum demanded by the negotiators was whittled down. After threats to freeze Portuguese assets in the United States, the State Department, in 1951, agreed to settle the matter largely on Portuguese terms. From the following year, it was West Germany which was the lead negotiator and it agreed to reimburse Portugal almost in full for the assets eventually surrendered to the gold commission to compensate former owners.[23] Salazar's obduracy meant that Portugal ended up with the world's second-largest gold reserve in relation to a country's gross domestic product, an estimated 383 tons of gold bullion stored away in the Bank of Portugal.

Salazar's steady hand on the Portuguese tiller for much of the 1950s ensured that torpor often characterised ties with the US. A degree of stability was provided at the American Embassy by an enigmatic figure who enjoyed an unusually long posting in Portugal, from 1945 to 1964. This was Theodore (Ted) Xanthaky whom ambassador Bonbright described as 'quite invaluable', somebody 'who knew everybody in town, in society, or official positions'.[24] He seems to have been the unofficial manager of the embassy at times and, according to another diplomat, 'overshadowed the DCM [deputy chief of Mission] and the ambassador himself in many ways'. His contacts were invariably with supporters of the regime and he could not conceal his distress when, meeting Salazar in 1961, he was required to translate Kennedy's letter exhorting Portugal to give up its colonies.[25] Delgado railed against him, warning against the influence of that 'Nazi ... the counsellor of all the wretched ambassadors that the State Department has sent to Lisbon'.[26] Salazar bid him a personal farewell in 1964 when his mission came to an end.[27]

In a 1963 letter to a US official, Xanthaky would observe: 'Portugal's overseas holdings are enormously important to every Portuguese as a vestigial link with the glories of the past when Portugal was in every sense of the word a world power and a world leader. To us this may seem romantic and unrealistic, but I am not sure that it is so in terms of Portuguese psychology.'[28]

Given his closeness to regime supporters, Xanthaky would probably have known at least some of the estimated crowd of fifteen to twenty thousand Portuguese who staged a demonstration outside his embassy on 27 March 1961. It was a mainly middle-class affair with several deputies of the National Assembly among the crowd. Police cordons were pushed aside and windows broken as the crowd yelled slogans like 'America for the Indians' and 'Get out of the Azores'.[29] The next day the government expressed 'deep regret' but Marcello Mathias, the foreign minister, pointed out, somewhat disingenuously, that 'manifestations could not be prohibited per se particularly because the public feeling is running so high against the United States'.[30]

Many of the protesters would have been even more outraged if they had known that a coup was being hatched with US encouragement. The coup was deep in the planning stage when, at an official event commemorating the twelfth anniversary of NATO, the health minister gave the oration. Martins de Carvalho had previously been head of the NATO section in the foreign ministry and he proclaimed the failure of the transatlantic entity: thanks to US behaviour, chaos was being sown.[31]

Botelho Moniz, the mutinous defence minister, did not share this outlook. He had been for the reorientation of Portuguese military towards NATO and European defence since 1959. He may not have felt it a great loss that Salazar pressed, without success, for the integration of Portuguese Africa into NATO's scheme of geostrategic protection, which was limited to the area north of the Tropic of Cancer. On

17 February 1961, he had an extended lunch with Elbrick and the chief of the local CIA station, Fred Hubbard. Moniz was accompanied by his close aide, Major Carlos Viana de Lemos. He later recounted that his boss was open about the growing rift between Salazar and much of the military leadership. He pointed out that it centred on colonial policy with the military preferring 'a political solution that included administrative decentralization, progressive political autonomy, and increased foreign investment'.[32]

Elbrick reported directly to Dean Rusk about the evolving coup up to the day before it was due to unfold. At his superior's suggestion, he informed Moniz (ahead of Salazar) that the United States was planning to line up with the Soviet Union against Portugal in the upcoming United Nations Security Council resolution condemning Portuguese colonialism.[33] With the involvement of the top figure in US foreign policy in the plan to unseat Salazar, it was no surprise that CIA operatives in Lisbon were busy utilising their Portuguese connections to ensure that a regime favourable to US interests emerged.[34] Feeling exposed, US officials drew back when there were signs that the regime would not go quietly. On the eve of its collapse Elbrick refused Moniz's request to extend 100 per cent support to the coup.[35] It would have been disastrous for the US image if there had been resistance and America was seen to be implicated in unrest that could easily be viewed as a throwback to the era of revolts in the 1920s.

Interestingly, Salazar did not suggest to Washington that Elbrick should be recalled. Nor was pressure put on the local CIA head to leave (though the PIDE would bug his telephone during his remaining time in Portugal, having earlier been shown how to do so by the same CIA).[36] The US envoy would have been apprehensive at his choice of a new foreign minister. Marcello Mathias, the outgoing minister, had been a faithful interpreter of Salazar's outlook on the world. Upon assuming the post in 1958, he had told the US ambassador that it was his view that American policy had been largely responsible for many of the setbacks which the Western world had suffered since the last war.[37]

The courteous but firm nationalist Mathias would go on to be a novelist. His successor, Alberto Franco Nogueira, had gained early fame as a literary critic. But he would prove to be a redoubtable foe of the Americans, portrayed by admiring nationalists as a sturdy bull skilfully avoiding the rapier thrusts of the Yankee foe. He was a republican realist, a professional who had climbed his way to the top of the foreign ministry by impressing Salazar with his abilities. He had no political ties to the regime and symbolised those Portuguese (who included military dissidents and long-term foes of the Estado Novo) who responded to the call for reconciliation and unity in order to defend the Ultramar.

Nogueira soon made Portuguese diplomacy far more combative and positive about Portugal's rights in Africa.[38] He refused to believe the Americans were being sincere in their anti-colonial stance and told them so, from the president down. He saw the bid to drive Portugal from Africa as merely the latest in a cycle of attacks and criticisms directed at Portugal's colonial presence. According to Jaime Nogueira Pinto, the foreign minister 'belonged to a world shaped by the paradigm of Hobbes. The egoism of states shaped his outlook. States and their purpose were eternal while the ideologies imposed upon them were ephemeral and would pass. This anti-ideological realism even made him consider an alliance with the People's Republic of China.'[39]

He had at least one ally in the US foreign policy establishment, Dean Acheson. As soon as Kennedy's decision to back early independence for colonies like those of Portugal was made, the US secretary of state in the previous Democrat administration wrote to Kennedy:

> Mr President, you have just made a mistaken and dangerous decision that will have grave consequences for Portugal and the United States.
>
> Concerning Africa, the main need is not to push yet more people towards independence who do not know how to use it any better than the Congolese. The big and serious challenge is to prepare them, not just through simple haste, to confront an inevitable future.
>
> … Any ruler, soldier or lawyer knows that the road to disaster consists of fighting on the terrain chosen by your adversary.[40]

Since Nogueira saw America as behind a series of hostile actions against Portugal, he thought it natural to treat his American partners at NATO meetings, the United Nations and in bilateral meetings as near foes. Dean Rusk's deputy, George W. Ball, believed his demeanour and approach was similar to what could be expected from a Czech foreign minister.[41] 'Bitter and unreconstructed', 'a long and highly disturbing conversation', 'caustic' comments, were some of the words used by Elbrick about him recording early encounters.[42]

Nogueira's defiance was a weapon of the weak. He thought it was the only way a small country could hold its own against what he viewed as an undisciplined giant with few claims to moral strength. Often US officials were horrified by his obduracy and the hint of menace in his remarks. But they never ceased to pay him attention. Perhaps at no other time has a senior Portuguese figure ever enjoyed such close access to the White House, where he was received during the early stages of the Cuban Missile Crisis. The Americans wanted to see him because they knew the Azores would be a vital air bridge in time of crisis.

Briefing Nogueira in advance, Rusk told him, 'anything could happen.' Rusk then asked Nogueira to tell the president that the United States could have unrestricted access to the Azores should the crisis precipitate an outbreak of war. He replied that he could not grant the request without consulting Lisbon. 'The rarely impassioned Rusk' pressed him harder.

As José Freire Antunes has recounted, 'Franco Nogueira looked at the Secretary and … in his imperious and impassive manner, [he] … replied: "It is more than two years that we, the Portuguese, are living in [a] permanent [state] of emergency, and it does not seem that many of our allies are much disturbed by this fact."'[43]

Nogueira refused to let the Cuban crisis moderate his hostility to what he viewed as naked and unprovoked US aggression against Portugal. Elbrick reported back to Washington about another difficult meeting on 12 January 1962:

> Nogueira was in a very unreasonable frame of mind. He said he felt US was working against Portugal, that dialogue which had begun so promisingly between us last year had produced nothing, that US is trying to achieve economic domination of Africa by its present policies, and he would not be surprised if US were trying to bring about political change in Metropolitan Portugal. I rejected these statements emphatically and pointed to fact we had always expressed desire to be of help to Portugal in most difficult situation. Nogueira merely replied he could no longer give any credence to such assurances.[44]

The ambassador in Washington at that time was Teotónio Pereira. He had been indispensable in keeping wartime Spain neutral. But now he was ageing and soon to be in very poor health. Perhaps many years spent away from Portugal on diplomatic assignments meant that he was ill suited to the task of still incisively advancing an official Portuguese viewpoint. Robert Kennedy, US attorney general and brother of the president, saw him as the Old World antithesis of the young American proconsuls who planned to remake the world of the 1960s in a progressive American image.[45] The unfortunate Pereira was kept waiting months before he could present his ambassadorial credentials while the ambassador from India, a country allied to the Soviet Union, was able to see the president straight away.[46]

Certainly Nogueira soon became Salazar's right-hand man across the foreign policy field. Initially, his chief had had to struggle to persuade his closest advisers that the untried Nogueira was a good choice for foreign minister. But soon Salazar was deferring to him and appreciative of the fact that he supplied him with original ideas for the defence of the Ultramar.[47] He proceeded to open up to him about the problems of the regime and its future in ways he did not with any other minister. With Nogueira's wife, a highly cultured Portuguese-Chinese woman, Vera Machado Duarte Wang, whom Nogueira had met when he was stationed in Japan at the end of the 1940s, he developed a warm friendship and she accompanied the leader to various official events and also to musical concerts.

Nogueira's fierce defence of the Portuguese position gradually appeared to yield results. In a meeting in the Oval Office on 29 May 1963, Kennedy told him that his decision of 1961 to oppose Portugal at the United Nations had been 'precipitate'.[48] Already by the summer of 1962, the 'Africanists' whom Kennedy had recruited to develop his pro-nationalist views in Africa were losing ground. Their main figure was Adlai Stevenson, the Illinois lawyer who had twice been a candidate for the US presidency. As America's ambassador at the United Nations, he and Nogueira clashed and one encounter degenerated into a public argument on 31 July 1963. The president later 'went through the roof' when he heard about the row and contacts with the Portuguese were temporarily scaled down.[49] But increasingly the US began to pursue a two-track approach, which it was hoped would mollify Salazar while keeping the Angolan nationalists of Holden Roberto still on side.

'We are trading our Africa policy for a few acres of asphalt in the Atlantic,' J.K. Galbraith complained. In a reversal of policy, secret arms shipments first intended for the Angolan nationalists were rerouted to Salazar to use against them.[50] American military chiefs, along with Acheson, were, by now, successfully emphasising the importance of those acres of asphalt, the Azores, for the defence capabilities of the US.

Kennedy's crusading zeal was eroded not only by resistance within the policy establishment but also by the disappointing character of many of the new nationalist regimes in Africa. The unrestrained violence and chaos of the Congo proved not to be a showcase for independence. The Salazar regime itself had also shown unexpected staying power. Military unrest had abated. The regime had attempted with some success to place the defence of Portugal overseas above internal politics. Critics of the policy within the military were given responsible positions. Salazar claimed to welcome collaborators from all sides. There may have been student unrest in 1961 and 1962, with young people from regime families involved, but Salazar seemed capable of overriding opposition at home.

Nogueira and Kennedy had a cordial meeting in the White House fifteen days before the President's assassination on 22 November 1963.[51] Perhaps the chief indication that the Kennedy administration was prepared to treat Salazar's perspective on African matters increasingly seriously came with the visit of George W. Ball, the under-secretary of state, to Lisbon on 31 August 1963. The veteran diplomat was intent on trying to reduce Portuguese suspicions of American intentions towards them. A report of his meeting with Salazar conveys this impression strongly:

> The Under Secretary emphasized that the continent of Africa was only of marginal interest to the US as far as American national interests are concerned. We feel that commercial possibilities in Africa are limited and we have no large economic ambitions there. We have, however, taken an active interest in African affairs for fear that the continent might be subjected to communist penetration. He said he would like to emphasize again that of all the areas in the world Africa was the least important from the point of view of American national interests, but our role there must be viewed in the light of the East/West struggle. The Under Secretary recognized that the Portuguese Government adopts a different approach and has a long-standing vital interest in Africa after 500 years of occupation and a sense of mission in the area.

We felt it is very useful to define clearly our separate points of departure, emphasizing that everything we do in Africa is in the fundamental interest of the protection of the free world.[52]

Ball found Salazar sufficiently absorbing to devote much of a chapter in his memoirs to what became a series of meetings with him. He provided an interesting description of a dictator who was defying what were then seen as the ineluctable tides of history with a quiet determination:

> When I went to see him in 1963, he was very much in command and never hesitant to use his full powers. In manner and appearance he seemed more the professor than the archetypal dictator. Dapper in dress, slightly built and pale, he was formally courteous in an Old World way. Consistent with his style of frugality and simplicity, his office was sparsely furnished and he gave an impression of frailty and shyness quite out of character for a notorious 'strong man'.

> The end of the Lusitanian presence in Africa would ... precipitate an acute and prolonged economic depression ... If Portugal were to lose ... she would forfeit even the shadow of respect as a small but solvent power and would sink to the level of an Iberian Graustark.

> Dr Salazar was determined this would not happen. In spite of its limited resources, he insisted that Portugal was improving and extending education in its African provinces. Racial discrimination, he stated flatly, did not exist as in other parts of the White Redoubt ...[53]

Not normally eager to linger in conversation with US diplomats, Salazar made a strange request to George Ball at the end of the meeting. He asked him to make an unscheduled halt in Lisbon on his way back from a trip to Pakistan so that their deliberations could continue.

At the conclusion of the second round, Ball recalled: 'Dr Salazar made a request that violated established protocol. "I have found our conversation useful and interesting," he said, "but I would like to give you a more reasoned reply. When you get back to Washington would you please write me a letter setting forth in detail the position you have outlined in our conversations. Write it to me personally and I will send you a personal reply."'[54]

The correspondence duly ensued, causing Ball to reflect twenty years later: 'Even today the exchange is, I think, of interest, not merely because each letter was an honest, thoughtful effort to express a point of view. Even though those points of view could not be reconciled by our two governments, we still understood one another better.'[55]

Even that most vigilant of sentries, Franco Nogueira, admired Ball for trying to rise above the previously cliché-ridden approach of the Americans towards Portugal.[56] Perhaps in a bid to mend fences, the US even agreed to provide $55 million (through a financial agency) to construct the first bridge spanning the river Tagus. It would be completed in 1967 and named after Salazar (even though he opposed the decision taken by a majority of his ministers).[57] By now Kennedy's successor as president, Lyndon B. Johnson, was prepared to listen to voices like that of Acheson who argued the need for the US to support Portugal in Africa without worrying about the reaction of the Third World.[58] But Johnson had little interest in Africa. It meant that a plan in the mid-1960s for a gradual transition to African independence, named after the then US ambassador, Admiral George Anderson, foundered.[59] The incentive for Portugal was large amounts of US aid both to it and its African territories. 'African'-minded officials like Chester Bowles, US ambassador-at-large, had already pushed for Portugal to be showered with cash in order for 'healthy political change' to get under way. While this might have appealed to some in the Lisbon power structure, Salazar was implacably opposed.[60] It was a misreading of his outlook.

When it was reported to him that oil in large quantities had been discovered in Cabinda, his response to the excited official was 'Oh what a pity'.[61] The sudden arrival of oil wealth would only be disruptive for his carefully modulated system of conservative order.

Admiral Anderson, the former US chief of naval operations, had been sent to Lisbon when he fell out of favour in Washington. His deputy chief of mission, William L. Blue, related that one of his main tasks was to keep an eye on the ambassador.[62] Once again, it seemed, the American approach to ties with Portugal was messy and disorganized, which placed the Portuguese at an advantage when dealing with them.

While muscular and proactive in its engagement with the United States, Portuguese diplomacy was feline and supple in its approach to France. In 1958, with the establishment of the Fifth Republic under Charles de Gaulle, that country emerged from a long period of intense division, punctuated occasionally by sharp national humiliations, from occupation by Nazi Germany to defeat by Vietnamese anti-colonialists at Dien Bien Phu.

De Gaulle would press ahead with granting independence to Algeria and, on the surface, it looked as if he would be likely to endorse Kennedy's drive to encourage Salazar to get out of Africa. Indeed, on the eve of Kennedy paying an official three-day visit to France in May 1961, de Gaulle was alerted that his guest would like Angola to be a prominent topic in the discussions. According to the French ambassador to Washington, this was due to the belief that, more than any other Western political leader, he was capable of bringing Salazar into line.[63] Kennedy had respect for the French leader. But at talks he found de Gaulle absorbed with defending 'the egotistical interests of his nation', according to a biographer of Kennedy.[64]

Kennedy soon found that France was unwilling to back him. The United Nations, de Gaulle observed, was not a suitable forum for seeking to alter Portugal's African policies. He also warned of the consequences if a violent position was adopted towards Portugal. 'Nobody knows what would then occur,' he remarked. He did not rule out 'a revolution' or the emergence of a communist regime. Overall, he didn't consider that either of their two countries had any need of a communist state in the Iberian peninsula.[65] Salazar was informed by Marcello Mathias, his ambassador in Paris in November 1961, that maintaining 'public order in the Iberian peninsula was of sufficient concern to the French government that it would contemplate becoming involved in a counter-coup if things went badly wrong there. By now Paris had made it clear to Washington that there was no support for putting pressure on Portugal. De Gaulle would also defy any arms embargo and furnish Salazar with what was needed militarily to defend itself overseas.[66]

The Kennedy administration had thus discovered that de Gaulle would not be taking its lead from the main Western superpower. The general would extract France from the military wing of NATO, forcing it to remove its headquarters from Paris. Kennedy's stance towards Portugal is likely to have confirmed the dismissive opinion that de Gaulle held about American statecraft, especially with regard to Europe. Like Salazar, he wished to keep the Americans as far as possible out of his country's affairs. He regarded Africa as a French sphere of influence and felt it was appropriate to defend Portugal's continued role. Such backing probably emboldened Nogueira. If de Gaulle had learned about the extent of his defiance, he might have considered him a model pupil. On 10 July 1961, the Portuguese foreign minister bluntly informed Elbrick, the US ambassador, that Portugal would go to the bitter end in maintaining its overseas territories and said that a world war might result. When the ambassador asked whether Portugal was ready to drag the whole world down because of Angola, Nogueira replied in the affirmative, saying that as far as Portugal was concerned, Angola was much more important than Berlin.[67]

There were times when Salazar saw the duel with the Kennedy White House in very personal terms: On 18 February 1963, Nogueira noted in his diary that Salazar had remarked to him earlier that 'either the Americans succeed in killing me or else I die. Or alternatively they will face years of struggle in order to put me under.'[68]

Some years later in 1969, after he had been debilitated by a stroke, the anti-Americanism of Salazar still shone though. When he was given a seventy-minute interrogation by Dr Houston Merritt, an American neurological expert, the doctor may have been surprised at the answer he got when he asked Salazar: 'What do you think of President Johnson?'

'That he is a good man, [but] not enough. One must know in depth the history, the culture and the politics of Europe, of Asia and of Africa. The Presidents of the United States do not know them.'

Then, when asked by Merritt to move his legs as if to give a kick, Salazar joked, 'In truth, the United States have been receiving quite a few kicks. And they'll receive many more!'[69]

De Gaulle and Salazar were both patient and extremely stubborn men with inexhaustible supplies of self-belief. When receiving the credentials of a new Portuguese ambassador in 1960, de Gaulle remarked: 'Both the people of France and I personally respect the exemplary work he [Salazar] has carried out and continues to perform to the benefit of Portugal and the world.'[70]

US diplomacy ought to have anticipated that Portugal would not stand alone in resisting its anti-colonial drive and that in France it could find a formidable ally. Marcello Mathias who spent many years as Portugal's ambassador in Paris, was extremely well-connected in elite policy-making circles. This smooth and supple figure, completely integrated into French life, was a highly effective envoy. 'I have quit a city as agreeable as Paris to be a minister' was his doleful comment when he answered Salazar's request to be foreign minister for three years in 1958.[71]

Any memories of the wartime period when both Salazar and Petain, the leader of the puppet regime at Vichy, proclaimed themselves as the leaders of 'a national revolution', were conveniently overlooked. De Gaulle ensured that the war years and their discordant happenings were a taboo subject, to be ignored by the French media. So it would be incongruous for his regime to have dwelt on past controversial aspects of Salazar's regime.

Military cooperation gathered pace. Four French frigates and four submarines were purchased by Portugal on very advantageous terms. Thanks to ambassador Mathias's footwork, the French offered Lisbon credit for their naval purchases and payment was to be extended over a lengthy period.[72] Alouette helicopters were also sold to Portugal from 1962 onwards. According to one military expert, they were Portugal's most useful military acquisition.[73] In return, France was offered a tracking station on the Azores, something that was required after it launched its own nuclear programme in 1963, at exactly the time Lisbon was threatening to tear up American base rights on the island chain.[74]

In the second half of the 1960s, Salazar found the French government less willing to defy UN sanctions by selling arms. It was also the case that not all policy-makers approved the close ties with Portugal, especially figures in the diplomatic service.[75] More than once, Mathias remarked that Portugal only enjoyed these advantages because it was de Gaulle who ruled in France.[76]

The Portuguese regime also enjoyed close ties with the French secret services. They possessed an unusual degree of weight in a democratic regime and de Gaulle regarded them as an essential adjunct of his rule. In 1965 their alleged role in the kidnapping of the Moroccan opposition leader Mehdi Ben Barka generated a scandal which dragged on for years. This event would be paralleled by the role of the PIDE in the killing of Humberto Delgado in the same year.[77]

Beyond Portugal itself, France easily furnished the greatest number of published works sympathetic to Salazar and many of the ideas behind his regime.[78] Prominent among the authors were Henri Massis and Jacques Ploncard d'Assac. The trauma of France's retreat from empire and frequent domestic political crises provided the basis for national conservative and far-right movements to thrive. Salazar's image was boosted in these circles by his decision to remain in contact with Charles Maurras upon his imprisonment for wartime collaboration. At one stage, he sent the veteran ideologue of the French right a case of port to ease his detention. Maurras, in turn, wrote to him in 1951 when rumours swirled that he was about to step down. 'Stay! hang on!' Maurras entreated. Salazar read the letter to cabinet colleagues and said he wasn't quitting.[79]

What helped to make Salazar much better known in France was a book written about him by a French conservative-minded journalist. Christine Garnier was thirty-six when she managed to obtain an interview with Salazar in 1951. She assumed it would be her first and last meeting with him, but it wasn't to be. He seemed charmed by her frankness and verve and invited her to visit him at his country retreat. A book based on their conversations appeared in 1952 called *Vacances avec Salazar*. It sold well and was translated into several other major languages.[80] It is one of the few works to give an account of his life away from the cares of office in Lisbon.

Garnier was the pseudonym for Raymonde Germaine Cagin (1915–87), a former model in French fashion magazines who went on to be a journalist.[81] It is quite likely that someone with her alertness would not have overlooked the significance of the fact that the individual who took the photographs of Salazar together with her was a longstanding secret policeman, António Rosa Casaco. He was a talented photographer who exhibited internationally.[82] Salazar seems to have enjoyed closer ties with several senior figures in the PIDE than he did with members of the military. This is perhaps not unusual, as for much of the time the vigilance of the secret police was more essential for the survival of himself and his regime than senior soldiers were.

Much of the interest in Garnier's book stems from her description of Salazar's unostentatious life on his small estate in Vimieiro. She depicts a man who was dignified and reserved but who enjoyed close ties with the villagers who tended his vine-laden property. As water from nearby wells and fountains tinkled in the background, he confessed that he was a peasant at heart who never felt more at ease than when inspecting the soil. She drew him out on man's existence. He reiterated his conviction that the link between enjoying happiness and possessing wealth was a false one: 'The political idea which reduces a spiritual sense to riches undoubtedly can forge a splendid society but not a true civilisation. Civilisation, at least as I understand, has to ensure the predominance of spiritual power.'[83]

She failed to challenge him on the fact that he could have improved the material lot of millions of Portuguese without having to alter the system of economic relations. She did momentarily quiz him about his views on liberty but did not press him when he repeated his long-held conviction that electoral democracy was not equivalent to freedom.

Garnier was sceptical when Salazar stated his belief in the power of French renewal. Later he himself grew somewhat despondent as the Fourth Republic staggered towards collapse. In 1956, when offering negative views on European integration, he noted that some nations appeared to be tired of their existence as nation-states. The Portuguese leader was puzzled that France welcomed what he considered as national suicide.[84]

Empathy grew between the austere dictator and his French muse. Even Dona Maria, ever suspicious of feminine intrusion into Salazar's private world, was taken by Madame Garnier and behaved well towards her. The French journalist was already married and Dona Maria may have sensed that she would be a good influence on her master. After the book was completed, he sent money to Mathias in Paris and asked him to buy a suitable jewel and present it to the journalist on his behalf. 'There's no point in bothering about the cost as money has never been any use to me', he told the diplomat.[85]

There was inevitably plenty of rumour and speculation about how close the attachment was between the pair. She continued to visit Salazar into the 1960s. By this time France had re-emerged as a strong European force and it was the most favoured destination of Portuguese emigrants. An estimated 1,033,030 people left between 1960 and 1970. Most were from northern and central Portugal, from villages not unlike Vimieiro.[86] Unenthusiastic in many cases (if they were men) about doing military service in Africa and desperately seeking higher wages, many failed to share the bucolic view Salazar had about Portugal as a rural idyll.

14

THE FADING OF THE LIGHT, 1964–70

It would take several years before the impact upon the regime of the escape from captivity of Portugal's leading communist would make itself felt. On 3 January 1960 Álvaro Cunhal and six other important party members were able to break out of the supposedly impenetrable prison fortress of Peniche.[1] It was situated up the coast from Lisbon on a promontory jutting into the Atlantic. Their deliverance from the Estado Novo had been brought about by Jorge Alves, one of their guards, who had become disaffected after having been passed over for promotion. He was also a heavy drinker who had been boasting in bars about being prepared to spring Cunhal. The efficient system of informers which the PIDE, the secret police, had supposedly devised nationwide was moribund in a place where it was needed most. Cunhal eventually made his way to Moscow. The efficiency of the PCP's underground network was shown by its ability to also spirit Alves and his family away to Romania. But things did not go well for them. Alves's drinking got worse and he beat his wife. Cunhal was there often as Bucharest was the headquarters of the PCP-in-exile. Alves was bluntly told by him: 'my friend, unless you fall into line, we are going to take away your family.'[2] When there was no improvement in his behavior, this is what happened and he hanged himself in 1967.

The head of the PIDE, António Neves Graça, was removed after this major security lapse. After years spent in solitary confinement, Cunhal would have been emboldened to see the limitations of the force whose main job was to hunt down communists. As leader of the PCP, he was one of the world communists most loyal to Moscow. Unlike his Spanish counterpart, Santiago Carrillo, he supported the crushing by the Soviet Union of the 1968 'Prague Spring' in Czechoslovakia.[3] The Soviets, on their side, had made plenty of effort to try and incite revolt in Portuguese Africa. Nikita Khrushchev in 1956, at a momentous party congress where he denounced his predecessor Stalin for his crimes, had announced the opening of a new front in the struggle to topple the capitalist West. Henceforth, championing Third World nationalist movements in a bid to hasten the demise of European colonialism was to be a key Soviet objective.

At a tense meeting in Vienna with Kennedy on 3 June 1961, Khrushchev raised the Portuguese Empire with him. He stressed that the Soviet Union viewed the recent violence in Angola as a popular war against colonialists and he accused the US of supporting them despite Kennedy's efforts to show otherwise.[4] Cunhal was enthusiastically behind the Soviets in this regard. Unlike some on the left, he had no emotional attachment to the Ultramar. He did not see it as an extension of Portugal. He was a world revolutionary and a coldly efficient one at that. He instructed the party to give full backing to Soviet efforts to organize subversion in Portuguese Guiné, where conflict got under way in 1963. It was close to the former French colony in Guinea, in whose capital of Conakry the Soviets had established their headquarters for promoting unrest across Africa. Naturally, Angola, Portugal's largest territory, acquired a special importance. The PCP would help to set up the *Popular Movement for the Liberation of Angola* (MPLA), which would rule there for decades after independence was granted by the Portuguese in 1976.[5]

In Portugal itself the influence of the communists was growing. The PCP consolidated its presence in cultural circles. Many artists and writers fell under the PCP's sway. Thus, it was unusual for major figures to continue to identify with the regime as much as José de Almada Negreiros did. He was arguably the most strikingly versatile artistic figure produced by 20th-century Portugal. He was an artist, caricacturist, writer, choreographer and dancer. Of mixed race, he had been born in 1893 in São Tomé to a Portuguese father and a São Toméan mother. He collaborated with the greatest Portuguese writer of the modern era, Fernando Pessoa, launching the futurist magazine *Orpheu*. He also worked with the architect Pardal Monteiro, whose building commissions transformed parts of the Lisbon cityscape during the Estado Novo.[6] He was an avant-garde figure who happened also to identify with the regime. The nationalist dimension to some of his works is shown in the *azulejo* tiles he designed for the ferry terminals along the banks of the river Tagus in the late 1940s.[7] Towards the end of his life (he died in 1970), he sat in the Corporative Chamber, as the representative for fine arts.[8]

Almada Negreiros was a hugely talented figure, very experimental in outlook, who in most dictatorships of the right might have been expected to identify with its left-wing adversaries. He remained beyond the reach of the communists, but this was increasingly less true of others in various sensitive areas of national life. Long before Cunhal's prison escape, the PCP had infiltrated the state labour associations. In time, its representatives would be the ones negotiating with major private firms. It also made steady advances in the university world despite students and academics being drawn from the middle and upper-middle classes.

True to its distaste for actively mobilising support, the regime had never sought to seriously implant itself in Portugal's three universities. Perhaps it assumed that the conventional backgrounds of most students and their orientation towards future careers made such a precaution unnecessary. It did show vigilance in the face of communist agitation and was prepared to mete out tough punishment on occasion. One such moment led to the outbreak of unrest in the universities of Lisbon and Coimbra in 1962. The regime had attempted to curb the activities of student associations. The spark for protests was the prohibition of an annual Student Day.[9] On 9–11 May, 800 students barricaded themselves in the student refectory of Lisbon University. Several of their leaders would later spring to prominence in national politics, such as Jorge Sampãio, a two-term president of the country. The authorities arrested some of them. Student ranks in Lisbon were dominated by the offspring of functionaries in an expanding state.[10] It is not unlikely some of their parents were able to persuade the authorities to show mildness. The protests coincided with the removal of a hardline head of the PIDE, Homero de Matos. He had cracked down on Jehovah's Witnesses, and a leading communist, the artist and teacher José Dias Coelho, had been shot dead in a Lisbon street in December 1961 as the PIDE sought to detain him.[11]

The regime could do without such unwelcome publicity as the searchlight was increasingly beamed upon it from abroad. The resignation of the rector of Lisbon University Marcello Caetano, because university autonomy had been breached, had brought further unwanted attention. An ex-foreign minister, Paulo Cunha, succeeded him and managed to defuse the crisis.[12] A careful watch was kept on the PCP's university activities. By contrast, the rest of the far left was somewhat overlooked and it was from Trotskyite and Maoist groups that the main challenge to the regime would arise in its last years.[13]

Meanwhile, at Coimbra less disruption occurred. Many of the students originated from the small and medium bourgeoisie in the provinces. Among them, a nucleus of right-wing nationalist students was to be found. The rector, Guilherme Braga da Cruz, was a traditional monarchist who was prepared to resist what he saw as subversion.[14] In still conservative Oporto, the climate of revolt was hardly visible.

Calm at home was badly needed as the regime wrestled with what to do in Africa. For nearly two years after the outbreak of violence in Luanda, there would be no settled position. Initially, it appeared that Salazar might opt for eventual self-government for the African territories within a Lusitanian federal framework. For nearly a year he had thrown his weight behind the innovatory approach of the man whom he had appointed as minister for the Ultramar on 13 April 1961. Adriano Moreira had told him in the late 1950s that standing still in Portuguese Africa was not an option. An ill-prepared regime was poised to be thrown into its biggest battle, and only a process of autonomy could enable it to hold on in Africa.[15] Salazar consented to his proposal that the indigenous statute under which the African population enjoyed far less rights than Europeans be abolished. Africans would enjoy the same civil and economic rights as everyone else, and the hated forced labour system for agricultural work would be abolished. There was to be an eight-hour day, collective bargaining and a two-week paid holiday.[16] Moreira was unimpeded on this reformist course for around a year. He seemed to be a bold and energetic maverick similar to Duarte Pacheco, the architect of sweeping public works. But Africa was a far more crucial policy area than the alteration of the face of central Lisbon. Different vested interests felt threatened or emboldened by Moreira's actions.

There were white settlers prepared to share power with local Africans who viewed him favourably. There were richer whites who may have lost out economically when he made it harder for them to exploit Africans. And there was the military, which held the governorship of Angola and found itself answerable to an assertive civilian, still only forty years old. General Venâncio Deslandes was appointed civil governor of Angola at the same time Moreira became minister. The divergence between them proved vast. The governor rushed ahead with costly investment projects for Angola. Moreira told the uncooperative general that funding wasn't available. At Moreira's request the Council of Ministers removed him in October 1962. This led to a backlash from privileged colonials. The minister, Correia de Oliveira, had close economic ties with Africa and was integrationist in outlook. He was probably more influenced by the economic rationale for Portugal remaining in Africa than many of his colleagues. The loss of its territorial holdings there meant an export market valued in 1960 at £160 million as well as cheap imports of raw foodstuffs and industrial raw materials, which were far more expensive on the world market.[17]

More seriously, some in the military viewed the sacking of Deslandes as a humiliation for the armed forces. The looming conflicts in Africa provided it with an enlarged national role and greater access to resources.[18] The toll on morale and stamina would take some time before it became a significant factor in shaping the military outlook.

Neither the Angolan whites nor the military had identical views on how to proceed in Africa. But Moreira may not have assisted his cause by revealing his own ambitions at the time. Probably his closest ally in the government then was Franco Nogueira, who remarked to me in October 1979: 'Power went to his head. He made very outspoken statements which he thought Salazar did not get to hear. But he did. Salazar used to say: "Why is he doing this. He only has to wait."'[19]

Later, a well-connected historian of the regime claimed that Moreira had been urging that a post of vice-president of the Council be created, charged with coordinating all public services at the national level, one that would have confined Salazar's influence to foreign policy.[20]

At no other time had as many articles about the state of the Salazar regime appeared in the foreign press. The political weekly the *New Statesman* of London described an atmosphere of feverish plotting in which ambitious civilians and soldiers, ultras and careerists, looked for the best moment to displace Salazar.[21]

Salazar may have feared that it was the nationalist officers in the military who would be the ones to oust him. They were more prominent than before as the army was now waging a war in what would soon be three theatres. Salazar summoned Moreira to a meeting early in December 1961. Moreira later related in a memoir what he claimed had transpired between them:

> [Salazar said:] 'When I invited you to the government, I said you could rely on my support and I think I fulfilled that promise.'
>
> I said: 'you did' ...
>
> Then his voice rose: 'Right now, the reaction against the reforms is so fierce that I'm not sure I can continue as President of the Council and this requires me to alter the policy.'
>
> And I said, spontaneously: 'Your Excellency, You'll have to change the minister.' ...
>
> Dr Salazar was very well-mannered and he accompanied me downstairs to the door.
>
> Almost there he said: 'Just one thing, Prof. Moreira, can we speak about this again in a week?'
>
> I responded: 'You will have to speak with the next minister.'
>
> And he: 'Who can I find to be minister?'
>
> 'To make reforms, I can't help you, but for a good administrator, consult the list of counsellors of the Council of the Ultramar and in each place there will be someone honest.'[22]

Salazar did not undo any of Moreira's policies and the assertive minister did not break with the regime. Much later, he observed, Salazar's 'unique intelligence remained but he was unable to summon up the will to resist the pressures bearing down on him'.[23]

It seems just to conclude that Salazar lacked the energy and resolve to try a new approach in order to ensure that Portugal remained a Euro-African concept. It may be worth briefly comparing his stance with that of Carmona, who, at the start of the 1930s already the pillar of the authoritarian regime, was nevertheless ready to allow a civilian, the younger Salazar, to dissolve the military dictatorship and give it a strikingly new form. Salazar, by the 1960s, may have grown too introspective to trust Adriano Moreira's judgement. Arguably, Moreira was far less skilful than Salazar had been in successfully traversing the factionalised world of Portuguese politics.

Perhaps, also, Salazar was simply too old to shed his paternalistic and at times racist approach to empire and embrace the ideas of Moreira based around a multiracial commonwealth. An incident which showed how blinkered he could still be occurred in 1964 when Jorge Jardim brought Pombeiro de Sousa, a Portuguese long resident in Blantyre, the capital of newly independent Malawi, to see him. Jardim hoped to persuade Salazar to cultivate Malawi and its leader, Dr Hastings Banda, in order to reduce the guerrilla threat which had just started up in neighbouring Mozambique. But the meeting did not go well, with Salazar referring on several occasions to 'little black folk'.

Jardim's friend eventually interrupted: 'Excuse me, Mr President, but there are black people who are as capable as, if not more so than, whites.'

Showing impatience, Salazar said: 'Don't you have an aeroplane to catch?'

'I was almost ordered out of the room,' his visitor recalled. At the same encounter, Jardim, when asked by Salazar what Banda was like, made the lapidary remark: 'Exactly like you, Your Excellency, except that he is black.'[24]

Jardim was credited with turning Banda's 'initially hardline views on settler colonialism in southern Africa into accommodation and cooperation'.[25] Persuasive and astute, Jardim ensured through his ties with its durable leader that strategically placed Malawi was not used as a launching pad for attacks on the Portuguese by Frelimo, the main guerrilla force in Mozambique.

The outbreak of fighting in Mozambique in 1964 was soon followed by an acute crisis in neighbouring Rhodesia, which put Portugal on a collision course with Britain, nominally in charge of the colony. Salazar had long concluded that Britain was hurtling off in a different orbit as it shed its imperial role. Under Harold Macmillan, prime minister from 1957 to 1963, much of the elite began to veer towards a European federalist outlook. Macmillan and some of his leading advisers have been described as 'part of an intellectual tradition that saw the salvation of the world in some form of world government based on regional federations'.[26]

However, Macmillan's successors soon found that withdrawing rapidly from Africa, never mind relegating Britain's Commonwealth ties, was complicated. The sizeable white minority in Rhodesia offered implacable resistance to London's plan for a rapid transition to majority rule. Under Ian Smith, the colony veered towards a declaration of independence in defiance of London. Portugal was in no mood to be accommodating to its oldest ally. At a NATO meeting in 1962, the British foreign minister, Lord Home, failed to talk Nogueira into scaling down the Anglo-Portuguese alliance to NATO defence matters.[27] Britain was already voting against Portugal at the United Nations, and orders for military equipment being submitted to British firms were being overruled by the government.[28]

Smith was urged to adopt a hardline approach towards Britain when he and Salazar met in September 1964. Perhaps dwelling on some of the recent experiences he had had with Britain, the Portuguese leader told Smith that if he was trusting, he would be double-crossed by London.[29] It may well have been a conclusion the laconic wartime fighter pilot in the British RAF had already come to. He harboured deep distrust of the desk-bound bureaucrats in London's Whitehall and of Harold Wilson, British prime minister during the first phase of the Rhodesia crisis. By contrast he had nothing but praise for the seventy-five-year-old Salazar, whom he described as one of the most remarkable men he had ever met. He wrote:

> his whole face displayed character and he spoke quietly and in measured tones ... everything about him depicted modesty, that characteristic which is probably the most important ingredient of a civilised man ... I found the simplicity, sincerity and determination of the man tremendously impressive, and the meeting will remain with me as an unforgettable experience. In my estimation, he was a man of great honesty and dedication who could be relied on to stand by his word. Sadly for us, he was not a young man, and time eventually caught up with him. Had he stayed on for an extra decade, Rhodesia would have survived.[30]

Common concerns about Soviet involvement in southern Africa, and the apparent apathy of Britain and America in the face of this geopolitical démarche, helped to strengthen the budding alliance. Smith was informed by Salazar that if he intended to defy Britain and declare independence, he would give him maximum support.[31] The port of Beira in Mozambique was a vital transit area for the transport of goods to Rhodesia, more accessible to the outside world than South Africa was. Portugal showed its commitment by allowing the Rhodesian rebels to open an unofficial diplomatic mission in Lisbon in mid-1965. It included military and intelligence attachés, and staff were granted all the privileges formally enjoyed by diplomats.

A few days after the declaration of Rhodesian independence on 11 November 1965, Salazar told Nogueira that the sanctions which Britain was going to impose on Rhodesia needed to be defied by Portugal. If the Smith regime failed to survive, it could have 'tragic consequences for the Portuguese position in Africa'.[32] Accordingly, Portugal attempted to foil the British blockade of the Mozambique Channel that had been imposed to prevent oil and other goods destined for Rhodesia being landed at Beira. It reinforced the military defences of the city in case of an attack by its formal ally.[33] However, both sides did not push for confrontation. Salazar thought it unlikely that Britain would turn on Portugal in the midst of the Cold War and because of the strategic importance of its NATO bases. He referred to a letter from Harold Wilson at the height of the crisis as 'threatening ... and an insult to the intelligence'.[34] In the end, British efforts to bring Rhodesia to heel with sanctions failed, and the willingness of Salazar to take a gamble on Rhodesia paid off, at least while he was still in charge.

There is no sign that Salazar developed any broader antipathy towards Britain as a result of growing apart from its policy-making elite. He may have been aware that Smith was held in high regard by many in Britain who did not decry its past imperial role. There were many such people resident in Portugal, middle-class Britons in the newly developing tourist areas of the Algarve as well as people involved with the port wine industry in the Douro valley. Salazar remained on the warmest of terms with several generations of the Gartons, an Anglo-Portuguese family who were domiciled in Madeira. From there Mrs Christiana (Cary) Garton regularly sent him orchids and birds of paradise to brighten up his spartan official dwelling. Politics rarely if ever entered into the correspondence that flowed between them. They were a solid middle-class British-orientated family whose domestic tastes and interests coincided with some of Salazar's own. During the last thirty months of his premiership, Cary Garton was his guest for Sunday lunch on no less than eighty occasions.[35] This durable friendship broadened the austere Salazar's social window on the world.[36]

Salazar's soulmate on foreign matters, Franco Nogueira, also had durable ties with Britain. After diplomatic pressure secured his release in May 1975 following eight months in a revolutionary jail, he moved to London and told an interviewer: 'I've known London for a long time, a place where I exercised official duties. I have numerous English friends and the English are a people whom I admire.'[37]

But with Franco next door in Spain, Salazar had little genuine rapport. Their final meeting in 1963 took place as Spain showed it lacked any real interest in defying Third World nationalism. Salazar, already alarmed by signs of liberalisation, concluded that Franco had ceased to be a useful partner in the struggle that he was waging on the world stage to try to maintain Portugal 'one and indivisible, from Minho to Timor'.[38]

The veteran Belgian politician André de Staercke drew a distinction between the two Iberian strongmen and suggested that their political relationship was purely transactional: 'He disliked Franco who was in sharp contrast to him: one was an amateur, the other was a technician; one was boastful, the other modest; one had sacrificed a nation for the sake of prestige politics, the other had shelved his prestige for the prosperity of the nation. Salazar lacked grandeur but was great; he was strong without being forceful; he was what he was without needing to project himself. He paid his dues to Christianity by how he acted. Franco embarrassed himself with his claims; Salazar made you forget he was a dictator; Franco reinforced the traits already present in the caricature through an unacceptably arbitrary display of power …'[39]

Franco left a stronger and more adaptable authoritarian regime where the succession question was not left hanging in the air, as it would be in Portugal. He also shed much of his reactionary baggage, which included aversion to Freemasonry and anti-Americanism. It is impossible to imagine Salazar sitting down on occasional evenings to enjoy a film set in the American 'Wild West' but this was one of Franco's favourite pastimes.[40]

Unlike Franco, who developed Parkinson's disease in the 1960s, Salazar remained free of any debilitating illness. But he was increasingly frail physically. In March 1964, he experienced one of several bouts of pneumonia which had laid him low already in 1959 and 1961, but the efficient and devoted care he received from Dona Maria meant that he pulled through. Under her watchful supervision, he kept to a brisk routine well into the 1960s. His physician for many decades, Dr Eduardo Coelho, believed that abiding by a habitual schedule explained why he retained considerable stamina for public affairs long after most people had retired.[41]

He was another who believed Don Maria played a major role in extending his years in power: 'She carried out an exceptional role in his life. Intelligent, discreet, with much common sense, she "divined" the likes of the chief and followed his steps … At the end of each day, she listened to the things that troubled him and calmed his spirits with phrases like "it doesn't matter", "don't let it get to you". She knew when to vanish into the background.'[42]

It is worthy of note that a ruler often characterised as a pro-clerical figure had no religious confidants in later years. His religiosity was not a crucial element in his approach to government. Spain's Franco saw his rule shaped by divine guidance and providence. His residence (admittedly far more palatial than either of the two used by Salazar) would include no fewer than ten different chapels, oratories and altars.[43]

Nogueira observed that his chief's pastimes were now limited to reading old Portuguese authors and the classics.[44] To his doctor he remarked that his reading 'verified that man was always the same in every epoch'.[45] He worried about society becoming detached from its Christian moorings. These views may have been strengthened by encounters he had with Otto von Habsburg and the historian Arnold Toynbee, whom he hosted in Lisbon in 1960. The son of the last Habsburg emperor (and later a member of the European Parliament) was an outspoken defender of Salazar's African policy. In 1965 he warned that 'China with its population of more than seven hundred millions sees in Africa, with its riches and sparsely inhabited regions, an ideal lebensraum for an excess population'.[46]

In the experimental 1960s, when boundaries were being swept aside on different fronts, few philosophers were now to be found reflecting

Salazar's conservative Christian perspective. The Russian dissident Alexander Solzhenitsyn would only become a figure of standing in the West after being released from a Soviet gulag in 1974. The Canadian philosopher Jordan Peterson, writing in 2019, echoed the belief of Salazar and other religious conservatives that human beings required a spiritual dimension in order to fulfil themselves and foster stable societies: 'There must have been some purpose in the universe having brought forth humanity, since if humanity's origin is purposeless then so is its existence and there is no basis for judging any action as right or wrong in any objective sense.'[47]

This unabashed traditionalist was seen as an advocate of narrow patriarchy in many quarters, though Salazar was perhaps a far too distant figure for any critic to make a direct parallel with him. Anyone familiar with the chaotic state of 1920s Portugal, where a century of poorly applied liberalism had helped to produce an unhappy, divided and dysfunctional polity, might have found echoes in the way Peterson described the Western world as it approached the 2020s.

Salazar never ceased to be concerned that the Catholic Church was prepared to make its peace with the new liberalism of the West even as secular progressives advanced ever more radical proposals for reordering society. In 1960 he criticised the young priests 'who go to Rome to study and return with the mad intention of mixing in politics'.[48] Relations were poor with the Portuguese church as it produced a growing number of malcontents who would challenge his regime, some of them playing prominent roles in the post-1974 revolution. The Vatican Council of 1962–5 revealed to a startled world that conservative instincts were in retreat at the summit of the church, but it may not have been such a surprise to Salazar, long aware of some of its failings.

The English novelist Evelyn Waugh was one of the most outspoken critics of the new progressive departure. He criticised the alterations in Catholic worship and the emphasis on vernacular languages over Latin. Salazar had acted as a sacristan at weekly Mass well into adulthood and he may have felt the changes to the Mass were jarring.[49] On the other hand, the replacement of Latin by Portuguese in the liturgy undoubtedly made it easier to diffuse Portuguese culture in the Ultramar.

Cardinal Fernando Cento, for many years papal nuncio in Portugal, has been described as someone who offered discreet encouragement to liberal Catholics.[50] The outbreak of fighting in the colonies placed individual Catholics and some elites in opposition to the regime's colonial policies.[51] Salazar warned the church more than once about the consequences if it disregarded article 2 of the 1940 Concordat, which obliged it to keep its distance from politics.

The appeal of Catholicism for a lifelong traditionalist like Salazar was its ability to transmit in an unbroken line a faith restraining some of mankind's worst instincts. He could be forgiven for fearing that a recasting of the church in a whole new progressive direction would harm his regime. In 1964, he told Franco Nogueira that the Apostolic nuncio ought to be bluntly informed that 'I hope to die before a visit is made by a Pope who has so aggravated my country.' He insisted to the foreign minister: 'As long as I live he won't come here. He is a foreign citizen whom we won't allow in because he doesn't conform to our tastes.'[52] Eventually, his resistance weakened and he was welcoming but somewhat distant when Pope Paul VI came to visit on the fiftieth anniversary of the apparition of Our Lady at Fátima. Photographs showed little cordiality and Salazar was careful not to be deferential. Soon after, in September 1967, when news reached him that the Pope had offered to mediate in Vietnam, Salazar mordantly remarked: 'I think the Pope talks too much, intervenes too much, delivers too many lectures. Nothing good can come of this.'[53]

In his twilight years, Salazar was determined not to adapt to the ascendant humanistic outlook of what to him was a shallow and overly materialistic world. Permanently installed in Lisbon, he remained quite unreconciled to urban life. He was determined to impede rapid modernisation because he believed 'urban life and the predominance of large industry will rapidly make such a disorganized population into a turbulent mass, envious, and always prone to revolt.'[54]

But the shift of population from the interior to the more built-up coastal centres of Portugal began during his time in charge and has never ceased since. He was unwilling to release the resources that might have slowed down the exodus from the countryside. Ricardo de Faria Blanc, his sub-secretary of state for the Treasury, told the story about the fate of his scheme for rural improvements in 1966. As part of a wider development scheme, he proposed a tripling of the expenditure already devoted to the interior. He arrived at Salazar's office keen to lay out his plan, only to encounter a very unenthusiastic political master. Part of the conversation went as follows:

Salazar: 'Where are you from?'

Faria Blanc: 'Azeitão, two steps from here.'

Salazar: 'I see. Well you don't have land and you don't know the interior of Portugal. The people there are wedded to their traditions ... If there is an abrupt arrival of progress, it will disturb the natural rhythm of life ...'[55]

In vain the sub-secretary tried to argue back, but Salazar had made up his mind about the need for his Portugal of the interior to be sheltered from modernity for some time longer. This display of irascibility is hardly surprising in the face of unsettling developments on all sides. He showed no sadness when he was informed in 1964 that a past foe, India's Jawaharlal Nehru, was dead. He replied to Nogueira: 'Well, politically he was dead for a long time already. Thank you for telling me.'[56]

It remains an open question how he really felt upon hearing the news in 1965 that his most troublesome internal foe, Humberto Delgado, had been found dead. His body had been discovered just across the frontier in Spain. He had been murdered on 13 February 1965 in an operation headed by Inspector António Rosa Casaco (well known to Salazar) and four other PIDE operatives. In 1981 a military tribunal found Casaco guilty of the deed and he was sentenced to eight years in prison. Three of the others were found to be accessories and received lesser sentences. But, living abroad, Casaco never served his punishment and, in 2001, the Supreme Tribunal of Justice decided to annul the case and the international arrest warrant for Casaco was lifted. He duly returned to Portugal, dying aged ninety-one, in the Lisbon area in 2005.[57]

The Spanish legal authorities were prepared to investigate the murder initially, but when Lisbon refused to cooperate it fizzled out.[58] Salazar's tactics were to retreat into silence. With elections for the National Assembly approaching, he tried to appear imperturbable. In a speech he referred to long years of close collaboration with Delgado, which contributed to personal regard. Salazar thought that his time in America had been disorientating, causing him to transport its political customs to Portugal 'where they collide with our traditions of hierarchy, restraint and dignity of power'. His 1958 campaign showed him to be 'a genius of agitation' but he did not represent a true danger 'in this calm land of placid habits'.[59]

This view was meant for external consumption, but in private Salazar was much gloomier. Delgado may have ended up an isolated figure who posed a diminishing threat to the regime, but he had exposed a depressing fact: 'Just look at the result when a country caves in to an adventurer. Change can be justified politically but not in this manner.'[60]

He undoubtedly regarded Delgado as a criminal who posed a threat to the state. Fernando Silva Pais, the head of the PIDE during the final twelve years of its existence, claimed to have written to Salazar in 1963 warning about Delgado's use of an opposition movement, the Patriotic Action Juntas, that was being allowed to operate out of Algiers by the regime of Ahmed Ben Bella.[61] But it is difficult to be sure of the veracity of actions taken or recommended, as much official documentation concerning the Delgado affair seems to have been destroyed.

A violent move against his bitterest foe still seemed completely out of character. Premeditated killing was not Salazar's style. According to some of his closest colleagues, upon hearing the news he is supposed to have responded: 'It's a bother and it's going to remain a bother. Delgado was only of use to us alive because he was an instrument of division and disarray in the opposition.'[62] However, he shielded the PIDE agents from punishment.[63] Perhaps he was confident that with East–West tensions still alarmingly high, the unsavoury killing of his most high-profile opponent would soon be forgotten. This turned out to be the case. There was little of the international uproar that greeted Franco's execution of the top underground communist leader, Julián Grimau, who was executed in 1963 despite direct appeals to Franco for clemency from the leaders of Britain and the Soviet Union.[64]

Nevertheless, Delgado's murder was a lawless act of the kind later associated with the regime of Vladimir Putin in Russia. It showed the regime's inability to manage the use of repression as effectively as it had done in the past, and it is perhaps the principal event during its lifetime which defenders of the regime have most difficulty in explaining away.

What can be viewed as the regime's gross mishandling of Delgado's challenge can be contrasted with the manner in which Franco next door steadily boosted his reputation as the end of his span in power approached. Initially, he had been viewed as 'a fascist beast', but memories of the bloodletting of the civil war faded except in European left-wing circles. With Spain outside NATO, he nevertheless cooperated more wholeheartedly with the US than Salazar did. He was at ease with American military and civilian figures in a way that Salazar usually was not. Without major colonial holdings Spain was not a target for anti-imperialist onslaughts in the media or at the United Nations. His ministers were increasingly technocratic figures rather than ideological holdovers from the civil war. The Spanish economy developed far more rapidly and the middle class grew faster than in Portugal. Dictatorial Spain appeared to many less anachronistic than Portugal by the 1960s despite the grim origins of the regime. Franco arguably established much smoother long-term relations with his armed forces and the church than Salazar would do in Portugal.

The counterpart to Portugal's colonial troubles was growing ethnic unrest among Spain's historic regions, above all the Basque country. But this festering problem caused far fewer problems on the international stage than the war in the Ultramar did for the Estado Novo.

The regime's image was further tarnished in 1967 with the unfolding of what became known as the Ballet Rose scandal, when a number of people in high society, including the economy minister, José Correia de Oliveira, were implicated in a prostitution racket involving young girls. The case was publicised in the London *Sunday Telegraph* on 10 December 1967 and three days later the opposition lawyer Mário Soares was arrested, accused of disseminating false information abroad liable to prejudice the good name of the country.[65] Divisions within the regime arose over how it should be handled. João Antunes Varela, the minister for justice, pushed for full disclosure and the punishment of those involved. He was a puritanical figure, but Salazar did not share his zeal. Accordingly, the investigations were suspended when they had reached quite an advanced stage.[66] Soares was packed off to exile in São Tomé (though he claimed not to have been the source of the leak). However, the justice minister quit soon after in protest at the investigation being blocked.

Costa Brochado, who gave strong personal loyalty to Salazar but was increasingly dismissive about the regime, persistently warned him during his final decade in charge that it was slipping from his grasp. With

Salazar no longer taking much of a role in filling positions, he was warned that opportunists who were reluctant to defend the regime when the chips were down increasingly prevailed in many sectors. He recounted how he confronted Salazar about it in 1960: 'We talked for two hours about the state of the regime, I having spelled out that Salazar was only living on accumulated prestige. That day I uttered things that perhaps had never been said to his face before: "Your Excellency, you found them expensive suits, restored their shrunken wealth, arranged well-remunerated posts in the administration, handed to them key political positions, and allowed them to consort with the men of money."'[67]

Long ago Salazar had chosen to keep his distance from the Lisbon bourgeoisie. He feared that the personal independence which he prized might be compromised if he was drawn into a world of petty intrigue. Marriage had been in the air in the mid-1940s when he took Carolina de Assesca, an aristocratic widow, to social gatherings, but as soon as the foreign press picked up the scent, he abruptly stopped seeing her.

In 1966, when Brochado sent him a congratulatory message after Salazar had delivered his final public speech, he remarked: for many 'it will appear that Your Excellency was speaking in a foreign language to people from another hemisphere.'[68]

There are conflicting views about the degree of control that Salazar exercised in his very last years. One authoritative source believes an increasingly fractious cabinet in 1967–8 shows that Salazar was losing his grip.[69] His authority was still most apparent in the area of foreign policy, which is what diplomats in the major embassies mainly reported about. In Nogueira he had someone who shared and reinforced his outlook on Portugal in Africa. He claims to have frequently been consulted by Salazar over the future and who might succeed him.[70] His views are noticeable in Salazar's last speech, given in Braga on the fortieth anniversary of the 1926 revolt:

> We live in a critical moment … in the history of the world. Everything is in crisis or subject to criticism—morality, religion, freedom of men, social organization, the interventionist extension of the State, economic regimes, the Nation itself and the advantages of its independence or integration with others for the formation of large economic and political spaces. The very notion of homeland is discussed in Europe. Revolutions such as the Soviet have continued the revolutions behind

the Reformation and the French Revolution in the realm of facts and philosophy, and, like all great movements possessing their initial force, tend to spread and dominate the world by poisoning us with visions and principles that are far from performing in their domains of origin. The purest spirits are uneasy, they are disturbed, they do not know how to orient themselves and, full of anguish, repeat Pilate's question to Christ himself: 'what is the truth?'[71]

In that year Salazar was told by António Castro Fernandes, the head of the National Union (UN), that it had proven impossible to organise a conference, after a decade without any formal gathering of the 'national front', because of massive lack of interest.[72] It was easy to detect an active clientele in Portugal eager to dispense the fruits of patronage, but it was harder to spot an authentic political class able to debate problems and plan for their resolution. But instead of a mood of crisis, there was torpor and a sense that the country was waiting for an interminably long order to end. At the same time, there was solid economic growth in Portugal and also in Angola and Mozambique, and militarily the situation would not be critical in any of the military theatres until the end of the 1960s. Indeed between 1961 and 1974, the total of 8,290 combatant deaths in Portuguese Africa was less than the total of fatal road accidents in Portugal (9,694 deaths) for the period 1990–4.[73] But military impatience with the war in Africa existed not far below the surface. In February 1965 Nogueira received a letter from General Deslandes in which it was proposed that Portugal withdraw to a few strategic colonial areas and grant independence to the rest.[74]

Contrary to what would prove to be the case, Salazar believed that Spain would face terrible problems after Franco went while the succession was likely to proceed smoothly in Portugal: 'the President will appoint a successor and that will be that', he told Nogueira in 1964.[75] Among a contrasting ensemble of confidants, helpers and advisers, Nogueira stood out as indispensable. Mathias in Paris was the diplomat who enjoyed most standing. Jorge Jardim was a peripatetic figure, seeking to forestall the guerrilla threat by ingenious counter-measures.

Some attention should also be paid to a curious figure who was easily overlooked but who revealed the flexible side of an apparently granite-like power structure. This was Cecilia Pereira de Carvalho, wife of Luís Supico Pinto, and known as 'Cilinha'. She flouted the rule that women ought to remain out of public life and got backing from her husband and from Salazar. She hailed from an aristocratic family with philanthropic inclinations and, unable to bear children, she decided to devote her life to caring for the welfare of the troops in Africa, of whom there were over 100,000 at the height of the conflict. To this end she set up the National Feminine Movement in May 1961.[76] She turned into a kind of female Robin Hood making innumerable trips to Africa and going out on patrol with soldiers. It is likely that not a few officers regarded her as a pest, but she had the ear of Salazar. He liked her directness and knew that, just like him, she was tenacious in defence of the Ultramar. She was able to have brutal commanders reprimanded and unblock shortages of life-protecting equipment and medical supplies. She was aged fifty-two when she returned from her last morale-boosting trip to Guinea-Bissau in early April 1974. By now, Salazar was gone, removed by an illness that struck as suddenly as the arrival of the regime's own end on 25 April 1974.

It was Portuguese Guiné which posed the biggest military headache for the Portuguese. Its complex marshy coastline riddled with numerous waterways and inlets would turn it into a nerve centre for the shipment of hard drugs to Europe in the future. But in the late 1960s this challenging geography enabled the PAIGC (led by Amílcar Cabral until his assassination in 1971) to mount a strong challenge to the Portuguese presence. General António de Spínola offered to become its governor. He came from a pro-regime family and had, in the past, been unafraid to offer Salazar views that combined flattery with candour. In May 1968, shortly before taking up his post, he took the opportunity to propound his thesis that territorial unity ought to be replaced by a new organising concept for the Ultramar—the solidarity of the Portuguese space. Five years later, he would set out this view in a book which would have profound consequences. Salazar heard him out and afterwards remarked to collaborators: 'Let's hope that local realities and his responsibilities make the governor realise that the world doesn't have room for his ideas, otherwise we have trouble.'[77]

May 1968 was the month in which strongman rule in France was challenged by protests which shook de Gaulle's regime to the core. Salazar was bound to be despondent. It was France at the start of the century which had provided an intellectual framework for Salazar's own conservatism. He viewed de Gaulle as a man who had partly restored political authority in Europe as well as being his firmest European ally. In a troubled frame of mind he wrote to Caetano on 6 June: 'The world is raving mad. The masses stumble into anarchy with fierce dictatorship being the sure outcome, and their leaders reckon that they can defend the people's best asset—order—with their liberalism.'[78]

In July, the American ambassador, William Tapley Bennett, underscored the mood of anxiety that gripped many within the regime: 'This country was badly shaken by the events in France in May. It was suddenly and starkly clear at various levels of Portuguese society how easily a strong-man system could be brought to the brink of revolution. Portugal is of course not France. It is presumably easier to hold down the lid in a country like this one, with a largely illiterate and unorganized people under a determined regime served by a pervasive police apparatus and a strictly controlled press.'[79]

He reported to Washington that earlier in July a delegation from the Brazilian government had found Salazar 'active and exercising his old charm and good humor but showing definite slow-down signs as regards physical vigor'. There was a definite 'end of an era' feeling, according to a well-disposed US envoy. But, in a land where strikes remained forbidden, he described the handling of a pay dispute on Lisbon's public transportation system, drawing the conclusion that it showed that the dictator still possessed his legendary acumen. There was 'a "folded arms" non-strike on Lisbon's public transportation system, when service was not interfered with while conductors simply refused to accept fares. After allowing this essentially jolly situation to go on for several days, government by fiat decided it was time for company (the fact that company was predominantly English-owned made the action easier) to accept bulk of wage demands. After this action the workers promptly appeared wearing Salazar buttons, and there has since been a carefully staged and widely publicized rally lauding Salazar as friend of working man and dispenser of all good things.'[80]

Franco Nogueira has noted that at a long cabinet meeting held on 12 June 1968, Salazar repeated almost verbatim an issue concerning the expulsion of a French dance choreographer, which everyone present assumed had been dealt with previously.[81] Nobody dared say anything, but at a further cabinet meeting in July, he seemed to recover his intellectual prowess. Two days of discussions resulted in a decision to build a vast hydroelectric project, the Cabora Bassa dam. It would enable Mozambique to become self-sufficient in energy and even be able to export it to South Africa. Nogueira and the army minister were in favour, but many more ministers were opposed, and the deadlock was broken when Salazar decided the costly project was merited.[82]

His next major task was to plan for a long-awaited government reshuffle, something that would involve the customary round of consultations. From the start of August he would be installed in his summer residence at the Fort of Estoril. There is disagreement over which day he suffered the fateful accident that would end his time as ruler of Portugal. But it seems likely that it occurred around 9 am on Saturday, 3 August. He was sitting on a deckchair in the presence of his hairdresser who had come to cut his hair. While glancing at a newspaper, the chair gave way from under him and he fell back, his head making violent contact with the stone surface.[83] His doctor, Eduardo Coelho, was only told about the accident when he came for a routine visit on 6 August. He couldn't find any external signs of damage but urged Salazar to contact him if he experienced the slightest headache. Salazar continued with his schedule. Several times he met with the president to plan the reshuffle. The new cabinet was duly sworn in on 19 August. Meanwhile, Salazar received many visitors—Christine Garnier, members of the Garton family, Nogueira and his wife, his adopted daughter Micas. Only Micas showed concern that he was suffering headaches.

At a cabinet meeting on 3 September, Salazar was very subdued and seemed unwell.[84] The next day the quality of the handwriting in the diary which he meticulously kept was poor. That night he suffered severe headaches which would not go away and Coelho was summoned. It was at this point, on 5 September, that he concluded Salazar was far from well. An examination made by a neuro-surgeon, Dr António de Vasconcelos Marques, confirmed this but there was no agreement about the extent of his malady. An operation carried out on 7 September found and removed a blood clot in his brain. He seemed to recover, visitors started to appear, and on 15 September a medical bulletin was released saying that he would be returning home. The statement even ended with the words 'this is the final medical bulletin'. But it wasn't. On the morning of 16 September, Salazar suffered a severe stroke and went into a coma. Having been summoned urgently, Cardinal Cerejeira administered the last sacraments to his old friend. Salazar clung to life and on the 18th he was examined by Dr Houston Merritt, director of the New York Neurological Institute. He considered that he had suffered a brain haemorrhage as a result of a burst artery.[85]

Tomás concluded that there was no point in further delay and a successor would have to be appointed. Constitutionally, the decision was wholly his to make. Days of intense consultations ensued. But there was no power struggle or split in the ranks. Often dismissed as a figurehead, the head of state strove to maintain unity and discipline at the heart of the regime and seemed to succeed.

What is striking is the lack of suitable choices. There was no political class with organised factions who could have been able to launch vigorous leadership bids. Instead, there was a sense of weary resignation from the president down that, in view of the incapacity of the chief, there was only one candidate who offered some minimal hopes that he could hold the regime together. This was Marcello Caetano, by now aged sixty-two. Although out of government for a decade, he knew the regime inside out, had many supporters within, and was one of its chief ideologues. His allies had advanced in the final cabinet reshuffle, which Tomás had counselled Salazar in August might have been too liberal.[86] He also knew about economics as well as administration. Only his heterodox views about the Ultramar may have given Tomás pause for concern.[87]

Upon being sworn in, Caetano declared: 'Life has to go on. Men of genius appear sporadically, sometimes at intervals of centuries, teaching directions, illuminating destinies, guessing solutions, but the normality of institutions rests on ordinary men. The country became accustomed for a long time to be led by a man of genius; from now on it has to adapt to the rule of men like others.'[88]

Those whose primary loyalty was to the man were unable to transfer it to another, especially to someone like Caetano who had been an inconvenient and querulous member of the 'situation' for lengthy periods.[89] Caetano was seen as a usurper in the eyes of some regime heavyweights. Censorship stimulated a feverish rumour mill and it is likely that Caetano's advice to medical staff in the Benefica hospital where Salazar was being treated was not long in coming out: 'Do not sacrifice the services staffed by regular doctors on their shifts in order to stand guard over a patient who might very well die. Saving emergency cases that arrive should be the priority.'[90]

Nogueira only consented to remain as foreign minister upon the insistence of Tomás. He was convinced that Caetano would be a weak chief inclined to make unacceptable concessions on colonial policy.[91]

To the stupefaction of many, Salazar emerged from his coma a month after what had been widely assumed to be his inexorable passage towards death. Further medical dramas ensued before, on 29 November, he began to breathe unaided and start to eat. But his right arm remained paralysed, he was almost blind in one eye, and he could only walk short distances with the aid of a stick.[92]

He remained in hospital for several months more. In January 1969, he was able to converse fluently in French when he was visited by Christine Garnier. To some of his visitors he asked: 'When I leave here, where do I go? I don't have a house, I've nowhere to go.'[93] Finally, on 5 February 1969, Salazar was taken back to his official residence on Rua da Imprensa. An unseemly power struggle had raged between Dr Coelho and Dr Vasconcelos about the wisdom of this step, which would spill into print years later. Salazar's physician prevailed, though some in the Salazar circle lobbied for him to be replaced, but Tomás refused to get involved.

After quitting the government, Nogueira visited Salazar on a regular basis. He had the unshakable conviction that Salazar was unaware that he was no longer president of the Council. He has written: 'it did not even occur to him that for health reasons this was now the case: he did not understand the seriousness of his illness, the length of time he had been unwell, nor the mental deterioration that he had suffered.' However, Nogueira goes on to add that his wife, who paid him separate visits and accompanied him on excursions by car, had an entirely different view. She was convinced that Salazar was aware that he was no longer in charge, but his own state of spirit prevented him from facing up to this fact.[94]

A year after his operation, Roland Faure, a journalist on the French newspaper *L'Aurore*, was able to interview Salazar. He was told: 'I am not completely fit and my only concern is to gather up my strength in order to resume my function.'[95]

He was asked: It is some time since he spoke of Marcello Caetano: what did he think of him? His reply may be viewed as an indication of the surprising level of pluralism that he had allowed at the top of the Estado Novo: 'I know him well. I respect him. Caetano likes power, not for personal benefits or to support his family since he is an honest man; but he likes power for the sake of it ... He continues to teach at the University. Sometimes he writes to me, letting me know what he thinks of my initiatives. He doesn't always approve and he has the courage to tell me this. I admire this courage. But he does not understand that in order to be effective, to make his mark on events, he has to be a member of the government.'

Faure prefaced his article: 'a strange and dramatic situation, shaped by the macabre grandeur of this Shakespearean character—the king who refuses to die'.

Nogueira believed the interview corresponded to the reality. Salazar was lucid but it was a lucidity bound up with the past. Salazar was in denial about his situation and this was proven in the interview.[96]

Tomás was also in no doubt that Salazar now lived wholly in the past and that his flashes of undoubted mental acuteness hid the fact that he had been stricken by a debilitating illness which had left him a shadow of himself. He wrote in his memoirs: 'The way in which he spoke about events prior to 16 September 1968 and his extraordinary memory gave his listeners a false idea about the true state of his mind. He was, it must be repeated, a man with an extraordinary willpower and a great intelligence, and this helped to fool others, especially those who were fanatically predisposed to believe that he might return to his old self.'[97]

Time magazine reported at the end of 1969: 'No one in Portugal has so far been able to summon up the nerve to say that his 36-year reign is over ... On several occasions ... Tomás has tried to break the news gently to Salazar ... Each time, Dona Maria recently told a friend, Tomás approached the old Premier's Lisbon quarters "with the firm intention of telling the truth, but he cannot find the words".'[98]

Caetano had proclaimed that the motto of his government would be 'evolution within continuity' and the clearest evidence of his new departure proved to be a rebranding exercise. The New State became the Social State, and it is true that much effort and resources were directed at improving health and social conditions. At the start of 1970, the União Nacional (National Union) was renamed Acção Nacional Popular (National Popular Action) and the government was filled with new people.

Salazar was kept in the dark that the political order which he had painstakingly constructed was now subject to a makeover. He did not know that Nogueira had quit as foreign minister in October 1969 over a clause in a constitutional revision which referred to 'new independences'. He had suspected that Salazar's successor wished to dilute Portugal's African presence. He told a historian: 'I wanted to maintain Africa; Marcello Caetano preferred to abandon it.'[99]

It is unclear how far Caetano had moved away from what he had written in the publication *O Mundo Português* back in 1935: 'Africa for us is a moral justification and a *raison d'être* as a power. Without it we would be a small nation; with it, we are a great power.'[100] He would have known that he was unlikely to last long in office if he was to attempt to scuttle the empire. Liberals and technocrats who were styled progressives were now omniscient, but Tomás and allies wielded power behind the scenes. He could perhaps have carved out a new policy on Africa if he had shown some of the ingenuity and boldness displayed by Salazar as he rose to power. But he was indecisive and too much of a theorist.

However innovative in social policy, he certainly remained unreconciled to party-based democracy. At a speech given in Setúbal in 1972 he invoked patriotism, the family, property, social justice. But he refused to invoke democracy. Like Salazar, he thought democracy suited some people but not others. In his famous 'Cursos e manuais' he referred to 'the good sense of the English' and the intrinsic 'disequilibrium of the Latins'.[101]

Salazar faced a new medical battle in July 1970 when he acquired a kidney infection. A week later he was on a dialysis machine and once again he showed great powers of resistance. But he finally passed away on Monday, 27 July, at 9.15 am.

The atmosphere across the nation was subdued. There was no outbreak of joy among Portuguese who possessed little esteem for Salazar. The press the next day grappled with the enormity of the event. *Diário de Manhã*, the official pro-regime newspaper, provided eleven pages of photos and text under a thick black banner which proclaimed 'the man who was Portugal for 40 years'.[102]

Correia do Minho, which covered the strongly Catholic north-west, proclaimed on its front page: 'Dr Professor António de Oliveira Salazar has died. A great Portuguese and eminent statesman who enters into the glorious history of eight centuries as one of the most lucid and effective servants of the nation.'

He was a servant who had received enormous personal fulfilment in this role without benefiting in financial terms. The state had been looking after him since he had fallen ill owing to his own lack of personal means. Besides an archive impossible to place a price on, his worldly possessions consisted of a small sum of money in two bank accounts, equivalent in value at that time to a three-bedroom apartment in an ordinary district of Lisbon.[103] There were also bits and pieces of land and property in his home village, of little value.[104]

NATO flags flew at half-mast at its Brussels headquarters until his state funeral on 30 July 1970. Beforehand his body lay in state in Jerónimos monastery at Belem (an unconsecrated building since the state had taken it over in 1833). It was built on the spot where Vasco da Gama and his men had spent a night in prayer before embarking on their voyage to the East in 1497. 'He is beside Vasco da Gama and Camões', the newspaper for long edited by his main press ally, Augusto de Castro, wrote.[105]

Many people filed past his open-topped coffin. The monastery was packed for the solemn funeral service at which Cardinal Cerejeira officiated. Religious figures and men in military uniform were ubiquitous but this was not emphasised in media coverage. According to one source, this was deliberately meant to show the subjugation of those powerful corporate bodies to the state.[106]

Salazar's coffin was then placed in a train and taken two hours northwards to Santa Comba Dão. Another religious service took place in his local church and a small pick-up truck, not unlike the kind used for transporting agricultural goods, conveyed his coffin to the small cemetery in Vimieiro where he was laid to rest.

15

THE AFTERLIFE OF SALAZAR

FIFTY YEARS OF CONTROVERSY

Upon the death of Salazar, seventy-six-year-old Dona Maria was given twenty-four hours to vacate São Bento and find alternative accommodation. The prime ministerial residence was also substantially renovated so that, except for the facade, little of the interior was preserved.

It was a small but telling sign that 'Marcello', as Caetano was universally known, wanted to impose his own authority and fully step out of the shadow of the autocrat whom he had served. But how far down a different path did he want to go? His brains trust of technocratic advisers came up with the slogan 'Evolution in Continuity'. Marcelismo was also much heard about in the initial period after he took office on 27 September 1968. But it hardly amounted to a fundamental break with the past; admittedly, after six years, the heavy atmosphere of late Salazarism had vanished. *Bien pensants* wrote in the most outspoken Marxist terms, while liberals increasingly filled university positions. People could speak without fear, certainly in urban centres.[1]

No new original body of ideas associated with the sixty-two-year-old law professor emerged.[2] It is hard to see how it could have done. Caetano did not undergo a late conversion to liberal democracy. According to his daughter Ana Maria Caetano, he was neither a dictator nor a democrat. He had lived through the First Republic and this had permanently marked him. His generation's desire for peace and order after a period of chaos had never left him.[3]

He wished to try and create an equilibrium between an autocratic regime and one where there were far more liberal openings. However, he had few adherents who were willing to join him on this arduous course. Unlike many of his protégés, he was also not an enthusiast for the burgeoning cause of European integration. Europe had to remain a cooperative forum of nation-states. The primary function of the EEC was to be an outlet for Portuguese exports, many of which derived from the Ultramar.[4] He remained committed to a Lusophone space benignly overseen from Lisbon but with the African territories increasingly at its core.

More and more this was not the outlook favoured by many in the educated bourgeoisie from whom his friends and helpers derived. Salazar had distrusted this stratum of society, which he saw as opportunistic and too willing to adapt to fashionable foreign ideas of doubtful merit.[5] He had devised his own political brand for the country in the 1930s but Caetano was unable to reveal anything deeper beyond the marketing symbol of the Estado Social (Social State).

To his credit Caetano did sponsor a modernisation drive without parallel in the history of modern Portugal.[6] The Constitution was also revised in 1971 to allow for an eventual federation of self-governing units. Nationalists were up in arms but Caetano had more to fear from the liberals who were the beneficiaries of his patronage in the public sector. His inability to blaze a radical new course meant that he faced growing desertions from their ranks. He grew to be as 'isolated as an island', in the words of his daughter.[7]

Perhaps the top job had come too late. He lacked the resolve to confront and weaken the hardliners on core policy issues and instead nibbled away at some of the fundamental principles of the regime in a covert way.[8] Adelino Amaro da Costa, a post-1974 centrist politician, remarked: 'One chooses one's own jailers, and the Prime Minister simply lacked the resolve to carry out genuine liberalisation.'[9]

There were expectations that seventy-eight-year-old Tomás would be politely asked to go into retirement by Caetano rather than be nominated for a third term in 1972.[10] Otherwise, the Constitution would permit him to block any major change, above all in colonial policy. Caetano himself assuming the presidency was also regarded as an option. But he disappointed his reformist backers, and perhaps sealed his own fate, by giving Tomás the option to stay on (which he accepted).[11]

Salazar had privately described Caetano in 1966 as 'a very difficult person, the most difficult I have encountered'.[12] Yet the regime had always found room for him and Tomás never seriously thought of dismissing him, perhaps because he had grown familiar with his ways and assumed that they would not be fatal to the regime.

It was ominous for the regime that Caetano lacked a tough attitude to power especially when crises loomed. He was disgusted when, on 1 July 1970, Pope Paul VI received in audience leaders of the African nationalist movements, Agostinho Neto, Amílcar Cabral and Marcelino dos Santos. He grew apart from Catholicism from that point on, writing to a friend: 'Sometimes faith is lost but respect for the Church in which it was lived is preserved; for me one disappeared and the other did not remain.'[13] He was similarly much affected by the strong public opposition that greeted his official visit to Britain in 1973 on the occasion of the 600th anniversary of the Anglo-Portuguese Alliance.[14] Of course, Salazar would never have submitted himself to such humiliation nor is it likely that he would have cracked under American pressure over the use of the Lajes airbase on the Azores. But in October 1973 Caetano was badgered by the Americans into allowing Portugal to grant refuelling rights to US planes rushing aid to Israel in the Yom Kippur war. No other NATO member would act similarly (nor did Spain) and the Arab oil producers promptly imposed a damaging embargo on Portugal.[15]

By this point a lot of junior and middle-ranking officers were prepared to take the law into their own hands. Their grievances initially were professional ones. In mid-1973 a new law had given conscripted officers (*milicianos*) parity in terms of pay and status with full-timers. This was a slap in the face for officers who had served successive terms in front-line positions. The government soon realised it had miscalculated and withdrew the bill. But in September 1973 an Armed Forces Movement (MFA) was quietly set up. It was a gesture of defiance towards desk-bound officers in Lisbon whose privileges were resented by combat officers. Many sat on the boards of large companies; merging the military and business elites had been seen, in the past, as a way of reducing the likelihood of a coup but it soured relations between senior and junior officers. The tedium, discomfort and occasional dangers presented by the war had destroyed most opportunities for social mobility that an army career might offer to young recruits from the provinces. Festering resentments soon ensured that the MFA evolved from a military trade union, ventilating grievances, to a tight-knit conspiratorial body.[16]

The catalyst for action turned out to be the publication of a book by Spínola advocating a Portuguese federation. *Portugal e o futuro* (Portugal and the Future) was read in advance by Caetano. He decided it could be published and, despite its turgid style, three editions were sold in a fortnight.[17] But there was a backlash from the old guard. A demoralised Caetano tried to resign. But Tomás's unyielding response was: 'You let the problem arise, now resolve it.'[18] The former president claimed in his memoirs that his last words to Caetano were: 'it is too late for any of us to abandon our position—we have to go on until the end.'[19]

Under pressure, Caetano summoned senior officers to a ceremony on 14 March 1974 where attendance would be seen as a sign of acquiescence in the existing colonial strategy. But the two most senior military figures refused to attend and were sacked.[20] Spínola was by now deputy chief of staff and his boss was General Francisco da Costa Gomes, the very man who had been involved in the conspiracy to oust Salazar thirteen years earlier. Only days earlier, 200 officers attended an assembly of the MFA in Cascais on 5 March 1974. This was a conspicuous location and the authorities were soon aware of the burgeoning revolt. But a melancholy Caetano was paralysed by indecision. His bleak mood would likely have been intensified by the letter he received from the former minister José Correia de Oliveira upon his return from a three-week trip to France, Switzerland and Britain. He had been horrified at the mood in the financial world about the future for Portugal. He wrote: 'Clearly, it is certain that these people are convinced that something new and terrible is going to overwhelm Portugal, reducing us to our European confines, a narrow and irrelevant spot. There is doubt about our ability to pay what we owe and even about our ability to construct what we need for the present and the future.'[21]

The PIDE was aware of the plotting but had grown too enfeebled to be able to swoop. A major step was the decision of Spínola to join the plotters who had drawn up a manifesto calling for democracy at home and decolonisation in Africa. Very rapidly, on 25 April 1974, the regime fell without a shot being fired in its defence. A spiritually broken Caetano was flown into exile in Brazil. He assumed Spínola was fully in charge, an impression that would have been strengthened by his being appointed provisional president of Portugal on 26 April. Initially, there was an air of optimism even among figures who had served the regime. Admiral Sarmento Rodrigues, a former colonial minister and leading promoter of the doctrine of Lusotropicalism, wrote to his Brazilian friend, the anthropologist Gilberto Freyre, in June: 'The leaders [of the coup] ... are in large part my friends. I have been seeing a lot of them and several have done me the honour of seeking my advice. They are good people full of good intentions.'[22]

Newly appointed as armed forces chief, Costa Gomes soon complacently proclaimed that the military had arranged 'the most dignified revolution in contemporary history'.[23] There was agreement on taking swift steps to dismantle the institutions of the old regime. But the differences piled up once the political left emerged from clandestinity. Its two best-known figures, Álvaro Cunhal of the Communist Party (PCP) and Mário Soares of the recently formed Socialist Party (PS), entered a provisional government. Disagreement rapidly surfaced over the pace of decolonisation and what form of political direction would occur at home. Spínola proved naive and completely out of his depth in an increasingly cut-throat power struggle. The communists used their links with the MPLA in Angola and Frelimo in Mozambique to deliver the main colonies in Africa to outwardly Marxist forces able to rely on the backing of the Soviet Union. They outclassed Spínola; by September 1974 he was no longer provisional president and in March 1975 he became a fugitive when he was manipulated into mounting an amateurish coup after he had been led to believe that a massacre of leading moderates was imminent.[24]

Sweeping nationalisations and land seizures promptly occurred. The publisher of Spínola's book, CUF, the main economic conglomerate, employing 30,000 people and accounting for more than ten per cent of industrial production, was taken over by self-proclaimed revolutionaries. No other Western country had ever seen such a radical switch in economic relations. The nationalisation of the Portuguese banks, insurance and transport companies, and the steel, chemical, petroleum and cement industries meant that 'the dorsal fin of Portuguese private capitalism' had been broken.[25]

Cunhal was convinced that Portugal was in the grip of an unstoppable revolutionary process. He was undeterred when elections for a constituent assembly on 25 April 1975 left the PCP and allies with only 16 per cent of the vote on a 90 per cent turnout and instead strongly endorsed moderate forces. He over-reached, trying to seize control of the media and the trade unions. He already faced a bitter challenge from an array of far-left parties which viewed the PCP as 'social fascists'. In an atmosphere of mounting sectarianism, Salazar was quickly lost sight of as a hate figure. The bridge over the Tagus that his ministers had named after him was quickly changed and a statue of him in his home town was decapitated, but this introspective ruler failed to turn into a permanent hate symbol.

The areas north of the Tagus which had given passive adherence to the Estado Novo now began to stir. As land seizures encroached on areas with prosperous family farms, well-organised resistance began. Cunhal and one thousand supporters were chased out of the historic town of Alcobaça on 18 August 1975 when they tried to hold a meeting in the teeth of local opposition. This was seen as revenge for the way the fiercely conservative archbishop of Braga, Francisco Maria da Silva, had been treated by communist customs officials at Lisbon airport while on his way to a religious conference in Brazil. Officials ordered him to strip after he was falsely accused of illegally exporting currency.

Later, on his return to Braga, he assailed communism as hostile to God in a town square speech on 10 August, which was followed by widespread attacks on communist offices.[26] Soon there was far more invective against 'the communist menace' than there ever had been against fascism. The atmosphere was inflamed by the return of hundreds of thousands of Portuguese settlers from Africa. The officers of the MFA were too inexperienced and divided among themselves to prevent such a mass exodus. Some, such as Admiral António Rosa Coutinho, in charge of Angola's decolonisation from July 1974, were thought to have worked to reinforce Soviet influence. It was self-serving of the prominent MFA figure Brigadier Pedro de Pezarat Correia to later claim that the behaviour of the post-1974 regime in the decolonisation process was 'coherent and honest', marred 'by the games of foreign interests at the height of the Cold War'.[27] Some of the most prominent military actors in the revolution were unbalanced characters. Otelo de Carvalho went from being a standard-bearer at Salazar's funeral where he had wept, to being the head of Copcon, a military police force that promoted property seizures while also preventing clashes between left-wing factions.[28] He at least had the presence of mind to admit after returning from a visit to Cuba in July 1975: 'I lack political coordinates. If I had them I could be the Fidel Castro of Europe but I have a limited culture.'[29]

By contrast, Colonel Vasco Gonçalves, the officer whom a naive Spínola appointed as prime minister in July 1974, had possessed underground loyalties to the PCP that stretched back several decades.[30] He placed no obstacles in the way of Cunhal's party attempting to disregard an unfavourable electoral verdict and place the country under communist control. Once Mário Soares took his fellow Socialists out of the government in June 1975, this intense soldier proved no match for the resolute and wily civilian. Deserted by other allies, he reshuffled his government on 8 August 1975 and appointed as his deputy the man who had been the chief theorist of corporativism at Coimbra University for decades. José Teixeira Ribeiro had survived the purges by throwing his fellow conservative professors to the wolves.[31] He would only survive in office until the end of the month when Gonçalves fell, but his appointment had a certain warped logic. The revolution could be said to have marked the ascension of a left-wing version of Salazar's corporativism. This is very much the view of the late Manuel de Lucena, who believed that in 1975, rather than a break with the past, there had instead been a continuation. The power of the state over the economy and civil society was taken much further than Salazar could have gone, and the levers of control over state, society and economy were left in few hands.[32] In 1976 a new pluralist constitution would be drawn up which he believed offered parallels with the 1933 one, given its strongly doctrinaire and paternalistic features, such as promising 'an irreversible transition to socialism'.[33]

Lucena was in no doubt that if the communist line had prevailed, it would have led to the existence of a corporative system even more enveloping than the previous one.[34] But in the former Portuguese space it was only in Angola that doctrinaire state management policies were adopted with rigour thanks to Cuban forces keeping the MPLA in power (amidst a prolonged civil war) after independence was hastily granted. For some months in the second half of 1975 Portugal seemed also to flirt with civil war as much of the world watched with amazement how a country with little news for forty years was now awash with social turmoil. It only took a year after the coup for the MFA to reveal itself to be a broken-backed force with no idea of how to calm a polarised country. The initiative swung to relative moderates around Major Ernesto Melo Antunes. He published a manifesto on 8 August which rejected both Soviet-style communism and West European social democracy, advocating instead socialism achieved by gradual means. With Gonçalves out and the Socialists back in government, tension remained high as vast numbers of guns disappeared from military arsenals. On 27 September 1975, a mob burned the Spanish Embassy. Just north of Lisbon, angry farmers threatened to cut the capital off from the rest of the country by blocking roads and discontinuing food, water and electricity supplies. If this failed, the far right threatened to blow up the bridges over the river Douro in Oporto and set up a breakaway regime. The government went on strike in October 1975 after 20,000 building workers trapped the prime minister and deputies inside parliament, a stone's throw from Salazar's old residence.

Although there had been a remarkably small number of people killed despite the enormity of the changes in the previous eighteen months, Portugal seemed to stand on the brink of civil war in November 1975. North and south, young middle-class revolutionaries and older conservatives, workers and farmers, urban and rural Portugal, would have been among the chief protagonists. But on 25 November 1975 professional military elements led by General Ramalho Eanes successfully moved against the far-left military units. Cunhal's communists, perhaps realising they had obtained the maximum they could hope to achieve in a non-revolutionary country, remained on the sidelines. Order was restored and the revolution fizzled out.[35]

25 April remains a totemic symbol for at least the 16 per cent of Portuguese (on a low turnout) who backed the far left in the parliamentary election of 2019. But the captains and majors of the MFA have mostly faded into obscurity, none achieving lasting renown. Only

Otelo de Carvalho has made occasional headlines. In 1984 he was imprisoned for some years after being found guilty of heading a terrorist organisation, Forças Populares 25 de Abril (FP-25), which had carried out a series of armed attacks. In 2011, by now in his seventies, he had reached doleful conclusions about the revolution. Beyond securing improvements in education and health care, he wondered what had been its point. Controversially, he went on to say: 'We need a man with the intelligence and honesty of Salazar but without the intention of imposing an Italian-style fascism.'[36]

Major Jaime Neves, who had played an instrumental role in winding up the revolution, much later also wondered if the revolution had been worth it. In 1999 he remarked: 'the truth is that, from many perspectives, the people feel they are worse off now than before 1974'.[37] The high-profile historian and veteran commentator Vasco Pulido Valente is Portugal's best-known contrarian and he put his disenchantment with the revolutionaries far more forcefully in 2014. He stated that 'we owe nothing to the captains of April: zero'. His scorn even extended to Major Melo Antunes, who, he believed, wanted to transform Portugal 'into something never seen before' and who was only moderate in the sense that he did not want to take orders from the communists.[38]

Under the 1976 Constitution, an elected president shared power with the government endorsed by the National Assembly. The composition of the constituent assembly which helped draw up this document was heavily weighted towards lawyers and educators.[39] The three main non-communist parties were dominated by figures with roots in the past. Freitas do Amaral of the Centre Social Democrats (CDS) belonged to an old Salazarist family. The Social Democrats (PSD) were led, until his death in a plane crash in 1980, by Francisco Sá Carneiro, the nephew of one of the longest-serving ministers in the former regime. Mário Soares had, of course, been a dissident, but he belonged to a prestigious republican family. For a decade Portugal was poorly governed by usually short-lived minority governments sometimes headed by non-party figures. The parties concentrated on inserting their members and influential clients into the sprawling bureaucratic system. It meant they became a magnet for job-seeking opportunists rather than a platform for people with vision and energy.[40] There was a shortage of good-quality politicians keen to build a new political order free of the vices of both the

First Republic and its authoritarian successor. It was no surprise that the very high turnouts at elections plunged over time as a kind of partyocracy took shape. Although the PSD would be instrumental in promoting a constitutional revision in 1989 which led to socialist clauses being dropped and the military's remaining influence being curtailed, each of the parties found it difficult to break free from the left-wing conditioning of the 1974–5 Revolution.

Even when a semi-privatisation of state assets took place and the old economic families regained control of some of their concerns, it was difficult to uproot the influence of state managers into whose control much of the industrial economy had fallen in 1975. Private capitalists needed to retain the goodwill of the bureaucracy and trade unions in order to function effectively. Foreign companies had more freedom to manoeuvre but, unsurprisingly, foreign investment slumped after the revolution. The story of the US-owned National Cash Register (NCR) helps to explain the downturn.

The firm had a factory in Lisbon for a long time until it was taken over in 1975 and run by a Workers' Committee, comprising nine people. The US Embassy tried to overturn what was an illegal expropriation. But the labour minister, José Costa Martins, an air force captain who had seized control of Lisbon airport on 25 April 1974, and was close to the PCP, was uncooperative. He initially refused to meet the US labour attaché and then said the government would do nothing against the workers. The state subsidised the plant for a while but then the spare parts ran out and none could be bought abroad because the value of the escudo had collapsed. Thereafter, the attitude of the workers' committee to the US owners quickly thawed. The embassy was asked to try and arrange their return. But the investment had been written off by the company, which thought it more prudent to invest in Ireland. The whole sorry affair probably cost 200 Portuguese their jobs.[41]

By 1977 Portugal had the worst unemployment (an estimated 25 per cent), balance of payments deficit and inflation in the whole of Europe. The Marshall Plan promised by Western countries if, in 1975, Marxist revolution was spurned had failed to materialise. The large emigrant community withheld remittances and bankruptcy seemed unavoidable. That is until Soares called in the IMF in 1978 and agreed to stiff deflationary terms in return for a large loan.[42] The far right returned to prominence and rallies in 1977 and 1978 led to clashes. General Kaúlza de Arriaga had set up a conservative nationalist party, MIRN, but it failed to prosper.[43] In 1978, there were clashes in Santa Comba Dão after attempts to restore a statue of Salazar which had sat in front of the courthouse from 1965 until February 1975. On that occasion its head had been blown off in a bomb explosion. In 1978, after the town council decided to restore the statue, the Lisbon parliament opposed the decision and clashes erupted on the streets of the town. A local woman, Herminia de Figueiredo, watching from her window, was killed by a police bullet and many others were injured. Within days a powerful bomb resulted in the statue being destroyed and Lisbon having its way.[44] Strong resistance would continue up to 2019 to any physical manifestation in Salazar's birthplace, whether it be a museum or an interpretative centre dedicated to Salazar and his regime (or its era) even in a neutral or censorious sense.[45]

However, the melancholy state of Portugal, economically moribund, divested of its African territories, and struggling to absorb 700,000 *retornados* (returned ones) from Africa, prompted fresh assessments of Salazar. The leading literary critic and political essayist António José Saraiva offered a particularly striking reappraisal. He wrote in the most prominent Lisbon weekly in 1979: 'Today we see, with a harsh clarity, how the period of history encapsulated by the Salazarist name was the last in which we merited being an Independent Nation. Now in full democracy and being a sovereign people, it merely remains for us to be a eucalyptus plant nation for use by an obscure economic entity which goes by the pseudonym of the EEC.'[46]

Unlike his brother José Hermano, who became education minister in the 1960s, he had been a Marxist for many years and had lost his teaching post, being forced into exile. So he had no store of affection for Salazar. Nevertheless, he praised him for reducing British hegemony over Portugal and keeping the country out of World War II, a feat he believed would have been beyond any of Portugal's post-1974 rulers. He acknowledged his authoritarian ways but could understand why, in the 1930s, he shrank from relying on the system of one person, one vote as a means of restoring Portugal's national health.[47]

With access to many of his papers, Franco Nogueira published a six-volume biography of Salazar from 1977 to 1984 which obtained respectful notice from critics though it was later dismissed as a panegyric in other quarters. He died in 1995, and the centenary of his birth in 2018 was marked by a respectful ceremony at the Portuguese foreign ministry.[48]

It was only in 2012 that anger erupted about the handling of the Salazar era in a major work of history. It was occasioned by the appearance of the monumental 997-page history of Portugal coordinated by Rui Ramos of the University of Lisbon.[49] Ramos described the Estado Novo as despotic but stopped far short of branding it as fascist and offered plenty of data to suggest that there had been considerable social and economic development especially from the 1950s onwards. His tome appeared at a time of flux in higher education: in common with much of the rest of Europe and North America, left-wing perspectives on sensitive topics were becoming dominant, and to challenge or merely modify them could be seen as highly provocative. A fierce polemic ensued which woke up the hitherto sleepy world of Portuguese historiography, only for it to quickly subside.[50]

Plenty of historical works appeared on the Estado Novo during the second decade of this century. Salazar's papers had already been gathered together in the national archival deposit in Lisbon at the Torre de Tombo. He had meticulously filed all correspondence and it managed to survive the upheavals of the revolution.[51] But Salazar himself was the subject of surprisingly few biographical studies in contrast to other major European contemporaries from de Gaulle and Franco to Hitler and Mussolini. Journalists who offered sometimes sensationalist portrayals of the regime and its period found the dictator a rather impenetrable figure, and often stock clichés were recycled about his supposedly unforgiving, mean-spirited and Machiavellian character.

Undoubtedly, Dona Maria, who had looked after all of Salazar's domestic needs, even down to buying his clothes, would have had a gripping story to relate. She had been 'attentive to everything' and was able to use her intuition to distinguish between people who were loyal or else hostile to the dictator, according to José Paulo Rodrigues, a close aide of Salazar's in the 1960s.[52] But she kept silent until her death in 1981 even though a lucrative book deal would have helped someone who had little money to fall back on.

Approaching old age, Salazar's adopted daughter, Maria da Conceição de Melo Rita, who for years had worked in the state tourist administration, did write a low-key and affectionate memoir. It emerges that Salazar never pulled strings to obtain any lucrative job for her and did not push her to attend university. Perhaps he sensed that his intelligent and personable ward would have an easier life after his death (or else removal from office) if she lived quietly.[53]

The most popular work on Salazar was a psycho-biography by Fernando Dacosta, which went into at least twenty-six editions after its appearance in 1997.[54] Various snapshots of Salazar were provided from his rural upbringing and seminary formation to his years in power and ultimately his mawkish final years. An author with a vivid imagination and a gifted pen embroidered his story in various stages, inventing dialogue and speculating about key moments in his personal life and political career. Inevitably, this kind of experimental study divided the Portuguese.

A retired diplomat, Fernando de Castro Brandão (who had been ambassador to Czechoslovakia and Venezuela after 1974), published a series of books documenting details of Salazar's personal life and public career in a bid to preserve accurate information about his life and prevent distortions accumulating.[55] Several of these books (based on painstaking research in the Salazar archive) are likely to be very useful to future historians, but they inevitably lacked the impact of *Horizons of Memory*, an evocation of Portugal's historical past, which began to be regularly presented on Portuguese state television from 1979 by the historian José Hermano Saraiva. He never hid his respect for Salazar though the programmes were far more concerned with buildings, landscapes, trade and human settlement than with politics. A very self-confident style as a presenter turned him into one of the few charismatic figures present on Portuguese television before or after 1974. His depiction of the Portuguese story, ultimately far beyond Portugal itself, brought him a cult following, especially among the older generation. His popularity and skills as a communicator on television meant that left-wing critics were powerless to impede his work and he was a regular on Portuguese television until shortly before his death (aged ninety-two) in 2012.[56]

Despite its growing strength in higher education and parts of the media, the political left was too weak (and also divided) to turn an anti-fascist narrative about Salazar and the Estado Novo ultimately into the only approved version. To some extent this was due to the restraint shown by Mário Soares. He was arguably the most important political figure in the first twenty years after 1974. He could have demonised the political right, but instead he promoted reconciliation, with himself being granted an outsized role as the man who enabled democracy to sink durable roots in hitherto inhospitable soil.

He had shown during the revolution a flair for the bold and unexpected, and he demonstrated this again in 1976 when, at the start of his two years as prime minister, he allowed Spínola to return from exile. He had been plotting insurrection against his former brother officer Costa Gomes, president of Portugal from April 1974 to June 1976, just a year previously. But he promptly retired from politics and top honours were bestowed on him later by Soares (for his civic and military heroism), during his ten years as president from 1985 to 1995. In a long profile that he wrote of Salazar in 1990, Soares underlined that 'he wasn't a duce ... always remaining a civilian, distant, secretive, composed: Doctor Salazar!'[57]

It is perhaps worth offering brief comparisons between Soares and Salazar. Economics was never much of a priority for the democratic statesman, who also lacked Salazar's appetite for detail. He enjoyed far more the ceremonial role of government, which enabled him to project his ego. He was an inveterate traveller reluctant to turn down tempting foreign invitations even when there was urgent business at home to attend to. Soares also was not afraid to strike out at former colleagues and allies whenever his power base seemed threatened. Salazar was the same but arguably, even as a dictator, he was skilful enough to make rather fewer enemies than Soares did during his thirty years in electoral politics. Both were also comfortable with the exercise of power, they usually managed to remain cool in a crisis, and were concerned with their respective legacies. Salazar published his speeches and interviews in six volumes known as *Os discursos* and today they are a collector's item, fetching high prices. Soares also published interviews, and the vehicle for preserving his influence was to be the Mário Soares Foundation. Unlike Salazar's opus, which was published privately, this foundation was built up with state backing and given the lease of an imposing property in central Lisbon (not far from the former PIDE headquarters).

This patronage was bestowed on Portugal's best-known democrat at a time when political conflicts had been blunted by Portugal's accession to the European Union. Its full membership after 1 January 1986 gave it access to transfer funds that were supposed to enable a new member to converge, in terms of levels of development, with established members. But there was a downside. Portuguese industry was unable to compete effectively against similar firms from bigger EU states which now had full access to the national market. Portuguese agriculture went into decline owing to the inability of a small national sector to compete against countries like Spain. The decline of the productive national economy gathered pace after Portugal took part in the launch of the single currency, the euro, in 1999. The new currency was pegged to suit the needs of Germany, grappling still with the challenges of unification. It accelerated the trends by which Portugal, along with other southern European economies, moved from being productive economies to essentially consumer ones, relying on tourism and property investment as well as the remittances of growing numbers of Portuguese abroad. They included a fast-growing Portuguese community in Angola, who comprised many skilled people who might have been absorbed into the economy at home if it had been better managed. After 2002 post-civil war Angola witnessed an industrial boom (still based largely on its oil wealth) and the explosion of a service sector based in the capital of Luanda. By 2019, with eight million people, it had become one of the largest cities in the Portuguese-speaking world (having had a population of only around half a million when Salazar died).[58]

It would be the PSD under Aníbal Cavaco Silva who presided over the first decade of Portugal's EU membership.[59] He had been a senior economic adviser of Caetano. The EU's bounty was disproportionately channelled into prestigious infrastructure projects by him. An overhaul of the antiquated transport system was badly overdue, but there was no equivalent drive to modernise education or improve the technical efficiency of state agencies given the continuing weight of the state in economic life. The quiet expectations held by small industrialists, thrifty peasants, parts of the Lisbon elite and the northern middle class that politics might be shaped around the country's real needs, rather than the power games of politicians, were soon dashed. Cavaco did not abuse his office, which could not be said of others on the right as well as the left. But given the vast sums coming from Brussels, the PSD soon became enmeshed in the politics of patronage. It suffered electoral defeat in 1995, and it and the Socialists alternated in office for the next quarter of a century, often with little distinguishing them in policy terms and governmental ethics.

For politics to lose its ideological edge was possibly a good thing so soon after a convulsive revolution. But the country continued to stagnate, held back by a cumbersome public bureaucracy and, arguably, one of the most inefficient state education systems in the Western world.[60] State-run utility companies found room for an army of relatives and allies of politicians, who were also prominent in semi-private banks. The bloated salaries which were acquired through such nepotism ensured that Portugal had one of the highest levels of income inequality in the developed world.[61] The excessive behaviour of political families contributed to the bankruptcy of the state, which, in May 2011, required an emergency bail-out from the European Central Bank to keep public services going.

A complacent political and intellectual elite received a jolt when, in 2007, viewers of the television series *Great Portuguese*—having been asked to vote for the greatest figure in Portuguese history—chose Salazar. A case was made for a candidate in an hour-long documentary. The candidates ranged from Portugal's more illustrious monarchs to the great explorers of the Age of Discovery and contemporary figures like Álvaro Cunhal and Aristides de Sousa Mendes. The conservative author and commentator Jaime Nogueira Pinto produced a programme which argued that Salazar was an honest man who, as an authoritarian ruler, had exercised his authority with restraint and had done great service to the nation by taking it from the edge of financial disaster and keeping it out of World War II.[62] Salazar received 41 per cent of the 159,245 votes cast for the state broadcaster RTP's competition, easily surpassing Cunhal, who was in second place. One commentator concluded that a long-dormant collective memory about Salazar had been rekindled by this media undertaking.[63]

The Socialist government of José Socrates was not best placed to launch any kind of 'anti-fascist' pushback. The party was increasingly dominated by figures originally from local government who used public money to boost their districts and were largely indifferent about holding the major state offices and governing effectively. Within weeks of the *Great Portuguese* drama, Socrates was facing embarrassing accusations, including the claim that he had obtained his university degree by irregular means. He clung on in government until 2011 and was arrested on suspicion of corruption and money-laundering three years later, which he claimed was a politically motivated attack on him.[64] Eventually, in 2017, he was charged with three counts of passive corruption while holding political office, sixteen counts of money-laundering, nine counts of forging documents, and three counts of tax fraud, committed between 2006 and 2015.[65]

Against a background of 'high levels of mistrust towards parties, the lack of clear alternative programs and the growing distance between parties and citizens', it was difficult to gain majority backing for the view that Salazar was a fascist with his regime deserving to be classed alongside those of Hitler and Mussolini.[66] My own view echoes that of the French political theorist Raymond Aron, who argued that Salazar's regime was a traditional autocracy, comprising a distinct category separate from pluralist systems but also totalitarian ones.[67] This was also the view of the ex-US secretary of state Madeleine Albright; when questioned in 2018 about her new book on fascism, she was careful to point out that 'he wasn't fascist, he saw Nazism as immoral' but he was an authoritarian figure.[68]

The regime acquired some fascist trappings for a temporary period in the late 1930s, but in terms of background, temperament, intentions and ambitions, Salazar was an unlikely fascist. He never had a mass party, his path to power was fairly conventional and not marked by any of the street action seen in Italy and Germany before 1922 and 1933, he put down communists but also the far-right Blueshirts, and never showed any appetite for developing an extremist phalanx which he could rely on in a crisis. He preferred to survive through his own wits rather than paramilitary movements or the secret police. Moreover, in time the PIDE declined in effectiveness, was prey to infighting, and was perhaps never as fearsome as its detractors often claimed.

Salazar possessed a resolutely empiricist mindset. He had set up the unwieldy corporative state, but his motivation may have been to ensure that he could influence the direction of the economy rather than build a fanciful new economic order that would be shaped by academic alchemists. He was careful in the 1930s and 1940s not to be swept away by dreams of war, endless conquest or permanent revolution. He elected to stay in Africa after 1961, but it was because he firmly believed that the colonies were an extension of Portugal. Today bustling and chaotic Luanda, the capital of Angola, may well be a city where the imprint of the ex-colonial power is more firmly implanted than in any other African capital.

Salazar wasn't a fascist but a reactionary, which, according to the French right-wing novelist Pierre Drieu La Rochelle, was the opposite.[69] He didn't share the revolutionary and racist preoccupations of Hitler and Mussolini but was always far more influenced by French right-wing thought in which Christian conservative themes often held sway. He went from being a cautious, conservative democrat in the early 1920s to being the constructor of a moderately authoritarian nationalist regime. He clung to the hope that the crises and opportunities of the 1930s would transform outlooks and mentalities. But his ambitions were steadily scaled down and his regime became a personal one in which he was assisted by administrators and technocrats whom he believed he could trust. It was a rule-based authoritarian government rather than a party dictatorship where informal and extreme forms of violence could periodically be unleashed.[70]

The nature of the Estado Novo encouraged a long-term depoliticisation. This tendency was reinforced by its post-1976 successor. It has tried to build a 'progressive consensus' around a consumerist democracy ready to be a well-behaved child in the European Union and managing to send one of its most artful politicians, António Guterres, to preside over the United Nations. Politics is reduced to debating which group of insiders, drawn from the legal profession and the bureaucratic classes, can be relied upon to manage the large social state and distribute funds from the EU.

The striking consensus displayed in favour of joining the EU stemmed from a desire to end isolation and reinforce a young democracy. But it may also have been due to the reluctance of many well-placed people to take responsibility for running Portugal. This reticence had been apparent early in Salazar's own political career and he turned it to his advantage. It is hard to detect a strong appetite among ambitious military figures to directly run Portugal after 1926. The country's problems appeared too daunting for many. If there had been a strong military drive to rule, then Salazar might have found it impossible to dissolve the military regime at the start of the 1930s. Paradoxically, the attempt to unseat Salazar hatched by senior officers thirty years later may have arisen for much the same reason. His then defence minister, Botelho Moniz, had no evident desire to rule on his own account but he was deeply unhappy about Salazar's colonialist instincts increasing the burden of responsibility which the military would face in Africa.

Salazar often found it hard to persuade what he thought were suitable people to join his government, perhaps on account of the demands that would be placed on them. There was usually less trouble in persuading people to join the National Assembly or the Corporative Chamber. These were largely honorific bodies whose demands on their members were light. He may have hung on for so long and been reluctant to delegate to a successor because of being unable to find enough capable people with a willingness to devote themselves completely to national affairs.

Perhaps it is the long-term pessimism of the elite about running a country as deficient in wealth as Portugal that helps to explain why Salazar was left to get on with ruling Portugal for so long. His democratic successors have not shown much aptitude or enthusiasm for tackling difficult tasks in areas like health and education, or modernising the bureaucracy. There is a ready acceptance to allow the European Union to oversee Portugal's broad development. The EU may have found Portugal one of its least troublesome members for much the same reason Salazar was able to be at the heart of power for nearly forty years. It may well be that the EU fulfils nowadays the same role as Salazar did before 1970 in a country where, within the political class, there are far more candidates to occupy sinecures or serve in the European Parliament than to tackle daunting problems corroding national life.

With so many productive and energetic Portuguese working abroad and much of the population now crammed into a few coastal cities, Portugal is one of the few European countries to escape a debate on national identity. The nation's diminished place in the world, and its dependence on decisions made by unaccountable forces in Brussels, means it is very hard for a discourse on patriotism to take shape.[71] With conservative nationalist movements flourishing electorally in most European countries, it was only in 2019 that the Portuguese equivalent, a party called Chega, led by André Ventura, managed to win a solitary parliamentary seat.

After the anger and betrayal felt during the five recessionary years stretching from 2010 to 2015, a degree of political calm has returned. The consensus is epitomised by President Marcelo Rebelo de Sousa (ironically the son of a leading Salazarist who, as a young child, was taken to top Estado Novo functions). Perhaps this tireless extrovert is continuing, in a different way, Salazar's policy of muffling sharp political differences. The low-key dictator, who died fifty years ago, still exerts appeal for many Portuguese on account of his personal rectitude. There is also a sense that, at least under him, the Portuguese as a national group were not always victims of fate, the subjects of decisions made by those 'others' whom they had absolutely no means of restraining. Turning to those beyond Portugal who are unhappy with the signs of social breakdown in the West, some can perhaps find solace in his conservative formula for managing society. He is bound to appeal to many who long for the depoliticisation of Western societies and who fear that the West in general is growing unhinged because so much that was once private, informal and even intimate has grown hopelessly politicised.

Salazar's traditional outlook is completely at variance, however, with radical forces in the West who have the ear of the media, the backing of corporate business, and the endorsement of many women, previously the bulwark of social conservatism. Today, in an age when middle-class radical youth protest against white privilege and patriarchy, Salazar appears to embody much of what they are against. For many of them, colonialism is perhaps the worst sin of white patriarchy and Salazar was the most stubborn and implacable 20th-century European colonial leader.

Preserving the national identity, which many devotees of radical identity politics are keen to sweep away, was always a primordial need for him. His Constitution upheld the family, which contemporary radicals see as a curb on the requirement to be experimental and nonconformist. He believed in fostering elites in order to guide society and would surely have been horrified by their vilification of successful individuals. He had no time for income guarantees, believing in the necessity for able-bodied people to work for a living. He also believed the economic victimhood that was a feature of communist doctrine was based on a false conception of humanity. And it is unlikely that he would have been impressed by an even bolder definition of victimhood encompassing not just classes but a range of minorities defined by gender, ethnicity and sexuality.

He would have prompted derision far beyond the 21st-century radical left for regularly insisting on 'the intrinsic value of religious truth to the individual and society'. As a professor of economics before beginning a marathon forty years at the centre of political life, today he would probably find it hard to acquire or keep an academic post. It is unlikely that he would find much sympathy among Green movement zealots even though he was an ecologist who reforested Portugal and only ever flew in an aircraft once in his life.

Salazar was a successful political figure who cast aside his humble origins to acquire and keep power for a remarkably lengthy period. He also used his political and diplomatic skills to keep his small but strategically placed country out of harm's way in an age of ruthless conflict. Much of the world (despite new-found prosperity) could be said to increasingly resemble the fractured, chaotic, ill-governed and spiritually moribund Portugal which he took charge of ninety years ago and ruled for another forty. The race to avoid the dissolution of once compact societies into ideologically riven battle zones may, in time, produce figures who display Salazar's steely will. They may not share his aversion to electoral democracy but will quite possibly possess a similar determination to prevent their lands becoming prey to heresies perhaps far worse than any that have laid waste to Europe in recent epochs.

As for Portugal itself, much of Salazar's political legacy has been erased. The removal of many of the repressive features of state power is surely an advance, but what progress there has been in other branches of politics and administration is the subject of much disagreement. However, Salazar the man is likely to retain a certain fascination because of his widely perceived honesty and asceticism, the simplicity of the life he led, and the strength of a patriotism that was acknowledged even by critics. Both his virtues and some of his vices also made him a somewhat un-Portuguese figure in several respects. His iron will, immense self-discipline and capacity for hard toil, as well as reserves of charm, calm under pressure, and an ability to inspire loyalty, enable him to stand out from a long procession of colourless rulers. (Only Pombal in the 18th century comes anywhere close in terms of statecraft.) There are no signs that the political class in 21st-century Portugal is capable of producing anyone with a fraction of his gifts, even though they may be needed if the technocratic European order in which the elite has invested faces deepening adversity.

He applied himself to governing the country in a dedicated but clearly overbearing manner that alienated many who preferred an alternative national path. Nevertheless, many Portuguese, beyond the reactionary sphere, are prepared to concede his dedication to public duties while recoiling from the way he projected his authority. Opinion polls have also frequently shown disenchantment with pluralist politicians for being far less serious in their approach to governance. Perhaps in a Europe struggling to recover from a coronavirus pandemic which is bound to leave great dislocation and hardship in its wake, there will be demand for national leaders of a not dissimilar stamp; ones who understand the need for active governance in order to prepare public institutions for tougher times.

Portugal may not be excluded if Europe is shaped by a new-found desire for elected rulers to govern primarily with the national interest uppermost in their minds and the interests of parties, clients, and foreign lobbies relegated to a lower plane. If customary political warfare is shelved, then Salazar may be invoked—not so much the dictator but the man who saw himself as the first servant of the nation; someone unlikely to flinch from rendering a full account of his stewardship to posterity.

John Maynard Keynes said of the French politician Georges Clemenceau that he 'had one illusion—France and one disillusion—mankind, including Frenchmen'.[72] Salazar doubted the ability of all segments of society, including the upper classes, to offer effective governance in modern conditions. This scepticism is shared by many of his own citizens and it has burst to the surface in countries historically more settled than Portugal has been.

It is perhaps hardly a reckless claim to say that for years into the future, Salazar is likely to remain synonymous with the country whose fortunes he guided during a crucial period in human affairs.

POSTSCRIPT

This biography about the life of Salazar, a micro-managing autocrat, was first published in the early months of an abnormal and disruptive situation that affected the whole world. The Covid-19 pandemic, a contagious infection which attacks the respiratory system, was in full spate. In a bid to control the spread of the virus, many Western democracies saw governments introduce unprecedented restraints on citizens going about their normal lives. In 2021, different states employed varying levels of pressure and urged their populations to take newly discovered vaccines. These vaccines were successful in reducing the death toll among the elderly and those whose pre-existing conditions made them more vulnerable. However, solidarity frayed when penalties for dissenting 'anti-vaxxers' were introduced, which acutely restricted their human rights. The ensuing public protests only increased when it became clear that none of the vaccines offered complete immunity from Covid-19. Vaccine 'refuseniks', and their sympathisers among the vaccinated, also expressed fears about the side effects of the vaccine. The scientific community was divided on the subject, although the range of opinion among experts was rarely shown by the corporate media, which was closely allied with state authorities. The polarisation and division did not recede when the evidence accumulated in the winter of 2021–2 showed that the pandemic appeared to be on the wane as natural immunity (by then, having been acquired by much of the population) acted as a barrier against its worst effects.

Some governments which had used the health emergency to establish a tight hold on the private lives of their citizens were reluctant to permit a return to the pre-Covid level of individual freedoms. Emergency powers, previously justified to tackle an exceptional occurrence, were retained. When what was seen as a centrally driven over-reaction sparked sizeable protests in Canada, the government arrested peaceable opponents, instructed financial institutions to seize individual financial assets, and threatened to remove the children of protesters if brought to illegal assemblies.[1]

Supporters of such bold moves offered justification on the grounds of the need for 'self-defending democracies' to resist social irresponsibility or insurgency. On the other hand, critics warned of the rise of a marked strain of 'authoritarian liberalism' whose enforcers were prepared to trample on long-established freedoms. Abrasive statements and tough actions from leaders in several states showed a preference for retaining emergency measures and rejecting dialogue and consultation with citizens.

Long-established and seemingly solid democracies, some of which, in the late 20th century, were involved in championing democracy elsewhere in the world, are among those which have seen a rapid advance in state power over the citizen. Australia, New Zealand and Canada have been much in the public eye for their forceful 'paternalistic' stance, with leaders very publicly slamming disobedient citizens and threatening to make an example of them for continued defiance.

Salazar was a determined paternalist who was prepared to use the state to enforce his will. Would he have been in his element had his rule coincided with such a medical emergency? Would he have extended his control over the daily lives of citizens, limiting contact with the outside world, and mobilising the media to create a synthetic sense of national unity? Would coercive measures have been adopted against whoever defied his emergency policies?

It is only possible to make speculations based on Salazar's inclinations in the face of unexpected challenges during his forty years at the centre of national affairs. How he responded to the acute economic difficulties of the early 1930s, the Spanish Civil War, World War II and, later, the colonial wars in Africa may offer clues. His regime was clearly an authoritarian one. But it was not one which expected citizens to participate intensively in the life of the state, nor did it closely supervise their private lives. There was an expansion of state power to handle economic coordination and strengthen national defence, but emergency powers that involved the close supervision of the lives of citizens on the scale of those acquired by many democracies in 2020–1 were never sought or acquired.

Perhaps a brief reminder of Salazar's conservative philosophy of life can give a clear indication of how he might have reacted to the pandemic. He strained every sinew to keep Portugal out of World War II, driven by the need to prevent mass civilian casualties and the collapse of the state, but he never believed that the Portuguese should be cocooned from the normal rigours and unexpected difficulties of life. He was not an advocate of *safetyism*, the now influential view that citizens need to be shielded from a variety of risks and dangers previously regarded as unavoidable parts of human existence. Salazar was a pessimist. He saw periodic calamities as an inevitable part of man's condition. Parts of Portugal near to where he had grown up, such as the Tagus River valley, had seen population levels decimated by the violence and destruction unleashed in the wake of the post-1807 Napoleonic invasion. It is quite possible that he would have used whatever means were at his disposal to protect the most vulnerable while trying to ensure that the economy and much of society functioned as normally as possible.

His belief in limited government meant that he thought the state ought to do far less than is customary today. He built a sizeable bureaucracy, but at the same time he had reservations about the motivations and intentions of regulators, rule-makers and wealth-holders. It stretches the imagination to assume that he would have been impressed by the qualifications of those at different levels of authority to whom power has been ceded during the pandemic.

It is quite likely that preserving a functioning economy would have been a strong priority. He was distrustful of foreign assistance, and he knew that keeping hunger and want at bay required the Portuguese to remain a productive people. So, it is hard to imagine him being a keen advocate of curfews and lockdowns of indeterminate length.

He might well have been surprised at the hectoring and abrasive tones leaders such as Emmanuel Macron in France and Mario Draghi in Italy used towards critics opposing the expansion of state power.[2] Salazar was unafraid of defending his undemocratic regime, but he was always careful to refrain from fuelling bitterness in his public statements. He was rarely if ever confrontational and he usually had no difficulty in admitting that his opponents were part of the national community, not outcasts. It is quite possible that the absence of a spirit of reconciliation in the pronouncements of Macron and Draghi would have strengthened Salazar's belief that, without strong institutional checks, the tendency in even well-known democracies is for them to evolve into a dictatorship of the majority (or the best-placed minority).

Internal divisions over the state's response to the pandemic were largely absent in Portugal. The vaccine take-up rate proved to be one of the highest in Europe. The age distribution of the population perhaps explains why. Twenty-four per cent of the population is over sixty-five and tends to look to the state for guidance. Thanks to emigration and a fast-decreasing birth rate, those under twenty-five now make up less than 13 per cent of the population.[3] Nearly everywhere, the elderly have been more receptive to the government line during the pandemic. They turn out in large numbers in elections. On 31 January 2022, they ensured that the ruling Socialists under António Costa, prime minister since 2015, obtained an absolute parliamentary majority. The quality of the left's rule has been variable as Portugal has fallen behind former communist states in Eastern Europe in terms of wealth and productivity. But its potent message of social paternalism chimes well in a country where 3.6 million, out of 10 million, have received pensions of various kinds from the state.

Salazar is likely to remain a figure of interest because of the way that he conserved power; as well as for his values, which shaped his actions and beliefs. It is hard now to draw as sharp a dividing line as before between his system of government and that of contemporary European democracies. Too many of them violated core elements of freedom during the pandemic by failing to heed the warning commonly attributed to the third President of the United States, Thomas Jefferson, that: 'There is no justification for taking away individuals' freedom in the guise of public safety.' Many of the reviews elicited by this biography in journals spanning the spectrum of ideas acknowledged that he was a ruler with evident failings but also distinctive qualities. His attachment to the national cause, which has gone out of fashion in the last seventy years, may appear less discordant because of an emerging tendency (one driven by events) to see politics as a matter of defending national objectives, rather than championing international goals.

The tragedy of Ukraine in 2022 has shown the limited ability of international forces to prevent civilisational norms from being assailed. The ability of an isolated democratic government to resist an invader, in no small part due to the depths of patriotic feeling and national solidarity, is also likely to improve the image of defensive nationalism in a ruthless and cruel world. Salazar's dictatorial style does not make him a comfortable emblem for small-state European nationalism in a fresh era of tyranny. But his ability to enable a country that was not very strong to survive in a predatory world is likely to be of continuing interest, given the present shattering of peace and stability in Europe.

NOTES

INTRODUCTION: A TENACIOUS DICTATOR IN A LIBERAL AGE

1. José Freire Antunes, *Cartas particulares a Marcello Caetano*, vol. 1, Lisbon: D. Quixote, 1985, p. 31.
2. Eduardo Coelho and António Macieira Coelho, *Salazar: o fim e a morte*, Lisbon: D. Quixote, 1995, p. 94.
3. Franco Nogueira, *Um político confessa-se: diário: 1960–1968*, Lisbon: Livraria Civilização Editora, 1986, p. 126.
4. Dan Bilefsky, 'Nostalgia for António de Oliveira Salazar Divides the Portuguese', *New York Times*, 23 July 2007.
5. Joel Kotkin, 'Our Suicidal Elites', *Quillette*, 23 April 2019, https://quillette.com/2019/04/30/our-suicidal-elites/ (accessed 30 April 2019).
6. See David Goodhart, *The Road to Somewhere: The Populist Revolt and the Future of Politics*, London: Hurst, 2017.
7. John Gray, 'You're Reaping What You Sowed, Liberals', *Unherd*, 7 February 2019, https://unherd.com/2019/02/youre-reaping-what-you-sowed-liberals/ (accessed 8 February 2019).

1. THE BOY FROM VIMIEIRO

1. Jaime Nogueira Pinto, *Salazar visto pelos seus próximos*, Lisbon: Ed. Bertrand, 2007 p. 23.
2. António Santos Luís, 'Pobreza', in António Barreto and Maria Filomena Mónica, *Dicionário de história de Portugal*, Suplemento P/Z, Lisbon: Figueirinhas, 1999, p. 104.
3. A.H. de Oliveira Marques, *História de Portugal*, vol. 3, Lisbon: Palas, 1981, p. 127.

4. Henrique Raposo, *História politicamente incorrecta de Portugal contemporâneo (de Salazar a Soares)*, Lisbon: Guerra & Paz, 2013, p. 81.

5. Quoted in Gabriel Paquette, *Imperial Portugal in the Age of Atlantic Revolutions: The Luso-Brazilian World, c.1780–1850*, Cambridge: Cambridge University Press, 2013, p. 319.

6. Leonor Freire Costa, Pedro Lains and Susana Münch Miranda, *An Economic History of Portugal 1143–2010*, Cambridge: Cambridge University Press, 2016 p. 235.

7. See Joaquin del Moral Ruiz, 'A independência brasileira e a sua repercussão no Portugal da época (1810–34)', *Analíse Social*, vol. 16, no. 64, 1980.

8. George W. Ball, *The Past Has Another Pattern: Memoirs*, New York: W.W. Norton, 1982, pp. 276–7.

9. Paquette, *Imperial Portugal*, pp. 318–19.

2. THE MAKING OF A CONSERVATIVE

1. Christine Garnier, *Vacances avec Salazar*, Paris: Grasset, 1952, p. 34.

2. 'Como surgiu a biografia (de Salazar) e quais as razões do seu exito' [interview with Franco Nogueira, 1977], *Observador*, https://observador.pt/especiais/franco-nogueira-a-entrevista-historica-salazar-a-revolucao-e-a-vida/ (accessed 30 August 2019).

3. Pedro Aires Oliveira, 'The Contemporary Era', *e-Journal of Portuguese History*, vol. 8, no. 2, Winter 2010, pp. 1–6.

4. Felícia Cabrita, *Mulheres de Salazar*, Lisbon: Editorial Notícias, 1999, pp. 20–32.

5. Manuel Catarino, *Salazar: só a cadeira o derrubou*, Lisbon: Correio da Manha, 2018, p. 110.

6. Catarino, *Salazar*, p. 26.

7. https://aviagemdosargonautas.net/2012/11/02/salazar-e-a-i-republica-9-por-jose-brandao/ (accessed 8 June 2019).

8. José Sollari Allegro, *A personalidade de Salazar e alguns aspectos da sua obra*, Lousã: Tipografia Lousanense, 1989, p. 4.

9. Pinto, *Salazar visto*, p. 31.

10. Howard J. Wiarda, *The Soul of Latin America: The Cultural and Political Tradition*, New Haven: Yale University Press, 2001, p. 44.

11. Franco Nogueira, *Salazar*, vol. I: *a mocidade e os princípios (1889–1928)*, Coimbra: Atlântida Editora, 1977, p. 88.

12. Allegro, *A personalidade*, p. 6.

13. Manuel de Lucena, 'Salazar', in António Barreto and Maria Filomena Mónica, *Dicionário de história de Portugal*, Suplemento P/Z, Lisbon: Figueirinhas, 1999, p. 319, n. 325.

14. The principal source for this paragraph was Pierre Goemaere, *Bissaya Barreto*, Lisbon: Livraria Bertrand, 1942. See also https://pt.wikipedia.org/wiki/Fernando_Bissaia_Barreto; https://journals.openedition.org/sociologico/1803

15. Catarino, *Salazar*, pp. 108–9.

16. Nogueira, *Salazar*, vol. I, p. 95.

17. Ibid., p. 168.

18. Cabrita, *Mulheres de Salazar*, p. 109.

19. Felipe Ribeiro de Meneses, *Salazar: A Political Biography*, New York: Enigma Books, 2009, p. 40.

20. See João Medina, 'Salazar, o ditador anti-português', *Mea Libra*, 3rd series, no. 20, Winter 2006–7, Viano do Castelo: Centro Cultural do Alto Minho; Cabrita, *Mulheres de Salazar*.

21. Manuel Braga da Cruz, 'O Integralismo Lusitano e o Estado Novo', in *O fascismo em Portugal*, Lisbon: Regra do Jogo, 1980, p. 114.

22. Irene Flunser Pimentel, *Fotobiografias, século XX—Cardeal Cerejeira*, Lisbon: Círculo de Leitores. 2002, p. 36, citing Alexandre Manuel, 'Cardeal Cerejeira', *Flama*, 18 May 1973, pp. 9–12.

23. *A minha resposta*, typewritten copy of 17-page document in possession of the municipal library in Povoa de Varzim, Portugal, p. 14.

24. *A minha resposta*, p. 3.

25. F.C.C. Egerton, *Salazar: Rebuilder of Portugal*, London: Hodder and Stoughton 1943, p. 107.

26. Yves Léonard, *Salazarisme et fascisme*, Paris: Chandeigne, 2003, pp. 34–5.

27. https://www.academia.edu/10375312/O_deputado_absentista_Salazar_e_o_parlamento_em_1921

28. *A minha resposta*, p. 11.

29. Ibid., p. 11.

3. SCALING THE HEIGHTS OF POWER

1. Nogueira, *Salazar*, vol. I, p. 194.

2. Fernando de Castro Brandão, *Cartas de Salazar para Gloria Castanheira, 1918–1923*, Lisbon: Europress, 2011, pp. 8–9.

3. Nogueira, *Salazar*, vol. I, pp. 215, 254.

4. Ibid., p. 252.

5. Fernando de Castro Brandão, 'A alegada ambição de Salazar, segundo o Padre Mateo', *Jornal O Diabo*, 25 June 2019, pp. 12–13.

6. José Freire Antunes, *Salazar e Caetano: cartas secretas, 1932–1968*, Lisbon: Circulo de Leitores, 1993, p. 14.

7. Duncan A.H. Simpson, 'Salazar's Patriarch: Political Aspects in the

Nomination of Manuel Gonçalves Cerejeira to the Patriarchate of Lisbon (April 1928—January 1930)', *Portuguese Studies*, vol. 25, no. 2, 2009, p. 140, n. 33.

8. Antunes, *Salazar e Caetano*, p. 14.

9. José António Saraiva, '28 de Maio: as verdades e os mitos', *Expresso*, Lisbon, 28 May 1979, p. 6 (review section).

10. Lucena, 'Salazar', p. 327.

11. Eugénio Montoito, *Henrique Galvão: ou a dissidência de um cadete de 28 de Maio (1927–1952)*, Lisbon: Centro de Historia, Universidade de Lisboa, 2005, p. 37.

12. José Luís Andrade, *Ditadura ou revolução: a verdadeira história do dilema ibérico nos anos decisivos de 1926–1936*, Lisbon: Casa das Letras, 2019, pp. 106–7.

13. David Neto, *Doa a quem doer*, Porto: Livraria Tavares Martins, 1933, pp. 190–1.

14. Léonard, *Salazarisme et fascisme*, p. 41.

15. Marques, *História de Portugal*, vol. 3, p. 210.

16. Nogueira, *Salazar*, vol. I, p. 337.

17. Garnier, *Vacances*, p. 73.

18. Freire Antunes, *Salazar e Caetano*, pp. 15–16.

19. Fátima Patriarca and Leal Marques, 'Diário de Leal Marques sobre a formação do primeiro governo de Salazar: apresentação', *Análise Social*, vol. 41, no. 178, 2006, p. 174.

20. António de Oliveira Salazar, *Doctrine and Action: Internal and Foreign Policy of the New Portugal 1928–1939*, trans. Edgar Broughton, London: Faber and Faber, 1939.

21. For this affair, see Francisco Carlos Palomanes Martinho, *Marcello Caetano and the Portuguese 'New State'*, Brighton: Sussex Academic Press, 2018, p. 21.

22. Franco Nogueira, *Salazar*, vol. 2: *os tempos aureos, 1928–1936*, Coimbra, Atlântida Editor, 1978, p. 62.

23. Fernando Rosas, *Salazar e o poder: a arte de saber a durar*, Lisbon: Tinta da Cina, 2013, pp. 96, 98.

24. Nogueira, *Salazar*, vol. 2, p. 62.

25. Joaquim Veríssimo Serrão, *História de Portugal*, vol. XIII *(1926–1935): do 28 Maio ao Estado Novo*, Lisbon: Editorial Verbo, 2000, p. 230.

26. Jaime Nogueira Pinto, *Portugal: ascensão e queda*, Lisbon: D. Quixote, 2013, p. 173.

27. António José Telo, *Economía e império no Portugal contemporâneo*, Lisbon: Ed. Cosmos, 1994, pp. 225–6.

28. Helena Matos, *Salazar: a construção do mito 1928–1933*, Lisbon: Circulo de Leitores, 2010, pp. 125–9.

29. Alan K. Smith, 'António Salazar and the Reversal of Portuguese Colonial Policy', *Journal of African History*, vol. 15, no. 4, October 1974, p. 663.
30. Manuel de Lucena, *Os lugar-tenentes de Salazar: biografías*, Lisbon: Aletheia Editora, 2015, pp. 11–16.
31. Valentim Alexandre, 'Ideologia, economía e política: a questão colonial na implantação do Estado Novo', *Análise Social*, vol. 28, nos. 123–124, 1993, pp. 1132–3.
32. Smith, 'António Salazar', p. 664.
33. Ibid., pp. 664–5.
34. Lucena, *Os lugar-tenentes*, p. 28.
35. See Douglas L. Wheeler, 'The Galvão Report on Forced Labour in Historical Context and Perspective: A Troubleshooter Who Was "Trouble"', *Portuguese Studies Review*, vol. 16, no. 1, 2009, pp. 115–52.
36. See Patriarca, 'Diário de Leal Marques'.
37. See Bernardo Futscher Pereira, *A diplomacia de Salazar (1932–1949)*, Lisbon: D. Quixote, 2012, pp. 32–3.
38. Vasco Pulido Valente, 'Marcello Caetano', in Barreto and Mónica, *Dicionário de história de Portugal*, vol. 7, Suplemento A/E, p. 200.
39. Lucena, *Os lugar-tenentes*, p. 70.
40. Ibid., p. 78.
41. Nogueira, *Salazar*, vol. 2, p. 79.
42. Ibid., p. 82.
43. Matos, *Salazar*, p. 143, n. 98.
44. Public Records Office (London), FO 371 15741, W7467/801/36, 25 June 1931, Frederick Adams, to Arthur Henderson, quoted in Tom Gallagher, *Portugal: A Twentieth Century Interpretation*, Manchester: Manchester University Press, 1983, p. 60, n. 38.
45. Francisco Cunha Leal, *As minhas memórias*, Lisbon: Edição do Autor, 1966, p. 307, quoted in Rui Ramos (ed.), *História de Portugal*, Lisbon: A Esfera dos Livros, 2009, p. 609.
46. Matos, *Salazar*, pp. 186–7.

4. SALAZAR CONSTRUCTS HIS 'NEW STATE'

1. Howard J. Wiarda, *Corporatism and Development: The Portuguese Experience*, Amherst: University of Massachusetts Press, 1977, p. 291.
2. Wiarda, *Corporatism*, pp. 282–3.
3. Cecília Barreiras, *Quirino de Jesus e outros estudos*, Lisbon: Edições Livro PT, 2017, p. 18.
4. Barreiras, *Quirino de Jesus*, p. 19.
5. António Sérgio, *Breve interpretaçaõ da história de Portugal*, Lisbon: Sá da Costa, 1974, p. 145.

6. Richard Robinson, *Contemporary Portugal: A History*, London: Allen and Unwin, 1979, p. 48; Matos, *Salazar*, p. 323.

7. Gustave Le Bon, *The Psychology of Socialism*, London: T. Fisher Unwin, 1919, p. ix.

8. Andrade, *Ditadura*, p. 292; Robinson, *Contemporary Portugal*, p. 48.

9. Rosas, *Salazar e o poder*, p. 124.

10. Goffredo Adinolfi and António Costa Pinto, 'Salazar's "New State": The Paradoxes of Hybridization in the Fascist Era', in António Costa Pinto and Aristotle Kallis (eds.), *Thinking Fascism and Dictatorship in Europe*, London: Palgrave Macmillan, 2014, p. 161.

11. Ramos, *História*, p. 653.

12. William C. Atkinson 'Institutions and Law', in Harold Livermore (ed.), *Portugal and Brazil: An Introduction*, Oxford: Clarendon Press, 1953, p. 81.

13. António Ferro, *Salazar, Portugal and Its Leader*, London: Faber and Faber, 1939, p. 244.

14. Adinolfi and Pinto, 'Salazar's "New State"', p. 161.

15. Quoted by Wiarda, *Corporatism*, p. 101.

16. *Discursos e notas políticas (1935–1937)*, p. 72, translation found in Patrícia Vieira, *Portuguese Film, 1930–1960: The Staging of the New State Regime*, London: Bloomsbury, 2013, p. 25.

17. Matos, *Salazar*, p. 338.

18. Marcello Caetano, *Manual de ciência política e direito constitucional*, 6th edn, vol. II, Coimbra: Coimbra Editora, 1972, p. 516.

19. See Mariana Canotilho, 'A Constituição Portuguesa de 1933', in António Simões do Paço (ed.), *Os anos de Salazar*, vol. 2: *a constituição do Estado Novo*, Lisbon: Planeta de Agostini, 2008, pp. 7–9.

20. Quoted in Lucena, 'Salazar', p. 313.

21. Frank Furedi, *First World War: Still No End in Sight*, London: Bloomsbury, 2007, p. 55.

22. Diogo Freitas do Amaral, *O antigo regime e a revolução: memórias políticas (1941–1975)*, Venda Nova: Livraria Bertrand/Noma, 1995, p. 69.

23. Adinolfi and Pinto, *Thinking Fascism*, p. 166.

24. Wiarda, *Corporatism*, p. 172.

25. Ibid., p. 142.

26. See Fátima Patriarca, *A revolta de 18 Janeiro de 1934*, Lisbon: Instituto de Ciências Sociais, 2000.

27. Wiarda, *Corporatism*, p. 10.

28. Lucena, *Os lugar-tenentes*, p. 78.

29. Philippe Schmitter, *Corporatism and Public Policy in Authoritarian Portugal*, London: Sage Publications, 1975, p. 22.

30. José Luís Cardoso and Nuno Estêvão Ferreira, 'A Câmara Corporativa

(1935–1974) e as políticas públicas no Estado Novo', *Ler História*, no. 64, 2013, https://journals.openedition.org/lerhistoria/290 (accessed 3 August 2019).

31. Steve Harrison, *A Tale of Two Cities: A Curious Tourist's Journey back to Povoa de Varzim in the 1950s*, Oporto: Blue Book, 2019, pp. 137–8.

32. Wolfgang Adler, 'Salazar and the Loss of the Business Elite', https://www.socialmatter.net/2017/12/06/salazar-loss-business-elite/ 6 December 2017 (accessed 18 February 2019).

33. See Jaime Reis, 'Portuguese Banking in the Inter-War Period', in C.H. Feinstein, *Banking, Currency and Finance in Europe between the Wars*, Oxford: Clarendon Press, 1995, p. 495.

34. 'Economy of the Salazar Regime', *Country Studies Series by Federal Research Division of the Library of Congress*, http://www.country-data.com/cgi-bin/query/r-10909.html, quoted in Adler, 'Salazar'.

35. David Corkill, *The Portuguese Economy since 1974*, Edinburgh: Edinburgh University Press, 1993, p. 11.

36. Cardoso e Estêvão Ferreira, 'A Câmara Corporativa'.

37. Wiarda, *Corporatism*, p. 162.

38. Ramos, *História*, p. 648.

39. Fernando Rosas, *História de Portugal*, vol. 7: *o Estado Novo (1926–1974)*, Lisbon: Editorial Estampa, n.d., p. 46.

40. See Salazar, *Doctrine*, p. 19.

41. Jorge Besada, 'Two Reasons Why Socialism Repeatedly Fails', *Mises Wire*, 29 May 2019, https://mises.org/wire/two-reasons-why-socialism-repeatedly-fails (accessed 19 June 2019).

42. A.H. de Oliveira Marques, *History of Portugal*, vol. II: *From Empire to Corporate State*, New York: Columbia University Press, 1973, p. 183.

43. Idelino Costa Brochado, *Memórias de Costa Brochado*, Lisbon: Livraria Popular Francisco Franco, 1987, p. 305.

44. See Gladden Pappin, 'Corporatism for the Twenty-First Century', *American Affairs*, vol. 4, no. 1, Spring 2020, https://americanaffairs-journal.org/2020/02/corporatism-for-the-twenty-first-century/ (accessed 20 February 2020); also Matthew Hilton et al., *The Politics of Expertise: How NGOs Shaped Modern Britain*, Oxford: Oxford University Press, 2013.

45. Wiarda, *Corporatism*, p. 171.

46. Maurice Glasman, 'Yes, the House of Lords Needs Reform: Why Not Create Vocational Peerages?', *The Guardian*, 20 October 2017.

47. Salazar, *Doctrine*, p. 247.

48. Quoted in Vieira, *Film*, p. 77.

49. Yoram Hazony, 'Conservative Rationalism Has Failed', *The American Mind*, 1 July 2019, https://americanmind.org/essays/conservative-rationalism-has-failed-2/ (accessed 10 July 2019).

50. *'O meu depoimento'* (no Palácio da Bolsa, em 7 de Janeiro de 1949, ao inaugurar-se a conferência da União Nacional e a campanha para a reeleição do Senhor Presidente da República, Lisbon: SNI, 1949.
51. Randall Morcka and Bernard Yeung, 'Corporatism and the Ghost of the Third Way', *SSRN*, 10 December 2010, p. 30, http://ssrn.com/abstract=1722350 (accessed 9 June 2019).

5. THE ART OF PERSUASION: ALLIES AND RIVALS SUBMIT TO SALAZARISM

1. See Paul Blanshard, *Freedom and Catholic Power in Spain and Portugal*, Boston: Beacon Press, 1962.
2. Luís Salgado Matos, 'Cardeal Cerejeira: universitário, militante, místico', *Análise Social*, vol. 36, no. 60, 2001, p. 803.
3. Pimentel, *Cardeal Cerejeira: fotobiografias*, p. 73.
4. Nogueira, *Salazar*, vol. 2, p. 152.
5. Salazar, *Doctrine*, p. 138.
6. Manuel Braga da Cruz, 'Centro Académico da Democracia Cristã', in Barreto and Mónica, *Dicionário de história de Portugal*, vol. 7, A/E, Lisbon: Figueirinhas, 1999, p. 291.
7. Lucena, 'Salazar', p. 332.
8. Anabela P. Parreira et al., 'O 1 Congresso da União Nacional', in *AAVV: o fascismo em Portugal*, Actas do Colóquio Realizado na Faculdade de Letras de Lisboa, Lisbon: Regra do Jogo, 1980, p. 228.
9. See Rui Ramos, 'O Estado Novo perante os poderes periféricos: o governo de Assis Gonçalves em Vila Real (1934–39)', *Análise Social*, vol. 22, no 90, 1986, p. 115.
10. See Álvaro Garrido, 'Henrique Tenreiro: "patrão das pescas" e guardião do Estado Novo', *Análise Social*, vol. 36, no. 160, 2001, pp. 839–62.
11. Ramos, 'O Estado Novo perante', pp. 133–4, n. 76.
12. See Jaime Nogueira Pinto, *O fim do Estado Novo e as origens do 25 de Abril*, Lisbon: Difel, 1995, p. 72.
13. Wiarda, *Corporatism*, p. 285.
14. *Gazette de Liège*, 9 September 1948.
15. For what happened in Fátima and its aftermath, see Jeffrey S. Bennett, *When the Sun Danced: Myth, Miracles, and Modernity in Early Twentieth-Century Portugal*, Charlottesville, VA: Virginia University Press, 2012.
16. Leonard, *Salazarisme et fascisme*, pp. 117–18.
17. Eugene Keefe, *Area Handbook for Portugal*, Washington DC: American University, 1977, p. 147.
18. Raposo, *História politicamente incorrecta*, pp. 26–7.

19. Franco Nogueira, *Salazar*, vol. 3: *as grandes crises 1936–1945*, Coimbra: Atlântida Editora, 1978, p. 262.
20. Lucena, 'Salazar', p. 379.
21. Pereira, *A diplomacia*, p. 407.
22. Raposo, *História politicamente incorrecta*, p. 27.
23. Fernando Dacosta, *Salazar fotobiografia*, Lisbon: Editorial Notícias, 2000, p. 59.
24. Stanley G. Payne and Jesús Palacios, *Franco: A Personal and Political Biography*, Madison: University of Wisconsin Press, 2014, p. 316.
25. Salazar, *Doctrine*, p. 136.
26. Nogueira, *Salazar*, vol. 3, p. 140.
27. Arnold Madureira, *Salazar anos de tensão*, Lisbon: Clube do Autor, 2017, p. 155.
28. Philip Rees, *Biographical Dictionary of the Extreme Right since 1890*, London: Simon and Schuster, 1990, p. 314.
29. Rees, *Biographical Dictionary*, p. 293.
30. Pinto, *Portugal: ascensão e queda*, p. 142.
31. Gallagher, *Portugal: A Twentieth Century Interpretation*, p. 90.
32. Rosas, *Salazar e o poder*, p. 135.
33. Raymond Aron, *Democracy and Totalitarianism*, London: Weidenfeld and Nicolson, 1968, pp. 154–5.
34. Rosas, *Salazar e o poder*, p. 140.
35. António Costa Pinto, *The Blueshirts: Portuguese Fascists and the New State*, New York: Columbia University Press, 2000, p. 168.
36. Pinto, *The Blueshirts*, p. 161.
37. Matos, *Salazar*, p. 318.
38. Ramos, *História*, p. 639.
39. Ferro, *Salazar*, p. 248.
40. Pinto, *The Blueshirts*, pp. 172–3.
41. Tom Gallagher, 'Portugal', in Martin Blinkhorn (ed.), *Fascists and Conservatives*, London: Routledge, 1990, p. 163.
42. 'As coisas que eles escreviam a Salazar', *Jornal O Diabo*, Lisbon: 30 August 2015, http://jornaldiabo.com/continuacao/salazar-cartas-ii/ (accessed 3 July 2019).
43. Luís Cabral de Moncada, *Memória: ao longo de uma vida (pessoas, factos, ideias), 1888–1974*, Lisbon: Verbo, 1992, pp. 182–3.
44. Salazar, *Doctrine*, p. 38.
45. Adriano Moreira and Vítor Gonçalves, *Este é o tempo: Portugal, o amor, a política e Salazar*, Lisbon: Clube do Autor, 2015.
46. José Pacheco Pereira, *Álvaro Cunhal: uma biografia política*, vol. 1: *1913–41*, Lisbon: Temas e Debates, 1999, pp. 443–4.

6. PORTUGUESE RUTHLESSNESS IN THE STRUGGLE FOR IBERIA

1. Madureira, *Salazar*, p. 301. Full article is reproduced in 'A geração que passou', http://doportugalprofundo.blogspot.com/2008/12/a-geracao-que-passou.html (accessed 30 June 2019).
2. Marcello Caetano, *Minhas memórias de Salazar*, Lisbon: Verbo, 1977, pp. 106–7.
3. Pedro Aires Oliveira, 'Taking Sides: Salazar's *Estado Novo*, the Nationalist Uprising and the Spanish Civil War', in Raanan Rein and Joan Maria Thomàs (eds.), *Spain 1936:Year Zero*, Brighton: University of Sussex Press, 2018.
4. Cesar Oliveira, 'Guerra Civil de Espanha', in Barreto and Mónica, *Dicionário de história de Portugal*, vol. 7, Suplemento F/O, p. 149
5. Peter Fryer and Patricia McGowan Pinheiro, *Oldest Ally: A Portrait of Salazar's Portugal*, London: Dennis Dobson, 1961, pp. 245 7.
6. Salazar, *Doctrine*, p. 312.
7. Oliveira, 'Taking Sides', p. 119.
8. 'Portuguese Naval Revolt', Australian Associated Press, 10 September 1936.
9. Oliveira, 'Taking Sides', p. 120.
10. Pereira, *A diplomacia*, p. 114.
11. Zara Steiner, *The Triumph of the Dark: European International History 1933–1939*, Oxford: Oxford University Press, 2011, p. 217.
12. Pereira, *A diplomacia*, p. 130.
13. Ibid., p. 117.
14. Oliveira, 'Guerra Civil', p. 151.
15. Lucena, *Os lugar-tenentes*, p. 91.
16. See Pereira, *A diplomacia*, p. 246.
17. Lucena, *Os lugar-tenentes*, p. 70.
18. Ibid., pp. 69–70.
19. Pereira, *A diplomacia*, p. 160.
20. Lucena, *Os lugar-tenentes*, p. 106.
21. Pereira, *A diplomacia*, p. 194.
22. Ibid., p. 12.
23. Lucena, *Os lugar-tenentes*, p. 114.
24. Pereira, *A diplomacia*, p. 199.
25. Ibid., p. 537.
26. Ibid., p. 194.
27. Interview with Fernando Santos Costa, Lisbon, 20 July 1981.
28. Ibid.
29. Madureira, *Salazar*, p. 180.
30. Brochado, *Memórias*, p. 164.

31. Brochado, *Memórias*, p. 164; Madureira, *Salazar anos*, p. 177.

32. José Javier Olivas Osuna, *Iberian Military Politics: Controlling the Armed Forces during Dictatorship and Democratisation*, London: Palgrave, 2014, p. 29.

33. Interview with Fernando Santos Costa, Lisbon, 20 July 1981.

34. Salazar, *Doctrine*, p. 388.

35. Ibid.

36. Ibid., p. 390.

37. Pereira, *A diplomacia*, p. 143.

38. Salazar, *Doctrine*, p. 362.

39. Ibid., p. 363.

40. Pedro Aires de Oliveira, 'Augusto Vasconcelos e o crise de SDN', *Relações Internaçionais*, 2004, p. 114, http://www.ipri.pt/images/publicacoes/revista_ri/pdf/r1/RI01_Artg14_PAO.pdf (accessed 30 June 2019).

41. Madureira, *Anos*, p. 21

42. Jaime Nogueira Pinto, 'As origens ideológicos do fascismo e do Estado Novo', *Futuro Presente*, no. 31, October–December 1990, p. 33.

43. Ramos, *História*, p. 653.

44. Aires de Oliveira, 'Augusto Vasconcelos', p. 114.

45. Quoted in Ramos, *História*, p. 649.

46. S. Kuin, 'A Mocidade Portuguesa nos anos trinta: anteprojectos e instauração de uma organização paramilitar de juventude', *Análise Social*, vol. 122, no. 28, 1993, pp. 584–5.

47. Raposo, *História politicamente incorrecta*, p. 30.

48. Madureira, *Salazar*, p. 193.

49. Kuin, 'A Mocidade', p. 572.

50. Ferro, *Salazar*, p. 176.

51. Salazar, *Doctrine*, p. 231; Ferro, *Salazar*, p. 176.

52. Ferro, *Salazar*, p. 248.

53. Margarida Magalhães Ramalho, 'Diplomacia em tempos de guerra', *Expresso*, 11 September 2018.

54. Vieira, *Film*, p. 53.

55. Orlando Raimundo, *António Ferro: o inventor do salazarismo*, Lisbon: D. Quixote, 2015, p. 149.

56. S.S. George West, lecturer in Portuguese at London University, from a lecture on 'The New Corporative State of Portugal', quoted by Michael Derrick, *The Portugal of Salazar*, London: Sands, 1938, p. 30.

57. Raimundo, *António Ferro*, p. 154.

58. Ibid., p. 176.

59. R.R. Reno, 'Eliot and Liberalism', *First Things*, 1 April 2016, https://

www.firstthings.com/blogs/firstthoughts/2016/01/eliot-and-liberalism (accessed 8 October 2019).

60. Margarida Acciaiuoli, *António Ferro: a vertigem da palavra*, Lisbon: Bizancio, 2013, p. 84.
61. Ferro, *Salazar*, p. 266.
62. Ibid., p. 270.
63. Raimundo, *António Ferro*, p. 166.
64. Ibid., p. 167.
65. Acciaiuoli, *António Ferro*, p. 8.
66. Raimundo, *António Ferro*, p. 153.
67. Ibid., p. 355.
68. Ibid., p. 338.
69. Garnier, *Vacances*, p. 84.
70. Ferro, *Salazar, Portugal*, p. 77.
71. Ibid., p. 77.
72. See José Gil, *Salazar: a retórica da invisibilidade*, Lisbon: Relógio D'Água, 1995.

7. SALAZAR'S PRIVATE WORLD

1. See Gerald Russell, 'Psychiatry and Politicians: The "Hubris Syndrome"', *The Psychiatrist*, vol. 35, no. 4, April 2011, pp. 140–5.
2. José Freire Antunes, 'Kennedy, Portugal and the Azores Base, 1961', in Douglas Brinkley and Richard T. Griffiths (eds.), *Kennedy and Europe*, Baton Rouge: Louisiana State University Press, 1999, p. 153.
3. For full accounts, see António de Araújo, *Matar o Salazar: o atentado de Julho de 1937*, Lisbon: Tinta da China, 2017; João Madeira, *1937—o atentado a Salazar: a frente popular em Portugal*, Lisbon: A Esfera dos Livros, 2013; Emídio Santana, *História de um atentado: o atentado a Salazar*, Lisbon: Forum, 1976.
4. See Araújo, *Matar o Salazar*.
5. Amaral, *O antigo regime*, p. 16.
6. Maria da Conceição de Melo Rita and Joaquim Vieira, *Os meus 35 anos com Salazar*, Lisbon: A Esfera dos Livros, 2007, p. 47.
7. Rosas, *Salazar e o poder*, p. 216.
8. Madureira, *Salazar anos*, p. 127.
9. Rita and Vieira, *Os meus 35 anos*, pp. 50–1.
10. Ibid., p. 53.
11. See Joaquim Vieira, *A governanta*, Lisbon: A Esfera dos Livros, 2010, ch. 9, 'A Caixa do Correio.'
12. Brochado, *Memórias*, p. 138.
13. Lumena Raposo, 'A mulher que humaniza o ditador', *Diário de Noticias*,

5 June 2010; 'Maria de Jesus: a governanta de Portugal', *History Passion*, 31 July 2018, https://gamepassion.blogs.sapo.pt/maria-de-jesus-a-governanta-de-portugal-23751 (accessed 4 July 2019).

14. Rita and Vieira, *Os meus 35 anos*, p. 40.
15. Caetano, *Minhas memórias*, p. 185.
16. Rita and Vieira, *Os meus 35 anos*, p. 63.
17. Martin Hume, *Through Portugal*, London: E.G. Richards, 1907, p. 233.
18. Neill Lochery, *Lisbon:War in the Shadows of the City of Light, 1939–1945*, New York: Public Affairs, 2011, p. 227.
19. Dean Acheson, *Sketches from Life of Men I Have Known*, London: Hamish Hamilton, 1961, pp. 115–16.
20. Nogueira, *Salazar*, vol. 3, p. 174.
21. See Amaral, *O antigo regime*, pp. 50–2.
22. 'Maria de Jesus: a governanta de Portugal', *History Passion*, 31 July 2018.
23. Lucena, 'Salazar', p. 380.
24. See Harrison, *A Tale of Two Cities*, pp. 175–6.
25. Miguel Carvalho, 'Estátuas, cabeças, nomes de ruas e a avenida que se abre para Soares', *Visão*, 11 January 2017.
26. Lucena, 'Salazar', p. 379.
27. Fernando de Castro Brandão, *Cartas singulares a Salazar*, Lisbon: Edição de Autor, 2015.
28. Mário Soares, *Portugal's Struggle for Liberty*, London: Allen and Unwin, 1975, pp. 94–5.
29. Pinto, *O fim*, p. 324.
30. Wiarda, *Corporatism*, p. 143.
31. Rosas, *História*, p. 111.
32. Brochado, *Memórias*, p. 380.
33. Rosas, *Salazar e o poder*, pp. 152–3.
34. Rita and Vieira, *Os meus 35 anos*, p. 45.
35. Mário Soares, 'Salazar, o retrato', *Público Magazin*, 29 July 1990.

8. WALKING EUROPE'S NEUTRAL TIGHTROPE, 1939–42

1. Raposo, *História politicamente incorrecta*, p. 96.
2. Fernando de Castro Brandão, *Salazar: uma cronologia*, Lisbon: Prefácio, 2011, p. 80.
3. See José Manuel Duarte de Jesus, *Dança sobre o vulcão: Portugal e o III Reich*, Lisbon: Edições 70, 2017.
4. Pereira, *A diplomacia*, p. 530.
5. Ibid., p. 191.
6. Ibid., p. 201.

7. Ibid., p. 201.
8. Stanley Payne, *Franco and Hitler: Spain, Germany and World War II*, New Haven and London: Yale University Press, 2009, p. 69.
9. Ibid., p. 75.
10. Ibid.
11. André de Staercke, *Mémoires sur la régence et la question royale*, Brussels: Éditions Racine, 2003, p. 290.
12. Pereira, *A diplomacia*, pp. 216–17.
13. Viscount Templewood, *Ambassador on a Special Mission*, London: Collins, 1946, p. 124.
14. Michael Bloch, *Operation Willi: The Plot to Kidnap the Duke of Windsor*, London: Weidenfeld, 1984, p. 73.
15. Ibid., p. 75.
16. David Eccles, *By Safe Hand: Letters of Sybil and David Eccles, 1939–42*, London: Bodley Head, 1983 p. 99.
17. Ibid., p. 100.
18. Ibid., p. 125.
19. W.N. Medlicott, *The Economic Blockade*, vol. II, London: HMSO, 1959, p. 314.
20. Payne, *Franco and Hitler*, p. 81.
21. Payne, *Franco and Hitler*, p. 88, n. 3; Javier Tussel, *Franco, Espana y la II Guerra Mundial*, p. 153.
22. Payne, *Franco and Hitler*, pp. 82–3, quoting *Documents on German Foreign Policy*, Washington DC, 1950, D, 11: 199–200.
23. Manuel Braga da Cruz, 'Pedro Teotónio Pereira, embaixador português em Espanha durante as Guerras', in *Estudos em homenagem a Luís António de Oliveira Ramos*, Oporto: Faculdade de Letras da Universidade do Porto, 2004, p. 436.
24. Paul Preston, 'Spain: Betting on a Nazi Victory', in R. Bosworth and J. Maiolo (eds.). *The Cambridge History of the Second World War*, vol. 2: *Politics and Ideology*, Cambridge: Cambridge University Press, 2015, pp. 327–8.
25. Preston, 'Spain', p. 327.
26. Payne, *Franco and Hitler*, pp. 103–4.
27. Preston, 'Spain', p. 327.
28. Payne, *Franco and Hitler*, p. 99.
29. Gerard F. Rutan, 'Factors Affecting the German Decision Not to Invade the Iberian Peninsula, 1940–1945', MA thesis, University of Montana, 1958.
30. Arthur Bryant, *The Turn of the Tide, 1939–1943*, London: Collins, 1959, p. 244.
31. Kenneth G. Weiss, *The Azores in Diplomacy and Strategy, 1940–1945*, Fort Belvoir, VA: Defence Technical Information Center, 1980, p. 5.

32. Ibid., p. 6.
33. Ibid.
34. Ibid., p. 7.
35. Ibid., p. 8.
36. Pereira, *A diplomacia*, p. 285.
37. Preston, 'Spain', p. 341.
38. Ibid., p. 334.
39. Cruz, 'Pedro', p. 437.
40. António Pina Amaral, 'Insólito pic-nic: o encontro Salazar/Franco', *Jornal O Diabo*, 15 November 2009, https://jornalodiabo.blogs.sapo.pt/tag/salazar (accessed 7 July 2019).
41. See Peter Conradi, *Hitler's Piano Player: The Rise and Fall of Ernst Hanfstaengl, Confidant of Hitler, Ally of FDR*, London: Duckworth, 2006.
42. Pereira, *A diplomacia*, p. 338.
43. Gonzague de Reynold, *Portugal*, Paris: Spas, 1936.
44. Ibid., pp. 333–4.
45. Letter of Salazar to Gonzague de Reynold, 2 March 1937. See Joana Gaspar de Freitas, *Gonzague de Reynold e Oliveira Salazar: 25 anos de correspondência*, Lisbon: Faculty of Letters, University of Lisbon, 2003, p. 4.
46. See Nicolau Andresen Leitão, 'The Salazar Regime and European Integration, 1947–72', in Pedro Aires Oliveira and Maria I. Rezola (eds.), *Estudos em homenagem a Jose Medeiros Ferreira*, Lisbon: Tinta da China, 2010, p. 468.
47. Roberts, *The Story of War*, p. 112.
48. Freitas, *Gonzague*, pp. 7–8.
49. Roberts, *The Story of War*, p. 301.
50. Cruz, 'Pedro Teotónio Pereira', p. 440.

9. NO SAFE HARBOUR FOR SALAZAR OR HIS REGIME

1. Harvey Klemmer, 'Lisbon: Gateway to Warring Europe', *National Geographic Magazine*, vol. 80, August 1941.
2. Klemmer, 'Lisbon', p. 273.
3. David Corkill and José Pina Almeida, 'Commemoration and Propaganda in Salazar's Portugal', *Journal of Contemporary History*, vol. 44, no. 3, 2009, p. 381.
4. Raimundo, *António Ferro*, p. 293.
5. See Rita Almeida de Carvalho, 'Ideology and Architecture in the Portuguese "Estado Novo": Cultural Innovation within a Para-Fascist State (1932–1945)', *Journal of Comparative Fascist Studies*, vol. 7, 2018, https://doi.org/10.1163/22116257–00702002 (accessed 3 April 2019).

6. Emília Caetano, 'Perfil Duarte Pacheco: mais depressa, sempre', *Visão História*, n.d.
7. Madureira, *Salazar anos*, p. 239.
8. Nogueira, *Salazar*, vol. 3, p. 589.
9. Pereira, *A diplomacia*, p. 245.
10. Ibid.
11. Bloch, *Operation Willi*, pp. 48–9.
12. Ibid.
13. This paragraph is partly drawn from the article by Margarida Ramalho, 'Os diplomatas de Berlin', *Expresso*, 18 August 2018, https://expresso. pt/internacional/2018–08–18-Os-diplomatas-de-Berlim (accessed 28 July 2019).
14. Pereira, *A diplomacia*, p. 303.
15. See Payne, *Franco and Hitler*, p. 170.
16. Lucena, *Os lugar-tenentes*, p. 44.
17. Carlos Fernandes, *O consul Aristides Sousa Mendes: a verdade e a mentira*, Lisbon: Edição de Grupo de Amigos do Autor, 2013, p. 40.
18. Lina Alves Madeira, 'Nacionalismo e Americanismo numa contenda jornalística Aristides de Sousa Mendes e a comunidade portuguesa de S. Francisco', *Estudos do Século XX* (University of Coimbra), vol. 7, no. 8, 2007, p. 2001 (accessed 24 July 2019).
19. Fernandes, *O consul*, p. 27.
20. See Fernandes, *O consul*, p. 46; Rui Afonso, *Um homem bom: o 'Wallenberg portugues'*, Lisbon: Editorial Caminho, 1995, p. 196.
21. Avraham Milgram, *Portugal, Salazar e os Judeus*, Lisbon: Gradiva, 2010, p. 84.
22. Lochery, *Lisbon*, pp. 42–3.
23. Milgram, *Portugal, Salazar e os Judeus*, p. 13.
24. Adolfo Benarus, *O anti-semitismo*, Lisbon: SNT, 1937, p. 31.
25. *Dez anos de politica externa*, vol. 1, Lisbon: Editor Imprensa Nacional, 1961, p. 137.
26. Irene Flunser Pimentel, *Judeus em Portugal durante a II Guerra Mundial*, Lisbon: A Esfera dos Livros, 2006, p. 41. The English translation of the title is 'How to Establish a State'.
27. Milgram, *Portugal, Salazar*, pp. 149–51.
28. Milgram, *Portugal, Salazar*, p. 102; Lochery, *Lisbon: War*, p. 47.
29. José Alain Fralon, *A Good Man in Evil Times: The Story of Aristides de Sousa Mendes*, London: Penguin, 2001, pp. 110–11.
30. Milgram, *Portugal, Salazar*, p. 102.
31. Afonso, *Um homem bom*, pp. 27–8, 301–2.
32. See Letter from the State Defence and Surveillance Police (PVDE) to the secretary-general of the Portuguese Foreign Ministry, dated 18 July

1940, from Ministry of Foreign Affairs Historical-Diplomatic Archive, contained in the Aristides de Sousa Mendes Virtual Museum, http://mvasm.sapo.pt/BC/Archives/en (accessed 10 October 2019).

33. See Fralon, *A Good Man*.
34. http://sousamendesfoundation.org/aristides-de-sousa-mendes-his-life-and-legacy/ (accessed 24 July 2019).
35. Afonso, *Um homem bom*, p. 257. For a state document confirming his salary status, see http://purl.sgmf.pt/326970/1/326970_item1/index.html.
36. http://sousamendesfoundation.org/aristides-de-sousa-mendes-his-life-and-legacy/ (accessed 24 July 2019).
37. Avraham Milgram, 'Portugal, the Consuls, and the Jewish Refugees, 1938–1941', Shoah Research Center, The International School for Holocaust Studies, p. 22.
38. Milgram, 'Portugal, the Consuls', pp. 22–3.
39. Pinto, *Salazar visto*, pp. 201–2.
40. José Freire Antunes, *Judeus em Portugal: o testemunho de 50 homens e mulheres*, Lisbon: Edeline Multimedia, 2002, p. 41.
41. http://visao.sapo.pt/actualidade/sociedade/opiniao-de-esther-mucznik=f521048.
42. Antunes, *Judeus*, p. 39.
43. Ibid., p. 42.
44. Afonso, *Um homem bom*, p. 145.
45. Irene Flunser Pimentel and Claudia Ninhos, *Salazar, Portugal e o Holocausto*, Lisbon: Temas e Debates, 2013, p. 656.
46. Milgram, *Portugal, Salazar e os Judeus*, p. 318.
47. Pereira, *A diplomacia*, pp. 412–14.
48. Weiss, *The Azores*, p. 12.
49. Ibid., p. 15
50. Ibid., p. 13.
51. Nogueira, *Salazar*, vol. 3, p. 358.
52. Medlicott, *The Economic Blockade*, p. 315.
53. Nogueira, *Salazar*, vol. 3, p. 366.
54. Ibid.
55. Peter Carey, 'Timor', in António Barreto and Maria Filomena Moníca, *Dicionário de história de Portugal*, Suplemento P/Z, Lisbon: Figueirinhas, 1999, p. 516.
56. Nogueira, *Salazar*, vol. 3, p. 212.
57. Ronald Bodley, *Flight into Portugal: The Dramatic Story of an Englishman's Escape from Paris to Lisbon*, Triptree: Anchor Press, 1941, pp. 199–200.
58. Pereira, *A diplomacia*, p. 330.
59. Rosas, *História de Portugal*, vol. 7, p. 308.

60. Mark Fox, 'The Battle of the Atlantic Has Much to Teach Us Today,', *Reaction Life*, 3 September 2019, https://reaction.life/the-battle-of-the-atlantic-has-much-to-teach-us-today/ (accessed 4 September 2019).

61. R.E. Vintras, *The Portuguese Connection*, London: Bachman and Turner, 1974, p. 104.

62. David Dilks (ed.), *The Diaries of Sir Alexander Cadogan O.M., 1938–1945*, London: Cassell, 1971, p. 530, 10 May 1943.

63. Pereira, *A diplomacia*, p. 361.

64. Lucena, *Os lugar-tenentes*, p. 47.

65. Amaral, *O antigo regime*, p. 66–7.

66. Ibid.

67. US Department of State Archive, Information released online prior to 20 January 2001, 'Allied Negotiations with Portugal', Department of State, https://1997–2001.state.gov/regions/eur/rpt_9806_ng_portugal.pdf

68. Lochery, *Lisbon*, p. 92.

69. António José Telo, *Portugal na segunda guerra (1941–1945)*, vol. II, Lisbon: Vega, 1991, p. 7.

70. Pereira, *Cunhal*, p. 245.

71. Rosas, *História de Portugal*, vol. 7, p. 41.

72. Telo, *Portugal*, p. 98.

73. Pereira, *A diplomacia*, p. 374.

74. Pereira, *Álvaro Cunhal*, vol. 1, p. 724.

75. Ibid.

76. Wiarda, *Corporatism*, pp. 97–8.

77. Pereira, *Álvaro Cunhal*, vol. 1, p. 451.

78. Lucena, *Os lugar-tenentes*, p. 48.

79. Ibid.

80. Telo, *Portugal*, p. 101.

81. Ibid.

82. Pereira, *Álvaro Cunhal*, vol. 1, p. 423.

83. Josef Joffe, 'A Cold Warrior and His Contradictions', *Wall Street Journal*, 6 July 2007.

84. John Lewis Gaddis, *George F. Kennan: An American Life*, New York: Penguin Press, 2011, p. 164.

85. Pereira, *A diplomacia*, p. 387.

86. Gaddis, *George F. Kennan*, p. 164.

87. FRUS (Foreign Relations of the United States), 1952–1954, Western Europe and Canada, vol. VI, Part 2, 'The Chargé in Portugal (Brown) to the Department of State', Lisbon, 2 November 1954. Secret, no. 269, Subject: Aspects of Portuguese–American Relations.

88. Pereira, *A diplomacia*, p. 422.

89. Ibid., p. 428.
90. Ibid., p. 430.
91. Franco Nogueira, *O Estado Novo 1933–1974*, Lisbon: Livraria Civilização Editora, 1991, pp. 217–18.
92. Nogueira, *Salazar*, vol. 3, p. 589.
93. Rita and Vieira, *Os meus*, pp. 71–3.
94. Ana Cláudia Carvalho, *António de Oliveira Salazar: discurso político e 'retórica' dos direitos humanos*, Salamanca: Ediciones Universidad de Salamanca, p. 370.

10. LOW SPIRITS, 1945–52

1. Conrad Black, 'The Indispensable Man', *New Criterion*, vol. 37, December 2018.
2. Pulido Valente, 'Marcello Caetano', p. 201.
3. Antunes, *Salazar–Caetano cartas secretas*, pp. 38–9.
4. *Votar é um grande dever*, Lisbon: SNI, 1945.
5. Antunes, *Salazar–Caetano*, pp. 46–7.
6. *Votar*, p. 18.
7. Telo, *Portugal na segunda guerra*, p. 8.
8. Raimundo, *António Ferro*, p. 337.
9. *Votar*, pp. 17–18.
10. Caetano, *Minhas memórias*, p. 248.
11. Telo, *Portugal na segunda guerra*, p. 132.
12. Caetano, *Minhas memórias*, p. 249.
13. Franco Nogueira, *Salazar*, vol. 4: *o ataque, 1945–1958*, Coimbra: Atlântida Editora, 1980, p. 23.
14. Raquel Ramalho Lopes, 'Ambiguidades na aliança entre Cerejeira e Salazar', RTP, 1 April 2010, https://www.rtpp.t/noticias/pais/ambiguidades-na-alianca-entre-cerejeira-e-salazar_n332839 (accessed 7 May 2019).
15. Raposo, *História politicamente incorrecta*, p. 30.
16. 'Portugal, How Bad Is the Best?', *Time*, 22 July 1946. The magazine was promptly banned from Portugal until 1950.
17. See Antunes, *Salazar–Caetano*, pp. 46–8.
18. Ibid., p. 48.
19. Pinto, *Portugal: ascensão e queda*, p. 162.
20. Riccardo Marchi, *Folhas ultras: as ideias da direita portuguesa (1939–50)*, Lisbon: Imprensa de Ciências Sociais, 2009, p. 223.
21. Political scientist Manuel Braga da Cruz, quoted by Martinho, *Marcello Caetano*, p. 112.
22. Martinho, *Marcello Caetano*, p. 111.

23. Wiarda, *Corporatism*, p. 171.
24. Ibid.
25. Ibid., p. 172.
26. Ibid., p. 185.
27. Ibid.
28. Nicolau Andresen Leitão, *Estado Novo, democracia e Europa, 1947–1986*, Lisbon: Imprensa de Ciênciais Sociais, 2007, p. 31.
29. Pedro Aires Oliveira, *Os despojos da aliança: a Grã-Bretanha e a questão colonial portuguesa*, Lisbon: Tinta da China, 2007, p. 48.
30. Nogueira, *Salazar*, vol. 4, p. 8.
31. Pereira, *Álvaro Cunhal*, vol. 1, p. 661.
32. Albano Nogueira, 'The Pull of the Continent', in André de Staercke et al., *NATO's Anxious Birth*, London: C. Hurst, 1985, p. 69.
33. John Gibbons, *I Gathered No Moss*, London: Robert Hale, 1939, pp. 98–9.
34. John Colville, *Footprints in Time*, London: William Collins, 1976, pp. 224–5.
35. Alberto Pedroso, 'Mecanismos da repressão', in *História de Portugal*, vol. XVI, Lisbon: SAPE, n.d.
36. Fernando Rosas, *Salazarismo e fomento económico*, Lisbon: Editorial Noticias, 2000, pp. 124–5.
37. Pereira, *Álvaro Cunhal*, vol. 1, pp. 776–7, 775.
38. See Paulo Drummond Braga, 'Os Ministros da Educação Nacional (1936–1974): sociologia de uma função', *Revista Lusófona de Educação*, vol. 16, 2010, pp. 23–38.
39. See Fernando Rosas and Cristina Sizifredo, *Estado Novo e a universidade: a perseguição aos professores*, Lisbon: Tinta da China, 2013, pp. 88–9; see also Luis Farínha, 'Os saneamentos no função publíco', in João Madeira, Irene Flunser Pimentel and Luís Farinha, *Vítimas de Salazar: Estado Novo e violência política*, Lisbon, A Esfera dos Livros, 2007, pp. 190–1.
40. See Álvaro Garrido, 'A universidade e o Estado Novo: de "corporação orgânica" do regime a território de dissidência social', *Revista Critica de Cienciais Sociais*, vol. 81, 2008, pp. 133–53.
41. Central Intelligence Agency Sr-31, 13 October 1949, subject 'Portugal'. SECRET. Copy no. 1 for the President of the United States. Harry S. Truman library, quoted by José Freire Antunes, *Kennedy e Salazar: o leão e a raposo*, Lisbon: Difusão Cultural, 1991, p. 31.
42. Questioned about the matter in 1978 by a later foreign minister, Franco Nogueira, Santos Costa does not recall being outspoken in his criticism and thinks the decisive intervention against Supico Pinto may

have come instead from Mário de Figueiredo (with whom he never raised the matter). See Cruz, *Correspondência*, pp. 121–2.

43. See Ana Soromenho and Isabel Lopes, 'Cilia, uma via gem ao Estado Novo', *Expresso*, 16 February 2008, https://oliveirasalazar.org/download/galeria/pdf___E6613A95-E62E-4C9A-BE22–6F33DDA619B8. pdf (accessed 14 September 2019).
44. *Correspondência de Santos Costa para Oliveira Salazar*, vol. 1: *1934–1950*, Lisbon: Comissão do Livro Negro Sobre Fascismo, 1988, p. 170.
45. Soares, *Portugal's Struggle*, p. 79.
46. José Magalhães Godinho, 'Salazar, Franco Nogueira e o MUD (2): o encontro com Carmona', *O Jornal*, 16 May 1980.
47. Fernando dos Santos Costa, 'No rescaldo do 10 Abril', *Diário de Notícias*, 26 May 1981.
48. Cruz, *Correspondência*, pp. 103–7.
49. Caetano, *Minhas memórias*, p. 250.
50. Pinto, *Salazar visto*, p. 74.
51. Rita and Vieira, *Os meus 35 anos*, p. 122.
52. Ibid., p. 111.
53. Castro Brandão, *Salazar: uma cronologia*, p. 291.
54. Luís Cabral de Moncada, 'A obra de Salazar à luz do sentimento histórico da sua época', in *Um grande português e uma grande Eeuropeu: Salazar*, Lisbon: União Nacional, 1948, pp. 19–20.
55. FRUS, 1952–1954, Western European Security, vol. V, part 1, 740.5/3–452, [1952]. Memorandum of Conversation, by Special Assistant Xanthaky.
56. André de Staercke, 'An Alliance Clamouring to Be Born: Anxious to Survive', in André de Staercke et al., *NATO's Anxious Birth*, p. 154.
57. Sir Nicholas Henderson, *The Birth of NATO*, London: Weidenfeld and Nicholson, 1982, p. 110.
58. Henderson, *The Birth*, p. 110.
59. Nogueira, 'The Pull', pp. 69–70.
60. Ibid., p. 72.
61. Henderson, *The Birth*, p. 111.
62. Nogueira, 'The Pull', pp. 73–4.
63. Henderson, *The Birth*, p. 111.
64. FRUS, 1949, Western Europe, vol. IV, The Ambassador in Portugal (MacVeagh) to the Secretary of State, secret, Lisbon, 7 December 1949.
65. Nogueira, *Um político confessa-se*, p. 171.
66. Pereira, *A diplomacia*, p. 487.
67. Freire Costa et al., *An Economic History*, p. 305.
68. Paris Gkartzonikas, 'The Effects of the Marshall Plan in Greece, Turkey

and Portugal', Athens: Greek Foreign Affairs Council, n.d. (accessed 28 March 2019).

69. Antunes, *Kennedy e Salazar*, p. 34.

70. For the background, see Maria Inácia Rezola, 'The Franco–Salazar Meetings: Foreign Policy and Iberian Relations during the Dictatorships (1942–1963)', *e-Journal of Portuguese History*, vol. 6, no. 1, Summer 2008 (accessed 19 May 2019).

71. Nogueira, *Salazar*, vol. IV, p. 164.

72. António Pedro Vicente, 'Franco em Portugal: o seu doutoramento honoris causa na Universidade de Coimbra—1949', *Revista de História das Ideias*, vol. 16, 1994, pp. 19–75.

73. The centenary tribute published in 2016 offers a detailed perspective on his role in the Estado Novo and his subsequent fate. See Gonçalo Sampaio e Mello, 'Guilherme Braga da Cruz: perfil biografico, para Guilherme Braga da Cruz no ano do seu centenário (1916–2016)', http://www.cidpp.t/revistas/rjlb/2016/4/2016_04_0827_0919.pdf (accessed 4 May 2019).

74. A photo of the two men taken during this visit adorns the front cover of Bernardo Futscher Pereira's book *A diplomacia*.

75. Hansard, House of Commons, 12 May 1949, vol. 464, col. 2011.

76. Payne and Palacios, *Franco*, p. 311.

77. Bruno Cardoso Reis, 'Portugal and the UN: A Rogue State Resisting the Norm of Decolonization (1956–1974)', *Portuguese Studies*, vol. 29, no. 2, 2013, p. 255.

78. Lucena, *Os lugar-tenentes*, pp. 318–19.

79. Ibid., pp. 319–20.

80. Michael S. Peres, '"Bewitched": Africa as a Determinant in the Career of Henrique Galvão, 1927–1970', *Bulletin for Spanish and Portuguese Historical Studies*, vol. 40, no. 1, Article 7, 2015, p. 134.

81. Peres, '"Bewitched"', p. 122.

82. Galvão's energy, talent and individualism are captured in the article by Wheeler, 'The Galvão Report', pp. 115–52.

83. Peres, '"Bewitched"', p. 123.

84. Montoito, *Henrique Galvão*, p. 64.

85. Luis Miguel Solla de Andrade, 'Henrique Galvão, 1895–1970: Aspects of a Euro-African Crusade', MA thesis, University of South Africa, March 2009, p. 48 (accessed 12 December 2018).

86. Andrade, 'Henrique Galvão', p. 51.

87. For this section of the 1930 Act, see Egerton, *Salazar*, p. 261.

88. Peres, '"Bewitched"', p. 127.

89. Caetano, *Minhas memórias*, p. 257.

90. Wheeler, 'The Galvão Report', p. 130, n. 6.

91. Nogueira, *Salazar*, vol. 1V, pp. 167, 176.
92. Peres, '"Bewitched"', p. 128.
93. Montoito, *Henrique Galvão*, pp. 130–2.
94. Pinto, *Portugal: ascensão e queda*, p. 215.
95. Henrique Galvão, *Santa Maria: My Crusade for Portugal*, London: Weidenfeld and Nicholson, 1961, pp. 210–11.
96. This information about ties between the two politicians is contained in de Staercke, *Mémoires*, pp. 23–24, 27–8, 284.
97. Acheson, *Sketches*, pp. 112–13.
98. 'My Country and NATO', https://www.nato.int/cps/en/natohq/declassified_162352.htm (accessed 12 November 2019).
99. Marcello Mathias, *Correspondência Marcello Mathias–Salazar, 1947–1958*, Lisbon: Editorial Difusão, 1984, p. 360.

11. THE GOLDEN AFTERNOON OF THE ESTADO NOVO, 1952–58

1. Soares, 'Salazar, o retrato', p. 9.
2. Yvonne Stolz, Joerg Baten and Jaime Reis, 'Portuguese living standards, 1720–1980, in European comparison: heights, income, and human capital', *Economic History Review*, vol. 66, no. 2, May 2013, p. 556.
3. José António Saraiva, *Salazar e Caetano: O Tempo em que Ambos Acreditavam Chefiar o Governo*, Lisbon: Gradiva, 2020, p. 36.
4. Stolz, Baten and Reis, 'Portuguese living standards, 1720–1980, in European comparison: heights, income, and human capital', p. 557.
5. Ibid., pp. 546–7.
6. The historian Jorge Borges de Macedo quoted by Pinto, *Salazar visto*, pp. 76–7.
7. Bernardo Futscher Pereira, *Crepúsculo do colonialism: a diplomacia do Estado Novo (1949–1961)*, Lisbon: D. Quixote, 2017, p. 64.
8. Vasco Pulido Valente, 'Marcello Caetano', in Barreto and Monica, *Dicionário*, Suplemento A/E, p. 202.
9. Nogueira, *Salazar*, vol. 4, p. 217.
10. Nigel Hamilton, *Monty, the Field Marshal, 1944–1976*, London: Hamish Hamilton, 1976, pp. 649–50.
11. Brochado, *Memórias*, p. 298.
12. de Staercke, *Mémoires*, pp. 290–1.
13. Garnier, *Vacances*, p. 62.
14. Antunes, *Cartas*, p. 246.
15. Pinto, *Salazar visto*, p. 98.
16. Ibid., pp. 69–70.
17. Office of Strategic Services, Research and Analysis Branch 1669,

19 January 1944. Subject: 'Salazar and the Crisis in Portugal', National Archives (Washington DC), quoted in Antunes, *Kennedy e Salazar*, p. 72.

18. Mendo Castro Henriques and Gonçalo Sampaio e Melo, *Salazar: pensamento e doutrina política—textos antólogicos*, Lisbon: Verbo, 1989, pp. 34–5.

19. Brochado, *Memórias*, pp. 305–6.

20. Ramos, *História*, p. 652.

21. 'S. Tomé e Príncipe: importância de massacre de Batepá tem sido ignorada', *Observador*, 8 June 2015, https://observador.pt/2015/06/08/s-tome-principe-importancia-massacre-batepa-sido-ignorada/ (accessed 22 October 2019).

22. Caetano, *Minhas memórias*, p. 507.

23. Daniel J. Mahoney, 'Two Critics of the Ideological "Lie": Raymond Aron and Aleksandr Solzhenitsyn', *VoegelinView*, 9 December 2015, https://voegelinview.com/two-critics-of-the-ideological-lie-raymond-arons-encounter-with-aleksandr-solzhenitsyn/ (accessed 11 August 2019).

24. Brochado, *Memórias*, p. 298.

25. Fernando Rosas, Rita Carvalho and Pedro Aires Oliveira, *Daniel Barbosa, Salazar e Caetano: correspondência política, 1947–1974*, vol. 1: *1945–1966*, Lisbon: Circulo de Leitores, 2002, pp. 12–13.

26. Meneses, *Salazar*, p. 336.

27. Daniel Nataf and Elizabeth Sammis, 'Classes, Hegemony and Portuguese Democratization', in Ronald H. Chilcote et al., *Transitions from Dictatorship to Democracy: Comparative Studies of Spain, Portugal and Greece*, London: Taylor and Francis, 1991, p. 79.

28. For a summary of the protectionist approach, see Corkill, *The Portuguese Economy*, pp. 6–8, 12–13.

29. David Corkill, *Development of the Portuguese Economy: A Case of Europeanization*, London: Routledge, 2002, p. 18.

30. Wiarda, *Corporatism*, p. 154.

31. José Luís Cardoso and Nuno Estêvão Ferreira, 'A Câmara Corporativa (1935–1974) e as políticas públicas no Estado Novo', p. 57, https://journals.openedition.org/lerhistoria/290

32. Wiarda, *Corporatism*, p. 214.

33. Ramos, *História*, p. 676.

34. Orlando Raimundo, *O último salazarista: a outra face de Américo Thomaz*, Lisbon: D. Quixote, 2017, p. 42.

35. A somewhat hostile account of his career and role in the regime is provided by Garrido, 'Henrique Tenreiro', pp. 839–62; the pro-Allied Costa Brochado is far more sympathetic in his *Memórias*, p. 360.

36. Pinto, *Salazar visto*, p. 76.
37. Antunes, *Salazar e Caetano*, p. 296.
38. Andrade, *Ditadura*, p. 296.
39. Leitão, *Estado Novo, democracia e Europa*, p. 33.
40. Antunes, *Salazar e Caetano*, pp. 71–2.
41. Lucena, *Os lugar-tenentes*, p. 130.
42. Leitão, 'The Salazar Regime', p. 466.
43. Leitão, *Estado Novo*, p. 58.
44. Wolfgang Adler, 'Salazar and the Loss of the Business Elite', *Social Matter*, 6 December 2017, https://www.socialmatter.net/2017/12/06/salazar-loss-business-elite/ (accessed 19 April 2019).
45. Leitão, 'The Salazar Regime', p. 466.
46. Ibid., p. 473.
47. António Costa Pinto and Nuno Severiano Teixeira, 'From Atlantic Past to European Destiny: Portugal', in Jurgen Elvert and Wolfram Kaiser (eds.), *European Union Enlargement: A Comparative History*, London: Routledge, 2004, p. 115.
48. Meneses, *Salazar*, pp. 354–5.
49. Leitão, *Estado Novo*, p. 55.
50. See Raposo, *História politicamente incorrecta*, pp. 48–54.
51. Nataf and Sammis 'Classes, Hegemony', p. 83.
52. Gerald J. Bender, *Angola under the Portuguese: The Myth and the Reality*, Stanford: Stanford University Press, 1977, p. 228.
53. See José Freire Antunes, *Jorge Jardim: agente secreto*, Lisbon: Bertrand, 1996.
54. A somewhat melodramatic interpretation of this alliance is found in João M. Cabrita, *Mozambique: The Tortuous Road to Democracy*, London: Palgrave, 2000, pp. 75–9.
55. José Maria dos Santos Coelho, 'Adriano Moreira e o Império Português', PhD thesis, University of Beira Interior, Portugal, 2015, p. 106.
56. Paul M. McGarr, *The Cold War in South Asia: Britain, the United States and the Indian Subcontinent, 1945–1965*, Cambridge: Cambridge University Press, 2013, p. 124.
57. See chapter 2 of Aires Oliver's, *Os despojos*.
58. McGarr, *The Cold War*, p. 121.
59. Foreign Relations of the United States, 1952–1954, Western Europe and Canada, vol. VI, part 2, The Ambassador in Portugal (Guggenheim) to the Department of State, Lisbon, 9 August 1954, https://history.state.gov/historicaldocuments/frus1952–54v06p2/d812
60. J. Ploncard d'Assac, *Salazar: a vida e a obra*, Lisbon: Verbo, 1989, p. 183.
61. Peter Burke and Maria Lúcia.G. Pallares-Burke, *Gilberto Freyre: Social Theory in the Tropics*, Oxford: Peter Lang 2008, p. 121.

62. Claudia Castelo, 'Um brasileiro em terras portuguesas', *Buala*, 31 March 2013, http://www.buala.org/pt/a-ler/um-brasileiro-em-terras-portuguesas-prefacio

63. Burke and Pallares-Burke, *Gilberto Freyre*, p. 119.

64. Castelo, 'Um brasileiro em terras portuguesas'.

65. Burke and Pallares-Burke, *Gilberto Freyre*, p. 120, quoting Gilberto Freyre, 'A propósito de criticas', *O Cruzeiro*, 15 November 1952; G. Freyre, *Aventura e rotina*, Rio de Janeiro: José Olympio, 1953.

66. Coelho, 'Adriano Moreira', p. 32.

67. Ibid., p. 118.

68. Ibid., p. 116.

69. Pinto, *O fim*, p. 108.

70. Joel Kotkin, 'Elites against Western Civilization', *New Geography*, 10 April 2019, http://www.newgeography.com/content/006431-elites-against-western-civilization (accessed 15 April 2019).

71. Lucena, *Os lugar-tenentes*, p. 125.

72. Graham Turner, 'The Real Elizabeth II', *Daily Telegraph*, 8 January 2002.

73. See Jonathan Conlin, *Mr Five Per Cent*, London: Profile Books, 2019.

74. Interview in *Corriere della Sera*, 30 March 1960 in Henriques and Melo, *Salazar*, p. 51.

75. Nogueira, *Salazar*, vol. IV, p. 448.

12. TORN CURTAIN, 1958–61: FRIENDS DESERT THE REGIME AND ENEMIES STRIKE

1. Caetano, *Minhas memórias*, pp. 493–4.

2. Ibid., pp. 495–6.

3. Gallagher, *Portugal: A Twentieth Century Interpretation*, p. 141.

4. J. de Hautecloque to the French Foreign Ministry, 8 February 1956, quoted in Conlin, *Mr Five Per Cent*, p. 308.

5. See Rosas et al., *Daniel Barbosa*.

6. Antunes, *Salazar e Caetano*, p. 73.

7. Ibid., p. 70.

8. Ibid., pp. 70–1.

9. Brochado, *Memórias*, p. 300.

10. Antunes, *Salazar e Caetano*, p. 69.

11. Caetano, *Minhas memórias*, p. 211.

12. Manuel José Homem de Mello, *Cartas de Salazar a Craveiro Lopes 1951–1958*, Lisbon: Moraes Editores, 1983, pp. 44–5.

13. Nogueira, *Salazar*, vol. IV, p. 489.

14. Rosas et al., *Daniel Barbosa*, p. 14.

15. Maria Manuela Cruzeiro, *Costa Gomes: o último marechal*, Lisbon: D. Quixote, 2014, pp. 13–14.
16. Caetano, *Minhas Memórias*, p. 424.
17. See his book *Da pulhice de homo sapiens*, Lisbon: Livraria Depositária, 1933.
18. Frederico Rosa Delgado, *Humberto Delgado: biografia do general sem medo*, Lisbon: A Esfera dos Livros, 2008, pp. 183–5, 192.
19. This was in an article for a journal catering for members of the Portuguese air force, *Revista AR*, no. 44, June 1941 and is quoted in Pimentel and Ninhos, *Salazar, Portugal e o Holocausto*, p. 129.
20. Cruzeiro, *Costa Gomes*, pp. 74–5.
21. Vieira, *Film*, pp. 166–7.
22. Ricardo Serrado, *O Estado Novo e o futebol*, Lisbon: Prime Books, 2012, p. 237.
23. Manuel Braga da Cruz, *O Estado Novo e a Igreja Católica*, Lisbon: Bizâncio, 1999, p. 103.
24. Harrison, *A Tale of Two Cities*, pp. 154–9.
25. Rosas et al., *Daniel Barbosa*, p. 257; author's italics.
26. See Manuel Beça Murias, *Obviamente demito-o*, Amadora: Regimprensa, 1980.
27. Nogueira, *Salazar*, vol. 5, p. 527.
28. Cruz, *Correspondência, 1936–1982*, pp. 420–1.
29. Interview with General Fernando Santos Costa, Lisbon, 20 July 1981.
30. Cruz, *Correspondência, 1936–1982*, p. 421.
31. Caetano, *Minhas memórias*, pp. 562–3.
32. D.L. Raby, 'Populism and the Portuguese Left: From Delgado to Otelo', in L. Graham and D. Wheeler (eds.), *In Search of Portugal: The Revolution and Its Antecedents*, Madison: University of Wisconsin Press, 1983, p. 64.
33. See Antunes, *Kennedy e Salazar*, p. 79.
34. 'Caminho do futuro', Lisbon: SNI, 1958. This was a speech given to the União Nacional on 1 July 1958.
35. Meneses, *Salazar*, p. 435, quoting Salazar, 'Não tenhemos receio', in *Discursos e notas políticas*, vol. 5: *1951–68*, Coimbra: Coimbra Editora, 1959, pp. 477–81.
36. See Tom Gallagher, 'Controlled Repression in Salazar's Portugal', *Journal of Contemporary History*, vol. 14, no. 3, July 1979, pp. 385–402 for a discussion of the careful use of repression by the regime.
37. Telmo Faria, 'Quem tem a tropa', in Iva Delgado, *Humberto Delgado: as eleições de 1958*, Lisbon: Vega, 1998, p. 238.
38. Irregularities in Braga and surrounding areas (long regarded as loyal to the Estado Novo) are set out in Iva Delgado, *Braga, cidade proibido:*

Humberto Delgado e as eleições de 1958, Braga: Governo Civil, 1988, pp. 95–105.

39. Ploncard d'Assac, *Salazar*, pp. 233–4.
40. Henriques and Melo, *Salazar*, p. 22.
41. Ibid., p. 43, quoting a speech delivered on 9 December 1934.
42. Amaral, *O antigo regime*, p. 56.
43. See Ana Mónica Fonseca and Daniel Marcos, 'French and German Support to Portugal: The Military Survival of the "Estado Novo"', *Portuguese Studies Review*, vol. 16, no. 2, 2008, p. 114.
44. Luís Nuno Rodrigues, 'The International Dimensions of the Portuguese Colonial Crisis', in Jerónimo Miguel Bandeira and António Costa Pinto (eds.), *The Ends of European Colonial Empires: Cases and Comparisons*, London: Palgrave Macmillan, 2015, p. 259.
45. Rodrigues, 'The International Dimensions', p. 259.
46. Oliveira, *Os despojos*, pp. 171–2.
47. Tom Gallagher, 'Fernando dos Santos Costa: guardião militar do Estado Novo 1944–58', in *O Estado Novo: das origens ão fim da autarcia 1926–59*, Lisbon: Fragmentos, 1986, p. 212. Espirito Santo died in 1956 and his influence is assessed in chapter 8.
48. See Lucena, *Os lugar-tenentes*, pp. 128–9.
49. Caetano, *Minhas memórias*, p. 579.
50. Tomás does not, however, seem to have removed him from that body.
51. Antunes, *Salazar e Caetano*, p. 78.
52. Jorge Alves Martins, 'O papel de Santos Costa no Estado Novo', *Público*, 11 April 2000.
53. Gallagher, 'Santos Costa', pp. 214–15.
54. Adriano Moreira, *A espuma do tempo*, pp. 180–1.
55. Ramos, *Historia*, p. 679.
56. See Cruz, *Correspondência*, pp. 416–17.
57. 'Carta do Bispo do Porto a Salazar (1958)', Entre as Brumas da memória, http://entreasbrumasdamemoria.blogspot.com/2007/07/carta-do-bispo-do-porto-salazar-1958.html (accessed 27 August 2019).
58. Luís Reis Torgal, *Estados novos, Estado Novo*, Coimbra: Imprensa da Universidade de Coimbra, 2009, pp. 459–60.
59. João Miguel Almeida, *A oposição católica ao Estado Novo: 1958–1974*, Lisbon: Edições Nelson de Matos, p. 480.
60. JB, 'Caso do Bispo do Porto', in Barreto and Mónica, *Dicionário*, A-E, pp. 183–7.
61. Lucena, *Salazar*, p. 312.
62. Luis Salgado de Matos, 'Manuel Gonçalves Cerejeira', in Barreto and Mónica, *Dicionário*, A-E.
63. Public Records Office, Foreign Office, FO 371 144851, 'Catholics in

Portugal': C.N. Stirling to London, 9 January 1959, quoted in Tom Gallagher, 'Portugal', in Tom Buchanan and Martin Conway (eds.), *Political Catholicism in Europe, 1918–1965*, Oxford: Clarendon Press, 1996, p. 149.

64. These details are taken from Gallagher, 'Portugal', pp. 149–50.
65. Nogueira, *Salazar*, vol. 5: *a resistência, 1958–1964*, Coimbra: Livraria Civilização Editora, p. 482.
66. Andrade, 'Henrique Galvão', p. 77.
67. See José Pedro Castanheira, Natal Vaz and António Caeiro, *A queda de Salazar: o princípio do fim da ditadura*, Lisbon: Tinta de China, 2018.
68. Brandão, *Salazar: uma cronologia*, pp. 435, 436.
69. Regarding the hijacking, use was made of Peres, '"Bewitched"', pp. 130–1.
70. Oliveira, *Os despojos*, pp. 224–5.
71. Douglas L. Wheeler and René Pélissier, *Angola*, New York: Greenwood Press, pp. 180–1; Glyn Stone, 'Britain and the Angolan Revolt of 1961', *Journal of Imperial and Commonwealth History*, vol. 27, no. 1, 1969, p. 113.
72. Cruz, *Correspondência, 1936–1982*, pp. 81–4.
73. Luís Nuno Rodrigues, 'Militares e política: a Abrilada de 1961 e a resistência do salazarismo', *Ler História*, no. 6565, 2013, http://journals.openedition.org/lerhistoria/447 (accessed 23 March 2019).
74. Americo Thomáz, *Últimas décadas de Portugal*, vol. III, Lisbon: Edições Fernando Pereira, n.d., p. 91.
75. Nogueira, *Salazar*, vol. 5, p. 238.
76. See Raimundo, *O último salazarista*.
77. Rodrigues, 'Militares e política', pp. 22–3.
78. Antunes, *Kennedy e Salazar*, p. 218.
79. Soromenho and Lopes, 'Cilinha'.
80. Nogueira, *Salazar*, vol. 5, p. 239.
81. Ibid., p. 209.
82. Rodrigues, 'Militares e política', pp. 24–5; Antunes, *Kennedy e Salazar*, p. 147.
83. Antunes, *Kennedy e Salazar*, p. 221.
84. Ibid., p. 223.
85. Cruzeiro, *Costa Gomes*, p. 96; Freire Antunes, *Kennedy e Salazar*, p. 225.
86. Rodrigues, 'Militares e política', p. 31.
87. Cruzeiro, *Costa Gomes*, pp. 116–17; Francisco da Costa Gomes, *Sobre Portugal: diálogos com Alexandre Manuel*, Lisbon: A Regra do Jogo, 1979, pp. 120–121.
88. Nogueira, *Salazar*, vol. 5, p. 244.
89. Antunes, *Kennedy e Salazar*, p. 215.

90. Nogueira, *Salazar*, vol. 5, p. 255.
91. 'Galvão Loses Post', *New York Times*, 31 October 1961.
92. Letter of Galvão to Manuel Sertório, 28 August 1962, quoted by Rosa Delgado, *Humberto Delgado*, p. 959.
93. Andrade, 'Henrique Galvão', p. 202.
94. Coelho, 'Adriano Moreira', p. 92.
95. See Orlando Ribeiro, 'Goa apenas uma mestiçagem espiritual', in *Goa em 1956: relatório ao governo*, Lisbon: CCP, 1999.
96. Maria Manuel Stocker, *Xeque-mate a Goa*, Lisbon: Temas e Debates, 2005, p. 259.
97. Oliveira, *Os despojos*, p. 132.
98. McGarr, *The Cold War*, p. 129.
99. Ibid.
100. Oliveira, *Os despojos*, p. 269.
101. McGarr, *The Cold War*, p. 132.
102. Ibid., p. 136.
103. Oliveira, *Os despojos*, pp. 280–1.
104. Allegro, *A personalidade*, p. 33. (The speech was read out by Mário de Figueiredo, president of the National Assembly.)
105. Oliveira, *Os despojos*, p. 281.
106. Ibid., p. 279.
107. Pinto, *O fim*, p. 92, n. 8.
108. See Pinto, *Salazar visto*, pp. 75–6, 233.
109. Antunes, *Kennedy e Salazar*, p. 123.

13. CONTRASTING ALLIES: PREDATORY AMERICA AND AMENABLE FRANCE

1. Antunes, 'Kennedy, Portugal', p. 150.
2. Ibid.
3. Wolfgang Adler, 'JFK's failed coup in Lisbon', *Social Matter*, 7 August 2017, https://www.socialmatter.net/2017/08/07/jfks-failed-coup-lisbon/ (accessed 28 March 2019).
4. Antunes, 'Kennedy, Portugal', p. 153.
5. Luís Nuno Rodrigues, 'About Face: The United States and Portuguese Colonialism 1961–1963', *e-Journal of Portuguese History*, vol. 2, no. 1, 2004.
6. Rodrigues, 'About Face'.
7. Pereira, *A diplomacia*, p. 389 (views of the author).
8. Nogueira, *Salazar*, vol. III, p. 266.
9. Ibid., p. 555.
10. Pereira, *A diplomacia*, p. 391.

11. FRUS, 1948, Western Europe, vol. III, The Ambassador in Portugal (MacVeagh) to the Secretary of State, 30 November 1948, https://history.state.gov/historicaldocuments/frus1948v03/d640 (accessed 22 October 2018).

12. Antunes, 'Kennedy, Portugal', p. 151.

13. Rodrigues, 'About Face'.

14. Words of Ambassador Elbrick, in FRUS, vol. XIII, Western Europe and Canada, Document 335, Telegram from the Embassy in Portugal to the Department of State, Lisbon, 18 December 1961, https://history.state.gov/historicaldocuments/frus1961–63v13/d335 (accessed 2 July 2019).

15. Pereira, *Crepúsculo*, pp. 251–3.

16. FRUS, 1961–1963, vol. XIII, Western Europe and Canada, Document 357, Telegram from the Embassy in France to the Department of State, 31 August 1963, https://history.state.gov/historicaldocuments/frus1961–63v13/d357 (accessed 11 August 2019).

17. Pereira, *A diplomacia*, p. 394.

18. FRUS, 1961–63, vol. XIII, Western Europe and Canada, Document 342, Memorandum from Secretary of State Rusk to President Kennedy, Washington, 12 June 1962. Subject: Negotiation of the Renewal of the Azores Base Agreement, Document 342, https://history.state.gov/historicaldocuments/frus1961–63v13/d342

19. Witney W. Schneidman, *Engaging Africa: Washington and the Fall of Portugal's Colonial Empire*, Lanham, MA: University Press of America, 2004, p. 5.

20. Interview with James Bonbright, 1986, 'Portugal, Country Reader', p. 34, http://adst.org/wp-contents/uploads/2012/09/Portugal.PDF (accessed 31 August 2019).

21. Pereira, *Crepúsculo*, pp. 141–2.

22. Interview with Joseph J. Jova, 1991, 'Portugal, Country Reader', p. 29, http://adst.org/wp-contents/uploads/2012/09/Portugal.PDF (accessed 31 August 2019).

23. See FRUS, 'Allied Relations and Negotiations with Portugal, Department of State', https://1997–2001.state.gov/regions/eur/rpt_9806_ng_portugal.pdf (accessed 19 July 2019).

24. Interview with James Bonbright, 1986.

25. Recollection of Franz-Paul de Almeida Langhans, Salazar's private secretary, 1951–61; see Pinto, Salazar visto, p. 126.

26. Rosa Delgado, *Humberto Delgado*, p. 955.

27. Brandão, *Salazar: uma cronologia*, p. 510.

28. Theodore Xanthaky to David Popper, 28 January 1963, quoted in Rodrigues, 'The International Dimensions', p. 263, n. 7.

29. Rodrigues, 'About Face'.
30. Antunes, 'Kennedy, Portugal', p. 15.
31. Antunes, *Kennedy e Salazar*, p. 212.
32. For the lunch, see Antunes, *Kennedy e Salazar*, pp. 153–5.
33. Antunes, *Kennedy e Salazar*, p. 48.
34. Alexander J. Marino, 'America's War in Angola, 1961–1976', MA thesis, University of Arkansas, 2015, p. 52; Antunes, *Kennedy Portugal*, p. 154.
35. Antunes, *Kennedy e Salazar*, p. 221.
36. Ibid., p. 107.
37. FRUS, 1958, Western Europe, vol. VII, part 2, document 282: Dispatch from the Embassy in Portugal to the Department of State, Lisbon, August 25, 1958, https://history.state.gov/historicaldocuments/frus1958–60v07p2/d282 (accessed 11 August 2019).
38. Felipe Ribeiro de Meneses and Robert McNamara, *White Redoubt: Great Powers and the Struggle for Southern Africa (1960–1980)*, London: Palgrave, 2018, p. 31.
39. Pinto, *Portugal: ascensão e queda*, p. 218.
40. Nogueira, *Salazar*, vol. 5, pp. 214–15.
41. Interview with William L. Blue (deputy chief of mission 1962–5), 1991, 'Portugal, Country Reader', p. 45, http://adst.org/wp-contents/uploads/2012/09/Portugal.PDF (accessed 31 August 2019).
42. FRUS, 1961–1963, vol. XIII, Western Europe and Canada, Document 336: Telegram from the Embassy in Portugal to the Department of State, Lisbon, 12 January 1962, https://adst.org/wp-content/uploads/2012/09/Portugal.pdf (accessed 11 August 2019).
43. Antunes, 'Kennedy, Portugal', pp. 34–5.
44. FRUS, 1961–1963, vol. XIII, Western Europe and Canada, Document 336: Telegram from the Embassy in Portugal to the Department of State, Lisbon, 12 January 1962, https://adst.org/wp-content/uploads/2012/09/Portugal.pdf (accessed 11 August 2019).
45. Antunes, *Kennedy e Salazar*, p. 282.
46. Ibid., p. 287.
47. Santos Coelho, 'Adriano Moreira e o império', p. 192.
48. Antunes, 'Kennedy, Portugal', p. 52.
49. Ibid., p. 54.
50. See Douglas Brinkley, *Dean Acheson: The Cold War Years, 1953–1971*, New Haven: Yale University Press 1992, p. 313.
51. Nogueira, *Um político confessa-se*, p. 81.
52. FRUS, 1961–1963, vol. XIII, Western Europe and Canada, Document 357: Telegram from the Embassy in France to the Department of State, 31 August 1963, https://history.state.gov/historicaldocuments/frus1961–63v13/d357 (accessed 4 September 2019).

53. Ball, *The Past*, p. 276.
54. Ibid., p. 276.
55. Ibid..
56. Nogueira, *Salazar*, vol. V, p. 519, n. 1.
57. Luís Nuno Rodrigues, 'The United States and Portuguese Decolonization', *Portuguese Studies*, vol. 29, no. 2, 2013, p. 173.
58. Franco Nogueira, *Salazar*, vol. VI: *o último combate, 1964–70*, Porto: Livraria Civilização Editora, p. 56.
59. See M.A. Samuels and Stephen M. Haykins, 'The Anderson Plan: An American Attempt to Seduce Portugal out of Africa', *Orbis*, vol. 23, 1979, pp. 649–69.
60. Mahoney, *JFK*, p. 199.
61. Neil Bruce, *Portugal: The Last Empire*, Newton Abbot: David and Charles, 1974, p. 41. In a slightly different version, a former minister of the regime, José Hermano Saraiva, relates this reaction: 'That's all we need. Now for the plotting', by which he assumed Salazar meant the US. *Jornal O Diabo*, 8 June 2004.
62. Interview with William L. Blue, 'Portugal, Country Reader', pp. 45–6.
63. Daniel Marcos, *Salazar e de Gaulle: a França e a questão colonial portuguesa (1958–1968)*, Lisbon: Ministério dos Negócios Estrangeiros, 2007, p. 90.
64. Robert Dallek, *An Unfinished Life: John F. Kennedy 1917–1963*, New York: Little, Brown and Company, 2003, pp. 394–7.
65. Marcos, *Salazar e de Gaulle*, p. 91.
66. Ibid., p. 243.
67. Antunes, 'Kennedy, Portugal', p. 159.
68. Quoted by Antunes, *Cartas particulares*, vol. 1, p. 31.
69. Meneses, *Salazar*, pp. 603–4, 435, quoting Coelho and Coelho, *Salazar*, p. 53.
70. Marcos, *Salazar e de Gaulle*, p. 65.
71. Antunes, *Kennedy e Salazar*, p. 93.
72. Marcos, *Salazar e de Gaulle*, p. 321.
73. John P. Cann, *Counterinsurgency in Africa: The Portuguese Way of War, 1961–74*, Warwick: Helion, 2012, p. 137.
74. Marcos, *Salazar e de Gaulle*, p. 161.
75. Ibid., p. 240.
76. Ibid., p. 442.
77. Irene Flunser Pimentel, *Os cinco pilares da PIDE*, Lisbon: A Esfera dos Livros, 2019, pp. 20, 274–5.
78. For an analysis of this literature, see Olivier Dard and Ana Isabel Sardinha-Desvignes, *Célébrer Salazar en France (1930–1974): du philo-salazarisme au salazarisme français*, Brussels: Peter Lang, 2017.

79. Eugen Weber, *Action Française: Royalism and Revolt in Twentieth Century France*, Stanford: Stanford University Press, 1962, p. 456.
80. Christine Garnier, *Vacances avec Salazar*, Paris: Grasset, 1952.
81. '1933: Salazar, le dictateur de glace ... et de feu (3)', 8 March 2013, http://laplumeetlerouleau.over-blog.com/article-1933-salazar-le-dictateur-de-glace-et-de-feu-3–115580554.html (accessed 5 September 2019).
82. Pimentel, *Os cinco pilares*, pp. 106–7.
83. Garnier, *Vacances*, p. 131.
84. Leitão, 'The Salazar Regime and European Integration', p. 468.
85. Brandão, *Salazar: uma cronologia*, p. 340.
86. Keefe, *Area Handbook for Portugal*, p. 83.

14. THE FADING OF THE LIGHT, 1964–70

1. For details of the escape see *Os anos de Salazar*, vol. 17: *1960, fuga do Forte de Peniche*, Lisbon: Planeta de Agostini, 2008, pp. 7–23.
2. Pedro Prostes de Fonseca, 'O Forte de Peniche a fuga de Cunhal e a história do guarda que o ajudou', *Observador*, 1 October 2016, https://observador.pt/especiais/forte-de-peniche-a-fuga-de-cunhal-e-a-historia-do-guarda-que-o-ajudou/ (accessed 11 September 2019).
3. See Pavel Szobi, 'From Enemies to Allies? Portugal's Carnation Revolution and Czechoslovakia, 1968–1989', *Contemporary European History*, vol. 26, no. 4.
4. Glyn Stone, 'Britain and Portuguese Africa, 1961–1965', in Ken Fedorowich and Martin Thomas (eds.), *International Diplomacy and Colonial Defeat*, London: Routledge, 2013, p. 171.
5. Jiri Valenti, 'Soviet Decision-Making on Angola', in David Albright (ed.), *Africa and International Communism*, London: Macmillan, 1980, p. 95.
6. 'Recordar Pardal Monteiro', *CM Jornal*, 1 June 2014, https://cm-sintra.pt/index.php?option=com_content&Itemid=1024&catid=220&id=2810&view=article (accessed 16 April 2019).
7. Jorge Pais de Sousa, 'O Estado Novo de Salazar como um fascismo de cátedra: fundamentação histórica de uma categoria política', *Storicamente*', 5, 2009, http://www.storicamente.org/05_studi_ricerche/estado-novo-como-fascismo-de-catedra.html (accessed 17 June 2019).
8. Pais de Sousa, 'O Estado Novo de Salazar'.
9. Guya Accornero, *The Revolution before the Revolution: Late Authoritarianism and Student Protest in Portugal*, New York: Berghahn, 2016, pp. 38–40.
10. Pinto, *O fim*, p. 247.
11. Gerhard Besier and Katarzyna Stoklosa, *Jehovah's Witnesses in Europe: Past and Present*, Cambridge: Cambridge Scholars Publishing, 2016, p. 302.

12. Pinto, *O fim*, p. 246.

13. Accornero, *The Revolution*, p. 43.

14. Pinto, *O fim*, p. 248.

15. Adelino Gomes, interview with Adriano Moreira, *Publico*, 22 April 1995, quoted in Coelho, 'Adriano Moreira', p. 137.

16. Bruce, *Portugal: The Last Empire*, pp. 97–8.

17. Stone, 'Britain and the Angolan Revolt', p. 133.

18. Ibid., p. 111.

19. Interview with Alberto Franco Nogueira, London, 6 October 1979.

20. Manuel de Lucena, 'Adriano Moreira', in Barreto and Monica, *Dicionário de história de Portugal*, Suplemento F-O, p. 541.

21. See Anthony Verrier, 'Portugal on the Brink', *New Statesman*, 19 October 1962.

22. Moreira and Gonçalves, *Este é o tempo*, pp. 86–8.

23. Lucena, 'Adriano Moreira', p. 542.

24. Antunes, *Jorge Jardim*, p. 172.

25. Owen J.M. Kalinga, 'Jorge Jardim', *Historical Dictionary of Malawi*, Plymouth: Scarecrow Press, 2012, p. 204.

26. Alan Sked, 'How a Secretive Elite Created the EU to Build a World Government', *Daily Telegraph*, 27 November 2015.

27. Stone, 'Britain and Portuguese Africa', p. 174.

28. Ibid., pp. 180–3.

29. Ian Smith, *The Great Betrayal*, London: Blake, 1997, p. 72.

30. Smith, *The Great Betrayal*, pp. 72–3.

31. Luís Fernando Machado Barroso, 'The Independence of Rhodesia in Salazar's Strategy for Southern Africa', *African Historical Review*, vol. 46, no. 2, 2014, p. 12.

32. Barroso, 'The Independence of Rhodesia', p. 21.

33. Ibid.

34. Brandão, *Salazar: uma cronologia*, p. 540.

35. 'Salazar e Christiana Garton', *Jornal O Diabo*, 19 Setembro 2017.

36. See Bárbara Reis, 'Cartas inéditas a Salazar relevam segredos e intimidade com três gerações de famíla inglesa', *Publico*, 26 November 2017, https://www.publico.pt/2017/11/26/sociedade/investigacao/cartas-ineditas-de-salazar-revelam-segredos-e-intimidade-com-tres-geracoes-de-familia-inglesa-1793601 (accessed 17 September 2019).

37. Maria João Avillez, 'Franco Nogueira: a entrevista histórica', *Observador*, 23 September 2018, https://observador.pt/especiais/franco-nogueira-a-entrevista-historica-salazar-a-revolucao-e-a-vida/ (accessed 3 August 2019).

38. Rezola, 'The Franco–Salazar Meetings'.

39. de Staercke, *Mémoires*, p. 294.

40. See Payne and Palacios, *Franco*, ch. 15.
41. Coelho and Coelho, *Salazar*, p. 92.
42. Ibid., p. 90.
43. Payne and Palacios, *Franco*, pp. 370–1.
44. Brandão, *Salazar: uma cronologia*, p. 521.
45. Coelho and Coelho, *Salazar*, p. 92.
46. Frederic P. Marjay and Otto von Habsburg, *Portugal: Pioneer of the New Horizons*, Lisbon: Bertrand, 1965, p. 9.
47. Will Jones, 'The Saturday Essay: Jordan Peterson and the Big Question', *Conservative Woman*, 30 March 2019, https://www.conservativewoman.co.uk/the-saturday-essay-jordan-peterson-and-the-big-question/ (accessed 5 April 2019).
48. Brandão, *Salazar: uma cronologia*, p. 447.
49. Casey Chalk, 'Evelyn Waugh Predicted the Collapse of Catholic England', *The American Conservative*, 2 May 2019, https://www.theamericanconservative.com/articles/evelyn-waugh-predicted-the-collapse-of-catholic-england/
50. Brochado, *Memórias*, p. 385.
51. Torgal, *Estados novos, Estado Novo*, pp. 459–60.
52. Nogueira, *Um político confessa-se*, pp. 102–3.
53. Brandão, *Salazar: uma cronologia*, p. 563.
54. Amaral, *O antigo regime*, p. 60, drawing upon Alberto Menano, *Economía política: apontamentos coligados das preelecoe do Exmo Senhor Doutor Oliveira Salazar*, Coimbra: Grafica Conimbricense, 1927.
55. Amaral, *O antigo regime*, pp. 61–2.
56. Brandão, *Salazar: uma cronologia*, p. 513.
57. 'Morreu Rosa Casaco o Inspector de Pide envolvido na morte de Humberto Delgado', *Publico*, 20 July 2006, https://www.publico.pt/2006/07/20/politica/noticia/morreu-rosa-casaco-o-inspector-da-pide-envolvido-na-morte-de-humberto-delgado-1264618 (accessed 18 September 2019).
58. Meneses, *Salazar*, p. 588.
59. Franco Nogueira, *Salazar*, vol. 6: *o último combate, 1964–1970*, Coimbra: Livraria Civilização Editora, 1985 p. 89.
60. Coelho and Coelho, *Salazar*, p. 95.
61. See Patricia McGowan, *O bando de Argêl*, Lisbon: Intervenção, 1979, p. 77.
62. Brandão, *Salazar: uma cronologia*, p. 526.
63. The various theories about the extent of Salazar's role are set out in Pedro Dordio, 'O que sabia e o que decidiu Salazar?', *Observador*, 12 February 2015, https://observador.pt/explicadores/humberto-delgado-quem-foi-e-como-morreu-o-general-sem-medo/12-o-que-sabia-e-o-que-decidiu-salazar/ (accessed 18 September 2019).

64. Payne and Palacios, *Franco*, p. 405.
65. Ana S. Lopes, 'Ballet Rose: e a moral salazarista deportou Soares a São Tomé', *Jornal I*, 23 December 2017, https://ionline.sapo.pt/artigo/593589/ballet-rose-e-a-moral-salazarista-deportou-soares-para-sao-tome?seccao=Portugal (accessed 18 September 2019).
66. Moita Flores, 'Para exibir a série tivemos que esperar a morte de um sacerdote', *Sol*, 23 December 2017, https://sol.sapo.pt/artigo/593591/moita-flores-para-exibir-a-serie-tivemos-que-esperar-a-morte-de-um-sacerdote- (accessed 18 September 2019).
67. Brochado, *Memórias*, p. 349.
68. Ibid., p. 361.
69. Nogueira, *O Estado Novo*, pp. 142–3.
70. Avillez, 'Franco Nogueira' (accessed 19 August 2019).
71. Luís Reis Torgal, '"Crise" e "crises" no discurso de Salazar', *Estudos do Século XX*, no. 10, 2010, Coimbra: Imprensa da Universidade de Coimbra, 2010, p. 417.
72. Meneses, *Salazar*, p. 589.
73. Pinto, *O fim*, p. 51, n. 22.
74. Nogueira, *Um político confessa-se*, pp. 115–16.
75. Ibid., p. 99.
76. This paragraph is drawn from two articles: Ana Soromenho and Isabel Lopes, 'Cilinha, uma viagem ao Estado Novo', *Expresso*, 16 February 2008, https://oliveirasalazar.org/download/galeria/pdf___E6613A95-E62E-4C9A-BE22–6F33DDA619B8.pdf (accessed 16 September 2019); and 'Primeira-dama de Salazar: Cilinha', *CM Jornal*, 21 January 2008, https://www.cmjornal.pt/mais-cm/domingo/detalhe/primeira-dama-de-salazar-cilinha (accessed 16 September 2019).
77. Nogueira, *Salazar*, vol. 6, p. 347.
78. Antunes, *Cartas particulares*, vol. 1, p. 247.
79. FRUS, vol. 12, Western Europe 1964–68, 'The Twilight of the Salazar Era', Document 71: Telegram from the Embassy in Portugal to the Department of State, 24 July 1968, https://history.state.gov/historicaldocuments/frus1964–68v12/d171 (accessed 26 February 2017).
80. FRUS, vol. 12, Western Europe 1964–68, 'The Twilight of the Salazar Era', Document 71.
81. Nogueira, *Salazar*, vol. 6, p. 360.
82. Meneses, *Salazar*, pp. 596–7.
83. Paulo Otero, *Os últimos meses de Salazar: Agosto de 1968 a Julho de 1970*, Lisbon: Almecina, 2008, pp. 30–7.
84. Nogueira, *Salazar*, vol. 6, p. 390.
85. Coelho and Coelho, *Salazar*, p. 29.
86. Thomáz, *Últimas décadas de Portugal*, vol. IV, pp. 291–2.

87. Amaral, *O antigo regime*, p. 85.
88. Nogueira, *Salazar*, vol. 6, p. 416.
89. Ibid. p. 417.
90. Coelho and Coelho, *Salazar*, p. 32; translation to be found in Meneses, *Salazar*, p. 602.
91. Lucena, *Os lugar-tenentes*, p. 138.
92. Tomás, *Últimas décadas*, vol. 4, p. 124.
93. Nogueira, *Salazar*, vol. 6, p. 424.
94. Ibid., pp. 427–8, n. 1.
95. Ibid., p. 433.
96. Ibid., p. 434.
97. Tomás, *Últimas décadas*, vol. 4, p. 124.
98. 'State Secret', *Time*, 19 December 1969.
99. José Freire Antunes, *O factor africano 1890–1990*, Lisbon: Bertrand Editora, 1990, p. 75.
100. Quoted in John P. Cann, *The Fuzileiros: Portuguese Marines in Africa, 1961–1974*, Solihull: Helion, 2016, p. 3.
101. Pulido Valente, 'Marcello Caetano', p. 204.
102. *Diário de Manhã*, 29 July 1970.
103. Fernando de Castro Brandão, 'O legado e a herança de um político honesto: Salazar', *Jornal O Diabo*, 11 July 2017.
104. Brandão, *Salazar: uma cronologia*, p. 557.
105. *Diário de Notícias*, 29 July 1970.
106. Rodrigo Lacerda Fernandes, 'A morte de um ditador: o visual e o olhar no funeral de António de Oliveira Salazar', MA, Faculty of Social and Human Sciences, New University of Lisbon, 2013, p. 110.

15. THE AFTERLIFE OF SALAZAR: FIFTY YEARS OF CONTROVERSY

1. Pulido Valente, 'Marcello Caetano', p. 206.
2. Torgal, *Estados novos*, pp. 615–16.
3. 'Isolado como uma ilha', *CM Jornal*, 7 October 2012, https://www.cmjornal.pt/mais-cm/domingo/detalhe/isolado-como-uma-ilha (accessed 3 October 2019).
4. Martinho, *Marcello Caetano*, pp. 205–6.
5. For an articulation of this perspective on the Lisbon bourgeoisie, see Pinto, *O fim*, pp. 185–7.
6. Pulido Valente, 'Marcello Caetano', p. 206.
7. 'Isolado como uma ilha'.
8. Pinto, *O fim*, p. 161.
9. Gallagher, *Portugal: A Twentieth Century Interpretation* p. 171.
10. Martinho, *Marcello Caetano*, p. 198.

11. Raimundo, *O último salazarista*, pp. 241–6.
12. Nogueira, *Um político confessa-se*, p. 114.
13. Martinho, *Marcello Caetano*, p. 245.
14. Gallagher, *Portugal: A Twentieth Century Interpretation*, p. 185.
15. See Rodrigues, Avelino, Cesário Borga and Mário Cardoso, *Portugal depois de 25 de Abril*, Lisbon: Intervoz, 1976, p. 14.
16. See Sunday Times Insight Team, *Insight on Portugal: The Year of the Captains*, London: Andre Deutsch, 1975, p. 35; and Phil Mailer, *Portugal: The Impossible Revolution*, Oakland, CA: PM Press, 2012, pp. 104–6.
17. Gallagher, *Portugal: A Twentieth Century Interpretation*, p. 184.
18. Martinho, *Marcello Caetano*, p. 217.
19. Thomáz, *Últimas décadas*, vol. III, p. 353.
20. Robert Harvey, *Portugal: Birth of a democracy*, London: Macmillan, 1978, pp. 17–18.
21. Letter from José Correia de Oliveira to Marcello Caetano, 13 March 1974, in José Freire Antunes (ed.), *Cartas particulares a Marcello Caetano*, vol. II, Lisbon: D. Quixote, 1985, p. 141.
22. João Alberto da Costa Pinto, 'Gilberto Freyre e a intelligentsia salazarista em defesa do Império Colonial Português (1951–1974)', *História*, vol. 28, no. 1, 2009, p. 482, n. 30.
23. Gallagher, *Portugal: A Twentieth Century Interpretation*, p. 192.
24. Douglas Porch, *The Portuguese Armed Forces and the Revolution*, London: Croom Helm, 1977, pp. 164–7; see also Kenneth Maxwell, 'The Hidden Revolution in Portugal', *New York Review of Books*, 17 April 1975, p. 34.
25. Manuel de Lucena, 'Reflexões sobre a queda do regime salazarista e o que se lhe seguiu', *Análise Social*, vol. 37, no. 162, 2002, pp. 20–1.
26. See 'The Anti-Communists Strike Back', *Time*, 25 August 1975, pp. 8–9.
27. *Diario de Coimbra*, 13 February 1992, quoted by John Andrade, *Dicionário de 25 de Abril*, Lisbon: Nova Arrancada, 2002, p. 301.
28. Gallagher, *Portugal: A Twentieth Century Interpretation*, p. 200.
29. Mailer, *Portugal*, p. 312.
30. 'Obituary of Vasco Gonçalves', *Independent* (London), 14 June 2005.
31. See Mello, 'Guilherme Braga da Cruz', pp. 909–10.
32. Lucena, 'Reflexões', pp. 32–3.
33. Ibid., pp. 16–18.
34. Ibid., pp. 31–2.
35. For the ending of the 'hot summer'of 1974, see José Freire Antunes, *O segredo de vinte cinco do Novembro*, Lisbon: Europa-America, 1980.
36. 'Otelo: precisamos de um homem honesto como Salazar', *Diário de*

Notícias, 21 April 2011, https://www.dn.pt/dossiers/tv-e-media/revistas-de-imprensa/noticias/otelo-precisamos-de-um-homem-honesto-como-salazar-1835446.html (accessed 13 October 2019).

37. *24 Horas*, 19 April 1999.
38. Vasco Pulido Valente, 'Não devemos nada aos capitães de Abril: zero', *Jornal i*, 21 April 2014, https://ionline.sapo.pt/artigo/325808/vasco-pulido-valente-nao-devemos-nada-aos-capitaes-de-abril-zero?seccao=Portugal (accessed 13 October 2019).
39. Ben Pimlott and Jean Seaton, 'Ferment of an Old Brew', *New Society*, 24 July 1975, p. 202.
40. See Tom Gallagher, 'Democracy in Portugal since the 1974 Revolution', *Parliamentary Affairs*, vol. 35, Spring 1985, pp. 202–18 for some of the negative features of the post-1976 democracy.
41. Interview with Robert S. Pastorino, US commercial attaché in Lisbon (1974–1977), 1998, 'Portugal, Country Reader', pp. 103–4, http://adst.org/wp-contents/uploads/2012/09/Portugal.PDF (accessed 27 July 2019).
42. Gallagher, *Portugal: A Twentieth Century Interpretation*, p. 233.
43. Robinson, *Contemporary Portugal*, p. 268.
44. Carvalho, 'Estátuas, cabeças'; see also Fernando de Castro Brandão, 'A estátua de Salazar em Santa Comba Dão', *Jornal O Diabo*, 17 January 2017; and 'Berlin and Santa Comba Dão', 26 February 2012, https://amidstinterpretation.wordpress.com/2012/02/ (accessed 13 October 2019).
45. Carvalho, 'Estátuas, cabeças'.
46. António José Saraiva, 'O salazarismo', *Expresso*, 22 April 1989.
47. Saraiva, 'O salazarismo'.
48. See 'Doação do espólio de Franco Nogueira ao Arquivo Diplomático no centenário do nascimento do diplomata português', Portuguese Ministry of Foreign Affairs, 17 September 2018, https://idi.mne.pt/pt/o-instituto/noticias/evocacao-do-centenario-do-nascimento-de-franco-nogueira (accessed 11 September 2019). See also Jaime Nogueira Pinto, 'O paradoxal itinerário político de Alberto Franco Nogueira e a chamada "crise da direita"', *Observador*, 3 July 2019, https://observador.pt/opiniao/o-paradoxal-itinerario-politico-de-alberto-franco-nogueira-e-a-chamada-crise-da-direita/ (accessed 17 July 2019).
49. See Rui Ramos, *História de Portugal*, Lisbon: A Esfera dos Livros, 2009.
50. The dispute may be said to have begun with the appearance of an article by the Marxist historian Manuel Loff, 'Uma história em fascículos ... (I)', *Público*, 2 August 2012, https://www.publico.pt/2012/08/02/jornal/uma-historia-em-fasciculos-i-24995274 (accessed 7 November

2016). A strong rejoinder came from Bruno Cardoso Reis, 'Este século não foi fascista: Salazar, Franco e a efémera nova ordem internacional nazi-fascista', *Relações Internacionais*, no. 27, September 2010, pp. 129–38; a balancing article summing up the debate came from Filipe Ribeiro de Meneses, 'Slander, Ideological Differences, or Academic Debate? The "Verão Quente" of 2012 and the State of Portuguese Historiography', *e-JPH*, vol. 10, no. 1, Summer 2012 (accessed 7 November 2016).

51. Brandão, 'O legado e a herança'.
52. Vieira, *A governanta*, p. 23.
53. See Rita and Vieira, *Os meus*.
54. Fernando Dacosta, *Máscaras de Salazar*, Lisbon: Casa das Letras, 2010.
55. These works can be found in the Bibliography.
56. 'Morreu o historiador José Hermano Saraiva', *JN*, 20 July 2012, https://www.jn.pt/artes/morreu-o-historiador-jose-hermano-saraiva-2677400.html (accessed 14 October 2019).
57. Soares, 'Salazar, o retrato'.
58. See Ricardo Soares de Oliveira, *Magnificent and Beggar Land: Angola since the Civil War*, London: Christopher Hurst, 2015, pp. 71–3, 77, 149, 159.
59. See José Magone, *Politics in Contemporary Portugal: Democracy Evolving*, Boulder, CO: Lynne Rienner, 2014, pp. 58–62.
60. Charles Forelle, 'A Nation of Drop-outs Shakes Europe', *Wall Street Journal*, 25 March 2011.
61. For its very low ranking in the EU, see António Barreto, 'Social Change in Portugal', in António Costa Pinto (ed.), *Contemporary Portugal: Politics, Society and Culture*, Boulder, CO: Lynne Rienner, 2011, p. 212, n. 46.
62. See 'O maior português de sempre: Oliveira Salazar' (Part 1) on YouTube, presented by Jaime Nogueira Pinto (RTP).
63. João José Brandão Ferreira, 'Salazar ganha e então?', http://nonasnonas.blogspot.com/2007/05/salazar-ganhou-e-ento-por-brando.html (accessed 14 May 2019).
64. Peter Wise, 'Portugal's ex-PM José Sócrates Detained on Suspected Tax Fraud', *Financial Times*, 22 November 2014.
65. Andrei Khalip, 'Portuguese ex-PM Sócrates Indicted on Corruption Charges', *Reuters*, 11 October 2017.
66. Marco Lisi, 'Portugal: Between Apathy and Crisis of Mainstream Parties', Centro Italiani Studi Elettorali, 12 June 2014, https://cise.luiss.it/cise/2014/06/12/portugal-between-apathy-and-crisis-of-mainstream-parties/ (accessed 16 October 2019).
67. See Aron, *Democracy and Totalitarianism*, pp. 154–5.

68. João Céu e Silva, 'Madeleine Albright: Salazar não era fascista', *Diário de Notícias*, 30 September 2018, https://www.dn.pt/edicao-do-dia/30-set-2018/interior/madeleine-albright-salazar-nao-era-fascista—9923234.html (accessed 26 January 2019).

69. Pinto, *O fim*, p. 111.

70. See Manuel Braga da Cruz, *O partido e o Estado no salazarismo*, Lisbon: Editorial Presenca, 1988.

71. See Jaime Nogueira Pinto, 'A excepção portuguesa: porque não temos uma direita radical?', *Observador*, 3 February 2019, https://observador.pt/opiniao/a-excepcao-portuguesa-porque-nao-temos-uma-direita-radical (accessed 11 June 2019).

72. Eugen Weber, *A Modern History of Europe*, New York: W.W. Norton, 1972, p. 775.

POSTSCRIPT

1. Ella Whelan, '"Liberals" are conspicuously silent on Canada's descent into tyranny', *Daily Telegraph*, 18 February 2022, https://www.telegraph.co.uk/news/2022/02/18/liberals-conspicuously-silent-canadas-descent-tyranny/ (accessed 26 April 2022).

2. Jon Henley, 'Macron declares his Covid strategy is to "piss off" the unvaccinated', *Guardian*, 4 January 2022, https://www.theguardian.com/world/2022/jan/04/macron-declares-his-covid-strategy-is-to-piss-off-the-unvaccinated (accessed 26 April 2022); 'Mario Draghi: "The unvaccinated are not part of our society."', One News Page, 19 February 2022, https://www.onenewspage.com/video/20220215/1434 6429/Mario-Draghi-quot-The-unvaccinated-are-not.htm (accessed 26 April 2022).

3. Carlos Abreu Amorim, 'PSD – tudo ao contrário', *Observador*, 12 February 2022, https://observador.pt/opiniao/psd-tudo-ao-contrario/ (accessed 26 April 2022).

BIBLIOGRAPHY

Acciaiuoli, Margarida, *António Ferro: a vertigem da palavra*, Lisbon: Bizâncio, 2013.

Accornero, Guya, *The Revolution before the Revolution: Late Authoritarianism and Student Protest in Portugal*, New York: Berghahn, 2016.

Acheson, Dean, *Sketches from Life of Men I Have Known*, London: Hamish Hamilton, 1961.

Adinolfi, Goffredo and António Costa Pinto, 'Salazar's "New State": The Paradoxes of Hybridization in the Fascist Era', in António Costa Pinto and Aristotle Kallis (eds.), *Thinking Fascism and Dictatorship in Europe*, London: Palgrave Macmillan 2014.

Adler, Wolfgang, 'JFK's Failed Coup in Lisbon', *Social Matter*, 7 August 2017, https://www.socialmatter.net/2017/08/07/jfks-failed-coup-lisbon/

Adler, Wolfgang, 'Salazar and the Loss of the Business Elite', *Social Matter*, 6 December 2017, https://www.socialmatter.net/2017/12/06/salazar-loss-business-elite/

Afonso, Rui, *Um homem bom*, Lisbon: Editorial Caminho, 1995.

Alexandre, Valentim, 'Ideologia, economia e política: a questão colonial na implantação do Estado Novo', *Análise Social*, vol. 28, nos. 123–124, 1993.

Allegro, José Sollari, *A personalidade de Salazar e alguns aspectos da sua obra*, Lousã: Tipografia Lousanense, 1989.

Amaral, Diogo Freitas do, *O antigo regime e a revolucão: memórias políticas (1941–1975)*, Lisbon: Livraria Bertrand, 1995.

Andrade, John, *Dicionário de 25 de Abril*, Lisbon: Nova Arrancada, 2002.

Andrade, José Luís, *Ditadura ou revolução: a verdadeira história do dilema ibérico nos anos decisivos de 1926–1936*, Lisbon: Casa das Letras, 2019.

Andrade, Luis Miguel Solla de, 'Henrique Galvão, 1895–1970: Aspects of a Euro-African Crusade', MA thesis, University of South Africa, March 2009.

Antunes, José Freire (ed.), *Cartas particulares a Marcello Caetano*, vol. I, Lisbon: D. Quixote, 1985.

BIBLIOGRAPHY

————— (ed.), *Cartas particulares a Marcello Caetano*, vol. II, Lisbon: D. Quixote, 1985.

—————, 'Kennedy, Portugal and the Azores Base, 1961', in Douglas Brinkley and Richard T. Griffiths (eds.), *Kennedy and Europe*, Baton Rouge: Louisiana State University Press, 1999.

—————, *Jorge Jardim: agente secreto*, Lisbon: Bertrand, 1996.

—————, *Judeus em Portugal: o testemunho de 50 homens e mulheres*, Lisbon: Edeline Multimedia, 2002.

—————, *Kennedy e Salazar: o leão e a raposa*, Lisbon: Difusão Cultural, 1991.

—————, *O factor africano, 1890–1990*, Lisbon: Bertrand Editora, 1990.

—————, *O segredo de vinte cinco do Novembro*, Lisbon: Europa-America, 1980.

—————, *Salazar e Caetano: cartas secretas, 1932–1968*, Lisbon: Círculo de Leitores, 1993.

Araújo, António de, *Matar o Salazar: o atentado de Julho de 1937*, Lisbon: Tinta da China, 2017.

Aristides de Sousa Mendes Virtual Museum, http://mvasm.sapo.pt/BC/Archives/en

Aron, Raymond, *Democracy and Totalitarianism*, London: Weidenfeld and Nicolson, 1968.

Atkinson, William C., 'Institutions and Law', in Harold Livermore (ed.), *Portugal and Brazil: An Introduction*, Oxford: Clarendon Press, 1953.

Avillez, Maria João, 'Franco Nogueira: The Historic Interview', *Observador*, 23 September 2018, https://observador.pt/especiais/franco-nogueira-a-entrevista-historica-salazar-a-revolucao-e-a-vida/

Ball, George W., *The Past Has Another Pattern: Memoirs*, New York: W.W. Norton, 1982.

Barreiras, Cecília, *Quirino de Jesus e outros estudos*, Lisbon: Edições Livro PT, 2017.

Barreto, António, 'Social Change in Portugal', in António Costa Pinto (ed.), *Contemporary Portugal: Politics, Society and Culture*, Boulder, CO: Lynne Rienner, 2011.

Barreto, José, 'O deputado absentista Salazar e o parlamento em 1921', www.academai.edu, 2013, https://www.academia.edu/10375312/O_deputado_absentista_Salazar_e_o_parlamento_em_1921

Barroso, Luís Fernando Machado, 'The Independence of Rhodesia in Salazar's Strategy for Southern Africa', *African Historical Review*, vol. 46, no. 2, 2014.

Benarus, Adolfo, *O anti-semitismo*, Lisbon: SNT, 1937.

Bender, Gerald J., *Angola under the Portuguese: The Myth and the Reality*, Stanford: Stanford University Press, 1977.

Bennett, Jeffrey S., *When the Sun Danced: Myth, Miracles, and Modernity in Early Twentieth-Century Portugal*, Charlottesville: Virginia University Press, 2012.

Besada, Jorge, 'Two Reasons Why Socialism Repeatedly Fails', *Mises Wire*,

29 May 2019, https://mises.org/wire/two-reasons-why-socialism-repeatedly-fails

Besier, Gerhard and Katarzyna Stoklosa, *Jehovah's Witnesses in Europe: Past and Present*, Cambridge: Cambridge Scholars Publishing, 2016.

Black, Conrad, 'The Indispensable Man', *New Criterion*, vol. 37, December 2018.

Blanshard, Paul, *Freedom and Catholic Power in Spain and Portugal*, Boston: Beacon Press, 1962.

Bloch, Michael, *Operation Willi: The Plot to Kidnap the Duke of Windsor*, London: Weidenfeld, 1984.

Bodley, Ronald, *Flight into Portugal: The Dramatic Story of an Englishman's Escape from Paris to Lisbon*, Triptree, Essex: Anchor Press, 1941.

Braga, Paulo Drummond, 'Os Ministros da Educação Nacional (1936–1974): sociologia de uma função', *Revista Lusófona de Educação*, vol. 16, 2010.

Brandão, Fernando de Castro, *Cartas de Salazar para Gloria Castanheira 1918–1923*, Lisbon: Europress, 2011.

———, *Cartas singulares a Salazar*, Lisbon: Edição de Autor, 2015.

———, *Salazar: citações*, Lisbon: Cosmos, 2008.

———, *Salazar: uma cronologia*, Lisbon: Prefácio 2011.

Brandão, José, 'Salazar e a 1 República', *A Viagem dos Argonautas*, 2 November 2012, https://aviagemdosargonautas.net/2012/11/02/salazar-e-a-i-republica-9-por-jose-brandao/

Brochado, Idelino Costa, *Memórias de Costa Brochado*, Lisbon: Livraria Popular Francisco Franco, 1987.

Bruce, Neil, *Portugal: The Last Empire*, Newton Abbot: David and Charles, 1974.

Bryant, Arthur, *The Turn of the Tide 1939–1943*, London: Collins, 1959.

Burke, Peter and Maria Lúcia Pallares-Burke, *Gilberto Freyre: Social Theory in the Tropics*, Oxford: Peter Lang, 2008.

Cabrita, Felícia, *Mulheres de Salazar*, Lisbon: Editorial Notícias, 1999.

Cabrita, João M., *Mozambique: The Tortuous Road to Democracy*, London: Palgrave, 2000.

Caetano, Marcello, *Manual de ciência política e direito constitucional*, vol. II, Coimbra: Coimbra Editora, 1972.

———, *Minhas memórias de Salazar*, Lisbon: Verbo, 1977.

Caminho do futuro, Lisbon: SNI, 1958.

Cann, John P., *Counterinsurgency in Africa: The Portuguese Way of War 1961–74*, Warwick: Helion, 2012.

———, *The Fuzileiros: Portuguese Marines in Africa, 1961–1974*, Solihull: Helion, 2016.

Canotilho, Mariana, 'A constituição portuguesa de 1933', in António Simões do Paço (ed.), *Os anos de Salazar*, vol. 2: *a constituição do Estado Novo*, Lisbon: Planeta de Agostini, 2008.

BIBLIOGRAPHY

Cardoso, José Luís and Nuno Estêvão Ferreira, 'A Câmara Corporativa (1935–1974) e as políticas públicas no Estado Novo', *Ler História*, no. 64, 2013, https://journals.openedition.org/lerhistoria/290.

Carey, Peter, 'Timor', in António Barreto and Maria Filomena Moníca, *Dicionário de história de Portugal*, Suplemento P/Z, Lisbon: Figueirinhas, 1999.

Carvalho, Rita Almeida de, 'Ideology and Architecture in the Portuguese "Estado Novo": Castanheira, José Pedro, Natal Vaz and António Caeiro, *A queda de Salazar: o princípio do fim da ditadura*, Lisbon: Tinta de China, 2018.

Cultural Innovation within a Para-Fascist State (1932–1945)', *Journal of Comparative Fascist Studies*, vol. 7, 2018, https://doi.org/10.1163/22116 25700702002

Castelo, Claudia, 'Um brasileiro em terras portuguesas', *Buala*, 31 March 2013,http://www.buala.org/pt/a-ler/um-brasileiro-em-terras-portuguesas-prefacio

Catarino, Manuel, *Salazar: só a cadeira o derrubou*, Lisbon: Correio da Manha, 2018.

Chalk, Casey, 'Evelyn Waugh Predicted the Collapse of Catholic England', *The American Conservative*, 2 May 2019, https://www.theamericanconservative. com/articles/evelyn-waugh-predicted-the-collapse-of-catholic-england/

Coelho, Eduardo and António Macieira Coelho, *Salazar: o fim e a morte*, Lisbon: D. Quixote, 1995.

Coelho, José Maria dos Santos, 'Adriano Moreira e o Império Português', PhD thesis, University of Beira Interior, Portugal, 2015.

Colville, John, *Footprints in Time*, London: William Collins, 1976.

'Como surgiu a biografia (de Salazar) e quais as razões do seu exito' [interview with Franco Nogueira, 1977], *Observador*, 23 September 2018, https://observador.pt/especiais/franco-nogueira-a-entrevista-historica-salazar-a-revolucao-e-a-vida/

Conlin, Jonathan, *Mr Five Per Cent*, London: Profile Books, 2019.

Conradi, Peter, *Hitler's Piano Player: The Rise and Fall of Ernst Hanfstaengl, Confidant of Hitler, Ally of FDR*, London: Duckworth, 2006.

Corkill, David, *Development of the Portuguese Economy: A Case of Europeanization*, London: Routledge, 2002.

———, *The Portuguese Economy since 1974*, Edinburgh: Edinburgh University Press 1993.

——— and José Pina Almeida, 'Commemoration and Propaganda in Salazar's Portugal', *Journal of Contemporary History*, vol. 44, no. 3, 2009.

Correspondência de Santos Costa para Oliveira Salazar, vol. 1: *1934–1950*, Lisbon: Comissão do Livro Negro Sobre Fascismo, 1988

Costa, Leonor Freire, Pedro Lains and Susana Münch Miranda, *An Economic History of Portugal, 1143–2010*, Cambridge: Cambridge University Press, 2016.

BIBLIOGRAPHY

Cruz, Manuel Braga da, 'Centro Académico da Democracia Cristã', in António Barreto and Maria Filomena Mónica, *Dicionário de história de Portugal*, vol. 7, A/E, Lisbon: Figueirinhas,1999.

————, 'Pedro Teotónio Pereira, embaixador português em Espanha durante as guerras', in *Estudos em homenagem a Luís António de Oliveira Ramos*, Oporto: Faculdade de Letras da Universidade do Porto, 2004.

————, *Correspondência de Santos Costa, 1936–1982*, Lisbon: Verbo, 1994.

————, *O Estado Novo e a Igreja Católica*, Lisbon: Bizâncio, 1999.

————, *O partido e o Estado no salazarismo*, Lisbon: Editorial Presenca, 1988.

————, 'O Integralismo Lusitano e o Estado Novo', in *O fascismo em Portugal*, Lisbon: Regra do Jogo, 1980.

Cruzeiro, Maria Manuela, *Costa Gomes: o último marechal*, Lisbon: D. Quixote, 2014.

Dacosta, Fernando, *Máscaras de Salazar*, Lisbon: Casa das Letras, 2007.

————, *Salazar fotobiografia*, Lisbon: Editorial Notícias, 2000.

Dallek, Robert, *An Unfinished Life: John F. Kennedy 1917–1963*, New York: Little, Brown, 1983.

Dard, Olivier and Ana Isabel Sardinha-Desvignes, *Célébrer Salazar en France (1930–1974): du philosalazarisme au salazarisme français*, Brussels: Peter Lang, 2018.

de Reynold, Gonzague, *Portugal*, Paris: Spas, 1936.

de Staercke, André, 'An Alliance Clamouring to Be Born: Anxious to Survive', in André de Staercke (ed.), *NATO's Anxious Birth*, London: C. Hurst, 1985.

————, *Mémoires sur la régence et la question royale*, Brussels: Éditions Racine, 2003.

Delgado, Frederico Rosa, *Humberto Delgado: biografia do general sem medo*, Lisbon: A Esfera dos Livros, 2008.

Delgado, Humberto, *Da pulhice de homo sapiens*, Lisbon: Livraria Depositária, 1933.

Delgado, Iva, *Braga, cidade proibido: Humberto Delgado e as eleições de 1958*, Braga: Governo Civil, 1988.

Derrick, Michael, *The Portugal of Salazar*, London: Sands, 1938.

Dez anos de politica externa, vol. 1, Lisbon: Editor Imprensa Nacional, 1961.

Dilks, David (ed.), *The Diaries of Sir Alexander Cadogan O.M., 1938–1945*, London: Cassell, 1971.

'Doação do espólio de Franco Nogueira ao Arquivo Diplomático no centenário do nascimento do diplomata português', Portuguese Ministry of Foreign Affairs, 17 September 2018, https://idi.mne.pt/pt/o-instituto/noticias/evocacao-do-centenario-do-nascimento-de-franco-nogueira

Dordio, Pedro, 'O que sabia e o que decidiu Salazar?', *Observador*, 12 February 2015, https://observador.pt/explicadores/humberto-delgado-quem-foi-e-como-morreu-o-general-sem-medo/12-o-que-sabia-e-o-que-decidiu-salazar/

BIBLIOGRAPHY

Eccles, David, *By Safe Hand: Letters of Sybil and David Eccles, 1939–42*, London: Bodley Head, 1983.

'Economy of the Salazar Regime', *Country Studies Series, Federal Research Division of the Library of Congress*, http://www.country-data.com/cgi-bin/query/r-10909.html

Egerton, F.C.C., *Salazar: Rebuilder of Portugal*, London: Hodder and Stoughton, 1943.

Faria, Telmo, 'Quem tem a tropa', in Iva Delgado, *Humberto Delgado: as eleições de 1958*, Lisbon: Vega, 1998.

Faria, Telmo, *Debaixo de fogo!*, Lisbon: Edições Cosmos, 2000.

Farínha, Luís, 'Os saneamentos no função publíco', in João Madeira, Irene Flunser Pimentel and Luís Farinha, *Vítimas de Salazar: Estado Novo e violência política*, Lisbon: A Esfera dos Livros, 2007.

Fernandes, Carlos, *O consul Aristides de Sousa Mendes: a verdade e a mentira*, Lisbon: Edição de Grupo de Amigos do Autor, 2013.

Fernandes, Rodrigo Lacerda, 'A morte de um ditador: o visual e o olhar no funeral de António de Oliveira Salazar', MA, Faculty of Social and Human Sciences, New University of Lisbon, 2013.

Ferreira, João José Brandão, 'Salazar ganha e então', http://nonas-nonas.blogspot.com/2007/05/salazar-ganhou-e-ento-por-brando.html

Ferro, António, *Salazar, Portugal and Its Leader*, London: Faber and Faber, 1939.

Flores, Moita, 'Para exibir a série tivemos que esperar a morte de um sacerdote', *Sol*, 23 December 2017, https://sol.sapo.pt/artigo/593591/moita-flores-para-exibir-a-serie-tivemos-que-esperar-a-morte-de-um-sacerdote-

Fonseca, Ana Mónica and Daniel Marcos, 'French and German Support to Portugal: The Military Survival of the "Estado Novo"', *Portuguese Studies Review*, vol. 16, no. 2, 2008.

Fonseca, Pedro Prostes de, 'O Forte de Peniche a fuga de Cunhal e a historia do guarda que o ajudou', *Observador*, 1 October 2016, https://observador.pt/especiais/forte-de-peniche-a-fuga-de-cunhal-e-a-historia-do-guarda-que-o-ajudou/

Foreign Relations of the United States (Washington: Department of State 1943–)

Fox, Mark, 'The Battle of the Atlantic Has Much to Teach Us Today,', *Reaction Life*, 3 September 2019, https://reaction.life/the-battle-of-the-atlantic-has-much-to-teach-us-today/

Fralon, José Alain, *A Good Man in Evil Times: The Story of Aristides de Sousa Mendes*, London: Penguin, 2001.

Freitas, Joana Gaspar de, *Gonzague de Reynold e Oliveira Salazar: 25 anos de correspondência*, Lisbon: Faculty of Letters, University of Lisbon, 2003.

Freyre, Gilberto, *Aventura e rotina*, Rio de Janeiro: José Olympio, 1953.

Fryer, Peter and Patricia McGowan Pinheiro, *Oldest Ally: A Portrait of Salazar's Portugal*, London: Dennis Dobson, 1961.

Furedi, Frank, *First World War: Still No End in Sight*, London: Bloomsbury, 2007.

Gaddis, John Lewis, *George F. Kennan: An American Life*, New York: Penguin Press, 2011.

Gallagher, Tom, 'Controlled Repression in Salazar's Portugal', *Journal of Contemporary History*, vol. 14, no 3, July 1979.

———, 'Democracy in *Portugal* since the 1974 Revolution', *Parliamentary Affairs*, vol. 35, Spring 1985.

———, 'Fernando dos Santos Costa: guardião militar do Estado Novo 1944–58', in *O Estado Novo das origens ão fim da autarcia 1926–59*, Lisbon: Fragmentos, 1986.

———, 'Portugal', in Martin Blinkhorn (ed.), *Fascists and Conservatives*, London: Routledge, 1990.

———, 'Portugal', in Tom Buchanan and Martin Conway (eds.), *Political Catholicism in Europe, 1918–1965*, Oxford: Clarendon Press, 1996.

———, *Portugal: A Twentieth Century Interpretation*, Manchester: Manchester University Press, 1983.

Galvão, Henrique, *Santa Maria: My Crusade for Portugal*, London: Weidenfeld and Nicolson, 1961.

Garrido, Álvaro 'A universidade e o Estado Novo: de "corporação orgânica" do regime a território de dissidência social', Revista Critica de Cienciais Sociais, vol. 81, 2008.

———, 'Henrique Tenreiro: "patrão das pescas" e guardião do Estado Novo', *Análise Social*, vol. 36, no. 160, 2001.

Gibbons, John, *I Gathered No Moss*, London: Robert Hale, 1939.

Gil, José, *Salazar: a retórica da invisibilidade*, Lisbon: Relógio D'Água, 1995.

Gkartzonikas, Paris, 'The Effects of the Marshall Plan in Greece, Turkey and Portugal', Athens: Greek Foreign Affairs Council, n.d.

Godhino, José Magalhães, 'Salazar, Franco Nogueira e o MUD (2): O encontro com Carmona', *O Jornal*, 16 May 1980.

Goemaere, Pierre, *Bissaya Barreto*, Lisbon: Livraria Bertrand, 1942.

Goodhart, David, *The Road to Somewhere: The Populist Revolt and the Future of Politics*, London: C. Hurst, 2017.

Gray, John, 'You're Reaping What You Sowed, Liberals', *Unherd*, 7 February 2019, https://unherd.com/2019/02/youre-reaping-what-you-sowed-liberals/

Hamilton, Nigel, *Monty, the Field Marshal, 1944–1976*, London: Hamish Hamilton, 1976.

Harrison, Steve, *A Tale of Two Cities: A Curious Tourist's Journey back to Povoa de Varzim in the 1950s*, Oporto: Blue Book, 2019.

Harvey, Robert, *Portugal: Birth of a Democracy*, London: Macmillan, 1978.

Hazony, Yoram, 'Conservative Rationalism Has Failed', *The American Mind*,

BIBLIOGRAPHY

1 July 2019, https://americanmind.org/essays/conservative-rationalism-has-failed-2/

Henderson, Sir Nicholas, *The Birth of NATO*, London: Weidenfeld and Nicolson, 1982.

Henriques, Mendo Castro and Gonçalo Sampaio e Melo, *Salazar: pensamento e doutrina política—textos antólogicos*, Lisbon: Verbo, 1989.

Hilton, Matthew, James McKay, Nicholas Crowson, and Jean-Francois Mouhot, *The Politics of Expertise: How NGOs Shaped Modern Britain*, Oxford: Oxford University Press, 2013.

Hume, Martin, *Through Portugal*, London: E.G. Richards, 1907.

'Isolado como uma ilha', *CM Jornal*, 7 October 2012, https://www.cmjornal.pt/mais-cm/domingo/detalhe/isolado-como-uma-ilha

Jesus, José Manuel Duarte de, *Dança sobre o vulcão: Portugal e o III Reich*, Lisbon: Edições 70, 2017.

Jones, Will, 'The Saturday Essay: Jordan Peterson and the Big Question', *Conservative Woman*, 30 March 2019, https://www.conservativewoman.co.uk/the-saturday-essay-jordan-peterson-and-the-big-question/

Kalinga, Owen J.M., 'Jorge Jardim', in *Historical Dictionary of Malawi*, Plymouth: Scarecrow Press, 2012.

Kay, Hugh, *Salazar and Modern Portugal*, London: Eyre and Spottiswoode, 1970.

Keefe, Eugene, *Area Handbook for Portugal*, Washington DC: American University, 1977.

Kotkin, Joel, 'Elites against Western Civilization', *New Geography*, 10 April 2019, http://www.newgeography.com/content/006431-elites-against-western-civilization

————, 'Our Suicidal Elites', *Quillette*, 23 April 2019, https://quillette.com/2019/04/30/our-suicidal-elites/

Kuin, S., 'A Mocidade Portuguesa nos anos trinta: anteprojectos e instauração de uma organização paramilitar de juventude', *Análise Social*, vol. 122, no. 28, 1993.

La Plume et la Rouleau, '1933: Salazar, le dictateur de glace … et de feu (3)', 8 March 2013, http://laplumeetlerouleau.over-blog.com/article-1933-salazar-le-dictateur-de-glace-et-de-feu-3-115580554.html

Leal, Francisco da Cunha, *As minhas memórias*, Lisbon: Edição de Autor, 1966.

Le Bon, Gustave, *The Psychology of Socialism*, London: T. Fisher Unwin, 1919.

Leitão, Nicolau Andresen, 'The Salazar Regime and European Integration, 1947–72', in Pedro Aires Oliveira and Maria I. Rezola (eds.), *Estudos em homenagem a Jose Medeiros Ferreira*, Lisbon: Tinta da China, 2010.

————, *Estado Novo, democracia e Europa, 1947–1986*, Lisbon: Imprensa de Ciências Sociais, 2007.

Léonard, Yves, *Salazarisme et fascisme*, Paris: Chandeigne, 2003.

BIBLIOGRAPHY

Lisi, Marco, 'Portugal: Between Apathy and Crisis of Mainstream Parties', Centro Italiani Studi Elettorali, 12 June 2014, https://cise.luiss.it/cise/2014/06/12/portugal-between-apathy-and-crisis-of-mainstream-parties/

Lochery, Neill, *Lisbon: War in the Shadows of the City of Light, 1939–1945*, New York: Public Affairs, 2011.

Loff, Manuel, 'Uma história em fascículos ... (I)', *Público*, 2 August 2012, https://www.publico.pt/2012/08/02/jornal/uma-historia-em-fasciculos-i-24995274

Lopes, Ana S., 'Ballet Rose: e a moral salazarista deportou Soares a São Tomé', *Jornal i*, 23 December 2017, https://ionline.sapo.pt/artigo/593589/ballet-rose-e-a-moral-salazarista-deportou-soares-para-sao-tome?seccao=Portugal

Lopes, Raquel Ramalho, 'Ambiguidades na aliança entre Cerejeira e Salazar', *RTP*, 1 April 2010, https://www.rtp.pt/noticias/pais/ambiguidades-na-alianca-entre-cerejeira-e-salazar_n332839

Lucena, Manuel de, 'Adriano Moreira', in Barreto, António and Maria Filomena Mónica, *Dicionário de história de Portugal*, Suplemento F-O, Lisbon: Figueirinhas, 1999.

———, 'Salazar', in Barreto, António and Maria Filomena Mónica, *Dicionário de História de Portugal*, Suplemento P-Z, Lisbon: Figueirinhas, 1999.

———, 'Reflexões sobre a queda do regime salazarista e o que se lhe seguiu', *Análise Social*, vol. 37, no. 162, 2002.

———, *Os lugar-tenentes de Salazar: biografias*, Lisbon: Aletheia Editora, 2015.

Madeira, João, *1937—o atentado a Salazar: a frente popular em Portugal*, Lisbon: A Esfera dos Livros, 2013.

Madeira, Lina Alves, 'Nacionalismo e Americanismo numa contenda jornalística Aristides de Sousa Mendes e a comunidade portuguesa de S. Francisco', *Estudos do Século XX*, University of Coimbra, vol. 7, no. 8, 2007.

Madureira, Arnaldo, *Salazar anos de tensão*, Lisbon: Clube do Autor, 2017.

Magone, José, *Politics in Contemporary Portugal: Democracy Evolving*, Boulder, CO: Lynne Rienner, 2014.

Mahoney, Richard D., JFK, *Ordeal in Africa*, Oxford: Oxford University Press, 1983.

Mailer, Phil, *Portugal: The Impossible Revolution*, Oakland, CA: PM Press, 2012.

Marchi, Riccardo, *Folhas ultras: as ideias da direita portuguesa (1939–50)*, Lisbon: Lisbon: Imprensa de Ciências Sociais, 2009.

Marcos, Daniel, *Salazar e de Gaulle: a França e a questão colonial portuguesa (1958–1968)*, Lisbon: Ministério dos Negócios Estrangeiros, 2007.

'Maria de Jesus: a governanta de Portugal', *History Passion*, 31 July 2018, https://gamepassion.blogs.sapo.pt/maria-de-jesus-a-governanta-de-portugal-23751

Marino, Alexander J., 'America's War in Angola, 1961–1976', MA thesis, University of Arkansas, 2015.

BIBLIOGRAPHY

Marjay, Frederic P. and Otto von Habsburg, *Portugal: Pioneer of the New Horizons*, Lisbon: Bertrand, 1965.

Marques, A.H. de Oliveira, *História de Portugal*, vol. 2, Lisbon: Palas, 1981.

————, *História de Portugal*, vol. 3, Lisbon: Palas, 1981.

————, *History of Portugal*, vol. II: *From Empire to Corporate State*, New York: Columbia University Press, 1973.

Martinho, Francisco Carlos Palomanes, *Marcello Caetano and the Portuguese 'New State'*, Brighton: Sussex Academic Press 2018.

Martins, Fernando, 'Pedro Theotónio Pereira: A Short Political and Ideological Biography. The Early Years (1920–1939)', *Santa Barbara Portuguese Studies*, Center for Portuguese Studies, UC Santa Barbara, vol. 9, 2007.

Mathias, Marcello, *Correspondência Marcello Mathias–Salazar, 1947–1958*, Lisbon: Editorial Difusão, 1984.

Matos, Helena, *Salazar: a construção do mito 1928–1933*, Lisbon: Círculo de Leitores, 2010.

Matos, Luís Salgado de, 'Cardeal Cerejeira: universitário, militante, místico', *Análise Social*, vol. 36, no. 60, 2001.

McGarr, Paul M., *The Cold War in South Asia: Britain, the United States and the Indian Subcontinent, 1945–1965*, Cambridge: Cambridge University Press, 2013.

McGowan, Patricia, *O bando de Argêl*, Lisbon: Intervenção, 1979.

Medina, João, 'Salazar, o ditador anti-português', *Mea Libra*, 3rd series, no. 20, Winter 2006–7, Viana do Castelo: Centro Cultural do Alto Minho.

Medlicott, W.N., *The Economic Blockade*, vol. II, London: HMSO, 1959.

Mello, Manuel José Homem de, *Cartas de Salazar a Craveiro Lopes, 1951–1958*, Lisbon: Moraes Editores, 1983.

Mello, Gonçalo Sampaio e, 'Guilherme Braga da Cruz: perfil biografico, para Guilherme Braga da Cruz no ano do seu centenário (1916–2016)', *A Revista Jurídica Luso-Brasileira*, vol. 2, no. 4, 2016.

Menano, Alberto, *Economia política: apontamentos coligados das prelecções do Exmo Senhor Doutor Oliveira Salazar*, Coimbra: Grafica Conimbricense, 1927.

Meneses, Filipe Ribeiro de, 'Slander, Ideological Differences, or Academic Debate? The "Verão Quente" of 2012 and the State of Portuguese Historiography', *e-Journal of Portuguese History*, vol. 10, no. 1, Summer 2012.

————, *Salazar: A Political Biography*, New York: Enigma Books, 2009.

———— and Robert McNamara, *White Redoubt: Great Powers and the Struggle for Southern Africa (1960–1980)*, London: Palgrave, 2018.

Milgram, Avraham, 'Portugal, the Consuls, and the Jewish Refugees, 1938–1941', Shoah Research Center, International School for Holocaust Studies.

————, *Portugal, Salazar e os judeus*, Lisbon: Gradiva, 2010.

Moncada, Luís Cabral de, 'A obra de Salazar à luz do sentimento histórico da sua época,' in Um grande português e uma grande europeu: Salazar, Lisbon: União Nacional, 1948.

————, Memórias: ao longo de uma vida (pessoas, factos, ideias), 1888–1974, Lisbon: Verbo, 1992.

Montoito, Eugénio, Henrique Galvão: ou a dissidência de um cadete de 28 de Maio (1927–1952), Lisbon: Centro de História, Universiade de Lisboa, 2005.

Morcka, Randall and Bernard Yeung, 'Corporatism and the Ghost of the Third Way', SSRN, 10 December 2010, http://ssrn.com/abstract=1722350

Moreira, Adriano and Vítor Gonçalves, Este é o tempo: Portugal, o amor, a política e Salazar, Lisbon: Clube do Autor, 2015.

'Morreu o historiador José Hermano Saraiva', JN, 20 July 2012, https://www.jn.pt/artes/morreu-o-historiador-jose-hermano-saraiva-2677400. html

'Morreu Rosa Casaco o Inspector de Pide envolvido na morte de Humberto Delgado', Publico, 20 July 2006, https://www.publico.pt/2006/07/20/politica/noticia/morreu-rosa-casaco-o-inspector-da-pide-envolvido-na-morte-de-humberto-delgado-1264618

Nataf, Daniel and Elizabeth Sammis, 'Classes, Hegemony and Portuguese Democratization', in Ronald H. Chilcote, Stylianos Hadjiyannis, Fred A. Lopez, Daniel Nataf, Elizabeth Sammis et al. (eds.), Transitions from Dictatorship to Democracy: Comparative Studies of Spain, Portugal and Greece, London: Taylor and Francis, 1991.

Neto, David, Doa a quem doer, Porto: Livraria Tavares Martins, 1933.

Nogueira, Albano, 'The Pull of the Continent', in André de Staercke et al., NATO's Anxious Birth, London: C. Hurst, 1985.

Nogueira, Franco, O Estado Novo, 1933–1974, Lisbon: Livraria Civilização Editora, 1991.

————, Salazar, vol. I: a mocidade e os princípios (1889–1928), Coimbra: Atlântida Editora, 1977.

————, Salazar, vol. 2: os tempos aureos, 1928–1936, Coimbra, Atlântida Editor, 1977.

————, Salazar, vol. 3: as grandes crises, 1936–1945, Coimbra: Atlântida Editora, 1978.

————, Salazar, vol. 4: o ataque, 1945–1958, Coimbra: Atlântida Editora, 1980.

————, Salazar, vol. 5: a resistência, 1958–1964, Coimbra: Livraria Civilização Editora, 1984.

————, Salazar, vol. 6: o último combate, 1964–1970, Coimbra: Livraria Civilização Editora, 1985.

————, Um político confessa-se: diário: 1960–1968, Lisbon: Livraria Civilização Editora, 1986.

Oliveira, Cesár, 'Guerra Civil de Espanha', in António Barreto and Maria

BIBLIOGRAPHY

Filomena Mónica, *Dicionário de história de Portugal*, vol. 7, Suplemento F/O, Lisbon: Figueirinhas, 1999.

Oliveira, Pedro Aires de, 'Augusto Vasconcelos e o crise de SDN', *Relações Internacionais*, 2004, http://www.ipri.pt/images/publicacoes/revista_ri/pdf/r1/RI01_Artg14_PAO.pdf

———, 'Taking Sides: Salazar's Estado Novo, the Nationalist Uprising and the Spanish Civil War', in Raanan Rein and Joan Maria Thomàs (eds.), *Spain 1936:Year Zero*, Brighton: University of Sussex Press, 2018.

———, 'The Contemporary Era', *e-Journal of Portuguese History*, vol. 8, no. 2, Winter 2010.

———, *Os despojos da aliança: a Grã-Bretanha e a questão colonial portuguesa*, Lisbon: Tinta da China, 2007.

Oliveira, Ricardo Soares de, *Magnificent and Beggar Land: Angola since the Civil War*, London: Christopher Hurst, 2015.

'O maior português de sempre: Oliveira Salazar (Part 1)' on YouTube, presented by Jaime Nogueira Pinto, RTP.

Os anos de Salazar, vol. 17: *1960: fuga do Forte de Peniche*, Lisbon: Planeta de Agostini, 2008.

Os anos de Salazar, vol. 2: *a constituição do Estado Novo*, Lisbon: Planeta de Agostini, 2008.

Osuna, José Javier Olivas, *Iberian Military Politics: Controlling the Armed Forces during Dictatorship and Democratisation*, London: Palgrave, 2014.

'Otelo: precisamos de um homem honesto como Salazar', *Diário de Notícias* online, 21 April 2011, https://www.dn.pt/dossiers/tv-e-media/revistas-de-imprensa/noticias/otelo-precisamos-de-um-homem-honesto-como-salazar-1835446.html

Otero, Paulo, *Os útimos meses de Salazar: Agosto de 68 a Julho de 1970*, Lisbon: Almecina, 2008.

Pais de Sousa, Jorge, 'O Estado Novo de Salazar como um fascismo de cátedra: fundamentação histórica de uma categoria política', *Storicamente*, vol. 5, 2009, http://www.storicamente.org/05_studi_ricerche/estado-novo-como-fascismo-de-catedra.html.

Pappin, Gladden, 'Corporatism for the Twenty-First Century,' *American Affairs*, vol. 4, no. 1, Spring 2020, https://americanaffairsjournal.org/2020/02/corporatism-for-the-twenty-first-century/

Paquette, Gabriel, *Imperial Portugal in the Age of Atlantic Revolutions: The Luso-Brazilian World, c.1780–1850*, Cambridge: Cambridge University Press, 2013.

Parreira, Anabela P. et al., 'O 1 Congresso da União Nacional', in *AAVV: o fascismo em Portugal*, Actas do Colóquio Realizado na Faculdade de Letras de Lisboa, Lisbon: Regra do Jogo, 1980.

Patriarca, Fátima, *A revolta de 18 Janeiro de 1934*, Lisbon: Instituto de Ciencias Soçiais, 2000.

————and Leal Marques, 'Diário de Leal Marques sobre a formação do primeiro governo de Salazar: apresentação', *Análise Social*, vol. 41, no. 178, 2006.

Payne, Stanley G., *Franco and Hitler: Spain, Germany and World War II*, New Haven and London: Yale University Press, 2009.

Payne, Stanley G. and Jesús Palacios, *Franco: A Personal and Political Biography*, Madison: University of Wisconsin Press, 2014.

Pereira, Bernardo Futscher, *A Diplomacia de Salazar (1932–1949)*, Lisbon: D. Quixote, 2012.

————, *Crepúsculo do Colonialismo, A Diplomacia do Estado Novo (1949–1961)*, Lisbon: D. Quixote, 2017.

Pereira, José Pacheco, *Álvaro Cunhal: uma biografia política*, vol. 1: *1913–41*, Lisbon: Temas e Debates, 1999.

Peres, Michael S., '"Bewitched": Africa as a Determinant in the Career of Henrique Galvão, 1927–1970', *Bulletin for Spanish and Portuguese Historical Studies*, vol. 40, no. 1, 2015.

Pimentel, Irene Flunser, *Fotobiografias, século XX: Cardeal Cerejeira*, Lisbon: Círculo de Leitores. 2002.

————, *Judeus em Portugal durante a II Guerra Mundial*, Lisbon: A Esfera dos Livros, 2006.

————, *Os cinco pilares da PIDE*, Lisbon: A Esfera dos Livros, 2019.

———— and Claudia Ninhos, *Salazar, Portugal e o Holocausto*, Lisbon: Temas e Debates, 2013.

Pinto, António Costa, *The Blueshirts: Portuguese Fascists and the New State*, New York: Columbia University Press, 2000 (Social Science Monographs Boulder).

———— and Nuno Severiano Teixeira, 'From Atlantic Past to European Destiny, Portugal,' in Elvert, Jurgen & Kaiser, Wolfram (editors), *European Union Enlargement: A Comparative History*, London: Routledge, 2004.

Pinto, Jaime Nogueira, 'A excepção portuguesa: porque não temos uma direita radical?', *Observador*, 3 February 2019, https://observador.pt/opiniao/a-excepcao-portuguesa-porque-nao-temos-uma-direita-radical

————, 'As origens ideológicos do fascismo e do Estado Novo', *Futuro Presente*, no. 31, October–December 1990.

————, 'O paradoxal itinerário político de Alberto Franco Nogueira e a chamada "crise da direita"', *Observador*, 3 July 2019, https://observador.pt/opiniao/o-paradoxal-itinerario-politico-de-alberto-franco-nogueira-e-a-chamada-crise-da-direita/

————, *O fim do Estado Novo e as origens do 25 de Abril*, Lisbon: Difel, 1995.

————, *Portugal: ascensão e queda*, Lisbon: D. Quixote, 2013.

————, *Salazar visto pelos seus próximos*, Lisbon: Bertrand Editora, 2007.

Pinto, João Alberto da Costa, 'Gilberto Freyre e a intelligentsia salazarista em

BIBLIOGRAPHY

defesa do Império Colonial Português (1951–1974)', *História* (São Paulo), vol. 28, no. 1, 2009.

Ploncard d'Assac, J., *Salazar: a vida e a obra*, Lisbon: Verbo, 1989.

Porch, Douglas, *The Portuguese Armed Forces and the Revolution*, London: Croom Helm, 1977.

Preston, Paul, 'Spain, Betting on a Nazi Victory', in R. Bosworth and J. Maiolo (eds.), *The Cambridge History of the Second World War*, vol. 2: *Politics and Ideology*, Cambridge: Cambridge University Press, 2015.

'Primeira-dama de Salazar: Cilinha', *CM Jornal*, 21 January 2008, https://www.cmjornal.pt/mais-cm/domingo/detalhe/primeira-dama-de-salazar-cilinha

Pulido Valente, Vasco, 'Marcello Caetano', in António Barreto and Maria Filomena Mónica, *Dicionário de história de Portugal*, Suplemento A/E, Lisbon: Figueirinhas, 1999.

Raby, D.L., 'Populism and the Portuguese Left: From Delgado to Otelo', in L. Graham and D. Wheeler (eds.), *In Search of Portugal: The Revolution and Its Antecedents*, Madison: University of Wisconsin Press, 1983.

Raimundo, Orlando, *António Ferro: o inventor do salazarismo*, Lisbon: D. Quixote, 2015.

————, *O último salazarista: a outra face de Américo Thomaz*, Lisbon: D. Quixote, 2017.

Ramos, Rui, 'O Estado Novo perante os poderes periféricos: o governo de Assis Gonçalves em Vila Real (1934–39)', *Análise Social*, vol. 22, no. 90, 1986.

———— (ed.), *História de Portugal*, Lisbon: A Esfera dos Livros, 2009.

Raposo, Henrique, *História politicamente incorrecta de Portugal contemporâneo (de Salazar a Soares)*, Lisbon: Guerra and Paz, 2013.

'Recordar Pardal Monteiro', *CM Jornal*, 1 June 2014, https://cm-sintra.pt/index.php?option=com_content&Itemid=1024&catid=220&id=2810&view=article

Rees, Philip, *Biographical Dictionary of the Extreme Right since 1890*, London: Simon and Schuster, 1990.

Reis, Bárbara, 'Cartas inéditas a Salazar relevam segredos e intimidade com três gerações de família inglesa', *Publico*, 26 November 2017, https://www.publico.pt/2017/11/26/sociedade/investigacao/cartas-ineditas-de-salazar-revelam-segredos-e-intimidade-com-tres-geracoes-de-familia-inglesa-1793601

Reis, Bruno Cardoso, 'Este século não foi fascista. Salazar, Franco e a efémera nova ordem internacional nazi-fascista,' *Relações Internacionais*, no. 27 (September 2010).

————, 'Portugal and the UN: A Rogue State Resisting the Norm of Decolonization (1956–1974)', *Portuguese Studies*, vol. 29, no. 2, 2013.

BIBLIOGRAPHY

Reis, Jaime, 'Portuguese Banking in the Inter-War Period', in C.H. Feinstein, *Banking, Currency and Finance in Europe between the Wars*, Oxford: Clarendon Press, 1995.

Reno, R.R., 'Eliot and Liberalism', *First Things*, 1 April 2016, https://www.firstthings.com/blogs/firstthoughts/2016/01/eliot-and-liberalism

Rezola, Maria Inácia, 'The Franco–Salazar Meetings: Foreign Policy and Iberian Relations during the Dictatorships (1942–1963)', *e-Journal of Portuguese History*, vol. 6, no. 1, Summer 2008.

Ribeiro, Orlando, 'Goa apenas uma mestiçagem espiritual', in *Goa em 1956: relatório ao governo*, Lisbon: CCP, 1999.

Rita, Maria da Conceição de Melo, and Joaquim Vieira, *Os meus 35 anos com Salazar*, Lisbon: A Esfera dos Livros, 2007.

Roberts, Andrew, *The Story of War: A New History of the Second World War*, London: Penguin, 2010.

Robinson, Richard, *Contemporary Portugal: A History*, London: Allen and Unwin, 1979.

Rodrigues, Avelino, Cesário Borga and Mário Cardoso, *Portugal depois de 25 de Abril*, Lisbon: Intervoz, 1976.

Rodrigues, Luís Nuno, 'About Face: The United States and Portuguese Colonialism, 1961–1963', *e-Journal of Portuguese History*, vol. 2, no. 1, 2004.

———, 'Militares e política: a Abrilada de 1961 e a resistência do salazarismo', *Ler História*, no. 6565, 2013, http://journals.openedition.org/lerhistoria/447.

———, 'The International Dimensions of the Portuguese Colonial Crisis', in Jerónimo Miguel Bandeira and António Costa Pinto (eds.), *The Ends of European Colonial Empires: Cases and Comparisons*, London: Palgrave Macmillan, 2015.

———, 'The United States and Portuguese Decolonization', *Portuguese Studies*, vol. 29, no. 2, 2013.

Rosas, Fernando and Cristina Sizifredo, *Estado Novo e a universidade: a perseguição aos professores*, Lisbon: Tinta da China, 2013.

Rosas, Fernando, *História de Portugal, vol. 7: o Estado Novo (1926–1974)*, Lisbon: Editorial Estampa, n.d.

———, *Salazar e o poder: a arte de saber a durar*, Lisbon: Tinta da China, 2013.

———, Rita Carvalho and Pedro Aires Oliveira, *Daniel Barbosa, Salazar e Caetano: correspondência política, 1947–1974*, vol. 1: *1945–1966*, Lisbon: Círculo de Leitores, 2002.

Ruiz, Joaquin del Moral, 'A independência brasileira e a sua repercussão no Portugal da época (1810–34)', *Análise Social*, vol. 16, no. 64, 1980.

Russell, Gerald, 'Psychiatry and Politicians: The "Hubris Syndrome"', *The Psychiatrist*, vol. 35, no. 4, April 2011.

BIBLIOGRAPHY

Rutan, Gerard F., 'Factors Affecting the German Decision Not to Invade the Iberian Peninsula, 1940–1945', MA thesis, University of Montana, 1958.

Salazar, António de Oliveira, *Doctrine and Action: Internal and Foreign Policy of the New Portugal 1928–1939*, trans. Edgar Broughton, London: Faber and Faber, 1939.

————, 'A Minha Resposta', typewritten copy of 17-page document in possession of the municipal library in Povoa de Varzim, n.d.

————, *O meu depoimento*, Lisbon: SNI, 1949.

Samuels, M.A., and Stephen M. Haykins, 'The Anderson Plan: An American Attempt to Seduce Portugal out of Africa', *Orbis*, vol. 23, 1979.

Santana, Emídio, *História de um atentado: o atentado a Salazar*, Lisbon: Forum, 1976.

Santos Luís, António, 'Pobreza', in António Barreto and Maria Filomena Monica, *Dicionário de história de Portugal*, Suplemento P/Z, Lisbon: Figueirinhas, 1999.

'S. Tomé e Príncipe: importância de massacre de Batepá tem sido ignorada', *Observador*, 8 June 2015, https://observador.pt/2015/06/08/s-tome-principe-importancia-massacre-batepa-sido-ignorada/

Schmitter, Philippe, *Corporatism and Public Policy in Authoritarian Portugal*, London: Sage Publications, 1975.

Schneidman, Witney W., *Engaging Africa: Washington and the Fall of Portugal's Colonial Empire*, Lanham, MA: University Press of America, 2004.

Sérgio António, *Breve interpretaçaõ da história de Portugal*, Lisbon: Sá da Costa, 1974.

Serrado, Ricardo, *O Estado Novo e o futebol: terá Salazar impedido Eusébio de sair do país?* Lisbon: Prime Books, 2012.

Silva, João Céu e, 'Madeleine Albright: Salazar não era fascista', *Diário de Notícias* online, 30 September 2018, https://www.dn.pt/edicao-do-dia/30-set-2018/interior/madeleine-albright-salazar-nao-era-fascista—9923234.html

Simpson, Duncan A.H., 'Salazar's Patriarch: Political Aspects in the Nomination of Manuel Gonçalves Cerejeira to the Patriarchate of Lisbon (April 1928–January 1930)', *Portuguese Studies*, vol. 25, no. 2, 2009.

Smith, Alan K., 'António Salazar and the Reversal of Portuguese Colonial Policy', *Journal of African History*, vol. 15, no. 4, October 1974.

Smith, Ian, *The Great Betrayal*, London: Blake, 1997.

Soares, Mário, *Portugal's Struggle for Liberty*, London: Allen and Unwin, 1975.

Soromenho, Ana and Isabel Lopes, 'Cilinha, uma viagem ao Estado Novo', *Expresso*, 16 February 2008, https://oliveirasalazar.org/download/galeria/pdf___E6613A95-E62E-4C9A-BE22–6F33DDA619B8.pdf

Steiner, Zara, *The Triumph of the Dark: European International History 1933–1939*, Oxford: Oxford University Press, 2011.

BIBLIOGRAPHY

Stocker, Maria Manuel, *Xeque-mate a Goa*, Lisbon: Temas a Debates, 2005.

Stone, Glyn, 'Britain and the Angolan Revolt of 1961,' *Journal of Imperial and Commonwealth History*, vol. 27, no. 1, 1969.

Stone, Glyn, 'Britain and Portuguese Africa, 1961–1965', in Ken Fedorowich and Martin Thomas (eds.), *International Diplomacy and Colonial Defeat*, London: Routledge, 2013.

Sunday Times Insight Team, *Insight on Portugal: The Year of the Captains*, London: André Deutsch, 1975.

Szobi, Pavel, 'From Enemies to Allies? Portugal's Carnation Revolution and Czechoslovakia, 1968–1989', *Contemporary European History*, vol. 26, no. 4, 2017.

Telo, António José, *Economía e império no Portugal contemporâneo*, Lisbon: Ed. Cosmos, 1994.

———, *Portugal na segunda guerra (1941–1945)*, vol. II, Lisbon: Vega, 1991.

Templewood, Viscount, *Ambassador on a Special Mission*, London: Collins, 1946.

Thomáz, Americo, *Últimas décadas de Portugal*, vol. III, Lisbon: Edições Fernando Pereira, n.d.

Torgal, Luís Reis, '"Crise" e "crises" no discurso de Salazar', *Estudos do Século XX*, no. 10, 2010.

———, *Estados novos, Estado Novo*, Coimbra: Imprensa da Universidade de Coimbra, 2009.

US Department of State Archives, Information released online prior to 20 January 2001.

US Library of Congress, *Federal Research Division*.

Valenti, Jiri, 'Soviet Decision-Making on Angola', in David Albright (ed.), *Africa and International Communism*, London: Macmillan, 1980.

Veríssimo Serrão, Joaquim, *História de Portugal*, vol. XIII *(1926–1935): do 28 Maio ao Estado Novo*, Lisbon: Editorial Verbo, 2000.

Vicente, António Pedro, 'Franco em Portugal: o seu doutoramento honoris causa na Universidade de Coimbra, 1949', *Revista de História das Ideias* (University of Coimbra), vol. 16, 1994.

Vieira, Joaquim, *A governanta*, Lisbon: A Esfera dos Livros, 2010.

Vieira, Patrícia, *Portuguese Film, 1930–1960: The Staging of the New State Regime*, London: Bloomsbury, 2013.

Vintras, R.E., *The Portuguese Connection*, London: Bachman and Turner, 1974.

Votar é um grande dever, Lisbon: SNI, 1945.

Weber, Eugen, *Action Française: Royalism and Revolt in Twentieth Century France*, Stanford: Stanford University Press, 1962.

———, *A Modern History of Europe*, New York: W.W. Norton, 1972.

Weiss, Kenneth G., *The Azores in Diplomacy and Strategy, 1940–1945*, Fort Belvoir, VA: Defence Technical Information Center, 1980.

BIBLIOGRAPHY

Wheeler, Douglas L., 'The Galvão Report on Forced Labour in Historical Context and Perspective: A Troubleshooter Who Was "Trouble"', *Portuguese Studies Review*, vol. 16, no. 1, 2009.

Wiarda, Howard J., *Corporatism and Development: The Portuguese Experience*, Amherst: University of Massachusetts Press, 1977.

————, *The Soul of Latin America: The Cultural and Political Tradition*, New Haven: Yale University Press, 2001.

Interviews

Gallagher, Tom, interview with Alberto Franco Nogueira, London, 6 October 1979.

————, interview with Adelino Amara da Costa, Lisbon, 11 December 1979.

————, interview with General Fernando Santos Costa, Lisbon, 20 July 1981.

Interviews with serving American diplomats in Portugal in 'Portugal Country Reader, Association for Diplomatic Studies and Training', http://adst.org/wp-contents/uploads/2012/09/Portugal.PDF

William L. Blue, deputy chief of mission 1962–5, 1991;

James Bonbright, ambassador 1955–8;

Joseph J. Jova, consular official, Oporto and Lisbon 1954–7;

Robert S. Pastorino, US commercial attaché in Lisbon 1974–7.

INDEX

INDEX